Modern Intellectual and Political History of the Middle East
Mehrzad Boroujerdi, *Series Editor*

Other titles in Modern Intellectual and Political History of the Middle East

GLOBALIZATION
and the Muslim World

Culture, Religion, and Modernity

Edited by Birgit Schaebler *and* Leif Stenberg

With a Foreword by Roy Mottahedeh

Syracuse University Press

First Edition 2004
10   11   12   13   14   15   6   5   4   3

Permission to reprint the following article is gratefully acknowledged: "Subduing
Globalization: The Challenge of the Indigenization Movement" by Mehrzad Boroujerdi,
in *Globalization at the Margins*, ed. Richard Grant and John Rennie Short,
copyright © Richard Grant and John Rennie Short. Reprinted with
permission of Palgrave Macmillan.

The paper used in this publication meets the minimum requirements of
American National Standard for Information Sciences—Permanence of
Paper for Printed Library Materials, ANSI Z39.48–1984. ™

Library of Congress Cataloging-in-Publication Data

Globalization and the Muslim world : culture, religion, and modernity / edited by
Birgit Schaebler and Leif Stenberg ; with a foreword by Roy Mottahedeh.— 1st ed.
p. cm. — (Modern intellectual and political history of the Middle East)
Includes bibliographical references and index.
ISBN 0-8156-3024-7 (hardcover : alk. paper) — ISBN 0-8156-3049-2 (pbk. : alk. paper)
1. Islamic countries—Civilization. 2. Globalization—Religious aspects—Islam.
3. Islam—20th century. I. Schäbler, Birgit. II. Stenberg, Leif. III. Series.
DS35.62.G58   2004
909'.09767083—dc22   2004008319

Manufactured in the United States of America

Contents

Figures

Tables

Foreword

ROY MOTTAHEDEH

Some of the most intellectually exciting activity at Harvard's Center for Middle Eastern Studies has been provided by its visiting fellows. In the academic year 1998–99 the center was particularly fortunate in that the interests of several of these fellows were convergent and produced the important conference that is the origin of the present volume.

Globalization and postmodernism are on the lips of scholars and intellectuals not only in the West, but also in the Middle East and the Islamic world. Titles with the Arabic word *'awlama,* the agreed neologism for "globalization," are everywhere to be seen in catalogues of Arabic books. And yet Middle Eastern and Islamic studies have often used the terms "globalization" and "postmodernism" without the self-reflexiveness of the authors of the essays in this volume; not the least of its contributions will be to make such use less acceptable. For example, economists tell us that about a century ago globalization in terms of exchange of goods and movement of populations was at a level that corresponds to the level again achieved recently. Can our understanding of the effects ascribed to the contemporary globalization be seen (or their absence accounted for) if we look back at the very beginning of the twentieth century?

"Postmodernism" also has its history. One of its points of departure for Middle Eastern studies was Edward Said's *Orientalism,* a book nearly a quarter of a century old. (It should be remembered that study of the Middle East and Islamic world, often blamed for being impoverished in "theory," was also a focus of interest for Clifford Geertz and Ernest Gellner as well as Edward Said.)

It has often been pointed out that postmodernism benefited from the shrinking of the intellectual approaches offered by Marxism and "development" studies, although these approaches are by no means mutually exclusive. We should also remember that the unexpected vigor of the supposedly "premodern" has given a great deal of energy to "postmodern" studies, a vigor that, at the very least, eliminated any simple dictionary definition of "traditional" and "modern." The continuing force of religions is the most obvious manifestation of this vigor.

Moreover it is clear that the "local" context is so important that it will always demand our scholarly attention, and cannot be dismissed simply as the "traditional" and "premodern." Even if we were fortunate enough to have a widely accepted definition of "modernity," its refraction through local contexts, both cultural and defined by the actual dialectic of events, would yield varieties of experience unpredictable from the definition of modernity itself.

If modernity is some ideal type extracted from contemporary European culture, it is not a real piece of history, and its interactions with non-European societies a matter more of theoretical consideration than of interest to the historian. The "European" world—however its boundaries are drawn—is not and never could be homogeneous synchronically just as it never has been diachronically. Moreover, as the authors of these essays emphasize over and over again, by definition interaction works in both directions. The first nondenominational British cemetery is not in England at Highgate, it is in Calcutta.

Of course, as a term, "Orientalism" has been grotesquely overextended and made into a sin so basic that it has at times blinded us to our dependence and gratitude for the work of our predecessors. The lexicons that non-Orientalists have carefully refined over the past two centuries provide one appropriate example. They are indispensable; they go beyond lexicons that existed earlier, while nevertheless often making judicious use of older traditions. God bless the men and women who made them. And the authors who made these lexicons had no sense that they were establishing "truths" in a positivist or any other sense. Every philologist will tell you that most of the words in definitions do not "exactly" correspond from one language to another. Lexicographers seek "approximate truths" and realize that some approximations are better than others.

Yet the very strength of the philological tradition gave it a slant that was to the disadvantage of historians. Philologists share a strong historical interest in the origins of both words and the other elements of language. Here too the "answers" as to questions of origin both were and are probabilities rather than certainties. Yet the etymological model increased the temptation to claim "facticity," to believe in an "essentialism" in the sense of a "core meaning," and to believe that tracing historical origins was a major part of historical explanation. Origins are, of course, interesting and help explain historical circumstances in the immediate environments of origins. But they may explain little more. The English word "pyjama" may have a Persian etymology but that origin would explain nothing of the history of pajamas in twentieth-century North America.

Historians of the Middle East have largely but not entirely freed us from these, and similar, bad habits of historical approach to our field. We must thank the editors and authors of this volume for taking us several steps further.

Cambridge, Massachusetts
Summer 2002

Contributors

Mehrzad Boroujerdi is an associate professor of political science at the Maxwell School of Citizenship and Public Affairs at Syracuse University. He received his Ph.D. in International Relations from the American University in Washington, D.C. He has been a postdoctoral fellow at Harvard, a Rockefeller Foundation fellow at the University of Texas at Austin and a scholar-in-residence at the Middle East Institute in Washington, D.C. In addition to numerous articles, Boroujerdi is the author of *Iranian Intellectuals and the West: The Tormented Triumph of Nativism* (Syracuse University Press).

Patrice C. Brodeur completed his doctorate at Harvard University in 1999. He is presently an assistant professor of religious studies at Connecticut College. His main area of interest is the relationship between contemporary Islam and Islamic studies within the broader academic study of religion, as reflected in his current book project on contemporary Arab Muslim perspectives on religious Others. He is also conducting research on Islam and globalization within the realm of transnational higher education and the participation of Muslims in interreligious dialogue. He is currently the book review editor of *Muslim World*.

Jocelyne Cesari is senior research fellow at CNRS and associate professor in the Department of Religious Studies at the Sorbonne. She has previously served as visiting professor at Columbia and New York Universities, as Fulbright scholar at the Center for Middle Eastern Studies at Harvard University in 1998, and she held a fellowship at the Center for the Study of World Religions in 1999. She is currently research associate at the Center for Middle Eastern Studies. As a political scientist, her areas of specialization are Muslim minorities in Europe and America; Islam, ethnicity, and politics; North African political and cultural life; and the cultural dimension of globalization. She has written several books and numerous articles on Islam and politics and on Muslims in the West.

Toby E. Huff is Chancellor Professor in the Department of Sociology and Anthropology at the University of Massachusetts, Dartmouth. He is author of *The Rise of Early Modern Science: Islam China and the West* (1993), which was recently translated into Arabic. A revised edition is now being translated into Indonesian. He is coeditor with Wolfgang Schluchter of *Max Weber and Islam* (1999). During the summer term of 2001 he was a visiting professor in the Department of Science and Technology Studies at the University of Malaya while conducting fieldwork on Malaysia's multimedia super corridor.

Anne Marie Oliver is a research affiliate at the Center for Middle Eastern Studies, Harvard University. Her book on Hamas and the Israeli-Palestinian conflict, *The Fate of Literalism,* is forthcoming.

Catharina Raudvere is an associate professor in the Department of History of Religions, Lund University, Sweden. Her main field of study is women and Islam in Turkey, where she has conducted fieldwork with particular focus on women's Sufi groups in contemporary Istanbul. Her monograph *The Book and the Roses: Sufi Women, Visibility, and* Zikr *in Contemporary Istanbul* was published in 2002. She is a member of the board of the Swedish Research Institute in Istanbul.

Sayres S. Rudy is completing a political science dissertation at Columbia University on the institutional sources of violent and peaceful social protests in diverse religious and secular contexts and movements. Currently he teaches comparative politics, social theory, and political philosophy in the Social Studies Program at Harvard University.

Birgit Schaebler is a professor of Middle Eastern history at the University of Erfurt, Germany. She has been a visiting professor at Duke University, a visiting scholar at the Center for Middle Eastern Studies, Harvard University, and a faculty member at the University of Erlangen, Germany, and at Georgia College and State University, USA. She is the author of *Aufstände im Drusenbergland: Ethnizität und Integration einer ländlichen Gesellschaft Syriens vom Osmanischen Reich bis zur Unabhängigkeit (Rebellions in the Druze Mountains: Ethnicity and Integration in Syria from the End of the Ottoman Empire until Independence)* (1996), which is appearing in Arabic with Dar an-Nahar. With Thomas Philipp she coedited *The Syrian Land: Processes of Integration and Fragmentation in Bilad al-Sham from the eighteenth to the twentieth century* (1998), and has published numerous articles, including "Practising Musha': Common Lands and the Common Good in Southern Syria under the Ottomans and the French," in *New Perspectives on Property and Land in the Middle East,* ed. Roger Owen (2000). She is a past president of the Syrian Studies Association of North America.

Heather J. Sharkey earned a Ph.D. in history from Princeton University in 1998. She taught for a year at the University of Massachusetts, Amherst, for two years at the Massachusetts Institute of Technology, and for two years at Trinity College (Connecticut). In 2002 she joined the faculty of the University of Pennsylvania, where she is an assistant professor of Middle Eastern and Islamic studies in the Department of Asian and Middle Eastern Studies. Her first book, *Living with Colonialism: Nationalism and Culture in the Anglo-Egyptian Sudan,* appeared in 2003.

Jakob Skovgaard-Petersen is an associate professor and head of the academic program at the Carsten Niebuhr Institute of Near Eastern Studies, University of Copenhagen, Denmark. He teaches courses on contemporary Islamic thought, television in the Arab world, and the history of Oriental studies. He is the author of *Defining Islam for the Egyptian State* (1997). His most recent publication is *Middle Eastern Cities, 1900–1950: Public Space and Public Spheres in Transition* (2001), coedited with Hans Christian Korsholm Nielsen.

Leif Stenberg is an associate professor in Islamology at Lund University, Sweden. He is also a professor in religious studies at Växjö University, Sweden. In 1996 Stenberg received his Ph.D. in History of Religions at Lund University. Between 1997 and 1999 he was a visiting scholar at the Center for Middle Eastern Studies, Harvard University, and during the academic year 1999–2000 he was a postdoctoral fellow at the Institut français d'études arabes de Damas (IFEAD) in Syria. Stenberg has published many articles in Swedish and English, primarily in relation to contemporary Islam, and he is the author of *The Islamization of Science: Four Muslim Positions Developing an Islamic Modernity* (1996).

Introduction

This volume is the product of a workshop held at the Center for Middle Eastern Studies at Harvard University in the summer of 1999. We were visiting fellows at the Center, and in between brown bag lunches, all kinds of lecture series, and countless cups of cafeteria coffee, we discussed how our work was influenced by what we thought to be the pressing theoretical issues of our day and age, the last year of a millennium: globalization and postmodernity.

We also agreed that we were living in times difficult to come to terms with, perhaps more so than in the preceding decades. A shift of millennium, the United States as the sole surviving superpower after half a century of conflict, and unchallenged capitalism as the foremost globalizing factor were all reasons enough to challenge our scholarly and also, often enough, our daily lives, in the "globalized life situation" that visiting fellowships entail. As a historian of the Middle East and an Islamicist, we represented different academic fields, yet found that difference, including its tensions, fruitful. Out of these discussions arose the idea to bring together more people from Middle Eastern and Islamic studies in a workshop. To provide some common basis for a discussion, we put together a reader of contributions that we found to be essential for the debate, including texts by Featherstone (1995), Fornäs (1995), Beyer (1994), Appadurai (1990), Jameson (1998a), Godzich (1986), and Foucault (1972). Participants were asked to reflect on the influence of globalization and postmodernity in their personal research as well as on the consequences for Middle Eastern and Islamic studies in general.

Globalization and postmodernity are, of course, highly contested phenomena, the sheer existence of which is debated. A political journal recently polled its readers on globalization, asking them to agree/disagree on the question of whether globalization was "a myth and shouldn't be taken seriously." Globalization, understood in a basic sense as the ever faster and ever denser streams of people, images, consumer goods, money markets, and communication networks around the world, is greeted by some, as we know, as victory, while others feel deeply threatened by it, and others again cautiously hint at the potential to "catch up" that might be inherent in these rather frantic developments, which are, however, not entirely new.

Three possibilities concerning the origins of globalization have been brought forward in the debate: that a form of globalization has been in progress throughout history as far back as the unrecorded, prehistoric movements of people across the planet; that it is an outcome of capitalism in the modern period; and that it is, more recently, the product of the "disorganized capital" of post-industrialism and postmodernity (Waters in Beynon and Dunkerley 2000).

The papers in this volume take up several of these possibilities and themes. The historical chapters (Schaebler and Sharkey) both assume that globalization has a history far further back than the twentieth, or even the nineteenth, century. The theoretical chapter (Rudy) sees globalization therefore as basically not theorizable, and also suggests a critical approach to it. Politically, the movement of the indigenization of knowledge can be interpreted as a resistance to globalization (Boroujerdi). Other chapters view globalization as a central condition for developments within Islam (Cesari), or, rather, as the very basis on which the proponents of a global Islam function (Stenberg). Two chapters concentrate on the obvious technological aspects and possibilities of globalization (Huff and Skovgaard-Petersen). One chapter seeks to locate where globalization actually happens in people's daily lives and activities (Raudvere), another takes clues from the language of global business to introduce a mediating concept between the global and the local (Brodeur), and the last chapter, in part, analyzes its effect on language itself (Oliver).

The papers thus, in a way, reflect the metaphor that Fredric Jameson used in the preface to a volume on globalization and culture, representing globalization as the proverbial elephant, which is described by its blind observers in so many diverse ways. Yet one can posit the existence of the elephant, even if there is no single persuasive or dominant theory to explain it (Jameson and Miyoshi 1998). It was the undefinedness of globalization, and the many tensions that seem to underlie it (global-local, East-West, modernity-postmodernity, self-other, and so forth), which positively demand interdisciplinary approaches, that made us choose it for the framework and the title of the volume. Necessarily, this is a flexible framework, and the essays in the volume should be seen as pointers in new directions rather than as final answers.

It has been argued that the debate on globalization as a paradigm is in many ways also the successor to the debates on modernity and postmodernity (Featherstone, Lash, and Robertson 1995). This collective of scholars has certainly established globalization as a central thematic in social theory and in the understanding of sociocultural change. A question that arises here is whether postmodernity, then, is the causal agent for globalization, or, rather, is caused by it? And, the most basic question that is still not answered, what is postmodernity? Postmodernity is usually identified by something it is not. It isn't modernity. But the sense exactly in which it is not modernity is open and contested. Is it the aftermath or a result of modernity? Does it have to do with time at all? Is it more correct to connect it to modifying processes in cultures? As such, is it the development, denial, or rejection of modernity? Or is it, rather, a reflective stage of modernity? Again, the papers in this volume do not take a unified approach, and they tackle these questions more implicitly than explicitly. The majority of contributors would also not refer to themselves as postmodernists. Yet they see postmodernity as a global condition that necessitates new approaches to the study of the Middle East and Islam.

Here lies a major concern of this volume. The intellectual currents linked to postmodernity, and most commonly also identified with the "post" prefix, are valuable because they subvert the "modernist certitudes, structural rigidities, Orientalist stereotypes and colonial and modernizing vanities" (Bose 1997) that formerly afflicted Middle Eastern and Islamic Studies. These postmodern, poststructural, post-Orientalist, and postcolonial perspectives have made it increasingly difficult to speak about the Middle East and Islam as fixed entities imbued with ahistorical religious and cultural essences, and to deny the people of this region or religion their agency in the making of history.

This view is, however, not universally held. Middle Eastern history, for example, dominated by the social history paradigm that fought its way in in the 1960s, still shares the unease of history as a general field about these new currents and their insistence on "culture" and about what has been called the "productive materiality of the text" (Poster 1997). Within Islamic studies, scholars all too often still see Islam simply as a "religion," and not also as a discursive field of contesting powers.

On the other hand, postcolonialism, with its radical critique of the hegemony of Western science and its legitimate challenge of the concept of Western modernity as universal modernity, can also reproduce dichotomies, or create new ones, as Sugata Bose has aptly laid out for the field of Asian Studies (1997). "Europe" and the "West" need to be seen as constructions, too, and not as ahistorical, monolithic entities. Thinking in global and comparative terms can perhaps help both sides in avoiding the trap of excessive "othering."

The first two essays of this volume take up this problematic. In the first, historian Birgit Schaebler seeks to stake out some middle ground where reflective Western social science and reflective postcolonial thought meet. Operating under the assumption that modernity is a global and conjunctural phenomenon, which implies the acknowledgment that the expansion of modernity has to be viewed not as a process of repetitive imitation of Europe, but as the crystallization of civilizations with their own discourses, dynamics, and self-perceptions, she looks at the globalization of a central concept of modernity, "civilization." Arguing that the debate on globalization helped to promote the emphasis of space over time in history as a field, she follows the invention and conceptualization of the term "civilization" and its counterpart, "savagery," from their French enlightenment origins to the colonial civilizing mission that strove to make them global.

In the process, she argues, they encountered and engendered complex processes of self-authentication, both in Europe and in the Middle East. In fact, it is processes of encounter that establish both Europe's modernity and that of its "others," such as the modern Middle East and modern Islam. Yet, Schaebler argues, conventional boundaries need to be redrawn. "Civilized" urban intellectuals in both the colonizing and the colonized world constructed their countrysides and certain people at their outer boundaries as ignoble savage others, and colonized elites came up with civilizing missions of their own. Indeed, the fault lines of modernity, she contends, have to be drawn not between civilizations, but within them.

Paradoxically, in the discourses on civilization, a concept representing modernity, Schaebler identifies archaism, the discovery and uses of elements of a premodern past, as playing an important part. Challenged by cultural encounters, Germans, Ottoman Turks, and Ottoman Arabs discover wild men and noble savages in their own reconstructed national pasts, in a movement of self-authentication and in order to counter dominating cultures. One such figure is the *ghazi,* the warrior for Islam, living in what came to be represented as a Golden Age of Islam, and these discourses then are the platforms on which nationalisms and Islamism would emerge. Such processes, Schaebler demonstrates, took place in Europe and the Muslim lands, yet, because the East has been constructed as being essentially different from the West, they were judged very differently, and Muslim cultures were long represented as passively importing or imitating Western ideas.

Taking up the issue of Western intellectual hegemony for the contemporary present, political scientist Mehrzad Boroujerdi defends the current project of knowledge indigenization, which, he contends, should not be dismissed as obscurantism, atavism, or an invidious and compulsive tendency to fetishize and celebrate difference. Rather, this project should be seen as a genuine endeavor by non-Western intellectuals seeking to end their condition of intellectual docility and to negotiate with the theoretical and practical challenges of the modern age.

These intellectuals argue that Eurocentric premises have, alas, colonized the social sciences and, in turn, perpetuated a Western-dominated world order. Their project of knowledge indigenization is a form of local resistance to globalization. What resonates among Third-World elites intellectually and politically is the desire to challenge the legitimacy of universalist claims by Euro-American-centered social scientists. Boroujerdi acknowledges that the project of knowledge indigenization is "fraught with epistemological difficulties and marked by vitriolic rhetoric," and he is especially skeptical about the Islamic experiment, an issue that is taken up by Stenberg in some detail. Yet Boroujerdi is cautiously optimistic that Third-World intellectuals may redefine separate paths to development without stigmatizing the other.

Introducing the category of subjectivity, political scientist Sayres S. Rudy takes a hard look at his field and its treatment of globalization, Islamism, and postmodernity. After the eruption, in the 1970s, of fundamentalism, globalization, and postmodernity as novel, predominant, and simultaneous social trends, analysts generally hesitated to combine these strands into a cohesive epochal shift. If they intuited linkages among these trends, they struggled to elaborate them. After all, theorizing these phenomena required rare aptitude across divided disciplines. The most influential works written in the 1990s echoed familiar theories of how Western political and economic formations and secular cultural valuation commingle, with fundamentalism pilloried across the ideological spectrum as nothing more than, in Rudy's words, the "minatory excrescence of unrealized modernity."

Globalization, then, the term of choice for the 1990s, was the title of an agenda for the diagnosis of worldwide economic, political, and cultural negotiations that solidified the trivialization of religious activism as uniform, insubstantial, and inessential. Yet, Rudy argues, there will never be a credible globalization theory, viz. a valid account of the direct social consequences of global unification. Globalization cannot be said to cause certain uniform social reactions because it acts upon societies, communities, and groups imbued with disparate tastes, desires, needs, and institutional or social resources to satisfy them. Thus, theorists can identify globalization's features and their systemic effects, but not their social effects. The regnant view, according to Rudy, is that globalization is a "secular, modern, and cosmopolitan process," while national, ethnic, or religious opposition to specific experiences of globalization is typically construed as resistance to secularism, modernity, and cosmopolitanism as such. Yet Islamism's multiplicity urges discrete accounts of personal, communitarian, and militant activities. They share external (global) pressures, but represent distinct domestic (local) struggles.

Here Rudy introduces the concept of choice. People's local reactions, he argues, are determined by their capacity to secure their initial or adapted desires, in light of their different social resources. By differentiating specific choices from choice itself, or desires from the ability to achieve or modify them, he arrives at the systemic position of choices and desires and their relation to subjectivity, which then can be systemic or anti-systemic. Where globalization gradually frustrates Muslims' desires, or, in contrast, socially disrupts desires, the reactions will be systemic, personal Islamism in one case, communitarian Islamism in the other. But when new choices are prevented, eliminating subjectivity, the reaction becomes anti-systemic, that is, militant Islamism. Each form of Islamism, Rudy argues, contains modern, anti-modern and postmodern elements in unique constellations.

Moving to "Western Islam," sociologist Jocelyne Cesari examines the "dramatically altered thought and practice" of the nearly seven million Muslims in Western Europe and the four to six million more living in the United States. These large numbers of Muslims residing in the West have shifted the debate over Islam and modernism from an Arab/Muslim context to a Western one. It is especially within global cities like Paris, London, Berlin, and New York, all of which favor both ethnicity and multiculturalism, that Muslims reconstitute themselves along ethnic lines, defending an ethnic vision of Islam rooted in their respective national cultures of origin. Cesari argues that the "culture of separateness" presupposes autonomy and independence in the religious realm, automatically deconstructing Western Muslim identities into religious, social, and ethnic components, contrary to more integrated identities in the Muslim world.

Western Islam cannot be viewed any longer as an isolated or marginalized part of the Islamic world, Cesari contends. Western Muslims constitute an important part of the *umma* and a new transnational Islam, which is making itself global through audio and video tapes, the broadcast of independent television satellite shows (of which Jakob Skovgaard-Petersen gives us an example), and, most significantly, burgeoning websites. In the Western context questions about democracy, religious freedom, and tolerance are raised, which are both a challenge to the Western democracies themselves and to authoritarian regimes in the Muslim world. Cesari sees globalization, in a way, as the condition for all these developments.

In the field of Islamic studies, Leif Stenberg takes a different approach. Interested in the process of knowledge production, he analyzes the International Institute of Islamic Thought (IIIT) and the School of Islamic and Social Sciences (SISS), both located in Virginia, and their conceptualization of religion and knowledge through the writings of Taha Jabir al-Alwani, who was the former president of IIIT and is currently the president of SISS. The goal of IIIT and SISS is, according to Stenberg, not only to establish an alternative social science that recognizes the revelation as a source of scientific knowledge, but also to promote Islam, worldwide, in a kind of missionary movement (da'wa). This discourse, despite its concentration on "traditional" themes (such as the Golden Age of Islam and so forth) implies, in fact, new understandings of Islam. It also constructs the "West" as its other.

Stenberg suggests viewing Islam as a "social product" and an "ongoing discourse, concerned with authority," because those who are active in the new discourse are mostly not trained religious experts, 'ulama'. Their response to the new kind of "free-floating" intellectuals can be quite critical, as in the case of Yusuf al-Qaradawi, himself a "global mufti" (Skovgaard-Petersen). The new global Islam, as also represented by Persian-American scholar Seyyed Hossein Nasr and British-Pakistani author Ziauddin Sardar, shapes a different understanding of the Muslim world, which, according to Stenberg, is less a geographical entity and more a world of ideas, thoughts, and practices. Traditional notions of center and periphery become obsolete, and Islamic experiments like the ongoing reinterpretation of Islam in Malaysia attract the attention of Muslims around the world. Stenberg thus sees globalization not only as a condition for these new developments within Islam and the Muslim world, but rather as the basis on which the proponents of a global Islam function.

The second part of this volume is concerned with concrete experiences and practices of globalization. Historian Heather J. Sharkey examines the implications of social contact for global, national, and local identities in the case of Muslim societies of Northern Sudan. Viewing globalization as "neither new nor modern," and the life of the fourteenth-century scholar and migrant Ibn Battuta as representing the epitome of an "Islamic global society in the years from 1000 to 1500," she looks at the physical movement of people and its nexus to the formation of Sudanese community consciousness. Interestingly, she finds that conceptions of community formed along the major routes traversed. She divides the history of migration into five distinct periods, from 1800 to the year 2000. These migrations of the past two centuries, she argues, fostered the expansion of Islamic and Arabic culture in the Sudan. Yet global, national, and local identities did not erase each other. Rather, they coexisted. By extension, she concludes, large-scale social changes do not homogenize cultures, but rather lead to new, ever-changing, and overlapping cultural formations.

Moving from physical migration to the rapid flow of information via the Internet, and from Africa to South Asia, sociologist Toby E. Huff's contribution looks at Malaysia's social experiment with a Multimedia Super Corridor (MSC). Because Malaysia cannot afford to wire the whole country, the MSC begins as a physical corridor, fifteen kilometers wide and fifty kilometers long, stretching from Kuala Lumpur south to the new international airport and two new cities. One of them, called "Cyberjaya," is Malaysia's new "e-commerce center," opened in 1999. The corridor, a high-speed, high-capacity fiber-optic Internet backbone, is intended to provide full access to the Web.

Basing his account on official information provided by the Malaysian government and on several visits, Huff examines the challenges of vision, growth, and control that Third-World economies, as well as others, have to face in the information-age economy. Huff is perhaps the most optimistic of all contributors to this volume, in his assessment that globalization and its related technologies can give developing economies the chance to catch up within the new global economy. On the other hand, it may leave Middle Eastern and North African countries far behind in Internet access and use, and relegate them to the status of having to adopt the unattractive "sunset" industries that strong economies continuously shed.

Assuming that "telecommunications is a central component, if not the very essence, of the current drive for globalization," Islamicist Jakob Skovgaard-Petersen compares two television shows featuring what he calls "global muftis," one on the by now omnipresent al-Jazeera satellite channel, the other on Egyptian state-sponsored television. The two "stars" are Yusuf al-Qaradawi, an Egyptian *'alim,* based in Qatar, with his show *Al-shar'ia wa-al-haya,* and "the most popular Islamic TV star ever," the late Shaykh Sha'rawi with his program *With Shaykh Sha'rawi.* Contrasting these two programs, Skovgaard-Petersen comes to the somewhat surprising conclusion that it is the Egyptian television channel that qualifies for some sort of postmodern televangelism, while al-Jazeera comes across as "the ultimate channel of the old modernist intellectual." In this sense, al-Jazeera is instrumental in helping to create a global *umma,* or a *watan 'arabi,* an Arab fatherland, very much in the tradition of Islamic modernism a hundred years ago.

Historian of religion Catharina Raudvere also states the importance of telecommunications, in a women's religious foundation in what she defines as "late modern" Turkey. Her opening scene in the *vakif* she studied has a teenage girl "using the television remote control to switch between the Islamist Kanal 7 and Kral (the Turkish answer to MTV), where Madonna's latest video was being shown," while the older women were planning new Qur'an lessons, food distribution to the poor, and street demonstrations. They also organize group pilgrimages to Mecca for women, an activity they often have to defend against male insistence on tradition. Raudvere's concern is the framework of globalization, or the question of where globalization actually takes place. Women should not be seen as victims of globalization, she argues, but rather as part of the changes connected with it. As such, women are empowered in their local communities, but not on the political scene. The women define themselves as keepers of traditional values. Raudvere contends that their religious activism is entirely in tune with late-modern society, although it is discursively anti-modern and holds nostalgia as one of its rhetorical key concepts.

Islamicist Patrice C. Brodeur draws a parallel between the dialectic of modernity/postmodernity and that of self/Other. Arguing that the dichotomy modernity/postmodernity may not be the most useful point of entry to describe present changes in the Muslim world, and that Muslim identities are never generated solely on the basis of "pure" internal Islamic developments, but are rather the fruit of a self/Other process, Brodeur suggests the concept of "glocalism" as an analytical tool to overcome the gaps between these dichotomous representations of reality. He defines "glocalism" as a "constant reflexive process by which a human being's philosophy/ideology/belief/perception and corresponding praxes understand and integrate reality." He then examines the usefulness of the concept for understanding contemporary Arab Muslim literature on religious Others, which is his term of choice for the Orientalist category of "Islamic heresiography." The participation of Muslims and non-Muslims in the construction of academic representations of Islam(s), he concludes, signals the end of a clearly demarcated *dar al-islam* Other as the object of study and reflects a healthy intersubjectivity that also reveals the multiplicity of ways in which Muslims today deal with religious diversity.

Looking in new ways at the Middle East and Islam, one cannot ignore the Israeli-Palestinian conflict. Not trying to offer any solution, however, the last essay of this volume is a literary one. Anne Marie Oliver takes up the Islamic Resistance Movement, Hamas, a player within the Israeli-Palestinian conflict, "that most literary and (alternately) literalist of conflicts," and places the movement and its literalization of sacred scripts of sacrifice, martyrdom, and apocalypticism in the context of what she calls "literalism." Islamism has inaugurated not only a political and religious revolution in the Muslim world, but also, and more importantly, she contends, a linguistic and aesthetic one. The Israeli-Palestinian conflict itself, she says, is "seen by countless people the world over . . . as the dramatic fulfillment of sacred texts and prophesies," which makes it a primary, vertical form of literalism and raises the question as to what function is served by transforming a twentieth-century conflict into a primeval rivalry. Oliver takes the fable of the frog and the scorpion, "the fable of enemies and tale of murder-suicide," to illustrate her point that the "suicide bomber, who constitutes his shadow," like the postmodern subject, seeks both to confirm himself through language, history, and judgment and to be rid of them completely, in that "great morality play, Manichaean drama, and scene of judgment, called the Israeli-Palestinian conflict," which, for her, is in essence a rediscovery of the "anxiety of civilization"—the intense ambivalence catalyzed by verticalism, the verticalism of both the scorpion and the frog.

It was owing to the unique academic environment of Harvard University that we were able to bring so many different perspectives, and fields, together. We believe that Middle Eastern societies and Islam are not the prerogative of any one field, and that one of the desiderata for future research is a more combined effort, with disciplines learning from each other. We hope that this volume might be of some inspiration for this effort.

The workshop on which this volume is based also included contributions by Farid Esack, Kambiz Ghanea Bassiri, Ramin Jahanbegloo, Jacques Kabbanji, Mohamed Mahmoud, Kristin Smith, Farzin Vahdat, Robert Wisnowsky, and Bill Graham that could not be published here. None of this, of course, would have been possible without the support of Harvard's professors of the Middle East and Islam. We wish to thank Roger Owen, then director of the Center for Middle Eastern Studies, for giving us the green light and pledging the Center's support for our project. Bill Graham encouraged us, helped us throughout the planning stages, and honored us with his presence and insight at the workshop. So did Roy Mottahedeh, who very kindly consented to write a foreword. We, and the volume, also benefited in various ways from generous support from the Swedish Research Council, the Swedish Foundation for International Cooperation in Research and Higher Education, and the German Research Association (DFG). We thank all the staff of Syracuse University Press, in particular the executive editor, Mary Selden Evans, for support and efficiency. Last but not least we also wish to thank Margaret Owen for her thoughtful editing.

Birgit Schaebler, Erfurt, Germany
Leif Stenberg, Lund, Sweden
May 2002

PART ONE | **Globalization Discussed**

1

Civilizing Others

Global Modernity and the Local Boundaries
(French/German, Ottoman, and Arab) of Savagery

BIRGIT SCHAEBLER

> European penetration of the peoples of the globe at the turn of the century
> had a threefold impact on them: It awakened them out of their traditionalism
> and lethargy to the influence of modern civilization, which thereby became
> the first universal civilization.
>
> —Hans Kohn, *The Age of Nationalism: The*
> *First Era of Global History* (1962)

> For several years now, I have tried to argue that modernity is historically a
> global and conjunctural phenomenon, not a virus that spreads from one
> place to another. It is located in a series of historical processes that brought
> hitherto relatively isolated societies into contact, and we must seek its roots
> in a set of diverse phenomena—the Mongol dream of world conquest,
> European voyages of exploration . . . the "globalization of microbes" . . .
> and so on.
>
> —Sanjay Subrahmanyam, in "Multiple Identities" (2000)

Discourses on "civilization," even the term "civilization" itself, a direct outcome of the French Enlightenment, are born in encounters with others. These
encounters, which have historically comprised ephemeral contact, intensive interaction, and violent clash (Bitterli 1991), are an important constituent of

I wish to thank the German Research Association (DFG) and its program on "The Interaction of Asian, Latin American, and African Societies with European-American Expansions from
the Sixteenth to the Twentieth Century" for generously funding my research for this chapter. I also
benefited from two workshops on "Islam and Modernity," organized by the German American
Academic Council (GAAC) within the Social Science Research Council (SSRC) in 1997–98.

3

modernity, understood as a global and conjunctural phenomenon. The concept of a global modernity implies the acknowledgment that the expansion of modernity has to be viewed not as a process of repetitive imitation of Europe, but as the crystallization of civilizations with their own discourses and dynamics (Eisenstadt and Schluchter 1998).[1] The concept of a global modernity also implies a critical rereading of "European modernity."

European colonialism, oft imbued with a civilizing mission, is but one, rather late, phase in a long history of encounter. Yet Eurocentric discourses, since the 1950s heavily influenced by theories of modernization, have long credited colonialism with the "Westernization" of "the peoples of the globe." In his work on the Europeanization of the Middle East, for example, Hans Kohn frames in an exemplary way the argument, still influential today, that "while Napoleon's emergence in Europe roused the nations of Europe from their lethargy, it accelerated the process of decay and dissolution in which the countries and peoples of the Levant were involved. These countries were brought within the sphere of world policy in the nineteenth century, but, just as in the economic field, only passively" (Kohn 1936, 186).

While the "lethargic" nations of Europe were invigorated by the civilizational challenge posed by France, the now quickly "decaying and dissolving" Levant was drawn into its powerful embrace and made over in its image. Europe, to use a metaphor that takes up undercurrents of Kohn's own language, is presented as a Sleeping Beauty, merely sleeping and waiting for prince Napoleon to kiss her back to life, while her passive Levantine sister is ravaged by the encounter and brought into the emperor's palace. I am borrowing this metaphor from feminist theory, because patriarchy and colonialism can be seen to exert analogous forms of domination over those they render subordinate. But, more importantly, the metaphor can explain the different ways in which local societies' reaction to the global project of French civilization are interpreted. In the view of Kohn and many others, Europe, "Sleeping Beauty," is still part of the same system of reference; she just had to be "awakened." Her Oriental sister is not. The Orient has indeed been stereotypically represented, often in a female metaphor, as "mysterious, decadent, and irrational" (but also as "fanatical, violent, barbarous") or "tra-

---

1. I am influenced here by the discussions on "Early Modernities" and "Multiple Modernities" in the journal *Daedalus,* clearly conceived as an answer of reflexive Western social science to the challenges of postcolonial and post-Orientalist scholarship, and by Featherstone, Lash, and Robertson (1995). In order to avoid new dichotomies, however, as in "our modernity" and "their modernities," I have used the term "global modernity" in the singular.

ditional," in opposition to "civilized," that is, "rational, scientific, well-ordered," or "modern" Europe (Said 1978).

I argue that the debate on globalization in the human sciences since the beginning of the 1990s can help us to rethink the history of the encounter of Europe and its modernity with the rest of the world, and provide us with new, local perspectives of the concepts of "civilization" and its dialectical antithesis, "savagery," which can, however, also serve as a means of self-authentication. In the process, this approach can also help subvert the binariness of the "us" versus "them" distinction, in the sense of Homi Bhabha's view that our point of intervention should shift from the *identification* of images as positive or negative to an understanding of the *processes of subjectification* made possible (and plausible) through stereotypical discourse (Bhabha 1986, 149). The point has recently been taken further, resulting in a critique of unhistorical culturalist (and globalist) critiques of Eurocentrism, which overlook that the meanings of "Europe" and its "modernity" are products of historical processes, if not themselves historical processes, inextricable from the invention of Europe's "Others" (Dirlik 2000, 33). Looking from the West to the East does not automatically legitimate Orientalism, but it can help us to understand the multiple and global processes of modernity, of which Europe is then a part.

It was postmodernism that inspired the swing away from the conceptualization of global culture in terms of alleged homogenizing processes, concentrating instead on the richness and variety of popular and local discourses, codes, and practices (Featherstone 1990, 2). It is exactly the notions of the potency and suggestive powers of Western civilization on the one hand, and non-Western societies' willingness to absorb them on the other, that are at stake here, expressed in the concepts of cultural homogeneity and heterogeneity. At least as rapidly as forces from various metropolises are brought into other societies they tend to become indigenized in one way or the other. Cultural expansions are also not necessarily Western (Appadurai 1990, 295). The Ottoman cultural expansion in the wake of the Tanzimat reforms of the nineteenth century was more directly important for the societies involved than the competing European one. The interplay of global and local cultural forces then is not a top-down form of domination, not a one-way street, but a transcultural process, a dialectic of dominant cultural forms and their adaptation, adoption, transformation, integration, disregard, or rejection by other cultures, a process that has to be interpreted as being in itself creative and not just as simple "imitation." D. Eleanor Westney (1987, 6) points out that even the successful imitation of foreign, in her case organizational, patterns requires innovation.

Globalization is a historical process that should not be confined to the last century. It came in stages, the periodization of which differs from author to author. In a general way it can be assumed that the first push of globalization came with the impetus of Orbis Universalis Christianus that ended with the victory over the Moors, the expulsion of the Jews in Spain, and the discovery of America. After a global system of trade in the thirteenth century (Abu-Lughod), the second push arrived with the establishment of the modern world system (Wallerstein) and the rise of the Netherlands, Britain, and France as new imperial powers. In this modern phase the Christian mission was secularized into a civilizational mission that went along with colonialism. The Christian mission did not cease to exist, however; it just played a secondary role. From the end of the nineteenth century until the Second World War, the European civilizing mission was remade in the United States in its rise to world power and was rearticulated with the Manifest Destiny (Mignolo 2000, 280). Since the Second World War, "modernization" and "development" have become key "civilizing projects," and since the end of the Cold War, it has been argued, a triumphant "democratization" carries with it "the aura of the civilizing mission of earlier colonialisms" (Spivak 1999, 223). The events of 11 September 2001 initiated a dangerously simplistic discourse on the "forces of civilization versus barbarity," enhancing my initial point that discourses of civilization come with encounters, even in the form of such violent attacks as the ones of 9/11.

Thinking historically about globalization means thinking about space and time. It is the prioritization of time over space that has been a central feature of discourses that understood social relationships, including those between cultures, in developmental terms. The move from "traditional" to "modern" societies is seen by Kohn and others in terms of a range of specific processes such as industrialization, urbanization, commodification, rationalization, and so forth. These processes, which arose within Western modernity, were imbued with a universalizing force. In effect, Western history was seen as universal world history. And the driving force, the inner logic incorporated within these theories in varying degrees of explicitness, was indeed the idea of progress (Featherstone 1995, 87). The idea of progress teleologically implies a direction, and a finitude, the eventual deliverance into or arrival at a society that its proponents would deem "civilized."

If we prioritize space over time, however, we obtain a different perspective. "Civilization," and its conceptual counterpart, "savagery," then need to be seen as concepts, constructed and imagined by certain intellectuals, as a part of their local history, in a certain space (and a certain time) and for a certain purpose.

From there this concept is regionalized and then globalized, in the sense that other intellectuals in other spaces make it part of their local history. They do so by adapting, adopting, transforming, integrating, ignoring, or rejecting it. In the same way as other Europeans (Sleeping Beauty in my metaphor), especially the Germans, had to come to terms with the spreading of the French concept of "civilization" and constructed their version of "culture" as an answer to the challenge, so the non-European peoples (the Eastern sister) had to conceptualize their own versions of "civilization" and also its "savage" counterpart, suiting their own needs. The processes are similar, yet, because "Western tradition" has made an essential difference between Europe and the East, they have been judged very differently, and the preponderant mode of explanation has been that Western civilization was imported into these cultures and was imitated by them. Yet, as already mentioned, the process of adapting, adopting, transforming, integrating, ignoring, or rejecting is itself a creative process. If we see the matter in this vein, we have advanced one more step toward "provincializing Europe" (Chakrabarty 2000), that is, making it part of a global modernity.

In this chapter, then, I do not deny that Western expansion had some cultural "push effect." But I do argue that it has to be interpreted within a global framework, which means that "European modernity" has to be qualified too. The fault-lines of civilization (modernity), as we shall see, have to be drawn not between Europe and its others, but within them. My aim is to take a comparative perspective, and to sketch the process of imagining and representing the modern image of the "civilized" and its "savage" other in France, the German lands, the Ottoman empire, and its Arab provinces. Everywhere it encountered and engendered complex processes of self-authentication, of which I will concentrate here on the popular and self-consciously archaic, romantic kind. It is in these processes that modern Europe, the modern Middle East, and even modern Islam have been constructed. I thus take clues from postcolonial theory, yet at the same time insist on its critique (as also formulated within its own ranks). And I will start in the West.

THE CONCEPT OF CIVILIZATION IN FRANCE

It was Napoleon's expedition to Egypt that constituted the first act of colonial aggression in which the mission was defined in terms of civilization, in Napoleon's own words to French soldiers on the passage to Egypt in 1798: "Soldiers, you are undertaking a conquest of which the consequences for civilization and world trade are unforeseeable!" The civilizing idea was manifest in his decision to take with him all the scientific and cultural apparatus for which the expedition became so famous. A little army of experts, engineers, Islamicists, printers, natural scientists, artists, mathematicians, and astronomers were all to study Egypt and then place their expertise at the service of the invading generals. Napoleon's idea was to lift Egypt out of the state of despotism and barbarism into which it had fallen after having had a glorious civilization of its own, and to bring to it all that French civilization had to offer: trade, the printing press, the French language, education, medicine, preventive hygiene, the arts, and principles of rational administration in fiscal, judicial, and land matters (Conklin 1997, 18).

The nineteenth-century empire builders no longer thought in terms of reintroducing civilization; they claimed to bring civilization into empty voids. And they began this last and decisive phase of the *mission civilisatrice* in Algeria in 1830. The actual term "mission civilisatrice" was not coined until the 1870s, in the journals of the geographic societies of the Third Republic, and it was then that it began to convey its notion of racial and cultural superiority over the "lesser breeds," so conspicuous in late nineteenth-century colonialism. When Ferry addressed parliament in the early 1880s, justifying the seizure of Tonkin and war with China, he did that by invoking the civilizing mission: "We must believe that if Providence deigned to confer upon us a mission by making us masters of the earth, [. . . this mission is] spreading or awakening [*sic*] among the other races the superior notions of which we are the guardians." Two years later he added: "The superior races have a right *vis-à-vis* the inferior races . . . the right to civilize them" (Conklin 1997, 13). This well-known colonial notion of the French civilizing mission is, however, the end-product of a process that stretched over two hundred years and had its beginnings in the Enlightenment.

The term "civilization" itself was coined in France as a neologism. In a French-German dictionary of 1740 "civilization" was still only defined as "a verdict, a sentence, that renders a criminal affair into a civil case." At that time, the French still used the verb *policer (un peuple policé)* to set up the boundary between civilized (and modern) societies and the others. The modern concept of civilization was born in the Enlightenment struggle between the advocates of the old order, the church, and the encyclopedists, between religious and secular thought. The earliest mention of the creation of civilization out of the verb *civiliser,* to civilize, is by the elder Mirabeau in 1756, which is itself quoted in the Jesuit counterpublication to the *Encyclopédie,* 1771: "Religion is the first resort of civilization" (Moras 1930, 5). Although the secular, republican concept of civilization wins out, it should not be overlooked that the religious, Catholic concept does not cease to exist. By the 1770s, the term "police" was obviously no longer deemed adequate because it failed to express French achievements in the moral and scientific spheres. By that time French *philosophes* were searching for a word that would connote the triumph and development of reason, not only in the constitutional, political, and administrative domain, but in the moral, religious, and intellectual spheres as well. "Civilization" represents the concept of modernity and was created, in its new sense, as the opposite of barbarism. On one side were the civilized (and modern) peoples, on the other, primitive savages or barbarians. The "noble savage" dear to Jean-Jacques Rousseau and his disciples, too, was not regarded as civilized, or modern (Braudel 1993, 4).

The concept of civilization started out as a universal concept. Until the end of the eighteenth century, neither Frenchmen nor Ottomans and Egyptians talked of civilizations in the plural. Instead, the assumption was that there existed a single universal human civilization that was capable of leading all peoples and nations out of savagery and barbarity, even if this civilization was thought to be French in inspiration. It features, from the very beginning, a twofold meaning, true civilization and false civilization *(la fausse civilisation)*, the former being an inner moral virtue, the latter being just an outer facade of manners, refinement, politeness, urbanity, and control of one's passions. These two levels of meaning would persist, pitching the dignity of spiritual concerns against the triviality of material affairs. Challenged by the French *mission civilisatrice,* the Germans would come up with their notion of culture versus (French) civilization that reflected exactly this dichotomy.

But civilization is also a process, intricately linked to the concepts of progress and reform. In fact, the standard formula of the Enlightenment is *progrès de la civilisation et des lumières, état de civilisation et des lumières.* Following Norbert Elias, this process plays itself out in three stages: In its first phase, the concept of civilization is a reform concept, half appreciating and half rejecting the existing order. Society, in the eyes of the reformers, has already reached a certain degree of civilization, but the process is not yet complete. In the hands and minds of the reform movement, namely the rising bourgeoisie, the notions of civilization broaden. Civilization then means civilizing the state, civilizing education, and civilizing broader strata of society, thus extinguishing all things barbaric and antirational. This means, according to Elias (1978–82), that civilization in its first stage is a kind of inner pacification of France herself under the guidance of reformist intellectuals.

And there was a whole wide world out there in France itself, beyond the boundaries of Paris and its orbit, that was utterly irrational and barbaric in the eyes of the city folks, far beyond the pale of modernity: the French countryside. "You don't need to go to America to see savages," mused Parisians strolling through Burgundy as late as 1840. The Landes was described as a "trackless desert, where one needs a compass to find one's way, inhabited by a people alien to civilization." It was compared to the wastes of Libya and Kamtschatka, waiting, like all such waste lands, to be claimed for civilization" (Eugen Weber 1976, 488). The modernizing state in France, driven by an inner *mission civilisatrice,* sought to push the boundary of civilization down into its savage other, the provincial countryside, whose population was represented as the childlike, backward, garrulous, unenterprising natives of undeveloped lands (Weber 1976, 487). Eugen Weber is not alone in making this argument. Natalie Zemon Davis, too, has suggested similarities between an encroaching (early) modern state in France and a civilizing mission overseas (Conklin 1997, viii). The boundary between civilization (modernity) and savagery, then, was not only drawn between France and the rest of the world, but also within France itself.

REDRAWING THE BOUNDARIES OF CIVILIZATION
AND SAVAGERY: THE COUNTRYSIDE AS THE
"IGNOBLE SAVAGE OTHER"

Several issues need to be clarified here. To view the countryside as the abode of the uncivilized, of objects in dire need of reform, was only one possible representation on the part of urban men of the pen. A poetic representation of *la douce France* would have described the sweetness of a classically well-ordered place where rivers, cultivated fields, orchards, vineyards, and woods were all in harmonious balance with each other (Schama 1996, 14), even if this idyllic place were an artificial playground, as in Marie Antoinette's royal gardens, a kind of early Disneyland. Raymond Williams has followed the path from the pastoral to the neopastoral, the inscription of the pastoral idylls into the real, in this case British, country estates, and the "civilizing effects" of a modernizing landowning class on their rural poor in poetry. Matthew Arnold, in *Culture and Anarchy,* voices his critique: "When I go through the country and see this and that beautiful and imposing seat of theirs crowning the landscape, 'There,' I say to myself, 'is a great fortified post of the Barbarians' " (Williams 1973, 104 f.). His conversion of the civilized landowners into barbarians, however, is more the exception than the rule. "The bourgeoisie has subjected the countryside to the rule of the towns," write Marx and Engels in the *Communist Manifesto,* another discourse of modernity; "it has created enormous cities ... [and] has made barbarian and semi-barbarian countries dependent on the civilized ones." Thus, it has rescued a considerable part of the population from the "idiocy of rural life" and, in the "barbarian and semi-barbarian countries, from barbarism" (Williams 1973, 303). Note, again, the way in which the European countryside and non-European countries are correlated. Marx and Engels, of course, believed in the civilizing (modernizing) forces of industrialization and its agent, the bourgeoisie, later to be expropriated by the urban proletariat.

In the colonized world, urban intellectuals and politicians blamed the state of dependency and backwardness of their respective countries on the savages and barbarians inhabiting them. For them civilization went together with technology and urbanization, and the areas of the world that needed to be civilized were those that had their reaches in their countryside and their countryside populated by "uncivilized" people. The Egyptian peasant, for example, has been blamed by more than one nineteenth-century urban reformer as the prime obstacle to progress and modernity, and has been represented as lazy, ignorant, dumb, "like a donkey at a water-wheel who is step by step trotting along slowly" (Qasim Amin, cited in Wild 1990). The Ottoman Sultan Abdülhamid told a European ambassador that in eastern Anatolia there were people "whose comportment was similar to savage tribes in America" (Deringil 1999, 41). Embarrassed by the primitives in their own backyard, and trying to demonstrate that their countries were part of the modern, civilized world to Europeans, non-European elites constructed their own countryside as an ignoble savage other.

"Othering" has been established by Spivak and other postcolonialist theorists as the process whereby a self achieves definition and value (as in "civilized") through creating and defining the "others" (as uncivilized). That which lies "beyond the pale," a metaphor invoking the fence in colonial Ireland, which separated the Protestant enclave of Dublin and the wild Catholic lands beyond, is often defined literally as the "other," the dark, the savage, and the wild (Ashcroft, Griffiths, and Tiffin 1998, 108). The concept of the "boundary," then, is of central importance for analyzing cultural encounters. It is one of the most important thought figures for Homi Bhabha, who begins his *Location of Culture* with a quotation from Heidegger: "A boundary is not something at which something stops but, as the Greeks recognized, the boundary is that from which something begins its presencing" (Bhabha 1994, 1). The boundary as a contact zone separates the constructed worlds of culture and nature, the male and the female, the urban and the rural, the scientific and the superstitious, or the civilized and the savage. The boundary also expresses the dimension of space and time and implies a spatial and temporal state of liminality. Such a state is beautifully expressed in Hans

Peter Duerr's image of the witch (Hagazussa) who, in medieval Europe, was believed to sit on the fence *(Hag)* that passed behind the gardens and separated the village from the wilderness. The witch was capable of crossing the boundary between wilderness and civilization, at least in her wild dreams (Duerr 1987, 46). A premodern creature, she was, in Duerr's words, "a being who participated in both worlds. In time, however, she lost her double features and evolved more and more into a representation of what was being expelled from culture, only to return, distorted, in the night."

The boundary as a zone of contact and encounter between "wildness" and "civilization," then, has to be drawn not only between the colonizing here and the colonized there, the colonizer and the colonized, but also within these cultural spaces. Bhabha's well-known demand "to push the conceptual boundaries of the west to their colonial periphery; to that limit where the west must face that peculiarly displaced and decentred image of itself 'in double duty bound,' at once a civilizing mission and a violent subjugating force" (Bhabha 1986, 148) needs to be qualified. The "double-bind" between the civilized and the savage is also an inner one. There is a contact zone at the inner boundary, as well as one located on the (outer) boundaries of societies of the "other."

SAVAGERY AS ANTITHESIS AND SELF-AUTHENTICATION

Until the actual discovery of the New World, geographical boundaries coincided with human boundaries. Unnatural creatures with two heads, gigantic feet or none at all, and other imagined deformities were thought to populate the unknown continents, and drawings of those creatures ornamented the margins of the world maps then in use (see Grafton 1995, 36, fig. 1.9). The limits of geography coincided with the limits of humanity. With the discovery of the new continent, the "outer boundary," the unknown, unnatural creatures, were replaced with the "savages" of the New World, who now first entered the imaginary of the modern world system (Mignolo 2000, 283). Over time, the difference of space became translated into the difference of time. Savages did not populate a different space any more; rather, they were chronologically inferiorized. Their perceived gap in human development then made them into objects represented as needy of European civilizing.

But savagery is a concept that is much more complex. The term "savagery" is in the West derived from the Latin *salvaticus* or *silvaticus*, meaning "of the woods," "wild." In the sense of "wild," "undomesticated," "untamed," it later acquired the contextual implication of ferocity. "Barbarous," by contrast, had in its

Greek origin probably a primary reference to speech, meaning non-Hellenic in language, foreign, then "outlandish, rude, brutal," and with the Romans, "uncivilized," "uncultured," and also "non-Christian." Ancient Arab lexicographers used the word *barbar* to describe the natives of North Africa west and south of Egypt, with some of them giving its origin as the verb *barbara,* "to talk noisily and confusedly," not derived from the Greek, and others seeing it as a foreign word, African, or possibly Greek.

Savagery in the sense of wildness and the figure of a "Wild Man" living in this state have a long history in European and Middle Eastern culture, even before Ibn Khaldun, as we shall see. In his archaeology of the figure of the "Wild Man," Hayden White undertakes an analysis of the function of "wildness" in premodern European thought. He finds that the notion of "wildness" belongs to a set of culturally self-authenticating devices like "civilization," used to confirm the value of their dialectical antitheses (1978, 151). With the extension of knowledge into those parts of the world, which though known about (but not actually known) had long served as the physical stages onto which the "civilized" imagination could project its fantasies and anxieties, concepts such as wildness, savagery, and barbarism were gradually demythologized in the process of modernity. In time the idea of the Wild Man (as Duerr's witch on the fence) was de-spatialized, and a compensatory process of psychic interiorization took place (White 1978, 153).

Despite the rationalism of the Enlightenment, it was the idea of natural man that fascinated educated, cosmopolitan Europeans (Bitterli 1985, 273). Urs Bitterli, among others, has convincingly shown that the imaginary figure of the noble savage played an important role between the sixteenth and the eighteenth centuries. The belief in the intrinsic virtue, innocence, and beatitude of man living according to the rules of nature, unspoilt by civilization, lasted from the very beginning of European colonial expansion until the age of imperialism (Bitterli 1991). The savage of the New World became an exotic object of fascination, idealized to formulate a critique of European civilization and society. An exotic version of the Wild Man, the savage was imagined as "noble," and it is precisely his "wildness" that makes him a metaphor so attractive for reformers discontent with civilization and modernity. In France, especially, the adoration of the noble savage over time developed into a social critique, even into a device to propagate ideas of revolution and anarchism (Cro 1990). He, and the tamed paradise of nature that he was thought to inhabit, were an excellent object on which to project ever-present images of a Golden Age long since past at home, and Diderot and Rousseau used the figure of the noble savage to attack the European social system of privilege, inherited power, and political oppression (White 1978, 191).

There are, then, two movements that we need to distinguish: a movement that idealizes the savage at an outer spatial boundary, and a movement that idealizes the savage at an inner temporal boundary. Primitivism, the idealization of an exotic noble savage at the outer boundary, holds up a vision of a lost world, insisting that this lost world is still latently present in modern, corrupt, and civilized man and is there for the taking (Hayden White 1978, 171).[2] Archaism, the movement at an inner temporal boundary, idealizes a real or legendary remote ancestor, often wild, and the Golden Age in which he lived. This figure of the premodern Wild Man, and the natural landscapes of wild sublimity in which he was imagined, inspired various romantic movements in Europe (Giesen 1998). Archaism, it has been argued, also inspired Luther's reformation (Hayden White 1978, 171).[3] Both archaism and primitivism have commonly been associated with a state of cultural crisis in a given society. The cultural crisis that interests us here is, of course, the crisis engendered by cultural encounter.

A good example of the cultural encounter within Europe is that between France and Germany. German playwrights and philosophers of the long eighteenth century felt frustrated and beleaguered by French civilization. Unlike France, where aristocratic society absorbed and assimilated the intellectual elite of the enlightenment who were of nonaristocratic background, German nobility, in many ways the poor cousin of the French model, closed ranks against the men of letters, who were left to think and write poetry *("dichten und denken")*, but who were effectively blocked from any other meaningful outlet for their creative reformist energies (Elias 1978–82). They rediscovered in self-consciously archaic ways the ancient Germanic tribes of the Hercynian forest, which Tacitus had so aptly described and used as a critique of Roman (decadent) civilization. Their rough-hewn vigor, "never . . . tainted by intermarriage with other peoples," was now instrumentalized, among many other things, to devise a counter-concept to civilization *à la française,* French-inspired courtly etiquette: (German) culture.

Tacitus's little book *De Origine et Situ Germanorum,* commonly known as the *Germania,* has been deployed across the centuries by countless publicists in Europe, of

2. To be sure, postcolonialists are right in pointing out that primitivism is guilty of the process of "othering." Even the most radical reformers engaging in primitivism were not really concerned with the actual fate of the savages they constructed as "noble." Their constructions only helped to sharpen the concept of their own civilization.

3. Archaism, it has to be added, can develop into primitivism. The primitivists' image of nature, the scenery of the Noble Savage, is usually an Arcadian, peaceful place. For archaism, the scenery in which its heroes act is animal nature, full of conflict and struggle, where only the strongest survive (White 1978, 172). Of course there are intermediate forms.

widely varying persuasions, some of them utterly nefarious. But when Alexander von Humboldt remarked that the "rediscovery of Tacitus was as important an event as the discovery of America by Columbus" (Rudé 1964, 279), he spoke about the discovery of savage worlds, one removed in time, the other in space. In his inaugural lecture as professor of history at Jena in 1789, the poet Friedrich von Schiller listed all the barbarous qualities imputed to primitive peoples by recent travelers and concluded: "We were like that. Caesar and Tacitus, eighteen centuries ago, found us to be little better" (Schiller 1972, 326). Schiller also referred to the "Four Stages Theory" of Adam Smith and the Scottish Enlightenment that postulated that society went through the four stages of hunting, shepherding (citing Tartars, Arabs, and North American Indians), agriculture, and commerce.

In 1784 Immanuel Kant formulated the philosophical antithesis to the French concept of *civilisation*. In his *Ideas on a Universal History from the Point of View of a Citizen of the World,* he wrote: "Cultivated to a high degree by art and science, we are civilized to the point where we are overburdened with all sorts of social propriety and decency . . . The idea of morality is a part of culture. But the application of this idea, when it results only in the similitude of morality, in the love of honor and in outward decency, amounts only to civilizing" (cited in Elias 1978–82, 7).

These two concepts, (German) culture and (French) civilization, would take on explicitly national overtones. In case there were any doubts as to why it was France that should be civilizing Europe, M. François Guizot, author of two books on civilization, drives home the point clearly: "There is something in the French génie, something social, something endearing, something that speaks for itself more gracefully and more effectively than the génie of any other people: be it the effect of our language, of our spirit (esprit) or our mores, our ideas are more popular, present themselves to the masses more clearly, spread among them faster, in one word: clarity, sociability and sympathy are the particular character of France and her civilization and these qualities render her eminently suitable to march at the head of European civilization" (Guizot 1829–32, 7).

As the German lands had to come to terms with the French concept of civilization, so had the others.[4]

---

4. The example of Germany should not be read as an apology. Germany was part of Europe and would of course engage in colonialism itself, even if belatedly, and come up with its own civilizing, euphemistically termed "healing," mission. The example of Germany helps to break up the concept of "Europe," however, as it shows that processes of self-authentication went on there too.

CIVILIZATION AND WILDNESS IN IBN KHALDUN:
HADARA, TAMADDUN, AND *BADAWA*

In Middle Eastern cultural history it was the fourteenth-century theorist Ibn Khaldun who had devised a concept of civilization/savagery in his *Muqaddima,* a cyclical theory of the rise and fall of great dynasties in the Maghrib. Given European preoccupations with the concepts of civilization/savagery, it is hardly astonishing that "it was in Europe that Ibn Khaldun was discovered and the importance of the Mukaddima realized" (Talbi in Lawrence 1989, 69). In Germany, he became a historian of civilization when the "history of civilization" was institutionalized as an academic discipline, comprising all nonpolitical history (al-Azmeh 1981, 190, n. 34). Yet, perhaps too much has been made of his career in Europe, while his impact on Middle Eastern thought has been neglected. The Ottomans, for one, incorporated him into their letters as early as the sixteenth century. Cornell Fleischer gives as the first firm date in the story of the Ottoman adoption of Ibn Khaldun the year 1598, when a learned man acquired a copy of the *Muqaddima* in Cairo. In the middle of the seventeenth century, Ottoman authors began to make explicit reference to Ibn Khaldun (Fleischer 1984, 47), and the *Muqaddima* seems to have been translated into Turkish in 1749. When the German Orientalist Hammer-Purgstall traveled and researched in the Ottoman empire at the beginning of the nineteenth century, he was surprised at the extent to which the *Muqaddima* was known within the empire's bureaucracy and at how frequently it was referred to. He called Ibn Khaldun the "Arab Montesquieu" (Tibi 1987, 285). The *Muqaddima* was also printed in Cairo in 1858.

The *Muqaddima* is an extended treatise of *'ilm al-'umran,* the "science of civilization," also sometimes translated as "culture," which is constructed from the Arabic root *'amara,* "to build." Ibn Khaldun examines the political and historical conditions under which *'umran* appears, flourishes, and declines. His discussion is not about an abstract framework such as the state. Political life is examined as the building and decay of cities, and the root of *'umran,* "to build," for him can mean to live, prosper, flourish, be full with life, inhabit, raise, be in good repair, build, and rebuild. The meanings of *'umran,* then, comprise activity, bustling life, fullness, prosperity, building (Mitchell 1991, 53). Ibn Khaldun distinguishes between *'umran hadari,* the civilization of the settled, and *'umran badawi,* the civilization of the nomadic people of the steppe or desert. *'Umran* thus comes in two forms, with the relation between these two forms being one of anteriority (*badawa* comes before *hadara* in time). The other related term Ibn Khaldun uses is *tamaddun,* the state of "living in the city," which then is "the empirical constituent of *hadara* and the telos of *badawa*" (al-Azmeh 1981, 20 f.). These two modes of existence are, however, interpenetrating, and *badawa*, the state of the bedouin or bedouindom, can in Ibn Khaldun's usage be translated in many cases with "wildness." He also uses *tawahhush*, "wildness." He defines *badawa* expressly as "natural livelihood" *(ma'ash tabi'i)*, and those who live in this state—Arabs, Turks, Turkomans, and Slavs—as "natural people." These "naturally wild people" have a vast potential of destructiveness, and the most savage among them he sees as the camel breeders, Arabs in the West and Turks and Turkomans in the East. Their harsh living conditions engender physical strength, and a personal prowess and courage that are lost in the cities, which make of them a reservoir of vast new energies, capable of ousting dynasties decadent from living in the cities for too long. Ibn Khaldun sees religion, Islam, as the sole medium capable of taming the wild Arabs (Ley 1982, 118 f.). *Badawa*, then, is not to be confounded with barbarity, but comes close to the concept of wildness we have identified in Western thought. It is for Ibn Khaldun, however, not the antithesis of civilization, since he uses the same word, *'umran*, with all its life-furthering meanings, for both the settled and the nonsettled modes of living. It is not entirely clear what values he associates with each mode, and scholars disagree about how neutrally he describes them. Antony Black is right, however, in pointing out that he is unique in seeing primitive society as providing the driving force toward statehood and empire, and settled cities (civility) as part cause and part effect of decay (2001, 181). Ibn Khaldun is certainly more sympathetic toward *badawa* than any other thinker, including modern ones and, especially, the Ottomans.

OTTOMAN DISCOURSES ON *MEDENIYET*, *TEMEDDÜN* AND *BEDEVIYET*

It was in the 1840s that Ottoman intellectuals at the center of the empire, in Istanbul, began to think about "civilization" and to grapple with the concept. They used the terms *medeniyet* and *temeddün* that appeared for the first time in Bianchi's *Dictionnaire français-turc*, in the second edition of 1843–46. In the first edition of 1831, neither *medeniyet* nor *temeddün* are given as entries for civilization. Instead, we find *edeb, erkan öğretmeklik*, and *insaniyet* (humanity). In G. Rhasis's *Vocabulaire français-turc* of 1828, *"civiliser"* is explained as *"polir les moeurs"* and consequently translated as *ahlaki tehzib etmek*, and civilization is rendered as *ünsiyet, tehzib-i ahlak*. Handjeri's *Dictionnaire français-arabe-persan et turc* of 1840–41 explains civilization as "état de ce qui est civilisé: zariflenme [refinement]," and tells readers, as a French example, that "the commerce of the Greeks has civilized the barbarians," translating barbarians by "illiterate" *(ümmi)* and "ignorant *(cahil)* people." Red-house's *English and Turkish Lexicon* of 1877 has *medeniyet* as the first and most important entry for civilization, and after 1882 *medeniyet* emerges as the generally acknowledged term (Baykara 2000, 23 f.).

Probably the first major modern discourse on civilization in the Ottoman empire took place on the pages of the journal *Mecmua-i Fünun,* published by an Ottoman Learned Society, the Cemiyet-i Ilmiye-i-Osmaniye, from 1862 until 1865 in Istanbul.[5] In a mission statement to the sultan, the founder of this society and Ottoman ambassador to St. Petersburg, Halil Bey, stated the goals of the society. He said that although the Ottoman sultan exerted great efforts for the advancement of science and practical knowledge, which led the European nations to the highest degree of civilization and power, Ottomans had not yet reached their desired goals. This was why some educated subjects of the empire had founded the society with the aim of disseminating the arts and sciences. Religion and politics were explicitly banned from the pages of the journal, yet, as we shall see, editorials had a political outlook. Members had to be Ottoman cosmopolitans and master one European language plus Arabic, Persian, and Turkish.

In the discourse on civilization in *Mecmua-i Fünun,* there is, explicitly, no room for the noble savage. In his first editorial, Münif Efendi, editor in chief and former teacher of Ibrahim Pasha of Egypt, takes on all those who (à la Rousseau, it seems) "prefer simplicity and a state of nomadism *(bedeviyet hali),*" clearly understood as barbarity, over civilization, which, he claims, is a fallacious idea. He and the other authors of the journal use the term *medeniyet* for civilization, and strictly oppose it to *bedeviyet,* which then means not so much "nomadism" as, rather, "barbarity." Even the qualities that people usually associate with *bedeviyet,* he argues, such as good health, physical strength, and hospitality, should not be understood as virtues, because civilization surpasses them all, with the comforts of paper money and hotels. And the hospitable bedouin, it is critically remarked, will not hesitate to rob his guest, once he is on his way again. Civilized people may not be as hospitable, then, but traveling is much safer and more comfortable in a civilized country. Münif Efendi also rejects the attribution of laziness and cowardice to civilized people, an indication that he is engaging with Ibn Khaldun's *Muqqadima.* Yet he seems to be familiar with Rousseau's "noble savage" theme too, because Ibn Khaldun, despite all his sympathy for *bedeviyet,* clearly does not "prefer simplicity and a state of nomadism over civilization."

Bedeviyet, "the state in which Arabs, Turkmen, and Kürd live," another phrase

5. All the information about the journal *Mecmua-i Fünun* is taken from Aydin 1995.

CIVILIZING OTHERS / 19

bringing Ibn Khaldun to mind, says Münif Effendi, is a little better than the cave stage of earliest man, but not much so. Civilization is represented as liberation from this primitive stage. With civilization man makes animals serve him, protects himself from natural disasters, turns raw materials into manufactured products, cures diseases, and achieves security and peace in society. Train, steam engine, and telegraph are all proudly cited as the three great discoveries of civilization in the nineteenth century. Civilization was explicitly interpreted by Münif Efendi as "city life," and for him also such rather mundane achievements as hotels, restaurants, and paper money were, as we have seen, an expression of "civilization."

Münif Efendi is clearly a modernizer, yet he locates his discussion within Middle Eastern and European (French) thought, taking on both Ibn Khaldun and Rousseau. Despite the bright and optimistic outlook of *Mecmua-i Fünun* concerning civilization in general and the Ottoman road toward it in particular, the link between civilization and power is also already clearly expressed. Civilization empowers nations and renders them militarily superior. The huge Chinese army was defeated by the British in the Opium War in 1848, the best evidence that uncivilized (nonmodern) nations simply have to civilize themselves in order to survive and not be humiliated. This is what the Ottomans, according to the journal, had to do as well in order to maintain their status as an empire. The Ottoman learned men identified with Britain. As Cemil Aydin (1995) notes, this is a striking contrast to the joyful and almost triumphant Ottoman reaction only five decades later toward the Japanese victory over Russia. In 1905, Japan was imagined as "one of us," an Eastern nation, and Russia as "one of them," a part of the West.

There is no sense yet of an East-West dichotomy in this cosmopolitan discourse of modernity. The notions of a weak Eastern civilization and a strong Western one have, indeed, not been constructed. In fact, the early Ottoman reformist authors, in the euphoria of progress, see the Europeans as bringing civilization wherever they go, and so the colonization of other societies is not seen as negative. On the contrary, it accelerates the civilizing process. In fact, in one article, Münif interprets the British empire's colonization of other countries as a very natural result of their higher civilization and something that befits the Ottomans as well. Clearly an imperial view.

It was especially the tribal, rural frontier regions of the empire, their inner boundary, that the Ottomans found wanting in civilization, and toward whom they developed a sense of their own *mission civilisatrice*. For them "the Arabs, Türkmen, and Kürd," as we have seen, were rather ignoble savages. This Ottoman mission to civilize was in many ways more important and more directly influential in the Arab provinces than the French *mission civilisatrice*, proving Arjun

Appadurai right when he points out that Western expansion and "Westerniza-tion" were often overrated by Western scholarship and that competing indige-nous cultural expansions were neglected (Appadurai 1990).

While the Ottoman *mission civilisatrice* still awaits exhaustive analysis, so far there is enough evidence to make the argument. For example, in the 1840s, the Ottomans saw the Maronites and Druzes of Mount Lebanon as barbarians (Makdisi 2000, 199). Ahmed Midhat Efendi described Iraq in 1870 as "waste land" and Iraq's tribes as "the roaming wild" *(ahalisi bedeviyet ve vahsiyeti)*, close to Ibn Khaldun's terms, but used with a clear value judgment (cited in Ursinus 1994, 161). Selim Deringil has identified the term *bedeviyet ve vahsiyet*, which he renders as "nomadism and savagery," as one of the stock phrases of Ottoman officialdom in the Hamidian regime (Deringil 1999, 41). In the 1890s, Ottoman officials de-scribed the Yezidi Kurds as living in this state. They needed to be "gradually brought into the fold of civilization" (Deringil 1999, 41). In a similar vein, and using the same language, the *vali* of the Hijaz declared in 1895 that the bedouin, who still lived "in a state of nomadism and savagery," had to be civilized by mak-ing them obey the laws of the Shari'a and obliging them to have their disputes settled in religious courts (Deringil 1991, 347).

Deringil seems to restrict the *mission civilisatrice* to nomads (Deringil 1999, 67). Yet, while for the Ottomans clearly the only good nomad was a settled nomad, their *mission civilisatrice* extended to the rural, especially the rebellious, countryside in general, if not to the provinces as a whole. It seems as if the Ottomans saw "the roaming wild" as indeed the lowest level of human development, but they used this expression as an image of "savagery" in the sense of "barbarity" in gen-eral. The (settled) Druzes of the Hawran, too, were considered to be in need of civilizing, which in 1888 included the demands that disputes should be settled in regular courts, children should be educated in Ottoman schools, all foreign mis-sionary teachers should be dismissed, and, in singular cases, even that local shaykhs should wear Ottoman instead of their own tribal garb (Schaebler 1996b, 150 f.). The Ottoman *mission civilisatrice* also included both religious and secular el-ements. Ottoman officials in the Hamidian and Young Turk eras attempted to "hanafize" heterodox frontier people like the Druzes (Schaebler 1996, 202), the Yezidi Kurds, and even nominally Muslim tribes found wanting in religious edu-cation, like the Hijazi bedouin. All of them, in official language, had to be "brought into the community of civilized people," that is, Ottomans of the Hanafi school (Deringil 1999, 100).

At the end of the empire, Ottoman officials would consider turning the *vi-layet* of tribal, rebellious Yemen into a colony explicitly modeled after French Algeria or British India (Sirma 1980; Kreiser 1983). One of Sultan Abdülhamid's palace translators, Mehmed Izzet, wrote in a book assessing the colonial penetration of Africa about a "dark continent, where civilized powers sent colonists." The Ottoman state was encouraged to do the same and to spread the "light of Islam" into "savage regions." Izzet's definition of colonialism was "the process whereby civilized countries send surplus populations to continents whose people are in a state of nomadism and savagery [sic], thereby rendering them prosperous" (Deringil 1999, 148). Deringil interprets the Ottoman notion of "civilizing nomads" as "clearly a migrant concept in a colonial setting." In my argument, civilizing missions are born out of modernizing discourses at the inner boundary. There is a link between modernizing one's own countryside and colonizing other countries, for which this Ottoman language is also proof.

At this time, the end of the empire, the *Mecmua-i Fünun* group's optimistic outlook toward a shared universal civilization had entirely disappeared. It had been ignored already by the Young Ottomans who followed them, who criticized cultural adoptions of European civilization within Ottoman society as "frequenting ballrooms, being liberal about the infidelities of one's wife and using European toilets" (Mardin 2000, 115). As Şerif Mardin has shown, Young Ottoman thought was, indeed, more political and philosophical in outlook. But in the historical writings of the major proponents of Young Ottomanism one rather romantic or self-consciously archaic element is striking: both Namik Kemal and Ziya Pasha seemed to place the spirit of *gaza* at the historical center of Ottoman history. For Namik Kemal, according to Mardin, *gaza* was the existing psychological substratum on which he built his patriotism and cult of the fatherland, with the preservation, rehabilitation, and development of the Ottoman state being his primary purpose (Mardin 2000, 321). According to Ziya, it was this spirit of *gaza* (often in conjunction with *fütüvvet* and in the sense of the "Ottoman pioneer spirit of conquest") that had provided the cohesive force in the Ottoman empire. In his opinion, the Ottoman army had relied for its strength on the "religious principle of rising to the beatific state of a *gazi*, while the men who made up European armies were dragged to the battlefield under the threat of the whip" (Mardin 2000, 356). That the original *ghazi* had not been an Ottoman was not a problem yet, but would of course become one when the Arabs of the empire would lay claim to the noble Arab *ghazi*s of the Arabian desert and Ottoman Turks would search for suitable Turkish ancestors.

Michael Ursinus has followed the archaistically romantic (then revisionist) "turn to the savage Turks" in the writings of popular historians such as Ahmed Midhat, Mehmed Murat, and especially Celal Nuri. In his *History of Ottoman De-*

cline of 1912, Nuri coined the provocative slogan "It was not the Turks who conquered Byzantium, it was Byzantium that conquered the Turks!" (Ursinus 1993, 56). What he meant was that the savage Turkish warriors of the Asian steppes and Turan who had conquered the city of Byzantium had been seduced by its maidens, corrupted by its luxury, and infected with its decadence. "Did this suggest that the Turks were degenerate?" was his equally provocative question, and the answer was an emphatic "No." After all, unlike the overcivilized urbanites of, especially, the capital still standing on the historical soil of Byzantium, the Turks (Türk in opposition to Osmanli), meaning the people *(ahalisi)* or the Turkish commoners *(avammi)*, had resisted degeneration and thus preserved some of the savage vigor of their ancestors (Ursinus 1993, 58). Such views illustrated the radical shift that had occurred within a short time. In 1890, "Türk" was still defined in the *Turkish and English Dictionary* of James Redhouse as a "country bumpkin," a "boor." In 1908 a British traveler still noted that "if you say to a Muhammedan in Turkey: 'Are you a Turk?' he is offended, and probably answers 'I am Osmanlı.' An Osmanlı Turk, if he says a man is a Turk, would mean that he was a lout or a clodhopper" (Ursinus 1993, 50). Ottoman cosmopolitanism rapidly developed into romantic Turkish nationalism. It was in the very last years of the empire, when it became ever more probable that it would not hold out in the "great game," that archaist visions became stronger, went back even further on the timeline, and resulted in a Turanian movement celebrating Attila, Jenghiz, and Oghuz Khan as proud ancestors of the Turks (Stoddard 1917).

Thus, after encountering an increasingly aggressive Europe, the civilizational optimism among Ottoman intellectuals waned. Out of the euphoria of civilization and modernity in the tradition of Ottoman cosmopolitanism and Enlightenment thought developed parochial thinking, which made use of what we have identified as archaist thought figures that could support both Islamism and an increasingly Turkish nationalism. Late Ottoman Turks were not the only ones to discover and idealize their "wild ancestors" and turn them into some kind of noble savage. Late Ottoman Arabs would do the same. This myth would also inspire the emergent Islamist movement, because the both wild and noble ancestor was imagined as a *ghazi,* a warrior for Islam.

TAMADDUN, BARBARIYYA, NOBLE SAVAGERY, AND ISLAM IN THE ARAB LANDS

It was Rif'at al-Tahtawi, the spiritual mentor of a delegation sent to Paris by fierce modernizer Muhammad 'Ali of Egypt to study French technological and scientific achievements, who used his five years in France, from 1826 to 1831, to learn French and become a keen observer of French society in all its aspects. Back in Egypt, he published a book, *Talkhis al-ibriz ila talkhis bariz* (1265/1848), in which he draws the temporal and spatial boundaries of civilization. He distinguishes three stages: the first stage of the "roaming wild," and here he uses *al-mutawahhishun* and gives "the countries of the blacks" as an example; then the second stage of the "raw barbarians," who in his example are the *'arab al-badiya*, the bedouin of the desert. It is interesting that he uses here the term *al-barabira*, and not, as the Ottoman learned men, the Ibn Khaldunian term *badawa*. The word *barbari* was, as we have seen, of ancient usage in Arabic. It was used to mean "certain people of the Maghrib, who were like the Arabs of the desert in hardness, coarseness or rudeness, and in slightness of religion and littleness of knowledge" (Lane 1863). The Arab bedouin are, notably, and unlike the Ottoman Münif Efendi's view, placed one stage above the "roaming wild" of Africa, or, in other words, African peoples are represented as the first stage of humankind. The third stage are the people of education *(adab)*, of refinement *(al-zarafa)*, of cultivation *(al-tahaddur)*, and of civilization *(al-tamaddun)*. And on this third level, the level of civilization and modernity, he counts Egypt, Syria, Yemen, the Ottoman empire, Persia, the European countries, and most of North America. Once again, there is no concept yet of a modern West and a non-modern East. Even if his own country admittedly could learn a few things from France (and vice versa), it belonged in al-Tahtawi's view to the civilized, modern world. The Sudan, however, did not.

Until about the end of the 1860s/70s, civilization was a universal concept of which Islamic societies perceived themselves to be part. In 1878, designated prime minister Nubar Pasha wrote a speech for the Egyptian Khedive Isma'il, in which he still euphorically exclaimed: "My country is not part of Africa anymore, we have become a part of Europe" (Schoelch 1991, 391). Africa, the Sudan especially, was clearly outside Isma'il's pale of civilization, a foreign, wild territory that needed to be militarily conquered. The Khedive spoke explicitly of Egypt's "destiny" and "civilizing mission" toward the Sudan. Because in European eyes Egypt was somewhere between Africa and Europe, to extend Egyptian authority into unexplored regions of the Sudan was thought by the Khedive to be an assertion of Egypt's mature and distinct civilization that would make it equal to and "part of Europe" (Troutt-Powell 1995, 38). Yet the Europeans closed their border: at the same time, in the 1860s, European politicians, journalists, and scientists drew a sharp line between their own civilization and the rest of the world. The French ascendant to the throne, Henri V, Comte de Chambord, spoke for many of them when he noted in his diary, during a journey through Egypt: "All these oriental peoples assume only the façade of civilization, with the barbarian ready to emerge at any minute" (Schulze 2000, 28).

Tahtawi's seems to be the first usage of the term *al-tamaddun* for civilization in its modern sense. In Kazimirski's *Dictionnaire arabe-français* of 1860, the verb *madana* is rendered as "to settle," with the second root to mean "to build cities," and the fifth root "to gather in a civil, political society (talking about the human family which has exchanged the state of savagery [*l'état sauvage*] for the social state [*l'état social*])." *Tamaddun*, then, is given as "état social, policé," in the French tradition before the term "civilisation" was coined. Kazimirski does not seem to want to credit Arab civilization with this modern term.

In Butrus al-Bustani's dictionary *Muhit al-Muhit* of 1870, the first dictionary of the *nahda*, the Arab awakening or Arab renaissance, the term *tamaddun* is of course also defined as deriving from the verb *tamaddana*, the fifth root, which has a reflexive meaning in Arabic. Much stronger than in Kazimirski's translation, however, it here means "to civilize oneself," "to become civilized by one's own effort," and is thus a truly self-authenticating (renaissance/awakening) term. Bustani makes this clear. The entry in his dictionary can be translated as: "And man civilizes himself means that he adopts the morals of the cities and moves from the stage of wildness *(al-khashuna)*, barbarity *(al-barbariyya)* and ignorance *(al-jahl)* to the stage of refinement *(al-zurf)*, and knowledge *(ma'rifa)*" *(al-Muhit)*. The three stages reflect Tahtawi's stages of civilization.

The discourse of the *nahda* is indeed a modern urban reform discourse, aiming at reviving some of the splendor of an Arab civilization of the past. In the more nostalgic aspects of his thinking, Butrus al-Bustani was probably the first to write with pride about the notion of Arab blood (Hourani 1983, 101), and in his dictionary the Arabic term that has acquired the meaning of nationalism, *qawmiyya*, is derived from the word *qawm*, which was a bedouin word describing the unit to which a bedouin belonged, to which he owed allegiance, especially in times of war, and that can be translated as "clan" or "tribe." As we have seen, Tahtawi saw the bedouin of the desert as a wild and barbarous lot, yet living already on the second stage of human development (out of three). Despite the strained relations between settlers and nomads in real life, there seemed always to have been an undercurrent that viewed this state of wildness also in a more positive light.

Ancient Arab lexicographers had recorded traditions, such as "the Arabs of the desert are the means of aiding the Muslims, and increasing their armies, and strengthening them by the contribution of their wealth as alms" (Lane 1863). Ibn

Khaldun has already been mentioned, representing, in a way, the bedouin as the driving force of civilization. The *nahda* movement would also rediscover the *Mu'allaqat*, the seven odes out of the considerable volume of poetry transmitted from the desert bards of the sixth century, collected in writing by Arab scholars of the eighth. Jurji Zaydan wrote of the pre-Islamic noble knights of the desert.

But it was the Aleppan 'Abd al-Rahman al-Kawakibi (1849–1903) who made popular the figure of a wild man turned noble. In his *Umm al-Qura,* a book about the future of the Muslim *umma,* which was published by Rashid Rida in installments in the journal *al-Manar* in 1902–3, he undertook a celebration of the Arab tribes and the Arabian Peninsula previously unheard of in Arab political literature. He was the first Arab Muslim writer to radically redefine the bedouin tribes of the Arabian desert. The Arabian Peninsula, halfway between the Far East and North Africa, and harboring the holy sites of Islam, was represented by Kawakibi as a special, almost sacred landscape. Because of its poverty and geographical remoteness, it had preserved the purity of both Islam and the Arab blood. Here was a truly Arabian Islam free from modern corruptions. He saw the Arab tribes as being free from the moral decay and the passivity that went along with despotism. They possessed the attributes of pride, independence, and ésprit de corps. The center of gravity, he famously demanded, should move back to Arabia. The caliphate should be in the hands of an Arab descended from the Prophet. Kawakibi's book, forbidden by the Ottoman authorities, was eagerly read in learned societies of the awakening movement *(jama'iyya)* in Egypt and Syria in the first decade of the twentieth century, and it influenced both emerging nationalism and modernist Islam.

At the end of the Ottoman empire, the savagery of Tahtawi's "raw barbarians" was being made over into noble savagery. When the German Orientalist Martin Hartmann visited Damascus in 1913, he recorded a conversation with the *vali,* Arif Bey, "of Arab origin but totally turkified," who insisted, not exactly to the liking of his German visitor, on singing the praises of the bedouin: these were noble, excellent people, still unspoilt by civilization. He knew these topics, Hartmann said, "the praises of *bedeviyet,* bedouindom, were a favorite essay subject in the schools, and a sheer inexhaustible source of conversation for the educated on social occasions" (Hartmann 1914, 19 f.). This was a change in attitude. Fifty years earlier, as we have seen, *bedeviyet* was seen as sheer barbarity in Ottoman literary magazines in Istanbul, which praised technical progress as civilization. Early Arab nationalists in exile in Paris turned the pre-Islamic desert folk hero 'Antar into the shining knight of Arab unity and brought him onto the theater stage. In 1910, the play *'Antar* by Shukri Ghanim premiered at the Odeon theatre. "Here 'Antar," wrote Khairallah Khairallah at the time, "the poet errant, is no longer the amorous paladin of the desert sands, but, in the novel conception of M. Ghanem the grand champion of Arab unity" (1919, 45). In a book on Syria published in 1912, Khairallah wrote a geographical and nationalist account of

> incorrigible nomads, [who] have remained, under their patriarchal tunics, what they were fourteen centuries ago, when a man of genius organized them and launched them onto the world. Living a life of freedom and deprivations, they regard with sovereign disdain all that is not part of this life of independence. Some of these ancient virtues are still with them: simplicity, pride, honor, and a certain majesty, even in their rags. But these are the Arabs. None of this is at all true of the Kurds, Turcomans, Tcherkesses, Yezidies, Nawars, or Isma'ilis. The Arab alone, downtrodden as he is, still possesses the remnants of the moral and intellectual qualities that render him suited for a proper civilization. (1912, 15)

As I have argued elsewhere, urban nationalists before the Arab Revolt discovered the ancient virtues of the noble Arabs of the desert in their tribal brothers within the emerging Arab *umma*.[6]

Under the onslaught of European (material) culture and an Ottomanism that developed increasingly missionary and Turkish nationalist traits, Arab intellectuals in the provinces found themselves under twofold pressure. To be sure, Arab intellectuals were also cultured Ottomans, who had appropriated the polished ways of the imperial culture. But in the steady process "from Ottomanism to Arabism" (Dawn) and in keeping with our argument, the cultural crisis in which they found themselves gave rise to self-consciously archaic rediscoveries of their own Golden Age and of some of its proponents, the noble Arabs of the desert. The Ottoman Arabs, like the Ottoman Turks, were discovering the premodern Wild Man turned Noble Savage in their cultural history, as had the Germans in the same global process.

It is especially in the popular imagined figure of the noble Arab of the desert and *ghazi* for Islam, that the *nahda* movement meets the other reform movement of the nineteenth century, the *salafiyya*. The *salafiyya* saw the early Islam of the pious forefathers *(al-salaf al-salih)* as the Golden Age to which Islamic civilization had to return in order to regenerate itself. As in Kawakibi's line of reasoning, the notion that Islam and Islamic society were to be found in their pure form on the Arabian Peninsula becomes almost a trope.

6. For an account of the shifting discourses on desert Arabs, and the role of the imaginary of the noble Arab of the desert in early nationalism, see Schaebler (forthcoming).

Archaism is an important factor in the modernist formulation of Islam. I contend that it is indeed the notion of "wildness," with its associated qualities of "vitality," "purity," and "uncorruptedness," that influenced the *salafi*s in their discovery of all these virtues in the "wild" Wahhabis of the Najd. The Najd, a desert region on the Arabian Peninsula, was, it has to be pointed out, one of the very few independent, noncolonized regions in the Middle East at the time. The *salafi*s brought the Wahhabiyya, who with their activism and Puritan version of Islam had long been regarded as extremist outsiders and dissidents, into the ranks of the *umma* and redefined them as "reformers." It is not astonishing that the *salafi*s were also influenced by Ibn Khaldun's *Muqaddima* (Lawrence 1984).

For al-Afghani (1838–1897), for example, the first Islamic intellectual who began to transform Islam into an ideology as opposed to traditional theology (Schulze 1990), the greatness of early Islam consisted primarily in its military conquest. It was at this point that the concept of *jihad,* holy war, was woven into the concept of civilization and acquired its double meaning: conquest of lands and peoples, as well as conquest of the self. Islam is more a civilization than a religion in the *salafi* discourse, with the concept of civilization being expressed in the language of Islam. It has been noted that Afghani was influenced by Guizot's writings on civilization and developed much of the more nostalgic elements of his vision of Islam while in exile in Paris, feeling estranged in the heart of Europe (Sharabi 1970, 39). *Al-tamaddun al-islami,* Islamic civilization, is above all activity, as expressed in the Qur'anic verse "God changes not what is in people, until they change what is in themselves" (13:10; Hourani 1983, 128). Man is responsible for his acts; no passive resignation, no fatalism is to be tolerated. Analyzing European modernity, that is, speculating about "the reasons for the transformation in the condition of Europe from barbarism to civilization," Afghani argued that the only reason was "the religious movement raised and spread by Luther" (Keddie 1972, 391). He reportedly saw himself as a kind of Luther. His colleague Muhammad 'Abduh (1849–1905) also considered the Reformation as the European breakthrough to modernity, but argued that with its demand for reform and for a return to the simplicities of the faith, it was in fact very much like Islam (Abduh 1966, 149). Modern Islam was clearly constructed as a discourse on civilization and modernity, and in an encounter with the West.

Rashid Rida (1865–1935) devised in a little textbook for Arab youth an answer to the question as to why God chose the Arabs for his divine revelation. This was because, and here we find Kawakibi's line of argument again, they were mentally and spiritually independent and their characteristics were courage, physical strength, virility, and honor; this was at a time when the rulers of the other peoples were completely corrupted by luxury and the other peoples themselves weakened by slavery and serfdom. The Arab tribes on the peninsula had equality, while the other societies had classes. In short, the Arabs were pure, intelligent, hospitable, and helpful, while the others were under the tyranny of their passions and generally morally corrupt. And they had a language that like no other language was able to express and develop the sciences and the arts. Thus, it was because of their wholesome nature that God chose the Arabs and prepared them for the Prophet Muhammad's mission and for their "religious and civilizational leadership" (Rida 1927, 5–8). In this spirit Rashid Rida opened a short-lived school for missionaries in Cairo in 1911–12. It was at this juncture that a *da'wa* movement, teaching Arabic and Islam, became active. The modern *umma* was to be an Arabic-speaking one, embracing modernist Islam.

Discourses of self-authentication created the platforms on which both Middle Eastern nationalisms as well as today's Islamism would emerge. They have proved to be far more potent in the contemporary world than proponents of the modernizing creed, who concentrated on "Westernization," ever deemed possible, because it was in such processes that a modern civilization with a distinct self-perception crystallized. Consequently, and as I have tried to demonstrate, the fault-lines of modernity today have to be drawn not between civilizations, but within them.

BEYOND DICHOTOMIES

Operating under the assumption that modernity is a global process of multiple, crossing paths, and arguing that the debate on globalization helped to promote the emphasis of space over time in history as a field, I have been following the process of globalizing the European (French) concept of civilization, from urban France to the French countryside, to the German lands, to the Ottoman capital and its Arab provinces. Everywhere, that is, also in Europe itself, as in the German example, it encountered and engendered complex processes of self-authentication. These processes are local reactions to global civilizing schemes and can imply civilizing missions of their own. They cannot be interpreted as imitation and repetition ("Westernization").

It is especially at the boundaries between the concepts of civilization and savagery, both inner and outer, and spatial and temporal, that we can observe these processes. Exotic noble savages at the outer boundaries are idealized to serve as a critique of the dominant civilization. At the contemporary inner boundary in space, proponents of the urban, cosmopolitan concept of civilization construct the countryside as its ignoble savage other.

Often at the same time, they romanticize premodern wildness. The wild men, often turned into noble savages, of times gone by, serve as a reservoir of energy and inspiration in times of cultural stress, and the Golden Age in which they lived serves as a model and inspiration for the future of crisis-ridden societies, beleaguered by the civilizing missions of dominant cultures.

My goal has been to show the historicity of the constructed and modern concept of civilization and its counterparts, which is true for both Europe and the societies it set out to "civilize" (read "dominate"). It is these processes of encounter and cultural self-authentication that, in the process, constitute both Europe and its others, and are part and parcel of modernity. In fact, it was in these processes that the notion of distinct civilizations was brought about, in the middle of the last century. Before, urban men of the pen in Istanbul, Cairo, and Paris could still write about one universal civilization of which all were a part, or well on their way to becoming part. After the 1860s this notion disappeared, and the "West" and the "East" were constructed as a dichotomy. A new understanding of Islam, and emerging nationalisms, then became the platforms of self-authentication in the face of European aggressiveness.

Yet, it has to be added that both Europe and its others engage in othering their own subaltern rural people as well as those at their outer boundaries, as in the case of the Sudan, and all of Africa, for that matter. This should not be read as an attempt to exonerate European colonialism, in the sense of "they did it too." "They" did it in the grip of a colonial world order. Let me conclude, as I began, by borrowing from feminist scholarship, where the concept of complicity has shown that the victims of patriarchy are imbued with some agency, too (Thuermer-Rohr et al. 1989; her German term *Mittäterschaft*, "co-agency," captures better what I am trying to say). In this sense, we must also recollect the compelling seductions of colonial power. In Leela Ghandi's words (1998, 4), the forgotten archive of the encounter between East and West narrates "multiple stories of contestation and its discomfiting other, complicity." If we want to be serious about sketching out the different but equally important paths to modernity, we cannot leave these stories out.

2

Subduing Globalization

The Challenge of the Indigenization Movement

MEHRZAD BOROUJERDI

Twenty-five years ago, Stanley Hoffmann (1977) described the discipline of International Relations (IR) as a peculiarly "American social science." He maintained that, traditionally, analysis of the international system had been equated with the study of U.S. foreign policy—not surprising given that scholars residing in the United States do much of the theorizing in IR. Ironically, however, IR scholars continue to view their discipline as a "global" social science within which theories and research methodologies can supposedly travel from one culture and location to another with little difficulty. Of late, postmodernist IR theorists have questioned the notion of IR as a "global" social science, insisting that all scholarship is radically situated within its own cultural and temporal frameworks. Postmodernists claim that there is no neutral vantage point or absolute standard of scientific objectivity from which scholars can observe human behavior.

Meanwhile, another emerging body of literature, not necessarily always in tune with postmodernism, has also challenged IR in particular and Euro-American-centered social sciences in general. I will refer to the authors of this literature as members of the "indigenization" movement. The proponents of indigenization argue that Eurocentric premises have, alas, colonized the social sciences and, in turn, helped to secure and perpetuate a Western-dominated world order. They argue that Third-World intellectuals have to be wary of the "Western," disguised as "universal," theories and research methodologies in the social sciences. Proponents of the indigenization movement have attacked such cherished assumptions and axiomatic principles of Western philosophy as objective reason, humanism, the idea of progress, culture-transcending knowledge,

30

and the radical dualism between religion and science. Instead they maintain that social scientists in the Third World should generate and use concepts and theories rooted in indigenous intellectual traditions, historical experiences, and cultural practices in order to explain in a more comprehensive fashion the world-views, sociohistorical contexts, and scholarship of their people.[1] Indigenization theorists maintain that social science is universal insofar as concepts and theories developed in one civilization are available to scholars in another civilization. However, they caution that we should not confuse universalization with generalization,[2] and that we should aspire to make social sciences more transcultural.

The brazen nature of their attacks on Western scholarship and Euro-American scholars' intellectual arrogance has not endeared the advocates of indigenization to Western academic circles. On the contrary, some Western opponents of knowledge indigenization have branded this movement as apologetic, chauvinist, essentialist, ideological, anti-modern, particularistic, and xenophobic. By contrast, I will argue that the project of knowledge indigenization should not be readily dismissed as obscurantism, atavism, militant particularism, or an invidious and compulsive tendency to fetishize and celebrate difference. Instead, I maintain that this is a largely genuine, albeit conflict-ridden, project by partisans of erstwhile civilizations seeking to end their condition of intellectual docility while negotiating with a compulsive and restless modernity. By looking at the ideological efficacy and travails of the indigenization project, I shall demonstrate how Third-World intellectuals wish to form their own discursive repertoire, not wanting to be a prolegomenon to Western philosophy. As a case study, I will briefly survey the "Islamization of knowledge" as one such enterprise.

1. For example, the ideas of the fourteenth-century Arab historical sociologist Ibn Khaldun on the rise and fall of states, Amin's "tributary mode of production," "the rentier-state" argument, and the Asiatic mode of production.

2. We should remember Raymond Williams's idea of "keywords" (words whose meanings change over time and differ across cultures). For example, some of the keywords in the liberal lexicon (that is, "liberalism," "individualism," "equality," "democracy," and "civilization") can be contested. Democracy may be a universal concept but its specific applicability often is not. You can have democracy in a Lockean form (checks and balance), as in Britain and the United States, or in a Rousseauian form (organic, centralized, unified rule), as in France or Latin America.

INDIGENIZATION: A HISTORICAL BATTLE CRY
FOR THIRD-WORLD SCHOLARS

The calls of Third-World thinkers for knowledge indigenization came on the heels of demands for political independence and cultural authenticity during the post-Second World War era. A host of movements—for example, Rastafaris and Négritude—and activist intellectuals—such as Samir Amin, Aimé Césaire, Frantz Fanon, C.L.R. James, Albert Memmi, and Léopold Sédar Senghore—argued that "intellectual decolonization" must accompany political liberation if the Third World is not to remain a nodal point on the Western imperialist map. The rise of "Third Worldism," starting in the mid-1950s, strengthened the calls for cultural authenticity because mimicry and submission were considered fraudulent and counterfeit modes of existence. Hence, the "decolonization" of Egyptian, Ghanaian, Indian, Indonesian, and numerous other national histories and historiographies began in earnest with much fanfare and vociferous rhetoric.

In 1972, the Malaysian scholar Syed Hussein Alatas lamented the "captive mind" of Third-World social scientists, defining this as "the product of higher institutions of learning, either at home or abroad, whose way of thinking is dominated by Western thought in an imitative and uncritical manner" (Alatas 1972, 691). He contended that Asians needed to create their own autonomous social science tradition. A few years later one of Alatas's counterparts in India, C. T. Kurien, wrote: "We are neither Asian nor scientists. Our knowledge about the problems of our own societies is largely bookish, and the books that we read are mainly from the West . . . We are beggars, all of us—we sneak under many an academic table to gather the crumbs under them. And we mix these bits and make a hash which we pretend to relish, but which we can hardly digest. We have hardly made a contribution to academic cuisine, and have thought it impossible to prepare a dish of our own, with a recipe we have made, using ingredients we have" (Atal 1981, 191).

Such developments as the precipitous decline of Third-Worldist solidarity, the end of the Cold War, and swift globalization of capitalism and modernity have moderated the rhetoric of the authenticity and indigenization movements. Yet these have not fallen into the dustbin of history. Quite the contrary: at the same time that all cultures have experienced the impact of globalization—the expansion of financial markets, the growing importance of information technology, and so forth—the calls for knowledge indigenization and cultural authenticity have intensified. While the global commodification of culture tends to homogenize the particulars, a robust counter-movement of local identity politics is concurrently rising. As Third-World societies try to engage, finesse, or incorporate Western modernity into their everyday life practices, they simultaneously alter that modernity by drawing upon their own reservoir of "cultural capital" and "habitus" (Bourdieu 1977).[3] Because the prerequisite for the realization of the ethos of Western modernity is the loss of non-Western peoples' former ontological identity, globalization and local resistance(s) to the process often go hand in hand.

KNOWLEDGE INDIGENIZATION:
THE PROJECT'S UTILITY

The movement to indigenize knowledge raises the following six questions: Is indigenization of knowledge a pernicious intellectual project? How legitimate are the non-Western charges against the precepts, and ethos, of the meta-narrative of Euro-American-centered social sciences? Should criticisms of Eurocentric ideologies lead to incrimination of Enlightenment principles or actual realization of some of them? How have non-Western intellectuals historicized and delimited Western thought? Have Third-World intellectuals formulated judicious "indigenous" epistemological principles in such fields as anthropology, economics, political science, psychology, and sociology? Finally, what are some of the obstacles to knowledge indigenization in the Third World?

According to Syed Farid Alatas, "The call to indigenization does not simply suggest approaching specifically indigenous problems in a social scientific manner with a view to developing suitable concepts and methods, and modifying what has been developed in Western settings. It goes beyond this and refers to the idea that social scientific theories, concepts, and methodologies can be derived from the histories and cultures of the various non-Western civilizations" (1993, 309).

The calls for indigenization gained particular momentum during the 1970s when numerous African, Asian, Latin American, and Middle Eastern intellectuals argued that Western culture and social sciences are not the only relevant and valid models. These intellectuals sought to narrate their respective societies' historical trajectories by developing a new set of conceptual vocabulary rooted in their own local conditions, needs, practices, and problems—yet obviously mediated

3. For example, the neo-Confucian cultural movement of Asia stresses the ethics of the bureaucratic public sphere by extracting from the cherished ideals of the family. This movement considers the individual an instrument of the group rather than an autonomous agent.

through their exposure to the West. As dependency theorists and the advocates of the New International Economic Order (NIEO) attacked the assumptions and arguments of modernization theory in the 1970s,[4] Third-World intellectuals called for an end to the sociocultural subjugation of Africa, Asia, Latin America, and the Middle East. Years of Western intellectual imperialism had produced a predominantly borrowed consciousness that rendered most social sciences esoteric and irrelevant in much of the Third World. Consequently, social scientists could play at best an ancillary role in Third-World societies; typically, however, the masses regarded social scientists as alienated from local realities.

The advocates of knowledge indigenization insisted that they did not see themselves through the Western gaze or mirror that had reduced them to mere echoes of American, British, and French scholarship under the false pretense of scientific universality. Intellectuals in the Third World had to focus on the historical and cultural specificities of their societies to offer theories and research methods reflective of their own goals, world-views, and sociocultural experience. Responding to those skeptics who denounced this "self awareness" as too subjective, the proponents of knowledge indigenization questioned the totalizing master narrative of Western modernity, which is based on an East-West binary construction, and the disguised partiality of Western science. Advocates of knowledge indigenization claim that they have the right to criticize the ideals, norms, and prescriptions of Western social scientists who are the children of the Enlightenment. Third-World intellectuals maintain that while "selective" and "constructive" integration of Western sciences is perfectly legitimate, one should not lose sight of the inherent ethnocentrism of Western academicians and their analysis.[5] Furthermore, these intellectuals underscore the intersubjective meanings between Western and non-Western settings that must not be minimized if social sciences are to become truly intercultural. Finally, they assert that like charity, social scientific research should begin at home. When local social scientists analyze their own realities, they expand both the substance and methodologies of their disciplines, offering alternative perspectives on human behavior.

While knowledge indigenization is fraught with epistemological difficulties and marked by vitriolic rhetoric, I cannot dismiss this project as a homoge-

4. For three classic examples of dependency theory, see Baran (1957), Frank (1969), and Amin (1976).

5. For example, during the 1970s, estimates put the number of American political scientists at 75 percent of the total worldwide. Similarly, Susan Strange (1971, 223) maintains that in 1971, nine-tenths of world's living economists were Americans.

neously rhetorical plot by Third-World demagogues. Central to the indigeniza-tion project are qualms about such pillars of Western intellectual tradition as ob-jective reality, universal rationality, and value-free science. Ironically, Western thinkers have raised similar objections, inspiring—albeit perhaps inadvertently—their counterparts in the Third World. For example, Peter Winch (1958) argues that various societies have different standards of "rationality." Roy Mottahedeh (1985, 202) describes reason as "one of the notorious weasel words of all lan-guages; it appears to designate a sanitized, universal area of discourse and yet in practice turns out to be as culturally determined and idiosyncratic [to say nothing of its gendered nature] as most of our ideas." As for the neutrality of science, the collective works of Jürgen Habermas and the Frankfurt School theorists demon-strate that all knowledge is rooted in some underlying interest or ideology. In ad-dition, Michel Foucault and postmodernist scholars substantiate the claim that social sciences are not power-free, value-free, or interest-free (Kleden 1986, 37).

The proponents of indigenization remind scholars: (a) that in science, they need to distinguish the universal from the particular; (b) that while the aim and method of science may be uniform throughout the world, the problem of sci-ence in relation to society is not; (c) that what constitutes science at a given period is determined by the prevailing system of values; and (d) that the radical dualisms of body and soul, fact and value, reason and faith so central to Western ontology and epistemology are not universally shared.[6] In other words, the protestation of positivists notwithstanding, indigenization theorists object to the scientism and epistemological/methodological imperialism of Western sciences. For example, a group of cross-cultural psychologists from the United States, New Zealand, Turkey, and India have maintained that instead of "thinking globally, acting lo-cally," American psychology is largely "thinking locally, acting globally." The strong commitment of Western psychology to foundationalism, empiricism, and the model of the self-contained individual often leads to the negation or igno-rance of the "local intelligibilities" of non-Westerners. Significantly, these psy-chologists conclude: "We see particular dangers inhering in the traditional attempt to establish culture free knowledge of human functioning regardless of the particular methods chosen for study. Not only do such attempts obscure or denigrate myriad traditions, in favour of the culture which 'calls the truth.' But, such inquiry does not appear to have significant promise in terms of the enor-mous practical problems confronting the world—both in local and international

6. The cosmopolitanism of Diderot—who believed that without the unity of physics, ethics, and poetry humans face a new "barbarianism"—exemplifies a Western idea not universally shared.

terms. Theories and methods with a strong grounding in or applicability to practical contexts are much to be sought" (Gergen et al. n.d.).

Contrary to the prophecy of modernization theorists, who contended that a priori identities (ethnic, religious, linguistic, and so forth) would dissipate with exposure to "the West," these identities have endured. Western social scientists must recognize and read the self-reflexive narratives of scholars seeking to build between cultures. Ignoring these narratives in fact reduces the explanatory power of Western social science. Worse yet, to underestimate non-Western scholars as they become increasingly self-assured and assertive in articulating their own historical narratives runs the risk of turning the principles of "intercultural interchange" and the "global village" into mere slogans. Humanity has overcome the condition of "historical pseudomorphosis" (Spengler 1939)—that situation in which an older alien culture's extensive hegemony hampers a young indigenous culture from developing self-consciousness. As Fred Dallmayr (1996) contends, humanity is in dire need of a new mode of cross-cultural encounter based on a "deconstructive dialogue or a hermeneutics of difference which respects otherness beyond assimilation."

Finally, a number of indigenization theorists pose the following questions: to what extent should reason and its corresponding values and goals be considered globally uniform and universal considering the absence of ideological syncretism or ecumenical brotherhood in the world today?[7] Even if reason were perceived as universal, to what extent should scholars embrace the scientific analysis that flows from reason without compromising cultural authenticity and specificity? Western thinkers such as Rousseau, Nietzsche, Heidegger, Sartre, Gramsci, and Kierkegaard would not favor the loss of authenticity, for they championed in one way or another the "be yourself" motto of authenticity. As Daniel J. Boorstin, former Librarian of Congress, inquires, "Can such an idea [the idea of progress], that grew from distinctively Western memory, experience, and imagination, take root and flourish elsewhere? Can it be credible in parts of the world that do not share the Judeo-Christian belief in a Creator God, a God of Novelty, and in a Creator Man, Apostle of Novelty? Can the idea of progress survive in societies that lack the melodramatic Western triumphs of science and technology? Can people be expected to share the intellectual product when they had not shared the process from which it came? . . . Would we not, perhaps, profit more from

7. As I have argued elsewhere (1997), Francis Fukuyama's argument (1992), that the growing appeal of economic and political liberalism in the Third World is tantamount to the "end of history," is short-sighted.

the diversity of human experience if we encouraged all people to make their own metaphor?" (1993, 60).

RISKS AND LIMITATIONS OF INDIGENIZATION:
THE ISLAMIC EXPERIMENT

The process of retrieving heritage while at the same time reckoning with modernity has rendered the knowledge indigenization project at once heroic and disjunctive. Yet hauteur toward the indigenization project should not necessarily translate into a blind acceptance of its fetishism of difference, cult of authenticity, or rancorous rhetoric. The efforts of certain indigenization theorists to short-circuit modernity through recourse to historical amnesia, exaltation of plebeian values, and invidious polarizing is ill-advised. Nor is "nativism"—the doctrine that calls for the resurgence, reinstatement, or continuance of native or indigenous cultural customs, beliefs, and values, especially in opposition to acculturation—a viable alternative to a modernity that has been simultaneously prodigious and perfidious.[8] In other words, countering the counterfeit "universalism" of the West cannot any longer be accomplished by embracing an arbitrary and intolerant "particularism."

For example, the Islamization of knowledge presently pursued by various Muslim intellectuals, who present Islam as a faith for all seasons, is an endeavor riven by epistemological flaws.[9] The hybrid that results from mutation of Islam into an ideology supposedly capable of guiding Muslims, through a shortcut, to the blessed land of an indigenous postmodern enlightenment often produces nothing but "cultural schizophrenia" (Shayegan 1997). While Islamization of knowledge is an effort by Muslim intellectuals not to suffocate in a secularist universe, where the commodification of everyday life is threatening the tenets of faith,[10] the thought of religiously sanctioned social sciences is disturbing.[11]

8. I have elaborated further on this issue in Boroujerdi (1996).

9. For two such examples, see Moten (1996) and the International Institute of Islamic Thought (1989).

10. For a discussion of how trends in the postmodern world have influenced Islam, see Ahmed (1992).

11. The heavy-handed nature of government-sponsored research in Muslim societies in particular and the Third World in general is of special concern. Because governments finance most research projects in the Third World, they often use the rhetoric of indigenization as a means to persuade or pressure social scientists to tailor their research to meet the state's needs for social engineering or its standards of public morality. Consequently, Third-World social sciences must often confront the vexing questions: what do I know? what should I think? and what shall I do?

More troubling is that the ardent appeals for Islamization have not produced rigorous theoretical alternatives to Western social sciences. Besides parochial and pedestrian critiques of Western models, and essentialist or indigenously ethnocentric alternatives, there is not much there. For example, "Islamic economics" is nothing but neoclassical economic theory in religious guise. Developing an authentically Islamic theory of sociohistorical change—not to speak of actual political practice based on such a new idea—has been extremely difficult.[12]

I do not wish to suggest that all Muslim intellectuals have wholeheartedly embraced the Islamization of knowledge project. Far from it; many have become rather critical of this whole endeavor. For example, a leading contemporary Iranian intellectual considers the attempt of the Muslim new Aristotelians to Islamicize sociology, economics, and law to be rather futile. He writes: "Water, for example, has a peculiar structure and essence. As such, we do not have religious and non-religious water or religious and non-religious wine. The same is true for justice, government, science, and philosophy. Even if these subjects were to have an essence then their Islamization would be rather meaningless. As such we can not have a science of sociology that is essentially religious or a philosophy that is essentially Islamic or Christian, the same way we can not have a system of government that is essentially religious" (Sorush 1995, 11).

In short, for the time being, to speak of indigenizing the substance of various social sciences is possible. However, I am skeptical about efforts to formulate an indigenous social science "methodology" because this entails altering and presumably improving the very logic of inquiry. Making allowance for the distinction between substance and methodology may expedite the closure of the Third World's scientific and technological gap with the West. In this way, Third-World intellectuals may pursue a homegrown rereading of sciences and redefine separate paths to development without resorting to invidious language, engaging demagogy, and stigmatizing the "other."

12. For expositions and discussions of such efforts, see Lee (1997), Mutahhari (1986), and Safi (1994).

3

Subjectivity, Political Evaluation, and Islamist Trajectories

SAYRES S. RUDY

There will never be a credible globalization theory, namely, a valid account of the direct social consequences of global unification. This statement remains true no matter how scrupulously a theory tries to link discrete global trends—market expansion, scientific cooperation, political convergence, legal standardization, cultural diffusion, isomorphic communications, or bureaucratic regulation—to particular social phenomena. First, we will unlikely ever know how "globalization" works. Is it new? Are its discrete elements coordinated, symbiotic, autonomous? Is it best seen as integration, convergence, or homogenization? How can it be process and end-point, a thing that leads to itself? Does it alter the dispensation of social power? Second, answers to such questions would not solve two far more significant snags. Universal, uniform causes cannot, in principle, explain particular, divergent effects; and global, general patterns do not, in practice, vary directly with local, specific patterns.

Globalization cannot be said to cause certain, uniform social reactions because it acts upon societies, communities, and groups imbued with disparate tastes, desires, needs, and institutional or social resources to satisfy them. But es-

My thanks to Birgit Schaebler and Leif Stenberg for generating the conference and book where these issues could be explored. For years of intellectual and personal inspiration I am deeply grateful to Ira Katznelson, David Waldner, Mark Kesselman, Amrita Basu, Yahya Sadowksi, and Seyla Benhabib. Manal Wardé, Robin Varghese, Chuck Tilly, Steven Solnick, Nathalie Silvestre, Brian Shaw, Birgit Schaebler, Hector Risemberg, Samantha Power, James Piscatori, Kris Palmer, Alex Motyl, Pratap Mehta, Albert Hirschman, Cassis Henry, Jona Hansen, Peter Hall, Muna el-Ghobashy, Raymond Geuss, Ophelia Dahl, Mark Blyth, Phineas Baxandall, Lisa Anderson, and Fouad Ajami have helped and influenced me enormously. Finally, thanks to Dillin, with whom I talked this through during many long walks.

pecially since 1989, several influential theorists have breezily ignored such complexity to link transnational commercialism to fundamentalism (Barber 1996) or intensified cross-cultural contact to nativism (Huntington 1996). Others reductively derive Western neo-imperialism from the hegemonic diffusion of late-capitalist cultural and economic forms (Jameson and Miyoshi 1998) or abstractly divine a non-hegemonic "Empire . . . composed of . . . national and supranational organisms united under a single logic of rule" (Hardt and Negri 2000, xii). Most social theorists and journalists portray globalization as a chaotic vortex that endangers social identities, political sovereignty, and human subjectivity, fostering protective exaggerations of existing identities: postmodernity in modern societies and fundamentalism in traditional societies.[1]

My programmatic position is the following, against such misleading simplifications. We may identify globalization's features and their systemic effects, but not their social effects. For example, we may link global capitalization to growing income disparities but not to specific social responses to either. Globalization's characteristics do matter but as causal contexts, phenomena whose indirect effects are mediated by local preferences and power. Complexity does not refute all causal theories *involving* globalization, just those that fail to conceptualize and differentiate global and local phenomena, only then to analyze them through their ideological and institutional mediation. We must distinguish among and within social movements so often caricatured and airily tied to globalization—multiculturalism, neo-fascism, and nationalist or religious fundamentalism—and then explore more precise intermediate factors, such as domestic political repression, that might explain their gravely diverse trajectories.

My special concern here is the ubiquitous mistreatment of religion. Ironically, many who respect religion as a social force flatten it as a cultural landscape (Huntington 1996), while many who acknowledge religious richness harbor secular prejudices derogating fundamentalism as the minatory excrescence of unrealized modernity. Edward Said (1993, 214, 230, 308), Benjamin Barber (1996, 205–10), and Fredric Jameson (1998b, 65–66) reduce religious activism to an anti-modern artifact of corrigible secular errors, a dangerous and ignorant revolt against nonetheless profane injustice, suffering, or objectification.[2]

1. This elision of social power confuses the sources and idioms of resistance. Islamist attacks on indigenous or colonial secular domination thus get attributed to Islam's cultural insularity or insecurity vis-à-vis modernity, rather than modernity's corrupt, coercive form (Said 1978).
2. In contrast to this functionalism, see Weber (1946, 270), Casanova (1994), Turner (1994), and Berger (1996).

This deeply ingrained Enlightenment paradigm that cobbles together non-scientific or nonsecular ideologies under the rubric "nonrational" underwrites the impulse to oppose globalization to various, especially agitated, strands of politicized "identities." The regnant view is that globalization, whether neutral or neo-imperial, is a secular, modern, and cosmopolitan process. National, ethnic, or religious opposition to specific experiences of globalization, then, is typically construed as resistance to secularism, modernity, and cosmopolitanism as such. A dichotomy has emerged between worldly, secular, modern globalization and parochial, sectarian, traditional separatism. Defined by ambiguous borders, evanescent meanings, and ethereal directions, globalization is ultra-modern: opportunistic, unpredictable, elastic, and unbounded. Its foil, nemesis, and menacing Other, fundamentalism, is ultra-backward: nihilistic, rigid, fixed, and parochial. This binary neatly marginalizes "nonrational" social movements as passionate outliers to modernity and to means-ends rationality and analysis.

My alternative assessment of identitarian social movements focuses on radically divergent Islamist groups, motivations, settings, and trajectories. This Islamist multiplicity impeaches general globalization accounts, urging discrete explanations of personal, communitarian, and militant Islamist activities under shared external pressures but distinct domestic struggles. The shared global environment presents "modernity" as economically, politically, or culturally prejudicial, coercive, and inegalitarian. Despite its self-presentation as universalizing, reciprocating, and equalizing, globalization is widely experienced as divisive, imposed, and hierarchic (thus hypocritical or deluded as well). But such potentially destabilizing forces underdetermine their consequences; like deracination, poverty, or alienation, globalization does not tell people how to react to it. Globalization directs but does not dictate its reception. Rather, the distinct domestic struggles determine the path of social protest.

Local reactions are determined by the capacity of people confronting globalization to secure their initial or adapted desires, given site-specific social resources. Idiosyncratic factors—such as class or cultural differentiation—shape any community's unique desires and capacity to realize them. But we can theorize how particular configurations are causally patterned in the globalization process. To do this, I differentiate specific choices from choice itself, or desires from the ability to achieve or modify them.[3] If I am freely offered something new to me, I

---

3. I use desires, choices, and preferences in one non-decisionistic sense; however "choice" connotes free will or "desire" unfree instinct. The experience of effective choice varies, whether or not "choices" are freely chosen.

have two choices: to refuse it based on my previous desires or to accept it based on a new desire. The choice I make is particular to how the offer and my desires interact, and is subjective, meaning I experience subjectivity in choosing. In this scenario, the actual choice can vary but choosing satisfies me invariably. But if something new is forced on me, I do not have the same options regarding my desires: I must subordinate my previous desires to, or radically exit, the new order. Crucially, the coercively imposed new order may satisfy my old or revised desires, yet leave me resentfully without choice. The experience of forced new orders is universal to coerced populations and is objective, meaning we experience lack of subjectivity in reacting. The distinction between the two scenarios is not the presence or absence of any choice; I make a choice in each situation. The difference lies in the systemic position of these choices. The first scenario allows me several choices within the new order, so my subjectivity is systemic. The second allows me no choice within the new order; my subjectivity is anti-systemic.[4]

Globalization's social effects involve, accordingly, two relationships, between (1) mundane global novelties and local—fixed or flexible—desires, and (2) the mode of globalization and local subjectivity. The latter relationship combines two inextricable components: (a) the coercive or optional nature of global diffusion and (b) the social resources for local resistance.

(1) and (2) above require distinct theoretical accounts. (1) Global-local contacts mix offerings and tastes and so must be assessed ideographically in anecdotal, process-traced narratives (Gallagher and Greenblatt 2000). But (2) the systemic permission or prevention of subjectivity may be nomothetically theorized, that is, analyzed in generalized causal terms. One has many potential choices, but one potential to choose. Choices are criteria of subjectivity; their evolution and realization gauge subjectivity. Choice is subjectivity itself, the capacity to realize noncoerced choices. The crucial distinction is between denying subjectivity and denying criteria of subjectivity. People change choices for many reasons, internal (private tastes) or external (public pressures). But choice itself, subjectivity, is precluded only when choices may not be made and realized within the dominant social order. Preventing subjectivity incurs uniform outcomes. Frustrating subjectivity radicalizes and militarizes populations; frustrating desires

---

4. Say a firm buys television stations in Countries A and B to show only American action films. Country A has many stations so the new schedule adds to the old: viewers have more options. Country B has one station, so the new replaces the old: viewers have fewer options. Country A viewers experience choice, Country B viewers do not. Relatively, Country B viewers react to lost subjectivity, not merely to lost programs. Globalization is constant; the mediation differs.

but allowing revised desires or alternative choices moderates populations. Globalization cannot impede subjectivity directly; rather, subjectivity is mediated (secured or foiled) locally, mainly by the state. As either guardian of local choices or tool of imperial designs, local state mediation drives the ideological-strategic trajectories of activists under global pressures. Thus, the more subjectivity itself is denied, the less globalization itself is directly responsible for and indeed targeted by anti-systemic protest activities.

Divergent Islamist trends, predictably, correspond to varied guarantees of local preferences regarding globalization. Where globalization gradually frustrates Muslims' desires, they adopt personal Islamism, an ethos of internalized blame and ascetic reconstitution reflecting a broadly naturalized or apolitical perception of social processes. In contrast, abrupt social disruption of a Muslim community's desires discredits political and state-co-opted religious elites, inspiring a communal moral reclamation project. The resulting call for publicly instilled Islamic conservatism, or communitarian Islamism, marks a novel choice tolerated by rulers and buoyed by institutional compromise. In these two Islamist forms, new social ideas, desires, or choices are actualized and stabilized. But when new choices are prevented, eliminating subjectivity, protest radicalizes into an anti-systemic and uncompromising militant Islamism that wars against the authoritarian state that has suppressed effective social will. Poignantly, the most violent, doctrinaire Islamist agitations correlate with (colonial or indigenous) tyranny, not with globalization.[5]

If global trends matter, the local mediation of their impact on subjectivity explains the systemic, peaceful acts of personal and communitarian Islamists or the anti-systemic, violent acts of militant Islamists. The hegemonic modernist view that fundamentalists vary by degree, not kind, links this variation to quantitative changes in one form of deprivation (material or cultural) rather than to qualitative changes in two forms of deprivation: of desires and of subjectivity (political). The section in this chapter on Islamist trajectories elaborates this corrective.

Finally, having shown how global trends and peripheral mediations combine to frustrate or satisfy local subjectivity, inspiring three disparate Islamist reactions, I map these reactions over a strict conceptualization of modernity, anti-

5. Neither is violent Islamism explained by its rejection of "freedom" or embrace of "evil," two handily meaningless evasions (see George W. Bush on al-Qa'ida, *Boston Globe,* 26 Sept. 2001, A8; 24 Oct. 2001, A6). The "Afghan Arabs" were created by domestic oppression of Islam in Algeria, Bosnia, Uzbekistan, Chechnya, Pakistan, and Egypt, among others, an oppression they reasonably perceived was subsidized by the only superpower, the United States.

modernity, and postmodernity. Each Islamism contains modern, anti-modern, and postmodern elements in unique constellations, despite stereotypes of them.

My argument proceeds, now, by scrutinizing globalization, Islamism, and modernity/nonmodernity while braiding them around an account of subjectivity supporting causal lineages of personal, communitarian, and militant Islamism.

GLOBALIZATION

The conceptualization and properties of globalization remain contentious. I will address briefly the pivotal question: can we attribute to "globalization" per se causal or facilitating influence on recent social movements in the periphery? Do globalization's cultural, political, and economic trends act directly or indirectly on social movements, in concert or independently? I argue that as a conditioning but not determining social environment, globalization affects local politics but must be subdivided and defined precisely to see how. I also argue that how local desires and resources mediate these global patterns is paramount in determining their effect on local subjectivity and thus on peripheral social agitation.

Concepts and theories of globalization must be parsed, theories being causal or correlational claims about concepts (Motyl 1999; Waldner 1999). Defining globalization as the weakening of states due to borderless capitalism or as the worldwide symbiosis of cultural and commercial homogenization violates this condition. Such typical departures build theories into definitions, leading to circular arguments. Rather, globalization must be defined and measured as a single effect, then hypothetically linked to some other effect(s). Once it is defined as, say, global capitalism, it becomes an independent variable for some testable theory, including defended social mechanisms, explaining some dependent variable; for instance, global capitalism causes religious aggression by threatening cultural values that people decide to defend. These steps comprise the minimal, clearly demanding, and routinely circumnavigated requirements of any valid globalization theory.

To be important in itself, globalization must have effects specific to globalness; it must suggest a new dynamic derived from globalization's unique qualities. A theory about globalization cannot be just an old social theory on a larger scale (Rosenberg 2000). The claim that capitalism endangers democracy, whether globally, nationally, or locally, theorizes capitalism, not globalization. Scale-insensitive theories actually demote globalization's significance. Most principal works now merely invoke globalization, unwittingly denigrating globalization theories (Beyer 1994, 14–44). A true globalization theory claims an effect of events occurring specifically at the global level, which requires that globalization have its own features. The only such feature I can identify is saturation, the potentiality of reaching the limits of planetary manifest destiny. A real globalization theory might argue that by finally losing its exit option due to world market saturation, global capitalism ceases to undermine unions. Arguments that do not link distinct qualities of globalization to novel social outcomes dismiss globalization itself as theoretically insignificant and are anyway wrong.[6]

This digression is important not because we need a globalization theory; we may not. Rather, I am clarifying limitations endemic to discussing what globalization does. Because globalization's unique feature must be the final endpoint of a globalized world, its valid theories are conjectures about the future. A valid globalization theory asks, "What will be the effect of a globalized world?" rather than "What happens when cultures, markets, and politics (perennially) aggregate or interact?" Globalization currently connotes a future condition and current process; globalizing events are commonly read off their presumed globalized endpoints. Theorists rarely perceive that globalization as expansion and as saturation suggest opposite projections. Globalization is apparently achieved when its features perish: when saturation eliminates expansion. That globalization theory remains derivative, conjectural, and incoherent does not, however, mean globalization is insignificant.

Globalization basically takes economic, political, and cultural forms, although "bureaucratic domination" is noteworthy (Offe 1996, 6). In examining each of these three realms in isolation for descriptive and theoretical clarity, I wish to avoid two tendencies in such synchronic delineations. One is to presume that in any epoch all realms of social life form a "totality" and are thus mutually identical instantiations of that epoch's spirit, mode of production, or ethos. The opposite tendency presumes that analytically distinct realms function and are graspable in isolation. The latter idea has infected globalization studies: specialization assigns political economists to capitalism, democratic theorists to governance, and "area specialists" to fundamentalism and nationalism.

Avoiding the totality and autonomy views of social spheres, I suggest that the affinities and tensions of cultural, economic, and political life form patterns that comprise historical periods or blocs. Social spheres are always mutually constitutive, interrelated by common features, causal connections, and complemen-

6. Old theories merely expanded to the global level have usually been discredited already at more precise levels of analysis, such as the direct equation of material deprivation with violence (Tilly 1978; Piven and Cloward 1979).

tary resistance (Held et al. 1999, 437). Globalization can be divided into three general periods: imperial (nineteenth century–1914), statist (1914–73), and neoliberal (1973-present). For each globalization phase, political, cultural, and economic trends must be studied individually and only then collectively for their reciprocal effects, core-periphery power distributions, and—against current economic bias (Sklair 1995)—variable influence over local subjective experience.

Economic Globalization

Economic globalization has conventionally referred to the cross-border integration of production, trade, financial transactions, and capital flows. In quantitative terms, these constituents of economic globalization are now merely returning to pre-First World War levels (Berger and Dore 1996; Boyer and Drache 1996). But statistical measures poorly capture innovations in economic globalization. Emphasis on "integration" or "convergence" fetishizes stable quantitative measurements of cross-border economic activity and obscures qualitative discontinuities (Portes and Rumbaut 1996, 6). Some analysts have thus emphasized qualitatively discrete stages of economic globalization, however similar aggregate figures now are to 1914 numbers. Political economists stress the pivot of the early 1970s, when the Bretton Woods system was scrapped, exchange rates floated, and monetarism, deregulation, and privatization undermined Keynesian management and Taylorist production (Brenner 1998). Economic dislocation resulted: global capital-flows abruptly outpaced trade, which surged ahead of Gross Domestic Product growth rates. Anarchic global capitalism constituted a new world system of financial and productive accumulation and distribution, replacing traditional risk with chaotic uncertainty (Schofield 1999; Eichengreen 1996).

But the meaning of this new disintegration of finance, trade, production, and growth for protest actions remains obscure, though social costs of neoliberal marketization have been high (Greider 1997; Luttwak 1999). Volatile and fragmented post-1970s capitalism resurrected age-old eulogies of the "autonomous" state but also reassurances of stability based on static gross long-term economic figures. No consensual or cogent social analysis of the global "new economy" emerged, partly because patterned outcomes are hidden by approaches stressing quantitative continuity over qualitative rupture. Analysts vaguely described economic globalization only as, for instance, compression or disintegration, a hapless variable for tracing discrete social effects. The missed novelty of current economic globalization—the dislocation of finance, production, and growth, and the intensified pace and propinquity of market activity—is the worldwide diffusion of capitalism.

The economic organization of imperialism consisted in a capitalist core and increasingly hierarchical, despotic, agrarian social and productive relations farther into the periphery (Mamdani 1996), with notable but few exceptions (Comaroff and Comaroff 1992; Pieterse and Parekh 1995). The postwar era until the 1960s upheld this pattern in an international division of labor that "underdeveloped" monocultural exporting countries economically, entrenching their noncapitalist place in the global market. The new industrial economies of the 1960s presaged the unification, homogenization, and standardization of world capitalism of the next decade. After two globalization phases of mixed and striated economic organization, capitalism universalized, bringing to wealthy Keynesian, middle-income industrial and poor, primary-goods-exporting countries alike commodification, deregulation, privatization, commercialization, wage-based labor markets, and welfare retrenchment (Callaghy 1993; Dolan 1993). Globalization seen abstractly as volatile or rapid integration or metaphorically as a "tidal wave" obscures globalization as capitalization, as the diffusion of a standard mode of production, distribution, and accumulation across countries (an exception: Calhoun 1995, 307).

We may now sketch capitalist globalization's outcomes, which evidently include increased income disparities, decreased accountability of political and economic elites, and unprecedented market volatility and dependency among the poor (Esping-Andersen 1996; UNDP 1999). It is the ubiquity, not the existence, of these patterns that is novel (Davis 2001) and that heightens the need to distinguish equal commodification from equal rights, opportunities, or capabilities (Sen 1999). This global diffusion of capitalist practices fosters neo-imperial inequality between north and south, while replicating these worsening income divisions within countries. Abundant evidence indicates a direct and internally irremediable (Offe 1984) correlation between radical capitalism and immiseration, exploitation, and inequality (MacEwan 1999; Rudy 2000), although debate persists over the long-term gains, limits, and traits of global capitalism (Weiss 1999; Bhagwati and Brecher 1980). Given paralyzing debt burdens and intra-LDC (Less Developed Countries) competition, capitalist globalization may get grafted to other protest ideologies (Keddie 1998).

The cultural effect of global capitalism is said to be the threat to authenticity and traditional solidarity. Thus Clifford Geertz (1996, 142–43) equivocates but claims that "[s]ecularism, commodification, corruption, selfishness, immorality, rootlessness, estrangement from the sources of value, all the ills attributed to the modern form of life as it has taken shape in the West (and especially, everyone's hard case, the US), loom, or seem to, as imminent threats." But the mechanisms connecting discrete social phenomena cannot be presumed (Elster 1999). Opposing capitalism to cultural cohesion—or "the market's universal church [to] a retribalizing politics of particularist identities" (Barber 1996, 7)—presumes that capitalism entails secularization via a rationalization process. Echoing an ancient duality (Koselleck 1985), this equation falsely opposes capitalist, scientific, and reasoned to religious, ethnic, and cultural valuation (Peter Berger 1996). This inculcated schema ignores multiple disconfirming findings, including "non-isomorphic" cultural, capitalist, and technological interactions across societies (Appadurai 1990); entrepreneurial Mormonism, "perhaps the most work-addicted culture in religious history" (Bloom 1992, 103); and the indigenization of capitalist currency (Zelizer 1997).

Despite this empirical compatibility of culture or religion and capitalist or scientific rationalization, the Enlightenment conviction about irreconcilable value-spheres frames the economic globalization discourse. This commitment posits a monistic signification process in which humans locate one meaning in the world at a time (Max Weber 1946). Positing a unified, autonomous subject, this outlook holds that religious and secular beliefs conflict until one supplies a coherent resolution to the theodicy problem that rationalization eventually renders otiose. This view, rejecting motivational, psychological, or ideological polyvalence, insists that people find comfort in only one mode of valuation. People do not sustain multiple needs or meanings in various value-spheres (religious, economic, political, erotic, or moral) simultaneously, but must choose an exclusive orientation. Under this calculus, modernity disenchants the world, dislodges religion, and undermines authentic culture; thus, religions or cultures accommodate the secular only artificially, unstably, or incoherently.

Competing paradigms have yet to dislodge this Enlightenment view of the subject, religion, and modernity (Blumenberg 1985; Schneewind 1998). One rebuttal elides the substantive polarity and thus tension of religious and secular value-orientations (Löwith 1949; Durkheim 1995). Another describes the negotiation of genuinely conflicting value-spheres as leading to new hybrid signifying systems. In this vein, context-sensitive analysts of this cross-value-sphere hybridization process disavow covering-rules for relationships between modern and traditional or rational and religious cultures (Taylor 1989; Kleinman 1999, 361, n. 10). Still others posit a pluralistic signification process in which separate value-spheres satisfy the permanent human need for multiple meanings (Geuss 1981, 9). Indeed, many diverse scholars now acknowledge the "systematic ambiguity" of cultural signification (Winch 1958, 18, 100), the multiplicity of overlapping "moral communities" (Simmel 1955, 125), and the particularity of resisting or accommodating secularization, capitalism, science, and technology. Thus, however global capitalism exacerbates social tensions, economic systems have no unambiguous, intrinsic, or regular impact on cultural identity or behavior. Unsurprisingly, no empirical link exists between global capitalism and religious or national radicalism (Sadowski 1998).

While capitalist globalization exacerbates economic inequality with an uncertain cultural effect, what are its political consequences? The predominant political anxiety is that globalization erodes people's secular or religious collective will (Kleinman and Kleinman 1997, 19). This worry reflects the broad modern concern that procedurally or instrumentally organized social systems stifle desirable collective valuation, or "colonize the lifeworld" (Habermas), obstruct species-being (Marx), erode social identity and cooperation (Mill, Tocqueville), trap us in a "steel-hard casing" (Weber), or elevate the social over the political (Arendt). Recent thinking about globalization and "civil society" or "the state"—either embodying collective will—reiterates this framework. All the rage in the early 1990s, civil society referred to whatever social activities secured human freedom. Defined against freedom-limiting conditions, then, civil society meant myriad activities, but conventionally ramified into capitalist market and associational life, two potentially conflicting axes of social organization (Taylor 1995). The globalization discourse has celebrated, then questioned, the freedom-restoring power of each civil society in turn. A group of civil-society-as-capitalism theorists around 1989 linked market activity to anti-authoritarianism, human rights, and world peace (Soto 1989; Fukuyama 1989; Mueller 1989). When capitalism itself impeded democratic and collective life, perpetrated human rights abuses, and privatized social power under new corporate license, civil society was neatly redefined as associational life that would confront capitalist excess.

But against capitalist globalization, local participation seemed the quaint repository of marginal identity, not the basis of a formidable collective challenge (Gowan 1999, 248 ff.). Hope for a meaningful public will or political sphere under globalization thus turned to the autonomous nation-state, traditionally the political ballast to the market. But the idea that the state will safeguard value, culture, rights, or political choice against capitalism just revives the age-old ideology of capitalist social equilibrium, namely, that capitalism provides political solutions to its economic costs.[7] Every stage of capitalist expansion has prompted

7. Alarmingly few statist anti-globalization arguments address the protean and rich legacy of state-capital collusion amply described by Smith, Marx, Gramsci, Charles Tilly, Michael Mann, Perry Anderson, and E. P. Thompson.

mourning and appeals for the savior-state, however implicated the state may be in the expansion itself.[8] That the state should inherit civil society's obligation to maintain political agency marks a further authoritarian capitulation given that civil society—market or community—always connoted the social defense of freedom against bad government. Indeed, the state has neither opposed capitalist globalization nor disappeared, but reoriented toward domestic security and international competition (Krasner 1999; Strange 1996; Cerny and Evans 1999). This security-competition state does not guarantee or preclude political collective action, but its priorities, constraints, and incentives encourage state elites to lure and ensure global capital and minimize outlays. Thus, even if collective action, such as labor activism (Thelen and Kume 1999; Adler 1996; Turnbull 2000; Shoch 2000), resists the "disembedding of social institutions" (Polanyi 2001; Giddens in Krieger 1999, 50) in borderless global capitalism, increasingly people feel disenfranchised and unprotected by the state-capital nexus.

Thus far I have argued that global capitalism has had clear, direct, and harsh economic results but an ambiguous cultural impact; it has also weakened civil associational politics and transformed the state into an elitist security-competition apparatus. These political diagnoses suggest intervening variables whose social effects remain murky (Rothschild 1999). Political disenfranchisement under the security-competition state must be understood with respect to the diverse conditions over which it universalizes. Recall the three broadly conceived periods of economic globalization, only the last of which is capitalist. First is modern imperialism (nineteenth century–1914), a set of despotic colonial regimes unifying an industrial core and agricultural periphery. Second is developmental statism (1914–73), the state-managed "governed economies" common to wealthy and poor countries, but encompassing distinct modes of production. Dependency and world-systems theories rightly situate the economic divisiveness of this period, when many LDCs remained subordinate primary goods exporters, within this statist convergence.[9] Third is global capitalism (about 1973-present).

These stages clarify the total and discrete features of the political economy of globalization (Wolf 1982, 3). First, modern imperial and developmental statism (nineteenth century–1973) are characterized globally by political isomor-

8. Many theorists fret about global capitalism's enervating state sovereignty from without but oddly not about domestic capitalism's enervating it from within. Hont (1995) shows the incoherence of this statist universalism.

9. Within developmental statism, inter-elite conflict-resolution varied with disparate results in economic growth and competitiveness (Waldner 1999).

phism and economic polymorphism, while global capitalism (1973–) has evinced political and economic isomorphism. Political homogeneity refers to underlying structural composition and policy orientation regarding government-market-citizen interaction whose social consequences outweigh superficially different "regime-types" (Moody 1999, 135–40). The similar political configurations of empires and autarkic, modernizing states sustained heterogeneous modes of economic production across rich and poor areas. Universal capitalization in the current phase is also underpinned by a single polity-type, the security-competition state. But this new political and economic homogenization does not override and may exacerbate the disparate conditions carved out by the previous globalization stages for rich and poor countries and classes. The experience of this new state thus politically differs across wealthy and poor populations. In advanced states welfare retrenchment, security reinvestment, and legal reorientation are accepted as the ineluctable telos and modernization of internal capitalist unfolding. In LDCs the emergent security-competition state is typically seen as the promiscuous guarantor of unaccountable external forces exacerbating local economic conditions. To attract global capital poorer countries must concoct new laws and property rights, stabilize the polity under worsening economic conditions, minimize outlays to meet international lending requirements, and all this while repaying or incurring massive debts.

Roughly sketched, the security-competition state entails legitimized diminution of the state in wealthy countries and the apparently parasitic expansion of the state in LDCs. These developments do not unambiguously produce "anti-Western" or "anti-capitalist" views, however. Rather, local activists evaluate their specific state-bourgeoisie performance, given local desires, and then determine their ideological reaction and political strategy. That evaluation, then, is a political or cultural judgment about the state's mediation of international capitalism, rather than a view of capitalism itself. Hence Islamists, like most Seattle anti-World Trade Organization protesters (1999), decry corruption but support capitalism if it promises the rule of law rather than merely an exploitable capitalist legal infrastructure (Scheuerman 1999). Because global capitalization systemically imposes a corrupt and undemocratic economic order, the ideological reception of capitalism combines separate political and economic criticisms. Three modest conclusions about the politics of economic globalization may now be drawn. (1) The security-competition state fostered by capitalist globalization poses different legitimation crises in rich and poor countries. The "lean" state seems inevitable in wealthy countries but an opportunist abrogation of public responsibility in LDCs. (2) Among developing countries, ancillary state structures mediate the appraisal of the security/competition state. Under similar capitalization and secularization, Islamists in democratic Turkey remain moderate while Islamists in authoritarian Iran launched a revolution. (3) Contesting positions across and within Islamic societies form unique mixtures of compromise and protest occasioned, not determined, by globalization (Geertz 1971).

My argument so far is twofold. First, capitalism exacerbates material hardships and universalizes the security-competition state, with an unclear cultural impact. Second, reactions to these tendencies depend on local case-specific desires and resources. It is logically and empirically wrong to link particular ideological reactions to universal trends associated with capitalism, such as nationalism to "global unification" (Ulrich Beck 1994, 1), "neo-tribal and fundamentalist tendencies" to "glocalization" (Bauman 1998, 3), identity-utopianism to global time-space compression (Giddens 1991), or, worst of all, "Jihad" to "McWorld" (Barber 1996).

Political Globalization

Political globalization refers not to the consolidation of democracy in each sovereign state but to the universal institutionalization of normative, ethical, and legal "governance," "a cosmopolitan law of global civil society" that trumps sovereignty (Habermas 1999, 264). Exemplified by a long-sought international human rights regime, the governance ideal has paralleled imperial control (Hochschild 1998; Lauren 1998). But its plausibility, benefits, and market-compatibility were urged earlier, as in Kant's influential argument that, guided by the "spirit of commerce," "nature irresistibly wills that right should eventually gain the upper hand" (Kant 1970, 113–14). Suspicious of such moral naturalism, most analysts now ground governance in noncommercial sources (Pogge 2002) and justifications (Pogge 1989, 1992). Political globalization must entail moral or legal activities with independent regulatory authority over other, particularly neo-imperial and capitalist, global phenomena (Held 1995). Under these strictures, governance appears merely possible. Democratic mechanisms can realize limited international norms and practices (Risse-Kappen 1995; Risse-Kappen et al. 1999), although skeptics doubt the scope and optimality of projected gains (Ruggie 1998).

Results so far are sobering. Governance now exhibits continued subordination, assistance, or blindness to the decreasingly inhibited privilege of private, corporate, and government realpolitik and profiteering. Political globalization passively oversees intensified medical inequalities (Kim et al., 1999; Farmer

1999), militarism (Silverstein 1999; Greider 1998), tendentious access to human rights (Chomsky 1999; Bales 1999), capitalization of "non-governmental organizations" (*Economist* 2000), and environmental devastation (Harvey 1996, 187 ff.). This partial list of capitulation to or support for unaccountable social power raises several points. First, successful global political interventions thus far have obeyed the policy requirements of dominant countries. Global human rights efforts either enforce U.S.-NATO foreign political and economic agendas or remain ineffectual and obedient, especially over social and cultural rights (Forsythe 1991; Beetham 1999; Press 2000). Second, the inefficacy of political globalization does not suggest a chaotic global landscape, but the directed, willful control of globalization by politically immunized groups. Third, international governance seems to serve special interests rather than universal principles, a combustible perception under exacerbating economic conditions. As Habermas warns, "the politics of human rights undertaken by a world organization turns into a fundamentalism of human rights only when it undertakes an intervention that is really nothing more than a struggle of one party against the other and thus uses a moral legitimation as a cover for a false juridical justification" (1997, 147). Contemporary political globalization—underwriting U.S.-led capitalization and foreign policy—projects precisely this false universalism, a partisan liberal "fundamentalism" that misconstrues principled resistance as nativist or backward (Hanssen 2000, 159). Peripheral activist reactions to the binding norms and rules of perceived "Western" hegemony vary widely depending on local circumstances, especially mediating institutions, initial cultural demands, and ideological flexibility. Yet the aggressive hypocrisy of global governance is a tinderbox easily appended to any other grievance emergent in especially but not exclusively poorer countries.

Cultural Globalization

Most discussion of cultural globalization dichotomizes rejection and accommodation, conflating within the latter two disparate responses to cultural contact: plural and hybrid identities (Featherstone 1995, 10). Philip Roth (1997, 86) on the "acculturating back-and-forth" of "the indigenous American berserk" and Ariel Dorfman (1998, 42) on "being double, the anxiety, the richness, the madness of being double" illustrate plural, divided selves. In contrast, Elias Canetti's (1979) and André Aciman's (1994) blended polyglot upbringings embody hybrid, unified selves. Plurality mixes established identities; hybridity forges new ones. Such memoirs clarify that cultural interaction is a historic constant distinct from cultural globalization, the latter marked by vertical (inter-class) and horizontal (intra-class) cross-cultural integration (Tomlinson 1999). Most important, they show that diverse cultural interactions yield various identities: new hybrids of world-views, old values in new contexts, new mixtures of old cultures, or innovative nativism (Greenblatt 1991; Hannerz 1996).

Cultures do not have intrinsic reactions to external events. Yet two leading views of cultural globalization ignore specific, idiosyncratic cultural reactivity. The first that claims ideological, aesthetic, or technological diffusion spawns cultural revanchism. In "the growing disjunctures between ethnoscapes, technoscapes, finanscapes, mediascapes, and ideoscapes" and the "sheer speed, scale, and volume of these flows," Arjun Appadurai arbitrarily detects that "de-territorialization . . . is now at the core of . . . Islamic and Hindu fundamentalism" (1990, 301; cf. Goonatilake 1995). A second view associates greater inter-cultural contact with cultural hostility (Huntington 1996). Conflict may ensue, though not necessarily (Bielefeldt 2000), when cultural communities must negotiate deeply held and opposed value-orientations in a confined space or in an inescapably shared social decision (Jones 1994). But cultural tensions result from abrupt confinement or threat and result in multiple outcomes ranging from rejection to hybridization to pluralism. Samuel Huntington (following Bernard Lewis) paradigmatically errs in equating different civilizations (description) with clashing civilizations (theory).

Even if the world is "shrinking" culturally, and not mainly for elites (Reynolds 2000, 650–53), the power distributions at each site of cultural interaction or dislocation determine local responses. Cultural contact will be resisted where forcibly imposed external cultural practices or beliefs endanger valued local customs. Similarly, cultural contact will be welcome where peaceably offered external cultural practices are desired. So the reaction to cultural globalization relates to the coercive content of the diffusion of the hegemonic culture's values, symbols, rituals, and ethics. Local reaction is not determined by the facticity of cultural encounter but by the coercive nature of that encounter. That coercion is measured (1) by the direct imposition of external cultural imperatives on preferred indigenous values, symbols, rituals, and ethics, and (2) relative to other threats to local desires and needs (Shklar 1990).

The moral reception of cultural incursion occurs in the coercive or emancipating tendencies of coterminous, especially economic and political, encroachments. Anti-imperialists resist cultural displacement and the domination that delivered it. This does not mean that cultural agitation is a function of political or economic deprivation; indeed cultural resistance in LDCs is likely where cultural diffusion imposes direct value-conflicts. But the costs and gains, coercion and emancipation, of mixed bundles of global trends, polymorphous across local settings, shape their social impact and reception.[10] How elements of globalization collectively affect local subjectivity is causally weightier than how each trend works individually. Even if external culture is offered rather than imposed, the context of cultural expansion affects local cultural response. Whether cultural penetration is seen to underwrite economic exploitation or redistribution, political complicity or justice, humanitarian corruption or assistance affects whether imported culture is enjoyed as amusing, adopted as enriching, or resisted as colonizing. Local reaction to cultural imposition will vary widely unless locals (elites and masses) have no choice in reacting (Fanon 1963; Memmi 1965). Finally, because economic, political, and cultural globalizations are autonomous relative to nineteenth-century imperialism, the experience and content of cultural incursion vary widely across and within regions.

Fittingly, "Americanization" (Spivak 1999, 341, 361; Jameson 1998; Brennan 1997, 12–65; Moretti 2001) of the world, however neo-imperial and monopolistic (Thompson 1990, 263), underdetermines its cultural and moral effects. Cultural globalization's three paradigmatic social outcomes—hybridity, doubleness, and rejection—correlate with power dynamics exogenous to, and incommensurate with, patterns of direct cultural contact (Sadowski 1998). Such variation and nuance overwhelm clunky catch-all models and exceed truisms about "contradictory tendencies . . . toward homogenization and . . . new distinctions" (Lévi-Strauss 1979, 20). Transcending schematic, tectonic theories and complacent reminders about social flux, multiplicity, construction, and intra-cultural contestation, we can link specifically combined globalization patterns to precise ideological and strategic responses. To do so, we model the coercion-choice nexus at the mediation between global trajectories and local perceptions.

Local activists respond to universalizing social trends as they experience them along three dimensions. First, universal trends exacerbate or instigate local power differentials and social divisiveness, so have divisive effects (across class, race, gender, ethnicity). Second, the ensemble of global pressures is site-specific, with disparate impacts across local populations. Third, the universal, unifying trends and their particular, divisive effects are modulated locally by distinct institutions, ideologies, histories, economies, resources, and desires that comprise the

---

10. LDC citizens, sectors, states, and firms act, rather than just react. But agency is power-dependent, unequal, and empirically discerned. Note, too, that push (core) and pull (periphery) effects drive globalization (Robinson 1972).

TABLE 3.1
REDEFINING AND MODELING GLOBALIZATION

1 *Value-Sphere*	2 *Universal Trends*	3 *Divisive Effects*	1 *Value-Sphere*
Economic	Capitalization	Income disparities Privatization of power	Welfare Wealth-creation
		Security/Competition State	Security
Political	Governance	Discriminatory Application	Political rights Civil Rights Social rights
Cultural	Cosmopolitanism	Cultural imperialism	Choice

Source: World Bank 2001, 310, table 19.

prism of their political perception, evaluation, and impact. Activism attending globalization will, then, be case-specific and patterned (Marcus and Fischer 1986).

Table 3.1 recapitulates my description of globalization trends. The columns include (I) the value-spheres of globalization trends, (II) their reconceptualization, (III) their divisive (non-universal) effects, and (IV) factors that mediate the universal trends and their divisive effects.

Globalization processes can be delineated basically by moving from left to right. For example, the move from "economic globalization" to "capitalization" shifts our focus from quantitative cross-border economic activity to the diffusion of qualitative capitalist practices (wage-labor, commerce, property rights). This substantive transformation, invisible to aggregate trade measures, creates the divisive effects of capitalization. Thus, the universal trends (II) cause and are coeval with the divisive effects (III), but neither establishes its reception by LDC social activists. A further cluster-variable decides the potential protest, resistance, or accommodation of incorporated populations. How the universal trends (II) and divisive effects (III) combine and are mediated (alleviated, stabilized, or exacerbated) by the social resources, institutional profiles, class relations, and preferences (IV) in peripheral communities explains consequent protest activities.

SUBJECTIVITY, IDEOLOGICAL DIVERSITY
AND GLOBALIZATION

I will presently apply this analytical framework to Islamism and modernity in pursuing the following hypothesis. Locally mediated, universal, and divisive globalization effects inspire (a) accommodation, reform, doubleness, hybridity, and humanism or (b) rejection, radicalism, purity, chauvinism, and anti-humanism depending on whether they permit communities self-determination, or subjectivity, namely, to choose and realize their desires. The core idea here is that the demand for at least initial choice is universal, while the content of choice is particular (Levi 1986; Gellner 1979). People make infinite choices, on many bases, but all demand an initial choice—even if it is to avoid future choice (Quine 1987, 68). This common human substrate, needed for social analysis, is prior to the contingent will to theodicy, meaning, democracy, coherence, or even basic sustenance (Moore 1978, 87). Because the will to subjectivity exerts itself in discrete social contexts, against multifarious constraints, it has no essential expression or natural final form (Foucault 1988, 214–18; 1980, 92–102). Subjectivity wills, in ideas and actions, the meanings, doctrines, ideologies, and strategies it needs given its precise obstacles. A good account of ideology, social evaluation, and action must show how the will to subjectivity generates activists' ideological and strategic choices.

But can a general theory cogently map universal trends and particular responses, or must we settle for isolated descriptions? I have emphasized that globalizations have uncertain consequences because respondents fortify, modify, or abandon choices idiosyncratically; but also that when denied the capacity to respond effectively—when denied choice itself—communities will always defend their subjectivity. Can we identify patterns in global-local dynamics if the forms of coercion and criteria of subjectivity vary by case? We can if we minimize our assumption of a universal human substrate and maximize our assumption of plural human desires in combining a broad causal account of denied subjectivity that respects diversity of desires, tastes, preferences, and choices.

The will to subjectivity is the minimal universal analytical locus because it is necessary for and antecedent to all diverse, substantive normative social choices. The will to subjectivity is thus the only universal baseline relevant to a theory of social change. Here we must distinguish between subjectivity and specific criteria of subjectivity. When denied, criteria of subjectivity (desires) can change to retain subjectivity (choice) (Friedrich 1982; Todorov 1996). As new criteria of subjectivity comprise political radicalization, pacification, or neutralization, they merit perusal. A community (1) has prioritized desires (Carter 1998, 9) and (2) evaluates the process of satisfying those desires. The assessment of the satisfaction of desires may or may not alter those desires (Fish 1999, 281 ff.). Dog owners who fail to limit leash laws continue to want fewer leash laws; failure to achieve their ends sustains those ends. Failed anti-meat campaigns often turn activists into vegetarians "just for health reasons"; failure narrows their ends by privatizing them. But striking workers denied raises often attack wage-levels and negotiation processes; failure to achieve the initial economic goal broadens their ends by politicizing them. So failure to satisfy desires may neutralize, narrow, or broaden those desires, or may politically stabilize, depoliticize, or politicize activists.

Desires or choices are criteria of subjectivity, the capacity to satisfy or change them the measure of subjectivity. Indeed, changing the criteria of subjectivity is subjectivity at work, just as revising desires expresses a secondary act of desiring. Only when this capacity to change criteria of subjectivity is thwarted is subjectivity prevented (Benhabib 1999, 346; James Miller 1999). Whether pliable criteria of subjectivity or subjectivity per se are frustrated determines intra-systemic (peaceful) and anti-systemic (violent) responses, respectively (Genovese 1979). While denying a community's criteria of subjectivity yields aleatory reactions, denying its subjectivity yields a universal, uniform, militant reaction. Despite the myriad tastes, moralities, desires, ideologies, and interests across communities, the prevention of their subjectivity spurs similar social reactions. We can describe conditions that deny all subjectivity more easily than we can conditions that deny all criteria of subjectivity (Bourdieu 1977, chap. 2; 1990, chap. 7; Gilligan 1996). This suggests a viable general theory of the interactions between global trends and local subjectivity that extrapolates social patterns from the "multiform, momentaneous, and almost unbearably precise world" (Borges 1998, 136).

So far I have disaggregated, re-specified, and complicated the sources, dynamics, and consequences of globalization and local action. I stressed that cultural, political, and economic trends have universal and divisive effects, mediated by peripheral institutions, given multiform desires and resources. I then outlined how subjectivity reacts to structural impositions to forge intra-systemic or anti-systemic political movements. Distilled, the analyses have clarified the unifying, fragmenting, and mediating aspects of globalization and subjectivity, represented in figure 3.1.

This schema transposes table 3.1, deleting the value-sphere and detailed columns and adding local reception of globalization. The figure illustrates that global developments and peripheral populations, or habitus, confront each other not as such but as the effect of divisive trends on the satisfaction of local desires.

FIGURE 3.1 SUBJECTIVITY, IDEOLOGY, AND GLOBALIZATION

Globalization				*Subjectivity*
General	Division	Mediation	Division	General
Universal Trends ◀▶ Disparities ◀▶		Criteria of Subject ◀▶ Will to Subjectivity ◀▶ Habitus		
		(desires, resources) (permitted/denied)		

Whether local tastes, choices, or desires persist depends on their fungibility, the communities' self-protective resources, and external coercion. How these combine to allow or impose the demise of antecedent values determines whether communities experience subjectivity.

Dissecting subjectivity is crucial. Subjectivity exerts itself in a habitus, a "durably installed generative principle of regulated improvisations" (Bourdieu 1977, 78). Subjectivity is a universal drive that expropriates cultural resources, creating the illusion that cultures use activists when it's the other way around. Radically diverse Islamist movements select from a shared repertoire of Islamic symbols, references, sources, and meanings; the repertoire itself cannot explain this selection. A habitus does not explain its permutations any more than a stage set explains actors' words. Rather, impediments to subjectivity inspire manipulation of the cultural backdrop from which the will to subjectivity draws its criteria and stabilizes, radicalizes, or meliorates those criteria.

There is no such thing, then, as globalization meeting habitus head on, as in "governance meets Buddhism," pace much of the literature. Divisive, particularized, interpreted, and eccentric versions of each meet at unique mediation points. If this contact allows subjectivity, the local reaction will be an idiosyncratic combination of global imports and local tastes; if it forbids subjectivity, local reaction will be to launch radicalized elements of the habitus against global or local power. The point is that social agitation forms in experienced subjectivity, not in globalized habitus; globalization and habitus cannot make direct contact but pass through thick layers of history, peculiarity, and will to subjectivity. We start not with mythically cohesive regions, civilizations, or religions or universal global trends, but with the social experiences, ideas, practices, innovations, and variations that only then drive activists to react further to globalization and habitus alike.

The priority, for social analysis, of subjective experience over "identity" in a habitus makes two further points. First, two communities of a common habitus but different circumstances will have less in common with each other than with communities of a different habitus in respectively similar circumstances. Commonalities across cultures, therefore, undergird our research model and case selection (Sen 2000). Rather than force Christians and Muslims into separate camps, we can compare communitarians (Iranian and American) and militants (American anti-abortionists and Algerian anti-feminists), for example. That the ideological trajectory runs from desires to subjectivity to habitus, not vice versa, negates idealist binaries such as American/Iranian or Christian/Muslim, and guides the sociology of religious politics to models of contextualized experience.

Globalizations thus diffuse to myriad locales, each a *Sittlichkeit* of institutional-ethical arrangements, principally the locus of the state (Stevens 1999). Self-determination of the peripheral community is measured by whether it chooses and satisfies its criteria of subjectivity, not by its defense of antecedent criteria; globalization may inspire modification of those criteria.[11] Every global-local interaction is particular vis-à-vis (1) the elements of globalization and subjectivity, (2) the elective affinity or alienation of those elements, and (3) the community's revaluation of the criteria of subjectivity given new possibilities. Outside forces may threaten, sustain, or improve communities' lives, provoking many secondary choices. But denied choice, communities respond uniformly. They defend their "iconic mental states" and social orders (Wollheim 1984, 63), often radicalizing their sense of self/other and violently reinterpreting their habitus. It is what happens to will, not desires, in the universal dialectics of subjectivity, that causally determines what the intersection of globality and community will produce.

We can now examine why Islamists pursue either (a) reform, accommodation, doubleness, hybridity, and humanism, or (b) radicalism, rejection, purity, militarism, and anti-humanism. Subjectivity is variously permitted by globalization across Muslim populations. How globalization—with or against local state efforts—excludes, weakens, facilitates, or encourages autochthonous commitments, ideals, and practices decides whether the will to subjectivity asserts itself as (a) or (b) above. As divergent trends attest in Iran, Algeria, Turkey, Jordan, Egypt, Palestine, Uzbekistan, Chechnya, Kashmir, Pakistan, and Muslim minorities in

11. Ideologies change from subjectivity's struggle for existence against constraints. Nietzsche (1998, 67) proclaims "the basic fact of the human will, its [horror of emptiness]: it needs a goal—and it would rather will nothingness than not will." Hegel claims individuality gains, recognizes, and develops its identity in confronting alterity (cf. Zizek 1999, 70–123; Wood 1990, chaps. 2, 4). The "unfathomable difficulty . . . in all its depth of contradiction" (Adorno 1978, 74) of the discovery and revision of subjectivity and identity only against alterity occurs when globalization politicizes criteria of subjectivity, urging their revaluation or conversion.

Europe and the United States, the greater the association between globalization and the absence of local political, economic, or cultural self-determination, the more militant and anti-humanist the response.

In the next section, I show that reactions (a) and (b) are distinct and discontinuous. Violent rejection and peaceful compromise do not inhabit one continuum of religious ideas and activities varying "only by degree," "in form but not content," or as "multiple means toward the same ends." Incommensurable Islamist trends—the uniqueness behind their commonality, not commonality behind their uniqueness—disprove the unity of causes and ends said to underlie "Islamism." The struggle for subjectivity under heterogeneous conditions—not the alleged struggle for authenticity under homogeneous conditions—cultivates multiple, non-spectral Islamist trends.

ISLAMISM

Islamic fundamentalism has divided Middle East scholars into two camps—idealists asserting a permanent Islamic ideological resistance to "Western" modernity and materialists calling religion a mere instrument for protests against political and economic deprivation (al-Azm 1993–94). Yet the call to explain Islamism has united these camps in an unwitting division of labor. The materialists have exposed the structural roots of suffering and the idealists have explicated the religious reaction to that suffering. Materialists (Beinin and Stork 1997) and idealists (Lewis 1998; Tibi 1998) thus have promoted rather than threatened each other's positions on Islamism. The more rigorous each research agenda, the more it yields to the other. Idealists privileging Islamic values turn to materialist explanations of Islamist ideological transformation and variation. Materialists stressing political and economic deprivation resort to idealism to explain the translation of nonreligious suffering into Islamist political discourse. This symbiotic endpoint draws not only on opposed and inadequate starting-points but also on a shared-continuum concept of Islamism. This section offers an empirically and theoretically stronger taxonomy and explanation of Islamist tendencies.

The materialist-idealist tempest echoes an old legacy of forcing the multiple miens of fundamentalism onto a continuum ranging from radical to quietist, militant to peaceful, revolutionary to reformist, presuming that they have greater similarity than difference and that they vary by degree and not by type. This continuum concept holds that fundamentalists vary strategically but not ideologically—militant, reformist, and private Islamists seek the same ends via different means. One typically ignorant essay descriptively, causally, and absurdly lumps together "the conservative and the radical wing of . . . Islamism . . . a movement of the urban and rural poor and . . . lower middle class . . . suffering . . . economic stagnation" (Laqueur 2001, 501–2). Muslims thus pursue their single ideology by whatever strategy eliminates impediments to its fruition; militancy reflects Islam impeded, communal legalism and individual quietism Islam permitted (Choueiri 1990, 12).

Notably, material and ideal explanations have united in one descriptive and explanatory "single-deprivation/continuum model" of Islamism. The former offers a single cause of all Islamisms and, following Karl Marx (1978, 28–46, 53–60) and Tocqueville (1969, 442 ff.), regards religious beliefs as the psychological effect of bureaucratic or capitalist stifling of humanity's essence. The latter posits a single Islamism adopting several strategic fronts and, following Hegel or later Durkheim, regards religious beliefs as fundamental to human striving, thus the cause of behavior in its name. Neither account—of religious belief as effect or cause of its social conditions—takes religious diversity seriously. In tandem, these views urge causal models relating degree-changes in one form of deprivation to what they consider "degrees of fundamentalism." The model's spectrums and causal (vertical) pairings are shown in figure 3.2.

Nomenclatures for fundamentalism vary (one work lists "revivalism, reformism, and radicalism") but occupy the same descriptive continuum. Types of deprivation inserted into this explanatory model include food, freedom, rights, equality, and authenticity. Whichever deprivation it stresses, each approach presumes that some single deprivation explains fundamentalism and its variety; into the same model go different terms and paradigms without a critique of the model itself. The continuum concept of Islamism forces explanations linking all its forms to degree-changes in one cause, for example "alienation" (Ayubi 1991). By this formulation, Islamist assassins are just more alienated than simply veiled women—any religious person is a ticking bomb a few alienation-units away from murder (Roy 1994). Typically, that model subsidizes globalization theories that correlate levels of economic, political, or cultural deprivation with "levels" of an allegedly single fundamentalism.

This single-deprivation/continuum model of fundamentalism has helpfully forced scholars to contextualize, historicize, and demystify religious identities

FIGURE 3.2 "DEGREES" OF FUNDAMENTALISM

Deprivation: Minimal ◀┈┈┈┈▶ Medium ◀┈┈┈┈▶ Maximal

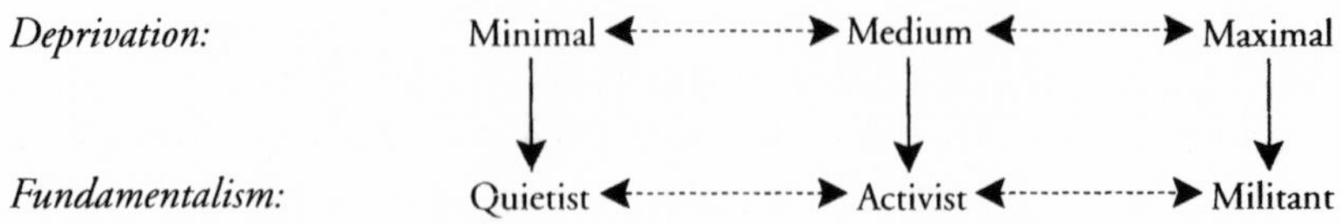

Fundamentalism: Quietist ◀┈┈┈┈▶ Activist ◀┈┈┈┈▶ Militant

and aspirations as "social constructions." Surely this insight alone upends only patently silly social determinism (Hacking 1999), but it rightly insists on studying religious activities in terms of interests, experiences, and evaluations rather than reflexes, impulses, and passions (Eickelman and Piscatori 1996). Recent interregional studies of religious resurgence have de-exoticized Islam while validating comparative sociological approaches (Kepel 1991), though often retaining the progress/reaction binary that homogenizes fundamentalism (Marty and Appleby 1992, 17–18). Some intraregional studies have emphasized the agential, creative, multifarious lives of Muslims (Zubaida 1993) against partisan caricatures (Sivan 1985). With similar nuance, specialists have deepened our appreciation of fundamentalism regarding modernity (Abrahamian 1993; Binder 1988; Burke and Lapidus 1988; Tripp 1999), democracy (Enayat 1982, 125 ff.), social theory (Euben 1999), and the nation-state (Piscatori 1986), all usually considered inimical to Islam(ism) (Salamé 1994). But such refinements, textures, and correctives do not de-essentialize or disaggregate Islamism or its sources—these works still see Islamist diversity as strategic adaptation by a cohesive ideology to intensities of some deprivation-type. In these works, what variety complicates, the single-deprivation/continuum model resimplifies; what agency de-essentializes, the model re-essentializes; what rationality humanizes, it renaturalizes.

The broader view of religion as maladaptation to uniform deprivation associated with secular progress uniquely hinders subtlety about fundamentalism. Other world-views are differentiated scrupulously, after all. We methodically distinguish between love of nation and rabid nationalism, between community and communalism (Kakar 1996; Daniel 1996), and between prejudicial and eliminationist anti-Semitism (Goldhagen 1996, 34–38) or racism (Outlaw 1996). The American communitarian, Polish Solidarity, and Indian Bharatiya Janata Party/Vishwa Hindu Parishad movements adhere to national identity, but no one considers them all "nationalists" to be explained by levels of poverty or industrialization. Just as social solidarity and sectarian violence differ in kind, not degree—and are not separated by a degree-change in one kind of deprivation—all "isms" take incommensurable forms requiring discretionary theoretical accounts.

Islamism includes three tendencies that I call personal, communitarian, and militant, each an ideological and behavioral composite. Each Islamist trend contains hierarchies or divisions of class, gender, education, and geography, as well as strategic nonbelievers (Macleod 1991; Kandiyoti 1991). But in principle and practice these groups are coherent and legible, their arguments are consistent, intelligible discourses resonant and accountable to active or passive observers. The tension between participant and observer, between religionists' beliefs and author's interpretations, is resoluble vis-à-vis Islamism (Fischer 1980; Bayat

1997).[12] Because religious reinterpretations are problem-solving ventures, Islamists tend to concur with analyses suspicious of "false consciousness" frameworks that impute dissonant strategic and ideological motivations to social movements. Hypotheses of political-entrepreneurial manipulation, for instance, must prove elite religious decrees and their popular advocacy to be disingenuous, instrumental, about something other than what they claim. Iranian Islamists were thus disgruntled *bazaris,* merchants "using religion to protest economic exclusion." But how does this challenge the authenticity, substance, and meaning of the religious expression? To account for and respect coextensive strategic-ideological choices, I take Islamism to comprise a set of ends-means cognitive and behavioral commitments held by religious believers (Bilgrami 1995).

Personal Islamism refers to the many Muslims of intensified religious observance who attend prayers, study the Qur'an, follow the Five Pillars, and conduct themselves with spiritual sobriety and ritualistic devotion. Resurgent personal religiosity resists easy measurement and general causal analysis because of its individualistic, private, and diffuse nature, and because it comprises in each context a heightened attention to a rich cultural identity (Bulliet 1994). The solemn practice and recalcitrance to social agitation or supra-mosque organization suggest individual discipline in a naturalized environment experienced as apolitical. This personal religiosity (positing the good, not the bad or evil) asserts itself against diffuse, gradual, and invisible constraints, internalizing the causes of private losses and gains, taking responsibility for failure and success. Personal Islamism achieves self-mastery through institutional support and obeisance without identifying enemies.

Communitarian Islamism is the public, concerted effort to formulate, inculcate, or institutionalize Islamic values procedurally within a political system (Sadowski 1996). Unlike personal religionists, communitarians proselytize for a clear set of solutions to impersonal, social deficiencies. This communal religiosity (positing good and bad, but not evil) asserts itself against specifically "immoral" developments, externalizing the causes of losses and gains, assigning blame elsewhere, and taking responsibility for moral reclamation. Communitarians target authoritarianism, corruption, and cultural "Westernization" that threaten their pre-activism beliefs (Goldberg 1992). Once mobilized, communitarians—like their American counterparts—increase their number directly through ideological

---

12. I conducted open-ended and follow-up interviews with secular and Islamist academics, feminists, refugees, activists, leaders, and rulers in 1986–87 (Jordan, Palestine, Israel, Turkey), 1990–92 (Egypt, Sudan, Israel, Syria, Sudan, Palestine, France, Algeria), 1993 (Lebanon), 1996 (Austria, Lebanon, Yemen). I thank my many interviewees for their trust, insights, and arguments.

recruitment and indirectly through cultural reform and social service provision. Their governmental tactic is to use the ministries of education and the interior to institute Arabization and Islamic teaching in public schools. Their anti-governmental strategy is to outperform the state in welfare distribution (day care, textbooks, disaster relief) and to equate their superior efficiency with religious-moral rectitude (Sadowski 1987). Several points stand out here. Communitarians are systemic participants who thrive on moral suasion, social example, arguments, and bargains, not coercion. Communitarian Islamism parallels the "action-oriented ideals" of Western civil society: "The normative principles underlying it, plurality, publicity, legality, equality, justice, voluntary association, and individual autonomy, constitute a self-limiting utopia that calls for a plurality of democratic form, a complex set of social, civil, and political rights compatible with a highly differentiated society" (Cohen 1997, 37). Personal and communitarian religious ideals, desires, negotiations, and moral stances are analogous to the moral, tolerant, inclusive, pragmatic endeavors of individual and collective actors carrying similar secular banners elsewhere (Nandy 1991).

Militant Islamism consists in the violent, revisionist, and manichean assault on perceived sites of morally bankrupt social control. Under secular authoritarian rule, militant Islamism ignites in sudden, sustained, and calculated violence when core activists and recruits ally against the abruptly total denial of their subjectivity.[13] Mobilizing rapidly, militant Islamists organize small, dispersed, underground cadres often led by intellectuals and scientists. These cells launch political violence against the denounced power structure (state, media, bureaucracy, protected sectors) and craft a propagandistic recruitment campaign. The violence against ruling figures and symbols draws state reprisal, instigating an abysmal cycle that engulfs the country, seducing recruits to fight heightened state-repression (Hasnayn Ibrahim 1992). Justifying murder, thievery, and rape for political conquest and moral reclamation, militants construe an "Islamic" theology of self-purification and other-demonization. This militant religiosity (positing good versus evil) excoriates alterity as immorality, malversation as tergiversation, dissent as sin. Setting moral purity and religious cleansing against dispirited technocracy and cancerous foes is fascist. Militants fuse "brutishness and terror" with political aestheticization, "the ideal of life as art, the cult of beauty, the fetishism of courage, the dissolution of alienation in ecstatic feelings of commu-

---

13. Algeria exemplifies the abruptness of militant Islamism. In 1992 civil war erupted in Algeria between Islamists and the state. Entelis (1986) had just argued that the secular revolution was "institutionalized" and Esposito (1990) had not even mentioned Algeria regarding the "global impact" of the Iranian revolution.

nity, the repudiation of the intellect, and the family of man" (Sontag 1981, 96; cf. McCole 1993, 179; Colas 1997; Benjamin 1968). But this aestheticized political violence also re-mythologizes "Islam" through its anti-doctrinal, metaphorical revaluation (Appiah 1992, 114 ff.; Berger 1967). The replacement of magic/tradition with science/modernity redirects religion from doctrinal literalism to theological exegesis, political invention, and metaphorical abstraction. When science/modernity appear to deny human subjectivity, militant reaction spurns both magic/tradition and science/modernity in an unprecedented archaic/modern theology of extremism (Ainslie 1986). Personal and communitarian Islamists revile the militants' atrocities and ideas as wholly irresponsible [14]—irrelevant to them, Islam, and even religion itself.

Most important in studying Islamism is that which ideologues blame for their dissatisfaction (self, bureaucracy, president) and what criteria of subjectivity (new, old) they value—both accessible through detailed, emic portrayals of distinct Islamist arguments and moral accounts. Thus I now describe the Islamist trends in terms of subjectivity and desires to discern their causal contexts.

Personal Islamists identify themselves as the object of critique and source of social progress, invoking rarely and abstractly an external constraint on their capacities or desires. Personal Islamists hold an ascetic ethic of responsibility, without a moral foe, that emphasizes private religiosity, often denouncing the conflation of political and religious life. As a social trend, this ascetic ideal emerges where gradual and morally naturalized conditions hinder people's pursuits, inspiring a revaluation in which actors remedy their undisciplined conduct or inadequate character. Reacting to incremental impoverishment or piecemeal disenfranchisement, Muslims intensify their commitments to existing Islamic beliefs and practices as agents reconstituting themselves. Personal Islamists thus blame themselves for their frustration and draw from the symbolic, spiritual, and intellectual resources of their habitus a moral and social regeneration. Personal Islamism results when Muslims, their desires hampered, can choose whether to retain those desires and, if so, to pursue them through religious rigor; the Islamist turn does not entail changed desires, just a new approach to those desires. The failing businessman may abandon his entrepreneurial ambitions or he may become disciplined via religious strictness to satisfy them. He chooses to drop or keep his ends (business) and, if he keeps them, what new means (Islamist disci-

14. Echoing Patocka's view that "[proper] religion exists once the secret of the sacred, orgiastic, or demonic mystery has been, if not destroyed, at least integrated, and finally subjected to the sphere of responsibility" (Derrida 1995, 2).

pline) will help. Personal Islamists exercise their subjectivity (choice) by changing not their criteria of subjectivity (desires) but their path to the same criteria.

Communitarian Islamists castigate themselves and the broader public for ethical turpitude, linking poor social values to government policies that frustrate people's capacities or desires. They focus on the corruption or victimization of classes, sectors, or the state, exemplified in recurrent crises and ineffectual policy responses (refugee issues, development, social provision, insulation from cultural invasion). Embarking on a public restoration, communitarians seek to resuscitate the collective, urging the adoption of acknowledged Islamic modes of probity, dignity, and discipline to reverse perceived losses. Yet for communitarian Islamism, social ends and means are co-implicated; spiritual and behavioral revival profound enough to resolve social problems must modify desires. Despite this aggressive moralization, communitarian ideology is equivocal, intellectual, and reflective—accepting blame, stressing choice over fate, identifying vague, malleable ambitions and critical targets. These Islamists debate, advocate, participate systemically, compromise, negotiate, and cohabit politically with their opponents; they are publicly accountable and personally responsible. Communitarian Islamism results when Muslims can exercise their subjectivity by changing their choices (selecting, amplifying, and following Islamic ethics) to eliminate social frustration.

Militant Islamists are dualistic moral secessionists incapable of self-criticism who massacre demonized power-holders, risking their lives "in a rain of blood, a snow of bone" (Amis 1991, 84). Absolutist, uncompromising monists seeking to conquer, not convince, to win, not win over, militant Islamists are secretive, unaccountable, and in this sense irresponsible. They battle elite groups (state and citizen) whose hegemonic organization and coercion have evidently frustrated their initial economic, political, or cultural ends and then denied them effective means of appeal. Militant Islamism results, then, when Muslims can neither satisfy their criteria of subjectivity nor modify them effectively, subjectively, within the dominant system, and thus erupt in anti-systemic violence.

This distillation insinuates causal contexts into the discussion that map over globalization. Recall that in the periphery the general globalization trends are variably crisis-prone, abrupt, traumatic, and imperious, and so variably implicate local-mediation as directly culpable. How does this variation relate to Islamist tendencies? Personal Islamists take responsibility for the gradual, systemic, naturalized frustration of their ends, where they experience nontraumatic economic, political, or cultural disfranchisement. Thus personal Islamism occurs where insidious trends slowly frustrate people's desires without apparent collusion or corruption of the state or local ruling classes (mediation of desires and external forces). Privately devout Muslims do not blame global or local forces that have disempowered them; the Islamist form most directly affected by globalization is, perhaps paradoxically, least directly critical of it. Because personal Islamists orient themselves within but also insulate themselves from these global forces, their identity is double.

Communitarians blame the moral tenor of all society for repeated policy failures, especially in crises, that frustrate popular desires. This evaluation occurs when dominant social actors appear unwilling or unable to offset traumatic setbacks to a peripheral community's conditions and when protesters can lead a moral, systemic protest against both the conditions and the failing elites. Because those setbacks often are caused by transparent exogenous shocks or policy impositions and appear unopposed or facilitated by local rule, communitarians criticize the link between globalization and inadequate local rule explicitly. But alternatively attacking globalization and blaming its mediators, they inveigh against both the coercive world order and ruling elites' past and present weakness of character, judgment, or courage. Communitarianism becomes a discourse of strong cultural and moderate economic and political protectionism, fortifying against a globalization unmediated by stalwart peripheral leadership. The Muslims of Turkey's former Refah party, Jordan's Brotherhood, Tunisia's al-Nahda party, or the United States Nation of Islam insulate themselves against "the West," a polyvalent metonym denoting admirable willfulness, looming domination, boorish secularism, or valueless utilitarianism. Criticizing globalization, communitarians yet display a "noble valuation" toward, not hatred of, the Western other; absorbing globalization on their own rigidified cultural terms, they cultivate a hybrid identity.

Militants execrate ruling elites for negating their desires and their capacity to pursue modified desires. Globalization may sponsor peripheral state coercion, but militant Islamists pointedly attack local power, not globalization. They may single out particular Western allies of the authoritarian governments suppressing them, but militants are far more likely to advocate globalization in appending it to their cause, in the common hope that international markets, law, or human rights regimes will undermine local dictatorship. The consequent identity of militant Islamism, forged in anti-autocratic combat, is—despite this instrumentalist, selective internationalism—rejectionist.

The globalization-Islamism nexus is as surprising, I suspect, as that each Islamism is singular, complex, and necessarily driven by a distinct deprivation. These correspondences are shown in table 3.2.

By now it should be clear that "more Westernization equals more Islamism" is a formula as irrelevant as it is popular, no matter how "Westernization" is de-

TABLE 3.2
ISLAMISM AND GLOBALIZATION

Variations	Personal	Communitarian	Militant
Mode of deprivation	material/cultural criteria of subj. gradual	material/cultural criteria of subj. crisis/episodic	political will to subj. abrupt
Target of inculpation	self	society (self/other) "West" as metonym for globalization	other (rulers) "West" as synonym for ally of local coercion
Type of inculpation	internalization individual responsibility	internal/ externalization common responsibility	externalization manichean purification
Identity	hybridity	doubleness	rejection
Globalization as focus of critique	absent (private vigilance, systemic naturalization)	shared w/ mediation (public vigilance, systemic moralization)	parasitic on mediation (public violence, anti-systemic moralization)
Globalization as causal factor	direct general, amorphous contact with criteria	mediated specific, state-centric contact with criteria	incidental occasion for local denial of will to subjectivity

fined. More interestingly, inserting globalization into this descriptive/explanatory disaggregation of Islamism provides counterintuitive findings. For one, militant Islamists' hatred of "the West" is not a reaction to its own values or practices but to its alliance with peripheral tyranny, as in pre-1979 Iran. In Algeria, South Lebanon, Afghanistan, and Palestine, "anti-West" anger has derived from country-specific Western collaboration with peripheral oppression, which is why globalization—say, of human rights—is often the Islamists' weapon in their campaigns. Similarly, the less acidulous discourse of communitarian Islamism is a reaction to globalization's imposition of competition-security states on Muslims, aided by weak local rule. Communitarians are more "anti-Western," meaning anti-globalization, than militants. Communitarianism, despite its systemic participation and seeming moderation, is thus more insular, reactionary, and persistent than either personal or militant Islamism.

I reemphasize the radically contrasting motivations, evaluations, contexts, and targets of these Islamist tendencies. I have often paired two against the third, especially vis-à-vis violence, because I am preoccupied with the dynamics of violent conflict. So a central distinction here has been that personal and communitarian Islamisms flourish when Muslims can successfully amplify, reinterpret, and deploy their religious heritage to counter frustration of their desires while militant Islamism emerges when Muslims are systematically denied effective self-determination. On this register militants seize on conditions opposite to those that foster personal and communitarian Islamism (Dabashi 1993). But any two strands can be placed against the third, depending on the register; militant and personal Islamists equally refuse formal public scrutiny of their positions, unlike communitarians, for example. The larger point that I hope is now agreeable is that conservative ascetic quietism against unnamed social impositions, revisionist social activism against discredited public institutions, and homicidal moral separatism against tyranny constitute distinct phenomena resulting from contrasting situations and experiences of subjectivity.

The trajectory of modern Algerian Islamism illustrates this argument. Postcolonial Algerian ruling elites implemented national educational policies, family laws, and Islamic discourse as concessions to observant Muslims despite official "socialist" ideology (Messaoudi 1995). Gradual mismanagement, global integration, and social dislocation nurtured a socially stable personal Islamism. But as crises multiplied, culminating in the October 1988 riots, Islamist activists and others assailed the political leadership for breaking the "egalitarian" social contract. Forming a dissident party and captivating adherents with vital religious language and sociopolitical skills, communitarian Islamists embraced the electoral contest their protests had secured and broadened. They thus satisfied their new desires for a legal Islamist party and participation in national elections, just as personal Islamists satisfied their desire for Arabization (1968) and the Family Code (1984). Cohabiting peacefully, both Islamist groups experienced subjectivity.

But after the communitarian Front Islamique du Salut's (FIS's) systemic, peaceful success in the 1990–91 communal, provincial, and initial national elections, the state canceled the final round of national elections in January 1992 and banned the FIS party. This reversal denied the opposition any effective recourse, collapsing the system, polarizing the population, and igniting civil war. The state's authoritarian maneuver enabled militants to supplant reformers, some of whom radicalized, creating an anti-systemic, violent rebellion. To casual observation, electoral participation and violent insurrection marked one ideology's (desire for Islamization) adapting strategies (from electoral to violent protest) to changed circumstances. But the electoral interruption changed the terms of Islamist political and moral evaluation (Martinez 1998). By annulling democratic reforms, the state eliminated the opposition's systemic subjectivity, triggering a radical critique, agitation, and revaluation of ends. In contrast, the Jordanian, Turkish, and Lebanese states have incorporated or accommodated, and thus de-radicalized, the Islamist resurgence by allowing them effective influence over policies. In Algeria the state did not merely extend the deprivation of some desire but annihilated activists' subjectivity, triggering an anti-systemic, militant attack on all previous social relations, symbols, and values.

MODERNITY

Islamism exemplifies all religions' tendency to subdivide into contentious interpretive and behavioral strains that, in turn, evince contradictory tendencies in diverse situations. For this complexity, religions have messy connections to modernity. But the tidy, standard view still insists that modernity, defined as rationalizing innovation, plays a zero-sum game against nonrational tradition, particularly religious belief. Human history, from this perspective, consists of a series of irrational world-views before, during, and after the triumph of modernity. Enlightenment gains are thus pitted against their antipodean Others, opposing materialism/secularism/positivism/ratiocination/democracy (or socialism)/experimentation/universalism to spiritualism/religion/faith/doctrine/authoritarianism (or fascism)/ritual/particularism. Like two tightly integrated teams, these lists usually play man-to-man but are allowed to play zone. For example, "material" protest is linked to interest, rationality, achievement, and universality, and so to modernity, but "identity" protest is attached to ideology, emotion, ascription, and particularity, and so to a rejection of modernity (Offe 1987; Inglehart 1997). This outlook casts fundamentalism as primitive ascription in revolt "against modernity" despite its contrasting behavioral, aesthetic, and intellectual manifestations.

In this conventional schema, Islamism epitomizes anti-modern delinquencies such as anti-falsificationism, universalism, and cosmopolitanism (Lawrence 1989).[15] Two narratives suggest this conflict. One says that Islamism arose when modern state-building politically marginalized Islam while subjecting it to secular rationalization (Humphreys 1999, 135). Thus, ancient "Islam" defies modern social fragmentation (Lewis 1998, 27–28). Another view holds that Islamism emerged not with the rise but with the fall of "high modern" political and economic conceits, such as rapid industrialization, bureaucratization, centralization, capitalization, and technocratic rigidities that benefited state control more than it

15. Thus *"jihad"* connotes one vast antimodern fight sprawling from "Islamic zeal" to "bloody holy war," such that "Jihad and McWorld . . . [are] moral antinomies" (Barber 1996, 9, 216).

did social welfare, competitiveness, development, stability, or international standing. Here Muslims angrily discover that humanism means only corrupt democracy, crony capitalism, authoritarian bureaucracy, or despotic socialism. Islamists putatively conceive these vices as the relentless assault of rationalization, Westernization, and secularization on community, agency, value, meaning, culture, and morality. But interpreted more dialectically (Bürger 1992, 32 ff.), Islamist ideologies reflect diverse experiences of modernity as an "internal textual struggle" in discrete settings (Pick 1989, 43).

This section first recasts the discussion of modernity and its others to enhance the conflicted modernity of Islamism. Islamist thought evinces intricate, counterintuitive stances toward modernity, and so to its cognates, such as postmodernity. Personal Islamists are least dogmatic and critical, most private and accountable, most worldly and apolitical. Communitarian Islamists are strident and compromising, public and insulated, disputatious and rigid. Militant Islamists are violent and doctrinal, scientific and eschatological, synthetic and purifying. Iranian rule has been intellectually anti-modern, discursively postmodern, and politically "high modern" (cf. Mosse 1978; Bartov 1996, 67 ff.). These positions reflect modernity's ambivalences and Islamists' fragmentary experience of modernity. This nuance explodes the fundamentalism-versus-modernity canard (Hafez 2000, 122, n. 9; Lifton 1986, 488) and its correlate that a spectrum from personal to communitarian to militant Islamism charts the intensification of anti-modernism.

Second, I read Islamist assertions of subjectivity as intra- or anti-systemic replies to particular aspects and appearances of modernity. Islamist movements react critically, heterogeneously, and purposefully against deprivations attributable to certain facets or expressions of modernity.[16] Frequently fundamentalists pursue elements of modernity that they have not experienced, often to offset or buttress those they have. Those hurt by capitalization demand democratic accountability or improved education, those disappointed by democracy's material benefits demand technological advances, and so on. Less typically, fundamental-

16. The opposite view is that "global reflexivization/mediatization generates its own brutal immediacy . . . [and] excessive non-functional cruelty . . . whose figures range from 'fundamentalist' racist and/or religious slaughter . . . a violence grounded in no utilitarian or ideological cause" (Zizek 2000, 8). Globalization's perceptual compression thus creates insane violence. This view commits every standard error: the single-deprivation/continuum model, acontextual abstraction, and undifferentiated psychologism. Indifference to specific political, institutional, or economic roots of violence in favor of alienation-and-violence clichés alas equally characterizes Keane (1996).

ists turn modern practices they have suffered against power-holders; for example, subjugated by modernity-as-bureaucratic-authoritarianism, militants reclaim their subjectivity through counter-authoritarian populist activism. The social mechanism is the same in both cases: different communities, experiencing modernity as discrete constellations of gains and losses to their desires or subjectivity, embrace those aspects of modernity that they believe will restore or protect their desires or subjectivity.

What then are the background concepts, commitments, and beliefs of "modernity" such that we may speak of its instances, effects, advocates, and critics? Distinguishing features of modernity can help us find the sources of "antimodern" ideologies. But my broader argument is that however we delineate periods and paradigms, however some other cognitive schema improves on mine, all social movements including Islamism will have an ambiguous, internally contradictory relationship to modernity. We can analyze ideologies against modern ideals even though modernity has empirically porous temporal-conceptual parameters. We need not essentialize "tradition," then, to assent to the grounding claim that "modernity can and will no longer . . . take its orientation from another epoch; it has to create its normativity out of itself" (Habermas 1991, 7; cf. Stephen Smith 1989, 57–61; Mill 1989). This baseline of modernity extends the criteria of "legitimizing legitimacy" to enlist reason in the innovation rather than mere consolidation, the revaluation rather than mere institutionalization, of the social order (Calasso 1994, 2). To achieve these criteria, modernity further specifies the noninstrumental content of "publicly significant" reason (Arendt 1958, 46 ff.; cf. Griffin 2000).

Modern thought affixes rational commitment to objectivity and universalism, and scientific dualism to emancipatory social progress (Flax 1990, 32 ff.). This initial definition distinguishes willful, rational human self-improvement as the ultimate end from specific means toward that end, such as secular liberal utilitarianism. Grafting certain practices to Enlightenment ideals tendentiously narrows modernity to Anglo-European conceptions, perforce deligitimating alternative paths toward subjectivity and reason (Geuss 1998, 299). Neutrally defined, modernity embraces multiple forms of willfully deliberated freedoms, including collective or religious orientations. But these familiar terms need clarification. Rationality here implies progressive internal critique, not mere rationalization, for Hegel the core of modern ratiocination. Objectivity refers to "the conviction that, whether with regard to physical nature or human culture, we can always discern the 'way the world is,' appropriately segregated from the perspectived conditions of human inquiry" (Margolis 1999, 5; Max Weber 1946, 139).

Universalism posits a human substrate enabling social translatability, regularity, predictability, and comparability, a locus of commensurability permitting human science (Marx 1978, 155 ff.; Durkheim 1995, 4). Scientific dualism claims that rational, philosophically realist methods distinguish falsity from truth, appearance from essence, and ideology from science. Finally, modernity harnesses these convictions to a robust theory of cumulative enlightenment.

Modernists, then, derive progress from the agential deployment of reason toward realizing evidently unspecified desires, or everyday ends. This implies that modernity delimits the means by which a community achieves its desires, not the desires themselves. But given the contribution of modern technology to unimaginable atrocities (Gourevitch 1998, 16; Bauman 1989), modernity must forbid desires that would vanquish reason. A people committed to scientific, objective, or technical means to satisfying certain desires must also desire a social order that ensures those means. These means and ends alone conjure a closed-system, rationalist modernity of soulless technocrats, stoic scientists, and ponderous methodologists. But modernity connotes the fastidious, methodical rationalist and the youthful, subjective, skeptical, even anti-intellectual dreamer (Krauss 1993, 2; Moretti 1987; Kermode 1971, 43–45; Hoffman 1989, 15). For Goethe, the quintessential modern, asks, fusing subjective and objective knowledge, "But is this really true—is it true for me?" (Trilling 1979, 5). Indeed, progressive rationalism not only allows but requires radical creativity or, as Weber says, "intoxication," however paradoxical it may seem that scientific experimentation must refuse teleology (Moretti 1987, 6). Modernity posits and interrogates, it does not master or eliminate, such tensions (Frisby 1986; Schorske 1998, chap. 3). It embraces the contradictory, symbiotic tendencies of reason, uncertainty, conjecture, and skepticism.

Rejecting modernity, then, is not tantamount to seeing its internal tensions. It is modernists who most worry that reason eventually favors procedural over substantive rationality, strategic over communicative action (Rousseau 1987, 67 ff.), private calculation over public deliberation (Kant, Arendt, Habermas), and scientific over ethical progress (Russell). Some despair that social rationalization dims human experience (Simpson 1995), cultivation (Tocqueville 1983, 77–96), knowledge (Scott 1998), and capabilities (Mill 1973, 47; Sen 1999) integral to human development and freedom. Others insist that reason itself, due to its "radical historicization" (Bourdieu 2000, 93 ff.), anti-foundationalist self-questioning (Lyotard 1984, 79), or paradoxical "modern critical stance" (Latour 1993, 10–12) strains the Enlightenment project. Such ambiguities and complexities define modern discourses of universalism, dualism, and objectivity. Modern problematics reject high modernist, positivist scientism (Quine 1981, 67–72), deepening rather than upending modernism.

Similarly, the "linguistic turn" from "subject-centered philosophy" relates ambiguously to rational agency (Habermas 1994, 208), just as the rejection of scientific dualism does not intrinsically confound reasoned moral progressivism (Putnam 1995, 7). The accredited place of imagination in historical representation (Finley 1960, 4–5) likewise underscores that "objectivity is a method of understanding" that "[deliberately] juxtaposes the internal and external or subjective and objective views at full strength, in order to achieve unification when it is possible and to recognize clearly when it is not" (Nagel 1986, 4). These diverse positions and sources illustrate that modernity is analytically equidistant from orthodox Enlightenment and fundamentalist world-views by its commitment to the ambiguities and dilemmas they both reject. Against this rich conception of modernity we may define the non-modern.

I have implied that it is not in observing modernity's internal complexity that one rejects modernity, but in conjuring a world without complexity, a tendency shared by ultra-rationalists, anti-modernists, and postmodernists. Leaving aside "high Positivism" (Danto 1999, 156; cf. Grafton [on Ranke] 1997, chaps. 2–3), rejecting modernity means denying the possibility, or relevance to social progress, of objectivity, universalism, and scientific dualism. Two versions of this denial are particularly relevant to contemporary protest ideologies: anti-modernism and postmodernism. I will portray these views and then integrate my accounts of globalization and Islamism into this discussion.

Anti-modernism is a protean recoiling from unfettered philosophical reflection, instrumental (versus value) rationality, social flux and instability, or secular, commercial, unprincipled life (Lears 1981). Primordial in recourse and reactionary in argument, anti-modernists associate purposive scientific reason with social folly or with the deracination and alienation of proper human ends (Hirschman 1991). Anti-modernists, as prickly Luddite romantics, stodgy Burkean aristocrats, or panicked Fichtean purists, applaud a value-grounded cultural standpoint that excoriates social progressivism. Anti-modernists, notably Heidegger, seek to reclaim a once-unified human essence by insulating it from technological and scientific mastery and alterity; in short, they agitate for the reintegration of social life based on an allegedly retrieved human or cultural authenticity.

Postmodernists, in contrast, distrust all fixed positions, scientific or identitarian, not because of reason's inherent folly or liminal progressive utility but because of its unreliable relationship to objectivity, universality, and science (Touraine 1995, 99 ff.). To avoid bowdlerizing postmodernism's complex ideas

(cf. Best and Kellner 1991; Kaplan 1988), I will summarize two critiques of objective, universal hermeneutics that capture the general postmodern attitude toward rationalism and progress. First, building on Heidegger's "ontological
radicalization of the relation between temporality and the historicity of existence," Gadamer and others espoused an "interpretative experience irreducible
to objective mirroring" (Vattimo 1997, 44,\q>ff.; cf. Palmer 1969 and Wolin
2000). However easily appended to anti-modernism, this rejection of objective
hermeneutics due to untranslatable cultural particularity is more typical of postmodern relativism (cf. Göle 1996, 87; al-Azmeh 1993, 39). Second, semioticians
isolated meaning, culture, and language from putatively genetic material or ideal
forces. Theorists from Ferdinand de Saussure to Jacques Derrida have held that
signification results from the differentiation of signs, not as a "reflection" of
some extrinsic "base" reality (Merleau-Ponty in Raschke 1989, 59). Post-
structuralists further deny "the existence of underlying systems of conventions
which enable elements to function individually as signs" (Saussure in White 1991,
15). Postmodernism thus centrally denies that "culture" (ideas, symbols, meanings) reflects either deeper social realities or any immanent organizing system. In
rejecting dualism, objectivity, universalism, and translatability, postmodernity
discounts them as sources of social progress.

Differentiating modern from anti-modern and postmodern convictions
rubbishes much ideological nonsense. For example, anything hybrid, hypocritical, symbolic, or chaotic in politics has become "postmodern." Nicolae
Ceaucescu was "the perfect postmodern despot" for being a "market Stalinist"
(Hitchens 1993, 130). The realpolitik of the "Middle East peace process" constitutes "postmodern politics" by involving religious symbols (Margalit 2000, 6).
Coffee becomes "the beverage of postmodernism" merely by expanding distribution (Roseberry 1996, 763). Far worse, violence in failed states morphs into
"postmodern war" just for being anarchic and "fought by irregulars" (Ignatieff
1998, 5–6). From such swamps we rescue concepts needed to connect, say, violence and modernity (Bauman 1995) or Islamism and postmodernity. The anti-
modern posture of militant Islamism, for one, combines multiple referents and
doctrines, a postmodern collage with modern political designs. Ideologies are,
too, textured by the overall balance and orientation of their conflicted attitudes
toward modernity (Davis 1999; Salvatore 1997).

Now I wish to link stances toward modernity to Islamist ideologies and then
to the global trends and local mediations molding them. I want, then, to thread
this section back through the previous sections to draw tentative inferences
about how globalizing forces politicize religious identity, shaping attitudes to-

ward modernity in the periphery. Recall the view that globalization, by imperiling cultural security (Huntington 1996; Barber 1996), prompts primordial anti-modernism. Recasting this logic, Bryan S. Turner (1994, 78 ff.; cf. Robertson 1989) portrays fundamentalism not as an instinctive retreat to ascriptive identity but "as the cultural defense of modernity against postmodernity," the willful, collective defense of "household" and "community" against global "de-differentiation." Here the agential, strategic, or humanist component of commu-nal mobilization upends primordialism. But this advance alone may replace one simplification with a better one: Islamism as active not reactive, modern not anti-modern, subject not object. This mirror-image refutation tends to re-homogen-ize fundamentalism, reinstating the model of a single (modern) ideology pursued via several strategies.

The non-continuum model of Islamist ideologies undermines both versions of attributing heightened religious conviction—as the instinctive rejection or subjective embrace of modernity—to the defense of endangered traditional identities. Both views hold that in reacting to sustained threats to their identities, cultures exaggerate their ideologies. So under globalization already-modern cul-tures exaggerate their modernity—progressing to postmodernism (Appiah 1992, 141)—and not-yet-modern cultures exaggerate their tradition—regressing to fundamentalism. By now subtler equations are in order. Personal, communi-tarian, and militant Islamisms are distinct constellations of modern and non-modern elements, sharing only core religious practices such as prayer and fasting.

Personal Islamists most closely approximate the criteria of modernity sketched above. Committed dualists, they evaluate public and private spheres, and matters of faith and science, by separate criteria. Ethical or aesthetic convic-tions are not universally or objectively justified while physics or capitalism may be. Personal Islamists accommodate neoteric technological deployments or so-cial institutions with religious equanimity, so live happily under secular law. Be-cause their religiosity is a private faith and practice, these Islamists individually embrace innovations and their lived burdens. Thus personal Islamists are toler-ant, nondogmatic, egalitarian, and denunciatory of public religiosity bent on cas-tigating outsiders or coercing women. Yet this cohabitation with social rationalization and moral secularization derives from a quintessentially postmod-ern anti-rationalism. Personal Islamism delinks reason and social progress, equat-ing the latter with private spirituality and salvation availed by insulating faith from secular politics and moral utilitarianism. Paradoxically, personal Islamism conjoins modernization by externalizing it from private, religious life, which—immured in this process—retains a uniquely traditional, simplified, ascetic form.

So as personal Islamists separate modern/public/rational and non-modern/ private/spiritual realms, purifying, endorsing, and embodying both, they create a doubled modern-postmodern Islamism.

Communitarian Islamists are more ambiguous about separating social and evaluative realms, especially demanding universalization of religious ethical and aesthetic values. But while they thus seek control of educational and cultural portfolios, communitarian Islamists acknowledge their views are not objective or scientific but partial or moral. Because their inculcation of religious values throughout society abolishes the public-private divide, however, communitarians have had to submit their plans and views to scrutiny, forcing a rationalization and intellectualization of their ideas that personal Islamists elude. The heightened deliberative ethos of communitarian Islamism applies reason to social progress, as do many ethically driven political movements that recognize the fact-value dilemma in moral philosophy. Communitarian Islamists internalize modernity into their strategy to externalize their convictions to the whole society. Paradoxically, then, the anti-modern cultural homogenization project heightens the public use of reason and often institutionalizes rational criteria of ethical justification for private and public life. Communitarian Islam is, then, a confection of intensified religiosity and rationalization that establishes a hybrid modern Islamism.

Militant Islamism represents an oddly more complicated mixture of modern and non-modern tendencies, despite its violent means, discourse of re-authentication, and totalitarian aestheticization. Militants wholly dissolve distinct social spheres, consistent with a moral unification across family, society, and state that demonizes outsiders and often subjugates women and minorities atrociously. Such patently fascist ideas are not, however, wholly anti-modern. Militant Islamist ideology does externalize from the community all moral, intellectual, and cultural uncertainty (Huyssen 1986, 180). But this effort foists a discursive "pastiche" mixing traditional meanings, references, and symbols with modernizing initiatives and avowals on inevitably suspicious populations. Hardly postmodern only to the outside analyst of such unprecedented social "texts," the radical statist rationalization (of bureaucracy, military, and police), cultural centralization, and religious secularization, all in the name of religious authenticity, form a deeply unstable doctrine (Herzfeld 1993, 65). Militant Islamism is anti-modernism appended to modernist schemes justified in a postmodern ideological collage.

To summarize briefly, discrete experiences shape distinct Islamist ideas, desires, criticisms, tactics, and their modern or non-modern commitments. Where political, economic, or cultural loss gradually impedes the satisfaction of desires without visible coercion or injustice, Muslims will adopt a devout, private, and apolitical Islamism compatible, even intertwined, with modern rationalization. If conditions abruptly and visibly hinder the realization of desires but permit effective, subjective modification or expectation to satisfy those desires, Muslims will collectively, publicly, peacefully, and systemically strive for a compromised Islamic modern public sphere. Where political coercion precludes both the satisfaction of given desires and the efficacious modification of those desires, Muslims will inventively radicalize and modernize their ideology to endorse anti-systemic violence and anti-rationalist chauvinism. Distinct Islamist approaches to globalization, the state, the "West," modernity, and Islam are conditioned by globalization's universal and divisive effects, but they are determined by how those effects are locally mediated to defend the desires and subjectivity of peripheral communities.

4

Islam in the West

Modernity and Globalization Revisited

JOCELYNE CESARI

Cultural globalization, one consequence of growth in world communication, is often depicted as a process of cultural homogenization. The best-known metaphor for such a depiction is the McDonaldization of the world. McDonald culture or—to use Benjamin Barber's term, McWorld culture—refers to the distribution of Western products, values, and lifestyles throughout the globe. Homogenization, however, is too simple as an interpretation. The global diffusion of Western goods and ideas does not necessarily lead to the emergence of one generalized Western culture. Along with homogenizing pressures comes a movement toward indigenization. That movement is reflected in an increasing diversification and syncretism of cultures and an aspiration on the part of non-dominant groups for authenticity. Despite the clean and coherent images that the West projects, the non-Western world increasingly questions McDonald culture. In this sense, globalization is actually linked to postmodernity—assuming we define that term as a reflexive stage of modernity, rather than as a successor to modernity that stands in opposition to it (Giddens 1991; Heller 1999). Thus, in the global era, postmodernity involves more than the cultural differentiation and social autonomization that are the definitive attributes of modernity. It also involves the defeat of the modernist ideologies of social progress, that is, the meta-narratives of socialism, democracy, and science.

It is no longer possible to conceive of a single world culture that defines for the planet a standard image of good society. Conflicting images abound. Non-Westerners, whether within Western or non-Western contexts, quest for authenticity in their pursuit of solutions to economic, political, or cultural problems. The Islamic revolution in Iran illustrated one such quest. Its initial success has encouraged groups throughout the Muslim world to frame their lives, rights, and needs in Islamic terms, making *asala,* the Arabic word for authenticity, the central theme of Islamist movements. Despite the potential for conflict in sphere values (to borrow Max Weber's terminology), one would be mistaken to reduce indigenization simply to an opposition to modernity. Even Muslims are trying to achieve modernization with authenticity. Their major question is: Can we be postmodern without being anti-modern? Speaking of the Muslim world, Robert D. Lee poses the following dilemma: "Does a world in search of authenticity create intolerant nationalisms, oppressive majorities or even a clash of civilizations as Samuel Huntington has argued? Or does it portend a coming together on new foundations as the context of authenticity itself expands towards universality? Which versions of authentic thought can be most plausibly reconciled with liberal democracy, with international tranquillity?" (1997, 3).

Some resolve the dilemma along the lines of Huntington's clash of civilizations. They regard Islam as the West's primary enemy and posit irreconcilable differences between Muslim and Western cultures that cause major international conflicts.[1] Others incline toward a postmodernist resolution. They explain the Islamic quest for authenticity as a definitive sign that Western enlightenment has been defeated. They agree with Bryan S. Turner, who understands an anti-consumerist ethic of moral purity based upon classical Islamic doctrine (1994, 92) as a reaction against the consumerist pressures of postmodernism and asserts that Muslims generally insulate themselves from crises of authority and identity through a strict fundamentalism that informs all issues, ranging from international politics to the minutiae of everyday life.

Along with Fred Halliday (1994), I reject as overly simplistic both proposed resolutions to Lee's dilemma—religion as either a cause of international conflict or a counter-postmodern force. The current study will focus upon the similarity, rather than the differences, between Islam and other religious systems as they are affected by globalization. It will employ a sociological analysis based upon world-system in place of the more common society-centered approach (Turner 1994). Sociological analysis of Islam at the global level in a comparison with other religious systems will overcome the Orientalist's sharp and artificial contrast between Orient and Occident. It will demonstrate that world religions can actually accelerate the process of globalization by promoting shifts from communal to

---

1. Huntington's vision, despite his background as a political scientist, seems subject to the "Orientalist effect," which spreads an essentialist and fixed vision of Muslim societies as religiously defined and intrinsically opposed to Western culture (Lee 1997, 12).

associative structures across nations. Religions will be shown not only to reinforce and recreate communal ties in response to globalization, but also to offer resources for new forms of individualization and modernization. The ideoscapes described by Arjun Appadurai will be seen to require more than members of a homogenized Western culture can provide.[2] Indigenous religious repertoires that rest upon shared ideas of justice, morality, dignity, and authenticity will be demonstrated to play as crucial a part in ideoscapes as do ideas, terms, and images, such as welfare, human rights, sovereignty, and democracy. In summary, to illustrate how religion in the postmodern era can accelerate as well as oppose global modernization, I shall examine the interplay among modernity, globalization, and Islam in the West.

MUSLIMS IN THE WEST

Between nine and twelve million Muslims live in Western Europe. Between four and six million more reside in America (Vertovec and Peach 1997, 3–48). In Europe, their presence is a direct, even if under-recognized, result of migrations that began in the 1950s from former colonies in Asia, Africa, and the Caribbean. In America, the Muslim presence is owing equally to migration from Asian and Middle Eastern countries and increasing conversion to Islam within the African American community.[3]

From the 1950s until 1974, Muslims served as transient workers within Western Europe. Under a cooperative agreement between former colonial powers and former colonies, annual quotas of lone Muslim laborers worked in European nations. Their transient status made both impractical and unnecessary any establishment of institutions around their culture and faith. The oil crisis of 1974 brought an end to Western Europe's "open door" policy for foreign workers. Although new arrivals were prohibited, Muslim laborers already in Europe were allowed to send for their families. This situation led to the establishment of a permanent Muslim population within Western Europe. With their presence has come a dramatically increasing need for mosques, halal butcheries, Qur'an schools, and Muslim cemeteries. Western Europeans, who had previously taken

2. "Ideoscapes are composed of elements of the Enlightenment world-view, which consists of concatenations of ideas, terms and images, including freedom, welfare, rights, sovereignty, representation and the master-term, democracy" (Appadurai 1990, 299).

3. Approximately half of the U.S. Muslim population is African American converts.

little notice of the Muslims in their midst, were surprised by the need to accept Muslims as their permanent and visible neighbors.

Heightened visibility of Islam in the West began in the 1980s, coinciding with the Islamic revolution in Iran and the growth of fundamentalist movements in Egypt, Palestine, Algeria, and Pakistan. Europeans and Americans, whose stereotypical understandings of Islam derived from demonized portrayals of warriors and terrorists, drew the mistaken conclusion that political activists in the Muslim world were inspiring an Islamic emergence within the West. They did not realize that Muslims do not practice their religion in Europe and America exactly as they do in their native lands. Exile and transplantation dramatically alter Islamic thought, practice, and community. As was the case several times before in Islamic history, Muslims in the West are revising and recreating Islamic culture by hybridizing their own heritage with the dominant norms and values of their host societies.

The settlement of Muslim groups in the West has shifted the debate over Islam and modernism from an Arab/Muslim context to a Western one. As early as the arrival of Napoleon Bonaparte in Cairo in 1798, the Muslim world has been engaged in a process of renewal in the face of modernity. During the century that followed, major figures in the *salafiyya* movement tried to prove that Islamic tenets could direct the adaptation of Muslim societies to a modern world.[4] Debate over the compatibility between Islamic values and Western political principles continues into the present with one momentous change: it is now also waged by Muslims residing within Western democratic contexts. For these Western Muslims, the debate no longer stresses issues of Islamic governance. Instead, it centers around issues of pluralism and tolerance.

Analysis of Western Islam must take into account the status of multiculturalism in host countries, as well as the status of Islam in countries of origin. Muslim communities develop unique characters, shaped as much by each Western country's specific approach to cultural diversity as by their own national backgrounds. Different ways of being Muslim emerge. Some Muslims live primarily

4. In 1880, the first reformist political-religious wave, the *salafiyya,* made famous by Jamal al-Din al-Afghani and Muhammad 'Abduh, based its vision on premises that are opposed to those of the Enlightenment, aiming for more rather than less religion. These thinkers attributed the decadence of the Ottoman empire to its political despotism and superstitious religious interpretations. Western superiority, they held, was solely material and technical, while true progress could only be spiritual and ethical. The rationalization of religious beliefs lay at the heart of the debate, as the chief proponents of the *salafiyya* sought to demonstrate the compatibility of Islam with the technologies and political principles of the West.

within the boundaries of their ethnic groups; others, especially among the Western-born, individualize and modernize their religious practice.

ISLAM VERSUS ETHNICITY

The incorporation of Muslims into the West now occurs within global cities such as Paris, London, Berlin, and New York (Sassen 1991), all of which favor both ethnicity and multiculturalism. Within such cities, new labor forces are integrated into existing labor markets along ever more segmented lines of race, gender, religion, and ethnicity. How do Muslims reconcile the demands of traditional Islamic lifestyle with those of their new homelands at urban, national, and international levels within such cities? According to Michael Humphrey, "The reconfiguring of Islam in the West has two axes: the localization of community and identity in the urban environment, and the resistance to the 'cultural imperialism' of the West. The latter is expressed through the conservation strategies of orthodox religious practice and the defense of patriarchal values in the Western family" (1998, 16).

Through their maintenance of family and regional ties, Muslims have traditionally reconstituted within the West their local religious communities of origin. As a natural consequence, immigrants from the same region, sometimes even the same village, established the first generation of Western mosques. This localization of Islamic communities has had two consequences. First, it has preserved cultural practices and protected against assimilation into the surrounding environment. Second, it has sustained a division of the Muslim population along lines of those national cultures within which Islam is embedded. Even within neighborhoods, where a single mosque might have served their needs based on religious practice alone, Muslims have preferred to establish multiple mosques on the basis of ethnicity—whether North African, Turkish, or Pakistani.

Without realizing it, some Muslims—primarily but not exclusively from the first generation of immigrants[5]—defend an ethnic vision of Islam rooted in national cultures of origin. Gender issues illustrate how their religious and cultural values interplay. One notes that Pakistani, Turkish, and North African males prefer wives from their countries of origin, rather than from among second-generation Muslim women in Europe and America. Their preference for "native daughters," who are by reputation more religiously observant, actually reflects a

5. For example, young Turks in Germany, France, or Belgium join Turkish rather than transnational Muslim organizations (Cesari forthcoming).

wish to remain close to native culture as much as a yearning to remain close to Islam. One also hears criticisms of Islam concerning violence and discrimination against women in the form of excision, mistreatment, and arranged marriages. Precisely speaking, such practices reflect patriarchal values rooted in a culture that predates Islam.[6]

On the political level, the braiding of national, ethnic, and religious identities means competition between ethnic groups. In those European countries where negotiation of religious interests necessitates dialogue between central political institutions and religious communities, difficulties in demarcating Muslim groups beyond their ethnic lines undermine their effective representation. Fragmentation spurs competition among various umbrella associations, each of which seeks to impose its ethnic influence upon the Muslim community at large. Even though problems of political representation do not exist in the United States, American Muslim populations also contain ethnic-based communities that promote segmentation (Cesari 1997; Cesari in press).

INDIVIDUALIZATION AND SECULARIZATION
OF ISLAM

The emergence of a "new Muslim" minority, whose membership is rapidly growing, has been an unexpected consequence of Muslim settlement in the West. Its novelty resides in its separation of religion from ethnicity. New Muslims have anchored their identity primarily within the transnational concept of *umma* (the timeless community of believers) rather than in national culture. Their solidarity with their "brothers" abroad was demonstrated by their protests against *The Satanic Verses,* their opposition to the Gulf War, and their support for peacekeeping efforts in Bosnia and Kosovo.

New Muslims exercise new levels of individual choice in the course of religious observance. Their encounter with democracy has fundamentally altered their relationship as individuals to Islamic tradition. They experience religion first and foremost as a matter of spirituality and personal ethics. In the Muslim world,

6. Although Islamic prescriptions can usually be reconciled with patriarchal values, they can also sometimes contradict them. One of the best examples of the contradiction between Islam and patriarchal values can be found in the Kabylia region of Algeria, where women are not entitled to inherit land. This restriction stands in contradiction to Islamic law, which gives women one part inheritance for every two parts received by men. To solve the problem, Kabyle tribes decided simply to ignore the requirements of Islamic law in this matter.

where Islam is a part of the dominant social norms as well as the religion of both state and majority, the group—not the individual—serves as the vehicle for Islamic identification. New Muslims have not only adjusted to postmodernity, urbanity, and globalization, they have also adapted to a "culture of separateness," one that presupposes autonomy and independence even in the religious realm (Gretty 2000). Consequently, identities that are integrated in Muslim countries are automatically deconstructed into religious, social, and ethnic components in the West.

Generally speaking, gains in autonomy are weakening Muslim ethnic and family ties within the West. In Islamic countries, children are taught to be deferential toward their parents, especially their usually authoritarian fathers. Muslim children in the West are acculturated within a relatively permissive society that explicitly represents authoritarian parenting practices as outdated, if not damaging, and implicitly denigrates Muslim fathers on the basis of socioeconomic status, educational background, and ethnicity. A "clash of civilizations" results within families, where a generation gap separates fathers from children, one that is considerably wider among Muslims than among first-generation non-Muslim immigrants. In extreme cases, children, generally males of adolescent age, develop adjustment difficulties when their efforts to reconcile incompatible values fail. Ironically enough, it is often the new Muslim who heals strains within his immigrant family by according respect to his parents as a freely exercised religious choice.

Abandonment of ancestral languages, such as Arabic, Turkish, and Urdu, as well as cultural habits also weakens ethnic identification. Loss of cultural practice and ancestral language, however, has not signaled the end of religious observance. Rather, it has led to the growth of "vernacular" forms of Islam in Europe and America, where sermons, religious literature, and public discussions are increasingly in English, which has now become the second language of Muslims all over the *umma*.

When they do not identify with an ethnic Islam, new Muslims within the West generally base their religious identities upon one of two foundations: either a secularized bond with Islam that relativizes its demands or a fundamentalist attitude that demands respect for Islamic tradition in its totality, minutiae included. Secularized Muslims resemble the "pickers and choosers" of other religions in the West. Like "consumers," they tailor their religious practice and tradition to their own subjective specifications. The devout among new Muslims define Islam as a faith-based, ethical system in which commitment of inner self takes precedence over rigid and public observances. Even their fundamentalist practice is the outcome of individual choice, as in the decision of women to wear the *hijab,* taken independently of male pressure, as an expression of spiritual self. Emphasis of meaning over display accords new Muslims a universalistic perspective that enables their dialogue with non-Muslims. Such dialogue highlights shared values that legitimize Islam in Western eyes.

New Muslims among the disadvantaged and marginalized are embracing Islam as a means to salvation. For these otherwise alienated groups within the global city, Islam facilitates integration into mainstream society. Islam has been mistakenly viewed as an obstacle to economic advancement, not only in Europe, but also in America, where a substantial Muslim presence is growing within the historically disenfranchised African American community. The reality is that adherence to Islam is protecting the disadvantaged against temptations to self-destructive activity such as crime, delinquency, drugs, and promiscuity. As one young Muslim told me in a low-income suburb of Paris, "We're not delinquents because we are Muslim. We are delinquents because we are not Muslim enough!"

If Islam is defined as a faith-based ethical religion,[7] what happens to its theological framework? The Islamic tradition is only now examining its principles as a minority within a non-Muslim country. A still small number of scholars and religious authorities are trying to renovate conventional interpretations of Islamic law.[8] While Western trends of Islamic thought are converging with recent developments within moderate Islamic movements in the Muslim world, how they will merge remains to be seen.

TRANSNATIONAL ISLAM

Religions have been transnational networks for centuries. New is their intensity and growing international influence as a consequence of migratory flows and advances in communication and technology. Individual actors, missionary organizations, sects, mystic movements, and informal networks—all are participating in transnational activities.[9] More easily than ever before they are conveying ideas,

7. For a longer explanation of this use of Islam, see Cesari 1998.

8. See, for example, the *Journal of the Institute of Muslim Minority Affairs,* published in England. For an attempt at renovation of Islamic theology, see Ramadan 1999.

9. The term "diaspora" is often used to describe these new forms of transnational ethnicity. Three major factors contribute to the definition of diaspora: awareness of ethnic identity, the existence of communal organizations, and the persistence of relations, even imaginary, with the homeland. In fact, diaspora refers to a specific relationship to time (memory) and space (Cesari 2000a; Sheffer 1996; Cesari 1996).

norms, and values throughout national societies and across national boundaries. Even the recent fragmentation of the Muslim world into different nation-states has not broken the power of the *umma*. Nor can Western Islam be viewed any longer as an isolated or marginalized part of the Islamic world.

Recent changes in religious practice are accelerating transnational Islamic developments. Firstly, "small-scale do-it-yourself societies of prayer and believers" (Rudolph 2000), which have always existed as amorphous forms of Islam, are today playing an increasing role at the international level. As Dale Eickelman has noticed, mass education and mass communication are actually yielding self-trained religious micro-intellectuals, who are competing with formally trained imams. The unprecedented access that ordinary people have gained to sources of religious information and knowledge make monopoly by official preachers more difficult, if not impossible.

Secondly, "electronic religiosity" is expanding Islam transnationally through circulation of audiocassettes and videocassettes, the broadcast of independent television satellite shows, and—most significant of all—the burgeoning of websites.[10] In particular, bulletin boards, chat rooms, and discussion forums on the Internet are promoting alternative, even contradictory, understandings of Islam, where only nationally based ones once existed. In so doing, they are exerting a moderating effect on Islamic discourse and breaking the monopoly of traditional religious authorities over the management of the sacred.

Transnational activities do not necessarily match those of national religious organizations. The distinction between national and transnational is not a distinction between high (organized) religion and low (popular, self-invented, spontaneous, local) religion. The term "transnational" refers to specific interactions between network organizations.[11] In the case of Islam, those networks can be

10. See Mandaville 2000. It would be misleading, however, to consider online Islam as an exclusive indicator of a new democratic public space without paying attention to specific social changes within specific Muslim contexts. In other words, to assess accurately what Muslim websites are accomplishing in terms of knowledge, perspective, and affiliation, sociologists must investigate how electronic religiosity is resonating with significant social changes in general.

11. Networks can be defined as a specific type of relation linking a defined set of persons, objects, or events." The set of persons, objects, or events by which a network is defined may be called the actors or modes. These actors or modes possess some attributes that identify them as members of the same equivalence class. Networks analysis stresses relational contents rather than structure and combines the study of group behavior with the analysis of interpersonal ties. It focuses on the achievement of goals through the instrumentalization of norms and values" (Knoke and Kuklinski 2000, 12).

distinguished according to the content and style of their message. The dominant categories are fundamentalist, traditionalist, and modernist.[12]

Contrary to Western stereotypical depictions, fundamentalists are puritanical revolutionaries who refuse blind and unquestioning adherence to the legal rulings of the theologian-jurists of the medieval Islamic era. They favor, instead, *ijtihad,* that is, intellectual exercise that draws independent conclusions on legal or other issues with the assistance of the Qur'an and the *sunna.* Muhammad Ibn 'Abd al-Wahhab, the founding father of Wahhabism; Sayyid Abu al-A'la Mawdudi, founder of the Jamaat-i-Islam in Pakistan; and Ayatollah Khomeini are the best-known figures of this fundamentalist movement. Traditionalists emphasize Islamic scholarship, teaching, and preaching. They follow the rules of the schools of the theologian-jurists of the medieval age. While they oppose Western modernization, they are generally apolitical pacifists. Jama'at al-Tabligh, whose organization is spreading throughout the Muslim world, is one such traditionalist movement. Muslim modernists represent the liberal and progressive current within Islamic revival. Although devout and practicing, they endorse Westernization and modernization without secularization. Through Islamic reform, they search for solutions to social and political problems. Hasan al-Banna, the founder of the Muslim Brothers in Egypt; Jamal al-Din al-Afghani; Muhammad 'Abduh, Muhammad Iqbal; and 'Ali Shariati, the intellectual father of modern revolutionary Shi'ism, are all figures within the modernist movement. Their attempts to reform religious tradition and societies can be compared to the efforts of the Christian theologians of liberation (Cesari 2000b).

Muslim communities in the West participate in the transnational networks described above, some of which are controlled by more active Muslim countries (for example, Saudi Arabia, Algeria, Morocco, and Pakistan) trying to extend their influence over Muslims beyond their borders. Still other networks are the

---

12. According to Husain (1995, 126), there is also a fourth category: the pragmatists. They are often only nominally Muslims who have been heavily influenced by secular education. The ruling elites of most Muslim countries are such. They adopt concepts and methods from the Western world without specific adaptations to their indigenous environment. They have an instrumental relationship with Islam that they can use as a means of propaganda or legitimization of domestic or international politics. The use of Islam by Saddam Hussein during the Gulf War is a good example of a pragmatic manipulation of Islamic symbols for opportunistic purpose. Within Muslim and Western countries, pragmatists are not limited to the ruling elite. Because they do not inspire social movements, or real renovation of Islamic thought, I do not include them in the typology of transnational activities. I also deliberately omit the Sufi transnational networks from this typology that concerns the globalization of the Islamic message.

products of transnational organizations, be they traditionalist, fundamentalist, modernist, or Sufi. Although transnational networks reflect diverse ideologies, a normative interpretation of Islam inspired by the *salafiyya* movement in either fundamentalist or modernist form is predominant throughout the world, especially within America and Western Europe.

Given the multiplicity of transnational activities, one must ask: Are religions, particularly Islam, promoting conflict or cooperation in the public arena? (Rudolph and Piscatori 1997). To answer this question, we must revisit the sociological debate on privatization and secularization (Bellah 1970). These terms refer to the interplay between individual choice and the restriction of religion to private life in Western culture and politics. They celebrate the contraction of the religious domain within the social as the hallmark of societies that have attained a high level of institutional differentiation. In these societies, the nature of religious experience is always optional and private and thereby extraneous to the formation of group identities. In our globalized, postmodern era, with religion no longer confined to the private realm, religious responses to social, economic, and political dilemmas become possible if they are conceptualized in Weberian terms as this-worldly, as opposed to other-worldly, expressions of religion. Even in the West, religious leaders are making forays into the public arena of politics. How they use religious references remains their prerogative—whether in liberal ways to solve problems that emerge as side effects of globalization, for example those relating to environment and bioethics, or in particularistic ways to oppose globalizing influences.

To understand how transnationalism has altered religion's political functions, analysts must go beyond simple contrasts between fundamentalism and conservatism. They must appreciate that the context in which transnational Islam operates determines its effects. In the West, for example, contrary to common belief, Muslim practices are both accelerating the integration and modernization of immigrant populations and challenging the pluralistic organization of societies, while in the Muslim world they are precipitating questions as to the legitimacy of authoritarian regimes.

TOWARD RECONCILIATION BETWEEN ISLAM AND THE WEST

Transnational Islam accentuates tensions between globalization and state authoritarianism in the Muslim world. Transnational networks demonstrate weaknesses in state control and fuel growing suspicions toward national institutions. They promote multiple loyalties and affiliations, as well as the means for political protest. Whether transnational Islam's various forms are forerunners to a more liberal civil society or to a repressive theocracy remains an open question. Under authoritarian regimes one now observes the creation of parallel institutions that resist repression. Such institutions function as alternative domains within which new values and styles of political participation are being forged, comparable with the parallel polity and society that characterized eastern Europe under Communist domination.

The presence of Muslims within the West, which extends the locus of their belonging beyond their traditional geographic constraints, complicates those narratives through which regimes have forged loyalties to state and nation. In abstract terms, Michael Humphrey explains: "The Western frontiers actually represented an opening which might engender skepticism about the authority of tradition; the possibility of challenging the World through the engagement of traditions in new spaces constructed by relations outside their control" (1998, 18). It is, therefore, not surprising to find that the modernist movement's emblematic figures nowadays live in Europe and America, where they are reconciling Islam and the West. Their presence alone constitutes a challenge to dominant historical narratives that claim Muslim oppression by Western imperialism.

In addition, as interpretations of Islam multiply, debate intensifies over the use of Islamic symbols:

> Increasingly, discussions in newspapers, on the Internet, on pirated cassettes, and on television cross-cut and overlap, contributing to a common public space. New and accessible modes of communication have made these contests increasingly global, so that even local issues take on transnational dimensions. The combination of new media and new contributors to religious and political debates fosters an awareness . . . of the diverse ways in which Islam and Islamic values can be created. It feeds into new senses of a public space that is discursive, performative, and participative, and not confined to formal institutions recognized by state authorities. (Eickelman 1999)

However appealing, one must resist romanticized visions of transnational religious networks as a precondition for democratization. Authoritarian regimes can commandeer or manipulate transnational groups, as the secular leader Saddam Hussein did when he invoked Islam in his media broadcasts during the Gulf War.

In a challenge to pluralistic democracy, transnational Islam also raises questions about religious freedom and tolerance, as well as about limits to public expressions of faith. Pluralism in Western secularized society no longer refers to the integration of socially subordinated groups or the representation of social diversity, but rather to the balance between cultural diversity and cohesion within the national community (Cesari in press). Thus democracies face these questions: Is a common agreement on cultural, political, and religious values possible?[13] Can we move beyond shallow civility toward true acceptance of other?

To recapitulate: In the global era, Western Muslims are reinventing debates on Islam, democracy, and modernization and translating Islam into more universalistic terms. Individualization is changing the meaning of Islamic observance and altering the relationship between individual and religious tradition. Western Islamic communities have become participants within transnational networks and Western Muslims are legitimate members of the *umma*. What challenges Islam in the West will pose to authoritarian regimes within the Muslim world remain to be seen.

13. This dilemma is illustrated by the opposition between liberals and communitarians in the United States.

5

Islam, Knowledge, and "the West"

The Making of a Global Islam

LEIF STENBERG

In a seminar held at the School of Islamic and Social Studies (SISS) in Leesburg, Virginia, in April 1998, I stated that religion cannot be perceived as an objective truth. From a scholarly point of view, the "objectification" causes a number of problems. This statement prompted a critical remark from a young Muslim participant. In his opinion I was making a truth claim, and the basis of my claim was that truth is horizontal and anthropocentric. He said that I was not taking into consideration the form of truth that is vertical, spiritual, and metaphysical. The latter referred to a higher, everlasting truth, given to humans in the form of a revelation—a truth that is spelled with a capital *T.* Contemplating his statement, I consider it correct to say that I may have presented and represented a truth claim. But it is, in a Weberian sense, a changeable and limited one, and it is, therefore, in opposition to his idea of *the* final truth. Furthermore, I consider his position as more or less fruitless considering the difficulty of subjecting a metaphysical truth to the trials of inductive reasoning and methodological falsification. Hence, at the seminar, I remarked that for me, trained at a secular university, the idea of a metaphysical Truth has no place in my theoretical and methodological framework. Despite this view, I find it appealing to examine and analyze ideas concerning the function of such a metaphysical truth.[1] After my response, the young Muslim repeated his statement and our discussion ended without agreement. However, our encounter triggered off an effort to sort out some of the ideas that

---

1. Theoretically I try to avoid making normative statements about the nature of Islam. My aim is to study and analyze what is stated about an Islamization of knowledge, that is, to study the dispute among Muslims about the nature of Islam. Like, for example, Robert Brenner (2001), I find this a tenable position in the study of ongoing discussion on Islam among contemporary Muslims.

I have been pursuing for the last few years, concerning how a certain group of contemporary Western European and North American Muslims conceptualize knowledge in general and how they understand the transmission of knowledge and authority in particular.

The term "knowledge" will not be precisely defined here. On the one hand it can refer to a specific body of knowledge, such as the Qur'an and *hadith*. On the other hand it can indicate what Michel Foucault has termed an *episteme*. That is, "the total set of relations that unite, at a given period, the discursive practices that give rise to epistemological figures, sciences, and possibly formalized systems" (Foucault 1972, 191). The former is a common conceptualization of the term "knowledge" in discussions among Muslims. The latter can be seen as an analytical statement about the floating use of the term "knowledge" in these discussions.

Moreover, my interest is in the relationship between the production of ideas and social contexts. These interests and topics—and my own outlook—seem to create a framework that considers the comprehension and conceptualization of knowledge and epistemological principles as key questions in attempts to forge a contemporary Islam among specific groups of Muslims in Western Europe and North America. In other words, they are key elements in a current production of Islam. Hence, in the present discussions of Islam among Muslims the term "knowledge" plays a significant role, and it is intimately related to notions of authority. Both are connected to the crucial question of who has the legitimate right to interpret—and to speak in the name of—Islam.

THE INTERNATIONAL INSTITUTE OF ISLAMIC THOUGHT AND ITS CONTEXT

It is often forgotten that the increased migration of Muslims to Western Europe and North America, especially since the late 1960s, had an impact on the intellectual debate among Muslims. In addition, a number of institutes and organizations were created starting in the 1970s that focused on questions concerning Islam and knowledge.[2] Today there are many competing projects established in the so-called West, with the aim to develop and/or reform Muslim thought in general. One project is entitled "The Islamization of Knowledge." There are a variety of ideas on the origin and meaning of the epithet "the Islamization of

2. It is to be noted in this context that ideas on a specifically Islamic economics have been expressed since the 1930s (Syed Farid Alatas 1995).

Knowledge."[3] This divergence in opinion is accompanied by a widespread disparity regarding the overall purpose of the project. One of its best-known exponents is the International Institute of Islamic Thought (IIIT) (Stenberg 1996 and 2000).

The IIIT was established in the United States in 1981 (<http://www.iiit.org>). The objectives of the IIIT and the general plan of the project were set forth by the well-known scholars Ismail Raji al-Faruqi and AbdulHamid AbuSulayman in a book entitled *Islamization of Knowledge: General Principles and Work Plan* (1989). The activities of the institute include the arranging of conferences, workshops, and seminars as well as the publishing of a number of monographs, pamphlets, and a journal—the *American Journal of Islamic Social Sciences* (AJISS). Today the network of the institute is global, and the IIIT has liaisons in many Muslim countries, Western Europe, the Middle East, and Asia.

The most important liaison office was the branch in Malaysia, and the institute's affiliation to Malaysia has traditionally been strong. One reason for the strong relationship with Malaysia is that much of the institute's financial support came from that country. However, political developments in the country and the arrest in 1998 of Deputy Prime Minister Anwar Ibrahim resulted in the loss of financial support to the IIIT and to its offspring, SISS.[4] The arrest of Anwar Ibrahim also led to the closing of the organization's liaison office in Kuala Lumpur and of its home page.

The IIIT also developed contacts with other Muslim organizations, and they cooperate with organizations in the United States and in Europe, such as the Islamic Foundation in England. So far, the formally institutionalized cooperation seems primarily to concern the distribution of books, pamphlets, and so forth. In addition, many of the institute's projects are today carried out in Egypt at Cairo University and al-Azhar. In a forthcoming book an Egyptian sociologist discusses the position of the IIIT office in Cairo (Abaza 2002). Apparently the office has offered a forum where various groups and individuals have come together to discuss the role of Islam in Egyptian society. It has become a new

3. The Malaysian intellectual Sayyid Muhammad Naguib al-Attas claims that he was the first to introduce the concept "Islamization of Knowledge." Today al-Attas is the head of the International Institute of Islamic Thought and Civilization (ISTAC), founded in Malaysia in 1987 (Alatas 1995, 95 f.).

4. It is to be noted that the head of SISS, Taha Jabir al-Alwani, issued a *fatwa* concerning the Anwar Ibrahim verdict. Al-Alwani stated that the verdict was contrary to the Shari'a and its principles of justice and was therefore not valid. According to al-Alwani, Anwar Ibrahim was innocent and should have been released immediately. See MSANEWS 2000.

public arena for communication of different and competing ideas concerning the interpretation of Islam and the Egyptian society in general. This arena has, of course, attracted the attention of the Egyptian security apparatus, and the office has been closed at various times. The IIIT has also been involved in the planning and development of Islamic universities and higher education in general in Muslim countries, for example in Algeria, Jordan, Malaysia, and Pakistan.

THE IDEAS OF TAHA JABIR AL-ALWANI, HEAD OF IIIT AND SISS

The example of the former president of the IIIT, Taha Jabir al-Alwani, can be used to highlight how the term "knowledge" is conceptualized within the IIIT. Al-Alwani is of Iraqi origin, and he received master's and doctoral degrees at al-Azhar in Cairo, the heart of Sunni theology. He came to the United States in 1984 and was the president of the IIIT from 1987 until 1996. Al-Alwani's academic specialization is in the field of *fiqh,* Islamic legal theory. He is a member of the Fiqh Academy of the Organization of the Islamic Conference (OIC) and holds a number of other positions: he is, for example, the chairman of the Fiqh Council of North America and a founding member of the Muslim World League in Mecca.

In 1996 he became the first director of the SISS—a newly established "school" for education and research in Leesburg, Virginia (<http://www.siss.edu>). To some extent the SISS appears to embody an ideological prolongation of the notions underlying the foundation of the IIIT. Basically, the IIIT can be seen as a Muslim "think tank" and SISS as an educational institution in which a variety of courses are offered to Muslims as well as non-Muslims. Although most students are Muslims, it is important to note that they represent a variety of ethnic groups and interpretations of Islam.

One of the most significant aims of SISS is to offer an education that is, according to al-Alwani, based on the amalgamation of what he describes as an "Islamic" and "Western" tradition of education and understanding of knowledge. The fundamental premise of SISS is that there is a "unity of human knowledge" and that this knowledge is rooted in "transcendent values drawing on the principle of unicity (the *tawhidi episteme*)."[5] The idea of combining the Arabic *tawhid* with the Greek *episteme* underlines the notion that Islam can be singled out as one comprehensive system of unity. To characterize the "unicity" as an *episteme* refers

5. Ideas on the *tawhidi episteme* are developed by Muna Abul-Fadl (1991).

to the original Greek meaning of the word, "knowing" or "knowledge." Especially in Platonic philosophy, *episteme* was a term designating a form of knowledge grounded on reason, something that was completely certain, a term in opposition to *doxa,* "assumption" or "belief." This comprehension is combined with an "understanding of the unity and purposefulness of life in a world attuned to the humanistic and civilizing vocation of the individual person on earth (*al-Khilafa*)"(SISS 1997–98, 1). These essential conditions of SISS materialize in an ambition to reconstruct the "current legacy of human knowledge." The idea is that a classical study of Islam joined with contemporary social science can provide the means to build a vision of a new academy.

These statements reveal that the vision of SISS is founded on a teleological understanding of knowledge. However, the more ideological ambitions of SISS are combined with practical desires. The institution wishes to establish itself in mainstream American academic life. One step in this direction is the offering of a master's degree in Islamic studies, including, for example, a core course entitled "Seminar in the Methodology of Comparative Religion and Civilization" and an elective course on "Comparative Religion" (SISS 1997–98, 25 f.). A general observation is that besides the variety of courses on Islam offered at SISS, the tendency among the courses offered in social sciences is toward political science. More interestingly, perhaps, is the school's development of a Master of Imamate degree, designed to meet the needs of the contemporary American Muslim community such as, for example, educating Muslim chaplains for the U.S. Army. The candidates for admission to the Master of Imamate program are required to be fluent in English, whereas "they may be admitted without a knowledge of Arabic" (SISS 1997–98, 45). However, the candidates are obliged to develop proficiency in classical Arabic. My point here is not that all this program is completely novel, but rather that it is carried out in a new fashion, different from the study of religions in Muslim countries. The Dutch scholar Jacques Waardenburg (1999) has pointed out that the study of religions as an academic discipline is almost nonexistent in Muslim countries.

Earlier articles by al-Alwani have been translations from Arabic, but during recent years he has been writing in English. One of the first articles he published in the IIIT's journal, entitled "Taqlid and Ijtihad," can be seen as a form of ideological manifesto.[6] It is in conformity with a style that is typical of most of those connected with the IIIT. He underlines the importance of using *ijtihad* in order to solve what he describes as the current crisis of the *umma*. The *umma* is, he says, in

6. Other articles by al-Alwani (1993 and 1996) touch upon the same themes.

a deplorable state, and it can no longer "present itself as having a unique culture, system of values, personality [sic!] or anything else which makes a civilization distinct from all others, for large scale borrowing from the West has undermined and distorted all of its inimitable features" (al-Alwani 1991, 130). This statement brings to mind the repeatedly expressed notion in the discourse on Islam and knowledge that the replacement of revelation by reason led to a negation of all metaphysical values. In general, participants in the discourse view nature as subordinate to Islam. One consequence of this assumption, related to educational objectives, is that academic disciplines studying nature will also be subordinate to Islam.

The indispensable tool for solving the crisis of the *umma* is, according to al-Alwani, the exercise of *ijtihad*. In his understanding, history reveals that the *umma* was brought to the contemporary crisis after *ijtihad* fell into disuse. It was gradually replaced by *taqlid* (al-Alwani 1991, 131). Al-Alwani stresses the notion that the study and correct use of *ijtihad* is one of the pillars of the Islamization of Knowledge project. It comes within the framework of a distinct Islamic methodology. If this Islamic methodology is applied, it will produce an Islamic understanding of sociological phenomena. He says: "What is needed is the erection of an Islamic methodology which can replace its Western counterpart. This is no easy undertaking, for it involves establishing a unique framework of knowledge, defining the sources of knowledge and the rules which govern their use, and initiating a critical review of all facets of both the Western and the Islamic methodologies so that those elements which are suitable can be retained, and those which are not can be either transformed and then accepted, or rejected outright" (Al-Alwani 1991, 131).

The aim of al-Alwani, and many other Muslims expressing views on Islam and knowledge, is to stress the need to establish an alternative social science that recognizes revelation as a source of scientific knowledge.[7] Behind this idea is the notion that revelation, correctly interpreted and materialized in a system of norms combined with social science, can explain relationships between phenomena in society and give solutions to various problems. It brings to mind the ideas of the early sociologists Auguste Comte and Emile Durkheim, especially Durkheim's way of seeing the function of religion in society as the primary cause of social cohesion.[8] This notion of al-Alwani's appears to support a form of social engineering founded on norms and values taken from the Qur'an.

7. See Louay Safi (1996) for a comparison.
8. See Fida Muhammad (1998) for a discussion of the similarities and differences between Ibn Khaldun, Hegel, Marx, and Dürkheim.

One enigma in al-Alwani's thinking is his exact aim when he suggests the creation of a specific Islamic methodology. At first, it appears that he would like to create an indigenous Muslim science, but in other texts it seems that the Islamization of knowledge in general has a global aim. Ideally, *all* science should be Islamized in order to be capable of studying *all* aspects of reality. This is a standpoint shared by many in the discourse, and it is founded on the widely accepted assumption within Muslim theology that Islam is a revelation aimed at all humans. The global striving to Islamize science can be interpreted as part of a larger project—or as a sub-discourse—that concerns the *da'wa* of Islam. The connection between the Islamization of Knowledge project and a more general aim of promoting Islam is particularly obvious in the frequent use of material—books, pamphlets, CD-ROMS, and videos—about, for example, Islam and natural sciences, in contacts with would-be converts.[9]

Another dilemma exposed in the quotation above is that methodologies can be rejected. The motive for a rejection is not clear in the quotation, but I imagine it is founded on the idea that if a certain methodology or technology is understood to run contrary to an interpretation of the Qur'an, the methodology or technology at hand should be rejected. Al-Alwani shares this attitude with a number of participants in the discourse (see Stenberg 1996 for a comparison). Yet, because the interpretation of Islam is not a static phenomenon, it is plausible to suggest that in the future we will see changes in the understanding of Islam. Today's sensitive scientific topics such as genetic engineering, and more general matters like abortion, will after a while be legitimized. According to the same logic, one can also expect things previously accepted to be reinterpreted as being against the "true" spirit of Islam. Moreover, these interpretations can be influential in public discourse, but more or less subordinate political, economic, and social concerns in society. One illustrative example is the rhetoric against contraceptives, colored by Islamic terminology launched during the Iranian revolution in the early 1980s. The new regime also encouraged Iranians to produce new citizens for the Islamic Republic. But today Islamic terminology is employed to motivate Iranians to use condoms or to perform vasectomy—the slogan is "Two is Enough." Companies in Iran also produce their own brands of condoms in order to lower the birth rate.

Ijtihad is captured as a key element in a "reformation" of Islam and as an essential part of the Islamization of Knowledge project. In al-Alwani's perception, *ijtihad* has to be exercised in new ways. He discards both what he describes as a "modernist" and a "traditional" approach to the term. He suggests that one

9. This has been noted by Pervez Hoodbhoy (1991) and Leif Stenberg (1996).

should view the *faqih* as a social scientist and involve him in scientific work. The *faqih* should be regarded as a complement to the existing social scientists. The impossibility of one individual's mastering all knowledge in modern society also leads al-Alwani to suggest the possibility of "group" *ijtihad*. The Indonesian scholar Nursholish Majid has suggested more or less the same idea. This group *ijtihad* requires the establishment of academic organizations or research institutions to support such an undertaking (al-Alwani 1991, 139). Al-Alwani emphasizes that neither those who claim that *ijtihad* is the province of a distinct group of religious experts only nor those who hold that its exercise is permissible for more or less everyone can solve the problems of the Muslim societies alone. Al-Alwani focuses on education as the source for carrying out *ijtihad* and as the source of authority. For example, in his understanding, authority seems not to be inherited.[10] Instead, the individual may be capable of creating his or her personal expertise, and therefore authority is intimately related to the individual's personal learning. Al-Alwani has also taken part in IIIT projects aimed at training scientists in their own religious tradition in order to give them the ability to individually perform *ijtihad*.

ISLAM, KNOWLEDGE, AND THE
INTERPRETATIONS OF HISTORY

In the discourse on the Islamization of knowledge and science, all participants refer frequently to three epochs in history. Their approach to history is selective and their focus is not on a historical continuity. However, on an abstract level they recognize a form of historic ideal such as "Islamic" values and norms that are not seen as tied to a historic moment, but as eternal. At the same time interpretations of history can provide boundaries between various standpoints in the discourse. The same Qur'anic verse, historical event, or historical person can be interpreted in different ways.

The first period is the time of the Prophet Muhammad. His lifetime is presented as an era of perfection, and especially the later part of his life is regarded as the most perfect of times. In the understanding of al-Alwani, the *sunna* of Muhammad plays a pivotal role in his creation of an "Islamic" cultural strategy.

10. In the discourse on the Islamization of knowledge and science, ideas expressed by, for example, Seyyed Hossein Nasr are in opposition to this statement by al-Alwani. Nasr, influenced by Sufism and other esoteric streams of thought, argues that at least religious authority and knowledge are hierarchical.

The *sunna* functions as a complement to the Qur'an and as a second source of interpretation. All in all, Muhammad is portrayed in very general terms in the discourse. The *ahadith* seem to be considered difficult to use as a source for a construction of an "Islamic" model. They are too many, too divergent, and it takes the ability of the religious scholar to bring order into the mass of traditions. It is to be noted that al-Alwani is an exception compared to other participants in the discourse, because he is trained as a religious scholar. Nevertheless, I consider it possible to maintain that the early history of Islam can be seen as a sacred history that contains a role model or a prototype that can create meaning for contemporary Muslims.[11] But the "Muhammadan" society of Medina should not be copied, but interpreted. The norms, values, and conditions of that particular society are to be transferred to the present time.

The second epoch is the "Golden Age of Islam." Most authors adhering to the ideas of the IIIT and the SISS seem to subscribe to the notion that the period from the ninth century up to around the thirteenth century was in terms of developments in knowledge and science a very prosperous period. This period coincides with the time in history when the Muslim empire was stabilized politically, economically, and socially. The notion of a Golden Age is certainly not unique. In the texts of several of the authors and academics following IIIT or SISS views, the Golden Age provides model institutions and model individuals for the present. Their texts suggest, for example, that an attempt be made to organize the IIIT on an idealized image of a medieval *dar al-'ilm* or *bayt al-hikma*. The connection between a contemporary institution and a historic one serves the present enterprise.

In the same manner, a set of individuals is picked out to serve as sources of inspiration. Some examples of such ideal historical personages within the IIIT and SISS sphere are Ibn Khaldun, al-Ghazzali, and Ibn Taymiyya. The emphasis on these three figures by adherents to the IIIT and SISS ideology can be compared with the choices other participants in the discourse make. The British-Pakistani author Ziauddin Sardar, for example, shares many of the ideas of the IIIT, and he also shares their emphasis on Ibn Khaldun and al-Ghazzali. But Sardar also emphasizes al-Biruni as an ideal person to emulate, and he likes to be portrayed as a modern al-Biruni himself. For Sardar, as I understand it, al-Biruni represents not only an omnipotent researcher, but he also stands for non-Islamism. And he is a person with an interest in Sardar's homeland.

11. The term "sacred history" can have multiple meanings. In this context I am trying to relate the term to the idea of a "sacred authority," as that particular term is used by Eickelman and Piscatori 1996, 46–79.

In general, though, the ideological positions that have developed around both IIIT/SISS and Ziauddin Sardar are connected to a group of more contemporary Muslim ideologists. Probably the three most frequently referred to are the Indo-Pakistani founder of the Jamaat-i Islami, Sayyid Abu 'Ala Mawdudi (d. 1979); the Egyptian Islamist Sayyid Qutb (d. 1966); and the American-Pakistani scholar Fazlur Rahman (d. 1988). It is important to note that in the discourse in general, references are commonly made to persons who share each individual's own ideological position. Another prolific participant in the discourse is the Persian-American scholar Seyyed Hossein Nasr. In his search for legitimacy he utilizes a different set of historical prototypes. Because he is strongly attached to various Sufi ideas, he turns primarily to Ibn 'Arabi and the so-called school of Illuminationists and its prime exponent, Shihab al-Din Yahya al-Suhrawardi (d. 1191). With some exceptions, all of the historical figures are presented in very broad terms and are used to support various statements.

The third period stretches from the late nineteenth century to the present—the colonial and postcolonial period. Particular emphasis is given to the present time. One assumption is the conception of the contemporary world as fragmented and/or compartmentalized. The world needs to be put together. In order to survive, human beings have to understand the world as a systematized totality, which is how it is constructed "in reality." This understanding of the true nature of the universe is part and parcel of an Islamic knowledge, given that such knowledge is firmly rooted in an organic world picture because of the inherent superiority of Islam. The statements contained in the discourse concerning this issue circle around ideas associated with the Islamic term *tawhid*. Hence, among adherents to the ideas prevailing at the IIIT and the SISS, a notion of a *tawhidi* or *tawhidic episteme* has been developed, as has been mentioned above. In the shaping of actual statements, the participants in the discourse also often support their arguments by references to various works criticizing science or the social structure in general in Western Europe and North America. In addition to creating concepts like the *tawhidic episteme*, they use terms from the social sciences, such as "holism" or "paradigm," to describe their approach. One example is Ziauddin Sardar's use of the concepts of the German sociologist Ferdinand Tönnies (d. 1936), *Gemeinschaft* (community) and *Gesellschaft* (association).[12]

12. Sardar's idea is to use Tönnies's studies of how societies transform from communal to associational relationships both as a critique of societies in North America and Europe and as evidence that humanity in the end will need the order of "Islam" to be able to create a society that works.

In comparison to the two earlier periods, the importance of the recent period lies not so much in the search for role models and ideals, but rather in demonstrating that Islam is a modern phenomenon and not antithetical to modern technology. Hence, Islam can be used today as a moral and/or societal as well as a scientific order.

In sum, I consider it fairly obvious that within the discourse concerning Islamization of knowledge and science the participants have an ideological relation to history. Their aim is to construct a normative history from which the individual as well as the collective can derive examples to follow. History also functions as a means to find a balance in life in a condition seen as marked by anxiety and lack of balance. One result is the projection of contemporary conditions and problems onto history. For example, in the perspective of participants in the discourse, the conditions of modernity are assimilated and internalized into the framework of Islam. All in all, their historiographic constructions of history vary, but rest on the same presupposition—that history provides a source for the norms and values of Islam. In addition, contemporary history is primarily understood as a period in time that has deviated and taken a fundamentally wrong direction. Therefore, history has the following interwoven purposes: references to history or Qur'anic terminology can support statements; history can provide a norm for behavior; history can provide solutions for contemporary problems. Prominent people and important events in history seem to point at an epistemology that can be resurrected and implemented today. Furthermore, within the discourse, the general critique of science and (post)modern debates are utilized to legitimate the types of interpretations of history presented above.

A CRITIQUE OF "THE WEST"—ESTABLISHING A DICHOTOMY

Among the individual Muslims and various movements in the discourse, a so-called "Western" science is seen as particularistic, fragmented, and without a holistic view. Science is judged as too specialized, which is why humans cannot solve large global problems such as the pollution of our environment. This view is not unique. It exists, for example, among Christian Creationists, Hindu fundamentalists, and adherents of New Age lifestyles. Connected to the notion of science as particularistic is also a critique of modern science as non-ethical. Seyyed Hossein Nasr and Ziauddin Sardar sometimes argue that today's science is superior to norms of ethics and morality in "the West." To give science such a position, they argue, is dangerous to society in general, but it is typical of the endeavor in Western societies toward a world without a God, characterized by materialism and secularism. The latter is interpreted as atheism. "The West" seems to carry an atheistic ideology striving for hegemony in the world. Paradoxically, "the West" is at the same time a civilization close to collapse. Problems with drugs, materialism, and so forth are used as examples of the forthcoming breakdown. In this endeavor to distinguish the good from the bad, a very essentialized form of everyday life in Europe and North America is compared to an ideal Islam. This view of "the West" and the construction of a dichotomy legitimize a subjective knowledge, bound to a specific culture.

Technically speaking the term "West" is conceptualized in the same sense as Qur'anic terms are. Hence, it is conceptualized in a rhetorical fashion serving an ideological purpose. Yet, in my opinion, the stereotype of "the West" encountered in the discourse is over-emphasized and too narrow. For example, South America, Eastern Europe, Japan, and Australia are not mentioned. The world is seen as polarized—"Islam" and "the West." The role ascribed to science is in my view also too strong. As I see it, the aim is to fabricate a dichotomy between the culture—and science—of the so-called Western world and the culture and science of the so-called Islamic world. The use of "the West" is reminiscent of the concept of "the stranger" outlined by Zygmunt Bauman (1990). Bauman's idea rests on earlier propositions developed by Georg Simmel. In Bauman's understanding, the stranger—in contrast to friends and enemies—undermines the order of the world and embodies a form of incongruity. The stranger comes uninvited and settles in an environment. He is not a distant enemy. Instead, he calls for attention in the same way as a friend. He represents something threatening. It is possible for the stranger to leave of his own free will, but he may also be forced to leave (Bauman 1991, 149 f.).

One interesting question here is what will come out of this form of Occidentalism—an Occidentalism that is primarily created in "the West." To compose a general critique of a Western civilization and a dichotomy between "the West" and Islam in which the latter is presented as the rational, natural, and harmonious society can backfire. It can be an apologetical trap in which the apologetics for Islam are strongly influenced by the argument of the other (Hjärpe 1999). Hence, if one leans toward, for example, ideas on modernity, postmodernity, and relativism, one runs the risk of being influenced by the very same ideas. Such an influence may consciously or unconsciously lead to new understandings of Islam. In the end, it is possible that the proponents of the idea that Islam is an all-encompassing order end up in a situation in which to be a Muslim means to follow a certain moral code—an individualized and marginalized form of Islam.

Paradoxically, this development is, of course, not in accordance with the ambition of most participants in the discourse.

It is, in my opinion, reasonable to ask, in accordance with Dale Eickelman and James Piscatori (1996), questions about distance and frontiers of "the West." All the changes in the world the last ten years or so, involving migration, globalization, the Internet, and so on, make notions of a monolithic "West" as well as a monolithic "Muslim World" obsolete. This is a fact that is of concern not only to Muslims engaged in the discourse on Islam and knowledge, but also to non-Muslim scholars studying Islam in general.

In sum, the constructed dichotomy between the so-called West and something abstract and idealized, called Islam, serves to legitimate the conceptualization of a specific Islamic knowledge and science. Notably, the understanding of knowledge as subjective, bound to a certain culture, is used by the participants in the discourse to formulate a universal epistemology. The subjective choice of Islam as the basis for science reveals the path to genuine knowledge and is in harmony with nature and creation. In this sense, what is supposedly an objectified Islamic science is the result of a subjective choice among Muslim scholars. The result is that the discourse on Islam and knowledge ends up in competing projects based on different epistemological understandings of "Islam."

HOW ONE CAN UNDERSTAND THE DISCOURSE

The "objectification" of Islam implies a form of *realism,* in the philosophical sense of the word, primarily in regard to Islamic terminology. Islamic terminology and Islamic terms are Arabic words stemming mainly from the Qur'an (Stenberg 1996, 17 f.). In its essence, Islamic terminology contains a sacred meaning that can be unveiled through a correct interpretation of words such as, for example, *tawhid.* The same type of fundamental notion underlies the comprehension of "Islam" in general among the participants in the discourse. That is, the correct form of "Islam" can be discovered through a careful interpretation of the sources. One condition within the discourse is that there is a need for "Islam" in the contemporary world. The world needs a religion that is in a sense an absolute ideology, embodying every aspect of human life, connecting the worldly life to the transcendental. Such suppositions compel science into the sphere of religion, and, therefore, the legal jurist, the *faqih,* should work together with social scientists. That cooperation would be ideal. It would ensure for the upholders of the religion the control not only of the interpretation of "Islam," but also of the possibility of putting limits to research in scientific disciplines such as physics, chemistry, or medicine. The notions about Islamic terminology and "Islam" also affect the views of history. History is seen as an interpretable source in the search for normative answers to topics discussed in the contemporary discourse. Naturally, different positions in the discourse can interpret the same historical event differently, and there is no fixed understanding of historical persons or events. Another consequence of the notion of "Islam" is that religion contains an epistemology. Essentially, the epistemology is founded on the idea that God created the world and therefore humans as his followers are obliged to study his creation. Such a study can be seen as an act of worship. However, ideas of epistemology or, for example, an Islamic social science always seem to be formed differently in different places. Yet, the IIIT has been fairly successful in spreading its message, and the literature of the institute is available in Muslim bookstores all over the world.

Unlike the notions of Islam existing in the discourse, I take my departure from a standpoint in which Islam is seen as a social product. This is a position that, as was noted at the beginning of this article, usually collides with Muslim positions in the discourse. In my understanding, religion is intimately related to society. To be even more explicit, contemporary Islam is forged by Muslims who live in a particular, historically grounded context that shapes their current understandings. In this comprehension, the relationship between modern society and religion is characterized by a balancing act—a state of tension—between religion captured as a conveyor of universal and timeless values, and pragmatically enforced interpretations carried out in close connection with developments in society. Hence, it is apparent that different interpretations of Islam compete, and a diversity of opinions exists among Muslim intellectuals engaged in a discourse regarding the "true" meaning of Islam. Accordingly, I view Islam as an ongoing discourse, in which different interpretations are engaged in a struggle, rethinking and reshaping the tradition of Islam. Each interpretation claims to represent the authenticity of Islam. Based on similar theoretical considerations, some examples of this process have been portrayed in books by Mehrzad Boroujerdi (1996) and Daniel Brown (1996).[13] From a believer's perspective, one can always argue that

13. Daniel Brown states that in this process Muslims "are engaged in an ongoing process of *rethinking* the traditions in which they participate. Some, of course, deny any connection with the tradition, and others deny that their activity can be called 'rethinking,' preferring to see it as the revival or preservation of some ideal and unchanging model. Nonetheless, even the most radical opponents of tradition are not departing from the tradition, but molding it, and seeking to lay claim to the authenticity it bestows. Likewise, even the most conservative defenders of tradition cannot help but reshape the very tradition that they seek to preserve unchanged" (1996, 3 f.). See also Boroujerdi 1996, 1–19 and Stenberg 1996 for the same type of statement.

the ongoing struggle and reinterpretation of Islam are an expression of the complexity of monotheism, having to do with unity and a plurality that always exist in a religion. But a believer can also deny, as Daniel Brown describes it, either "the connection with the tradition" or "that their activity can be called rethinking."

A presupposition for viewing Islam as an ongoing discourse concerned with authority is the idea that contemporary Muslim intellectuals, pseudo-intellectuals, and scholars, irrespective of their position in society and their standards as intellectuals and/or scholars, are often part of contending positions, each striving for dominance and authority. In my theoretical framework their interpretations of the Qur'an and *sunna,* their work as Muslim intellectuals, are reflections of debates, discussions, and developments in the society at large. These statements on the position of Muslim intellectuals and scholars do not have the intention of reducing the relationship between religion and the social cohesion. My aim is to stress that the appearance of modernity, and especially late modernity or postmodernity, has modified both the role of religious scholars in society and the actions taken by them to cope with changing realities. Friday sermons all over the world can relate to what happened yesterday in Palestine or Chechnya. The interpretation of events can also be made with references to the work of disparate persons such as the French converts Roger Garaudy and Maurice Bucaille on one hand and, on the other, academic scholars such as Karl Popper, Max Weber, Louis Althusser, and Michel Foucault. The possibilities of choosing legitimate sources and developing personal interpretations of Islam undermine the authority of formally educated religious scholars.

SOME FINAL REMARKS AND QUESTIONS
TO ANSWER

The paucity of references to the Shari'a and the focus on personal morality and ethics provide an interesting phenomenon within the discourse on Islam and knowledge. The fact that most of the participants are religious experts lacking formal religious education and that they are anti-authoritarian can explain this phenomenon in part. Their effort to open up the exercise of *ijtihad* to individuals without formal religious education to perform is important, but not without restrictions. The point is that people without formal religious education can exercise *ijtihad.* But they have to have other credentials such as education, position in society, connections, and so forth. The focus of the reinterpretation is the Islamic terminology—how to understand key words and texts in relation to contemporary society. Hence, the discourse can be characterized as a struggle concerning the meaning of Islamic terms. All participants strive to appropriate the meaning of certain terms. They generally go directly to the Qur'anic revelation in search of solutions to perceived problems, and not to the traditions of Muhammad or to interpretations made by *'ulama'*, the formally educated religious scholars. Often the latter are collectively seen as unable to deal with today's problems, and they are not recognized as legitimate authorities. Within the discourse, the *'ulama'* are generally stereotyped, portrayed as a negative and closed force in Muslim societies. A common problem for all participants in the discourse is the absence of a single principal religious authority that can make accepted judgments for Muslims in general on matters concerning Islam and knowledge.

Will we see a response from formally trained religious scholars? The fear of losing the initiative in the formulation of Islam has forced religious scholars to take part in the discussions of Islam and science. And besides al-Alwani, such disparate scholars as the Egyptian Qatari-based Yusuf al-Qaradawi and the Syrian Grand Mufti Ahmad Kaftaru have indeed stated that the religious scholars have an important role to play in the development of their societies, in cooperation with other specialists. Otherwise, they say, Muslim societies and Islam run the risk of being hijacked by extremists. In relation to modern science it appears that religious scholars have restricted their attention to limited domains, mainly certain natural phenomena and subjects such as astronomy. Even so, today there is a rapidly increasing number of opinions of traditionally educated religious scholars on the Internet. They are now meeting the challenge of lay interpretations of Islam to show that they are the ones qualified to understand the meaning of Islam. However, these discussions have not helped the modern Muslim natural scientist to bridge the gap between his or her roles at work and at home. In relation to power over interpretation, one can ask whether it is possible that secularization, globalization, the end of "grand narratives," and the death of world-views will produce a situation where power struggles—processes of conceptualization—become more visible. Will one interpretation come out on top or will various trends be prolonged and make it difficult for those of us who study contemporary Islam to use the word "Islam" without a mass of reservations?

If we deal with the various movements trying to Islamize knowledge and science as social movements and to Islamize their interpretations of Islam as a way to motivate and justify acts, is it then possible that the movements will turn to other sources to justify acts in the future? Socially constructed groups can transform or be dissolved, and in this process they change motive and find support in other sources. In the search for legitimacy, they choose other sets of ideas in order to express a collective or individual critique. This does not have to be a radical change. Rather, it can be a slow process where various ideas amalgamate, typical of how the understanding of Islam is formed among Muslim movements in Europe and North America. More explicitly, is it possible that if an Islamization of knowledge does not solve their problems, they will turn to other histories (grand narratives) for historiographic constructions? And/or will they turn to ideologies such as liberalism or bring Marxism or Arabism back to life? At the least, it is worth noting that the turn toward Islam is a subjective choice today.

One can view the idea of an Islamization of knowledge as a nostalgic appeal to the past, the aim of which is basically to formulate a critique of modern society. Sardar can be seen as attempting to bring new ideas of authority and knowledge into Islam, and Nasr as holding older values in trust. However, both of them share the view that science has a meaning, a form of teleological perspective on science. Moreover, they are both elitist, especially Nasr. On matters concerning authority and knowledge in the Muslim tradition, he often states that knowledge is given. A person cannot fully gain knowledge of a subject himself; he has to be enlightened—a view in which knowledge comes from above. Hierarchical and elitist views open the possibility of a discussion of an Islamic knowledge and/or science in modern society. Can Nasr's view on how knowledge is distributed in society fit with ideas of a democratic society?

The existence of pluralism, self-criticism, critical evaluation of science, and discussions of scientific method by writers such as Paul Feyerabend, Karl Popper, Michel Foucault, Louis Althusser, and many others are, according to followers of the IIIT, signs of a deep crisis. One method they suggest to come to terms with the crisis is to use a *tawhidic* approach. In their understanding such an approach would create a holistic perspective and, in the end, a unitive science. This is a science that puts the world together into a systematized totality. In this picture nature and humans are not separated. That is, ideas are firmly rooted in an organic world picture. Often, a writer will back up his views by restricting his references to other people who share the same ideas and belong to the same position. In addition, the writer takes a position in which he or she acts as a vessel presenting undeniable "facts" (Potter 1996, 157 f.). This is an important strategy in the discourse, and it reveals the artificially constructed and pseudoscientific character of the discourse, as well as the fact that it is basically a struggle for the power of the privilege to define Islam. Furthermore, science is assigned metaphysical aspects. One obvious problem is that science that contradicts the word of God will not be tolerated.

It seems that within the discussions of the meaning of Islam in general, a group of free-floating intellectuals has developed. This development is underlined by the peculiar location of the IIIT and SISS headquarters in Virginia. Muslims such as Sardar, Nasr, and representatives of the IIIT belong to an international Muslim jet set going from conference to conference, and from government to government, presenting their form of Islamic science. The idea of a geographically located Muslim world, or of a center and periphery, becomes somewhat obsolete. The Malaysian endeavor to build an Islamic state has attracted the attention of the rest of the Muslim countries as well as of the participants in the discourse on Islam and knowledge/science. And it comes as no surprise that Nasr, Sardar, and persons connected to the IIIT have all been in Malaysia as advisers. The International Islamic University in Kuala Lumpur also had the former head of the IIIT, AbdulHamid AbuSulayman, as president.

One interesting question is whether the idea of a global Islam can function on the local level. To what extent is the global influenced by the local understanding of Islam and vice versa? One can interpret the discourse on Islam and knowledge as an expression of a situation in which "Islam" is exposed to challenges from other value systems. That exposure would also explain why the discourse on Islam and knowledge appears to be more dynamic in Europe and North America than in Muslim countries. Following the ideas of the sociologist Roland Robertson, such a challenge would cause local ideas on "Islam" to become essentialized and proclaimed as being universal (Robertson 1992, 164 ff.).

Related to the question of the global is the fact that the language of communication within the discourse is English. In order to be able to communicate, Muslims from Malaysia, India, Pakistan, Africa, Europe, North America, and the Middle East tend to use English when communicating on matters concerning knowledge and science (Stenberg 1996).

Finally, one often-repeated argument is that there is nothing wrong with Islam. Frequently the participants in the discourse say that the enigma of today's Muslim has to do with the un-Islamic behavior of Muslims. If they returned to correct Islam all problems would be solved. One obvious dilemma for Muslims, as well as for students of Islam, Muslims and non-Muslims, is the large number of interpretations claiming to be the One and True form of Islam. In my opinion, one consequence for students of Islam is that to study the specific Islamic or Qur'anic opinion on various matters is almost impossible, because no such thing exists. One cannot trace the transcendental meaning of Islam, or the absolute or final Islamic view of science. For me, the solution is to look at the Muslims as actors and not at Islam in its entirety, that is, to focus on the study of interpretations and on relations between interpretations.

| Globalization Experienced
and Practiced

6

Globalization, Migration, and Identity

Sudan, 1800–2000

HEATHER J. SHARKEY

The meaning and impact of globalization riveted debate at the end of the twentieth century. As networks of mass communications and trade tied far-flung communities more closely together, some identified the emergence of a "global society." But others pointed to organizations that were countering this trend, by nurturing difference within the world order. They pointed, for example, to nation-states, which were mitigating the growth of global society through legal barriers and border controls that restricted contact to inter-national terms (Featherstone 1995, 1–14; Beyer 1994, 21–25; Cvetkovich and Kellner 1997, 1–30). This tension between the global and the local, the universal and the particular, or the "macro-" and the "micro-" led to a semantic dilemma of choosing between singular and plural forms to describe groups. Should one speak of society, or societies; culture, or cultures? Challenging the notion of a monolithic Islam in practice, for example, some academics began to write of "Islams." Hence the title of the conference at which these essays were first presented: "Muslims and Islams in the Age of Globalization and Postmodernity."

GLOBALIZATION AND HISTORY

Musing over the implications of social contact for global, national, and local identities, one may pose the following two questions. First, how and in what forms does community consciousness take shape (Anderson 1991)? Second, do the "global economy" and "global communications" foster cultural simplicity ("homogenization") or the opposite, complexity (Appadurai 1990)?

Historians wishing to take these debates beyond a contemporary setting

113

must examine them in light of their timing, by addressing another query: Was globalization a new phenomenon in the late twentieth century, or did it exist, in other forms, places, and eras, before computers and the Internet, and even before the printing press? Answers will rest on a definition of terms. If one defines globalization as a process of intense exchange among economies and cultures within "world systems" (Wallerstein 1974), then globalization is neither new nor modern in the Middle East or in the wider world (Manger 1999; Brook and Schmid 2000). One could, for example, speak of an "Islamic global society" in the years from 1000 to 1500—a society epitomized by the fourteenth-century scholar Ibn Battuta, whose travels from Morocco to the Moluccas testified to the wide web of trade and culture that linked his world together (Irwin 1996; Dunn 1989). Thinking about identity issues, historians must also question nationalism's genesis, to ask how modern (or originally European) a phenomenon it was (Hastings 1997; Brook and Schmid 2000).

Identity-building exchanges take many forms, but all, seen in the abstract, occur through a process of conveyance or migration. Like Ibn Battuta, people may move from place to place, but so may ideas and objects, which have social lives of their own (Appadurai 1986). Whatever the mode of their conveyance, peoples, commodities, and concepts move together, collectively making links that forge identities.

Working from the premise that social identities are the product of interactions across distances, this essay examines the role of migration in the formation of community consciousness. For the sake of simplicity, it restricts migration to the physical movement of peoples and concentrates on one historical case: the Muslim societies of the Northern Sudan in the past two centuries (1800–2000). Study of population movement in this region shows that conceptions of community formed along the major routes traversed in each period, and entailed constant interactions between global and local processes.

MIGRATION TO ABOUT 1820

Because peoples, historically, have always migrated, social identities have always been in flux. While the Northern Sudan confirms this pattern,[1] its history from 1800 warrants study as a unit, for two reasons. First, historical sources are richest for this "modern" era. Second, the past two centuries show a certain cultural unity. By 1800, the circulation of people and ideas along routes of migration had

1. See, for example, Spaulding 1998.

established Islam and Arabic as primary features of Northern Sudanese culture, and had linked the region into a Muslim global society.

It is assumed that Islam and Arabic came to the Northern Sudan together, as Arab Muslim nomads trickled into the region from Arabia (via Sinai and Egypt) after the earliest forays of Muslim armies into Nubia. Islam spread slowly in the centuries that followed, first as the religion of bedouin and traders. Conversion among indigenous peoples accelerated from the early fourteenth century, when Islam displaced Christianity among Nubian elites. By the late fifteenth century, Sufi itinerants (religious migrants), many of whom dabbled in trade, had helped to propagate Islam along the Nile and the Red Sea coast (Hasan 1967). Intermarriage and the assimilation of slaves also contributed to Islam's dissemination.[2]

The Arabic language spread in concert with Islam, until by the sixteenth century it was displacing Nubian languages around the confluence of the White and Blue Niles. This linguistic trend accompanied the spread of "Arab" ethnic identity, so that by 1800 many Muslim groups in the riverain Northern Sudan traced genealogies back to Arab progenitors (O'Fahey and Spaulding 1974, 33, 81). But in the east, west, and far north, certain communities accepted Islam while retaining indigenous languages as "mother tongues," coming to regard themselves as "Muslims" but not "Arabs." Included in this category were Nubians, Fur, Beja, and others (Adams 1977; Kapteijns 1985; Ewald 1990).[3] Such communities adopted Arabic only as a lingua franca, in trade, and as the language of Islamic study. These trends suggest, first, that language proved more resistant to change than religion in the Northern Sudan; and second, that men, not women, were the primary bearers of Arabic and Islam, because of male dominance in trade and scholarship.[4]

Islamization and Arabicization continued apace after the founding of two Muslim states, the Funj sultanate (about 1500–1820) based at Sennar, near the junction of the Niles, and the Kayra sultanate (about 1600–1874), based in Darfur, along the Darb al-Arba'in trade route connecting Lake Chad to Cairo (O'Fa-

2. This trend persisted into the late nineteenth century. For one striking case in the 1880s, see Beswick 1998, 153–54.

3. These changes may have had something to do with the prevalence of migration. It appears that Nubian languages, for example, persisted north of the Nile cataracts partly because the harsh climate and terrain in their "Belly of Rocks" (Batn al-Hajar) repelled immigrants, as they had done in Pharaonic times (Adams 1977).

4. In a late-twentieth-century parallel, male Ethiopian refugees in the Sudan proved more likely than females to learn Arabic, because males had a greater range of social contacts beyond the home (Bulcha 1988, 177).

hey and Spaulding 1974; Walz 1979). By 1800, Muslims from the Red Sea coast to the Darfur savannahs were drawing guidance and solace from an Islam of Sufism and holy men, buttressed by a legal framework of courts and *qadis* (McHugh 1994). Moving southward, however, the influence of Islam waned, particularly as savannah gave way to seasonal swampland (Beswick 1994).

As the nineteenth century dawned, new intellectual currents were circulating in the Islamic world, radiating from a hub in Mecca. Reform was in the air. The global shift of power toward Europe and away from Muslim empires (made clear through European encroachment into Ottoman and Mughal domains) may have prompted Muslim thinkers, at this juncture, to reappraise Islamic practice (Voll 1982). The Arabian Wahhabi movement illustrated this trend forcefully. Through its call for a return to Muslim fundamentals, Wahhabism inspired many Sufi thinkers, including several who returned to, or set out for, Africa. There, such men began to advocate new forms of Sufi practice, characterized by greater self-discipline in worship and attention to scriptural norms (Martin 1976; O'Fahey 1990; Karrar 1992). With its more close-knit organization, "neo-Sufism" in Africa also stimulated trade, by joining affiliate branches and members into networks for spiritual and material exchange (Evans-Pritchard 1949, 79).

This spirit of Islamic reform inspired or invigorated the series of *jihad* movements that marked African history in the nineteenth and early twentieth centuries. The first of these occurred in 1804, in the Hausa-speaking territories of West Africa, when the Fulani intellectual Uthman dan Fodio (1754–1817) declared war against the pagan and semi-Islamized communities of the region. This *jihad,* aiming to purge "un-Islamic" practices, introduced the Hausa masses to two ideas that had important repercussions for the Northern Sudan.

The first idea concerned the virtue of pilgrimage *(hajj)* to Mecca—an undertaking hitherto more common among African Muslim elites, but now emphasized as a general Muslim duty. Compelled by religious devotion and by the economic and social upheavals of post-*jihad* society, West Africans began to set out on pilgrimage in greater numbers. Their routing was significant. Whereas West African pilgrims in past centuries had taken Saharan routes to transit centers on the North African coast, they now began to favor a route along the eastern grasslands, passing through the Northern Sudan to Red Sea ports. This route had only become attractive in the eighteenth century, when, for the first time, Muslim governments were in control of the lands from Lake Chad to the Red Sea (Birks 1978, 12–14; Yamba 1995, 30–47; al-Naqar 1985; O'Fahey and Spaulding 1974, 165).

The second idea of the Hausaland jihad was millennarian. Uthman dan

Fodio and his associates circulated predictions about the imminent coming of the Mahdi, the Rightly Guided One, whose arrival in the East would herald the end of time. Mahdist beliefs, a feature of folk Sunni Islam for centuries, gained special credence as the fourteenth Muslim century (A.H. 1300/A.D. 1882) approached (al-Hajj 1967). West African pilgrims bore mahdist expectations into the Northern Sudan and thus set the stage for Muhammad Ahmad, a Sufi thinker from Aba Island on the White Nile, who declared himself Mahdi in 1881.

1820–1881

In the years between 1820 and 1881 the Northern Sudan became part of a Turco-Egyptian empire controlled by the dynasty of Muhammad 'Ali, an enterprising Albanian officer in the Ottoman Empire who had struck out on his own in Egypt. The Turco-Egyptian state brought the Nile Valley into formal union and thereby drew nineteenth-century Sudan and Egypt more closely together politically, economically, and socially. This period also witnessed the burgeoning of an extant slave trade, which served as a vehicle for Islamization and Arabicization among enslaved populations. Finally, through the emphasis it placed on export commodities (not only slaves, but indigo, ivory, and other cash "crops") the Turco-Egyptian regime ushered the Northern Sudan into a monetized global economy (Hill 1959; Bjørkelo 1989).

When Muhammad 'Ali authorized conquest of the Northern Sudan in 1820, he hoped to secure sources of gold for his coffers and slaves for his armies. Though gold proved to be lacking, slaves were plentiful. At a time when interpretations of Islamic law endorsed enslavement within non-Muslim communities, the Nuba Mountains in Kordofan and the far reaches of the Blue and White Nile basins—the immediate non-Muslim peripheries of the riverain Northern Sudan—were deemed acceptable targets for raiding.

Slavery was a major reason for migration into the Northern Sudan in the nineteenth century. In the Turco-Egyptian period, the market for slaves (men, women, and children) grew not only in Egypt (which had been an importer since ancient times), but also in Arabia and in the Northern Sudan itself. Consequently, slaves between Wadi Halfa and the Fourth Cataract, estimated as 4 percent of the population by 1820, constituted about one-third of the population by the end of the nineteenth century (Spaulding 1982, 9, 11). Settled in the North, slaves became Muslims and Arabic speakers. But in the eyes of the slave-owning classes, slaves did not automatically become "Arabs," even after manumission, because "Arab" identity implied high status. Instead, by the late nineteenth century, many slaves, ex-slaves, and their descendants were known as "Sudanese" (singular *su-dani*, plural *sud*), that is, "Blacks," a usage that prevailed until the early twentieth century, when "Sudanese" began to serve as a nationalist label (Sharkey 1998, 34–75).

In the years after 1820, the newly enslaved (or "coerced migrants") came to perform the bulk of farm work, at a time when growing land shortages along the Nile and the pressures of Turco-Egyptian taxation were compelling many free Muslims to seek opportunities elsewhere (Spaulding 1982; Bjørkelo 1989). These free migrants fell into two main groups, each with its own trajectory of migration. They were the *jallaba* and the Nubians.

The *jallaba*, as they came to be known, were "Arab" men who left riverain villages to take up trade in the west or south, where, in the mid-nineteenth century, they dealt in slaves especially. Settled in Kordofan, some had wives and family members join them, while others established new families locally (Bjørkelo 1989, 137–38). A *jallaba* community and identity persisted into the late twentieth century, partly because members of this minority retained links to family in the riverain North. In functional terms, the *jallaba* acted not only as traders but as cultural conduits, transmitting the normative Islamic and Arabic culture of the riverain North to the agricultural and nomadic societies in which they settled or traded (Saavedra 1998, 227–28; Beck 1998, 265–68).[5]

The Nubian pattern of migration, by contrast, tended toward Lower Egypt, thereby continuing an ancient migratory trend. In the mid-nineteenth century, Nubian men filled specific niches in the booming economies of Cairo and Alexandria, supplanting slaves as domestic servants, guards, and carriage drivers (Adams 1977, 61; Sørbø 1985, 63). Most Nubian migrants preserved links to the women, children, and elders of their home villages, sending remittances and returning to retire. This pattern of Nubian male emigration continued throughout the twentieth century as well (Hale 1979, 279–80). In 1906, one observer estimated that 40 percent of Nubian males over ten years old were away from their villages (Sudan Government 1911, 240); in 1997, demographers were still discussing the phenomenon of Nubian male out-migration (Abusharaf 1997, 516).

Nubians were not the only migrants to Egypt in the nineteenth century. Another small but significant migration of men consisted of Northern Sudanese students. Encouraged by the Turco-Egyptian regime as a matter of policy, these students went to Cairo to study the Islamic sciences at al-Azhar, where, from

---

5. On the continued economic prominence of the Jallaba in the late twentieth century, see Mahmoud 1984, 73–74, 84.

1846, they were able to stay in a special Sudanese student hostel (Sulayman 1985, 55–56). Educated in the legalistic tradition of "official" Islam, some stayed in Cairo, adding to the city's "Sudanese" community, while others returned, serving the Turco-Egyptian, Mahdist, or early Anglo-Egyptian regimes as *qadi*s and teachers ('Abd al-Rahim 1936).

As an episode in colonial control, the period from 1820 to 1881 drew the Northern Sudan into a Turco-Egyptian empire. Imperial logistics fostered a migration of bureaucrats, notably through the importation of "Ottoman Turks" (including ethnic Albanians, Circassians, Kurds, and others) to serve as military rulers (Hill 1959, 1). Many "Egyptians"—distinguished from "Turks" by their use of Arabic as a first language—followed on their heels as traders, petty bureaucrats, and Islamic scholars. As "Egyptian" men married local women, children of intermediate ethnicity, known as *muwalladin* (meaning "born-in-the-place," or half-breeds), resulted. Along with the movements of Nubian peoples, these migrations in the Turco-Egyptian period forged new bonds of kinship that transcended the fixed Sudan-Egypt borders of the twentieth century.

1881–1898

In 1881 Muhammad Ahmad declared himself Mahdi, with Islamic reform and anti-imperialism as platforms of his mission. Declaring *jihad* against the Turco-Egyptian regime, he founded a state that ultimately fell prey to a second, British, colonialism in 1898. The Mahdist movement was not only millennarian in inspiration, it was also pan-Islamic. The Mahdi's emphasis on Islamic integrity connected his movement to broader trends (circulating in Africa and Asia) that asserted the importance of a unified Muslim identity to counteract European imperialism (Voll 1982, 87–147; Sharkey 1994).

As a first step toward realizing his agendas, the Mahdi called for expulsion of the Turco-Egyptians from the Northern Sudan, on several grounds (Shuqayr 1972, 631–34). They taxed excessively and ruled badly. They were decadent, foreign, and unjust, as their occasional use of cruel punishments, such as impalement, showed (Bjørkelo 1989, 52). And their ostensible allies, European Christians, who were growing increasingly visible in the Turco-Egyptian hierarchy, were pressuring Egypt to ban the slave trade—a legitimate Muslim practice that was essential to the local economy. Tapping into local resentments on these and other issues, Muhammad Ahmad al-Mahdi attracted mass support for his movement. Unified by calls to *jihad*, his supporters defeated Turco-Egyptian armies beginning in 1881. Mahdist victories culminated in 1885, when Khartoum, the capital, fell to their side. By this time communities in the riverain north, Kordofan, and Red Sea region had given their oaths of allegiance or had been forced to submit (Holt 1970).

The Mahdi died in 1885. Under his successor, al-Khalifa Abdullahi, the Mahdist state combined expansionist ideals with isolationist practices, and regarded states in neighboring Egypt and Ethiopia as its most immediate external foes. Although the Mahdist state was officially an Islamic state, it prohibited the *hajj* to Mecca, because it was wary both of Turco-Egyptian and European ships plying the Red Sea waters and the possibility of "pilgrim" espionage. However, the ban on the *hajj* did not dissuade many West Africans, who, upon receiving news of the Mahdi's appearance, migrated eastward in droves (Birks 1978; al-Naqar 1985; Yamba 1995).

One of the most important migrations of the Mahdist era involved coercion. Aware of the fragility of the state after the death of the Mahdi, and anxious to consolidate control over the wide expanses of the region, the Khalifa Abdullahi forced many groups (particularly Baggara cattle nomads from the west) to migrate to the new capital at Omdurman in a policy known as *tahjir*. He did so to mobilize troops, ensure control over potentially disloyal groups, indoctrinate local leaders, and integrate tribes by contracting marriage alliances (Kramer 1991, 69; Kapteijns 1985, 79–83). As a result of these migrations, Omdurman swelled from a village to a city. By 1898, it had some 250,000 residents, approximately three-quarters of whom were female (Kramer 1991, 90–101). Many of these women, distributed as wives and concubines, had been taken as booty in war, particularly from southern and southwestern Kordofan (Decker 1998). However, the Omdurman population did not stay rooted. Following the fall of the city to the Anglo-Egyptian army in 1898, many of the forced immigrants went back to their former homes, and the city shrank to a fraction of its size (Kramer 1991, 255–64). A population tally from 1905 suggested that Omdurman had fewer than 40,000 inhabitants (Sudan Government 1905, 94).

Northern Sudanese historians argue hotly over the effects of Mahdist policies—including migration policy—on culture and identity in the Northern Sudan. Some claim that the Mahdi was a symbol of national liberation in the struggle against foreign oppression, and that the Mahdist era unified the region's tribes under the aegis of a shared Islamic heritage (al-Qaddal 1992). Others claim the opposite, pointing out that the Khalifa's preferential hirings of kinsmen and supporters sowed tribal discord and undermined the religious universalism of the Mahdist movement's aims (Malik 1987). In this case as in others, cultural homogeneity and heterogeneity appeared to move hand-in-hand.

1898–1956

The Scramble for Africa was well under way when Britain "reconquered" the Sudan for Egypt in 1898, thwarting French designs in the process. Although an 1899 agreement constituted the Sudan's new regime as an Anglo-Egyptian partnership or Condominium, Britain made the Sudan into its virtual colony. Taking account of the territorial claims of the other European powers, Britain applied arbitrary but fixed borders to map the "Anglo-Egyptian Sudan." By defining a territory and then elaborating a state within it, British colonialism laid the framework for the future Sudanese "nation-state" and for a Sudanese national identity.

Britain had justified its conquest to home audiences on the grounds of a civilizing mission, one platform of which was abolitionism. But for men on the spot, economic pragmatism prevailed over humanitarian ideals. To reconstruct the Northern Sudanese economy in the aftermath of war and to build up a tax base that could make the colony pay, labor—slave or free—was critical. Abolition might not only destabilize the labor force and hence the economy, it might also alienate influential members of Northern Sudanese society. British authorities therefore tiptoed around the issue by banning the slave trade but accepting the continuation of extant slavery. While they sometimes granted manumission papers to those who pled for them, they tried to dissuade slaves from leaving owners, anxious to keep workers rooted on farms, where their labor was crucial to subsistence agriculture (Hargey 1981).

Notwithstanding restrictive laws, many slaves fled from their owners, claiming freedom with their feet. Ex-slave migrants headed to the towns, especially to Khartoum, which the Anglo-Egyptian regime rebuilt as a capital. Labor was short on every front. Hence jobs abounded, particularly in the construction and public works sectors, where men and women alike engaged in heavy manual labor (Sikainga 1996). Unable to control the flow of slaves to cities, the regime passed a law against vagabonds, to signal that while ex-slaves might migrate, they could not loaf. Meanwhile, landowners, who were desperate for workers, made their children do the work of slaves who fled (Sudan Government 1907, 190). Lacking the coercive force of an Islamic state structure, labor control devolved on the family, where elders used various tactics—including exhortations in initiation songs—to persuade young males of the merit of farm work (Abdullahi Ali Ibrahim 1994, 10).

Young men needed convincing if they were going to stay on their fathers' farms. In the riverain North, wage-paying jobs were plentiful and attractive. Following a trend throughout Africa, the Anglo-Egyptian regime promoted the development of cash crops that would yield monetary revenues through sale in world markets. To transport bulk goods for export, the regime built railways, which were a major source of wage-paying jobs. Stability after years of war favored economic growth in general. Businesses boomed, towns grew, the bureaucracy and social services expanded, and the communications network spread. All of these ventures required skilled and unskilled labor of different kinds—labor for laying rails, building dams, and erecting telegraph poles; labor for delivering mail and manning steamboats, and so on.

Desperate for laborers, the regime welcomed immigrants from abroad. Beginning in 1906, for example, with the opening of a new port city at Port Sudan, the regime recruited men from Jidda and Yemen as harbor workers, to compensate for the lack of interest among local Beja (Perkins 1993, 125–28). In the 1920s, after the dismantling of the Ottoman empire, the government welcomed many skilled laborers from Asia Minor, including Greeks and Armenians (Hamid 1996, 20). In the same decade, the traditional flow of Nubian migration reversed, as villagers from near Idfu, in Upper Egypt, migrated to Wadi Halfa, just over the Sudan border. Initially attracted by jobs in the porterage, construction, and transport sectors, many of these "Basalwa" settled permanently in the Sudan, becoming Sudanese citizens after independence in 1956 but retaining a distinct ethnic identity (Sørbø 1985, 119–35). Environmental factors also played a role in this particular migration, as impounded Nile waters dislocated Egyptian Nubian communities after the initial building and subsequent enlargements of the Aswan Dam (Adams 1977, 652–53).

Nubian migration also changed direction on the Sudan side of the border. With the development of the Sudanese economy, Khartoum rather than Cairo became an urban magnet. Moreover, as legal residents of the colonial territory, Sudanese Nubians stood to benefit from hiring policies that increasingly discriminated against "Egyptians," particularly for jobs in the Sudan government bureaucracy (Hale 1979, 91–93; Sørbø 1985, 64; Sharkey 1998, 64–69). Having assisted Anglo-Egyptian forces during the Mahdist and Reconquest eras, Sudanese Nubian men had a head start in getting bureaucratic posts, including those that required advanced Arabic literacy. The early development of government schools in Wadi Halfa confirmed this trend by producing cadres of formally educated Nubian men who could compete "nationally" for high-caliber jobs.

The largest immigrant sector of the colonial period came from West Africa. Attracted by the possibility of performing the *hajj,* and still inspired, in some cases, by mahdist faith, West Africans continued to migrate to the Northern

Sudan. The British conquest of northern Nigeria in 1903, together with French expansion into Niger, accelerated their eastward migrations. Colonial rule also made pilgrimage easier, because of the growth of transport and public security. After 1909, for example, the railway reached El Obeid from Khartoum. Although many pilgrims were too poor to afford tickets, it helped that they could follow tracks east (Birks 1978, 18). Once arrived in the Sudan, many West Africans established community support networks by participating in Sufi orders. Some of these, like the Tijaniyya *tariqa* in Kordofan, helped to transcend ethnic divisions by incorporating members of diverse backgrounds and facilitating intermarriage with local "Arabs" (al-Karsani 1998). Ultimately such organizations were agents of Arabicization (spreading the Arabic language) and, to a lesser extent, Arabization (spreading Arab ethnic identity).

British officials noted the arrival of West Africans with approval. A report from 1908 declared, "Some 5,000 Fellatas from West Africa have arrived during the past seven months and more are expected. These people are nominally on their pilgrimage to Mecca but finding Omdurman a good place to halt and earn money in, by far the greater majority stop the best part of the year and not a few settle. These Fellatas are an energetic and cheery people. They have few wants and seem to greatly appreciate the benefits of the Sudan government. I am informed that the fame of Omdurman has spread West and that numerous other tribes are about to follow the example of the Fellatas and that indeed some are already en route" (Sudan Government 1909, 557). West Africans (also known as the "Fellata") settled in all the major towns of the North. After 1925, with the start of the cotton-growing Gezira Scheme, many moved into the Blue Nile region to work on farms, where landowners were relieved to have them.

West Africans continued to migrate into the Northern Sudan throughout the twentieth century. In the 1956 Sudanese census, 908,686 people (over 8 percent of the total population) were of "professed West African origin," a figure that may have reflected acute undercounting (Balamoan 1981, 5, 54, 65). Once arrived, West Africans radiated toward specific cities and regions, as regional and city-based population figures show (Balamoan 1981, 67). These migrations peaked in the colonial era but did not end. By the late twentieth century, West Africans were still immigrating, evading the postcolonial border patrols of Nigeria, Chad, and the Sudan (Yamba 1995, 65–67).

While many West Africans came to the Sudan, few moved to Mecca or returned whence they came. Their migration, in other words, was permanent—a trend reflected in contemporary language maps of Africa that mark a Hausa language zone in the midst of the Northern Sudanese Arabic belt (Griffiths 1994,

29). Research from the Blue Nile region, undertaken in the 1980s and 1990s, showed that many members of the West African migrant community there were choosing to resist assimilation and to retain a self-consciously distinct identity. Indeed, many Hausa speakers whose progenitors settled in the Blue Nile region three, four, or five generations ago still identified themselves as pilgrims and clung to the dream of performing the *hajj*—though few ever succeeded. In spite of their settledness (which was compounded by debts that tied them down), these "pilgrims" stressed their transience and difference vis-à-vis the Arabic-speaking "Sudanese"—for example, by building impermanent houses, practicing distinct customs (such as wife seclusion), and maintaining separate Qur'an schools. Those who went to seek better jobs or education outside the community were often ostracized by fellow West Africans and were thereby obliged to cultivate Sudanese-Arabic identities instead. These "permanent pilgrims" viewed assimilation as an all-or-nothing affair (Yamba 1995, 75–81).

Among groups immigrating into the Sudan during the Anglo-Egyptian era, foreign traders were also important. The arrival of Greeks and others, beginning almost immediately after the conquest, signaled a continuation and acceleration of a Turco-Egyptian-era trend (Stiansen 1993). In 1930, a British official captured the spirit of these migrations in a ditty that ran, "Khartum was captured by Kitchener in 1898. / A Greek with a parcel of groceries was the first man through the gate. / Then came the Copts and the Syrians to help the country grow; / And still they keep on coming until everywhere you go—There's the Cypriots and the Syrians, the Armenians and the Greeks" (Henderson and Owen 1963, 64). Many of the children and grandchildren of these traders left the Sudan in the postcolonial era (particularly after the government "nationalized" businesses in 1970), but some persisted into the 1990s, finding niches in the service and import-export sectors (Niblock 1987, 53–59, 233–89). Members of this "minority" business community hold "Sudanese" passports without considering themselves, or being considered by others, as "Sudanese." Their "foreignness" derives above all from their non-Muslim status, endogamous marriage practices, and European social customs and business connections. Their small number (according to one study, for example, Greeks and Syrians constituted only 3 percent of "leading businessmen" in 1976 [Mahmoud 1984, 73]) belies their economic importance (Tignor 1987, 187, 195–96).

Bureaucratic migrations, a feature of the Turco-Egyptian era, also intensified in the Anglo-Egyptian period. In the first half of the twentieth century, elite administrative cadres came from Britain, most being males in their twenties, thirties, and forties, who returned home upon retirement (Warburg 1971; Collins 1983; Daly 1986 and 1991). Middle-ranking bureaucrats came from Egypt and

Lebanon (Murqus 1984, 308–33; Hourani 1992; Sharkey-Balasubramanian 2000). Though many of the latter left the country when their service ended, some settled permanently in the Sudan with their families, acquiring citizenship and moving into the private sector.

Most importantly for the region in the long run, the regime groomed an elite cadre of Northern Sudanese males for bureaucratic jobs by educating them in new government schools. Initially placed in lower-tier positions, these Northern Sudanese employees rose through the system as the colonial era advanced (and inherited political control of the country at independence in 1956). Sent throughout the colonial territory on transfer, these men came to conceive of the territory as a geographical whole. Their bureaucratic migrations thereby inspired the development of a nationalist identity predicated upon colonial borders (Sharkey 1998).

Although many northerners went on job migrations to remote regions of the territory, virtually all—including those who had been raised in villages—retired to urban locations, especially to the "Three Towns" of Khartoum, Khartoum North, and Omdurman. Urbanization among these educated classes represented a small part of a much larger rural-to-urban migration that continued apace over the twentieth century. Estimates suggest that the population of the Three Towns and its vicinity grew from fewer than 90,000 in 1905 to nearly 245,000 in 1955—before quintupling again in the first twenty-five years after decolonization (Sudan Government 1905, 94; Hamid 1996, 27; Abu Salim 1991, 197).

Although British authorities were prepared to send educated Northern Sudanese men on job postings within the territory, they were eager to restrict their movement out of it, particularly in the direction of Egypt where, they feared, dangerous ideologies might "infect" them. Indeed, young educated males were increasingly dazzled by ideas of Arab nationalism and anti-colonialism emanating from Cairo. From the mid-1920s, therefore, British authorities tightened controls along the Sudan-Egypt border, requiring educated northerners to apply for travel visas if they wished to cross (Hamad 1980, 32–36). In one publicized case, a few Northern Sudanese students defied these restrictions, "escaping" to Cairo as fugitives (haribun) and becoming a cause célèbre among nationalists who extolled the ideal of Nile Valley unity (Najila 1964, 128–41). Among the politically quiescent, however, border crossing posed little difficulty, particularly for those who had family in Egypt.[6]

6. Documentation in personnel files at the National Records Office in Khartoum supports this claim. See, for example, NRO Personnel 3A/6/13: Personnel file of Hamza al-Malik Tambal and NRO Personnel 1A/2/4: Personnel file of Da'ud Iskandar.

British authorities were also eager to regulate migration across another border—the cultural line that divided the "Northern" and "Southern" Sudans. By the early twentieth century, Islam and Arabic prevailed in the arid and semi-arid "North," while local religions and Nilotic and other languages prevailed in the wetter "South," where clumps of water weeds (the *sudd*) had impeded southward navigation and slowed the spread of Islam in precolonial times. In the Anglo-Egyptian era, the refrain among British officials was that "Africa" (which to them meant the South, and was discrete from the Arab world) "begins at Malakal," around 10 degrees latitude on the White Nile (Collins 1988).

Believing that southern societies needed to be protected, first from the slave-raiding propensities of the Muslim North and second from the corruptive forces of modernity (which would threaten its pristine state), the British applied isolationist policies. While the colonial government directed educational development in the North, comparatively underfunded Christian missionary groups had free rein over education in the South (Sanderson and Sanderson 1981). Cash-crop promotion in the North—notably cotton in the Gezira and gum arabic in Kordofan—had no parallels in the South (Daly 1991, 6–7, 91, 100). Nor were railway lines extended there. And while Arabic remained the main language of instruction and administration in the North, English or local vernaculars served the same purpose in the South. Through these and other policies, British rule enhanced the religious, linguistic, and economic distinctions that reified the North-South divide (Spaulding and Kapteijns 1991).

Border controls dividing North from South gained force through law following passage of the Closed District Ordinance in 1922, which barred Northern Sudanese from traveling south of Malakal without the permission of the local British authority. The regime expanded on this practice in 1930 with the adoption of a "Southern Policy" that aimed to cultivate indigenous southern culture "untrammeled by Arabic, Muslim influence from the North" (Collins 1988). From 1922 to 1932, British officials pursued a similar policy in the Nuba Mountains, aiming in the words of one official "to preserve or evolve an authentic Nuba civilisation and culture as against a bastard type of arabicisation" (Salih 1982, 2, 7–10). The Arabic language spread anyway, as the stability of the colonial period encouraged Nuba farmers to move from the mountains to the plains and thereby to have greater contact with lowland "Arab" communities (Nasr 1979, 1).

These policies also entailed isolationism for the army, which (continuing a Turco-Egyptian and Mahdist-era trend) recruited heavily from the South and Nuba Mountains. Like their bureaucratic counterparts, soldiers had moved widely in the colonial territory, although policies increasingly restricted southern and Nuba units to regional postings. Urgent demands in the Second World War put army isolationism in reverse, as the regime sent Nuba soldiers to fronts in Eritrea and Libya (Salih 1982, 337–94). These long-distance postings of the mid-twentieth century were far more limited than their nineteenth-century counterparts, when Sudanese soldiers had served as far afield as Greece, Mexico, and Tanganyika (Johnson 1989, 73; Hill and Hogg 1995). By broadening the physical and social horizons of soldiers (and of the wives and family members who accompanied them), the colonial army fostered community conceptions on a larger scale—regionally, nationally, and globally.

The colonial army also served as a major vehicle for the spread of Islam, for two reasons. First, the army's working culture was strongly Muslim—a legacy of the Turco-Egyptian practice of hiring 'ulama' as Muslim army chaplains—and soldiers often converted to Islam as a matter of course. Second, Islam's scope was appealing, for as a global religion it could transcend local ethnic divisions and provide a sense of corporate membership and social solidarity among men who were otherwise diverse. Upon retirement, those who returned to rural areas of the South and Nuba Mountains helped to spread Islam locally (Nasr 1979, 26, 36). Meanwhile, those who moved to towns often settled among fellow ex-army people, giving rise to so-called "Nubi" communities that retained distinct identities into the late twentieth century (Johnson 1989, 82–83). Returned soldiers also helped to propagate Arabic as a lingua franca in Southern and Nuba towns, giving rise thereby to local Arabic dialects (Miller 1991).

By the time the Second World War ended, the Sudan's British rulers knew that decolonization would occur—if not in ten years, then in twenty or thirty. After having practiced "divide and rule" for nearly fifty years, "unite and quit" became the order of the day (Austin 1980, 19). At the Juba Conference in 1947, British policy-setters signaled that North and South would gain independence as a unit. Anointed as nationalist leaders, educated Northern Sudanese now implemented policies to reverse regional isolationism and to accelerate the spread of Arabic and Islamic culture in the South and Nuba Mountains. Counteracting the influence of Christian missionaries was at the top of their agenda. From 1949, therefore, Arabic displaced English as the official language of instruction in Southern schools, while Islamic schools gained favor. Northern politicians gained greater latitude with independence in 1956, so that they were able to nationalize Christian missionary schools in 1957 and expel foreign missionaries in 1964. According to a Southern observer, Northerners also promoted Arabicization and Islamization through small-scale measures such as requiring Southern children to adopt Arabic Muslim names for classroom use (Malek 1991, 29–34).

Northern and Southern Sudanese historians disagree sharply in interpreting the Juba Conference and its aftermath. Northerners are likely to hail it as a triumph in the quest for a national unity based on Islamic and Arabic culture, and as a victory against the divisive policies of colonial rule (al-Rahman 1972). Southerners, by contrast, are more likely to see it as a betrayal by the British, who left a disempowered South open to cultural assault from the North (Ruay 1994). This clash in interpretation gained grounding in fact when civil war broke out in 1955, months before independence.

1956–1983

In 1956 the Sudan became independent within its colonial borders and gained recognition from the international "community." Viewing the country as a unit, its subsequent migrations fall into "national" and "international" categories.

Whereas educated elites in the Anglo-Egyptian period had undertaken migrations within the colonial territory, sent on job transfer in their capacity as bureaucrats, educated elites in the postcolonial period were more likely to travel abroad—to pursue higher education or to find jobs. Because Khartoum University was able to award undergraduate degrees of its own starting in 1956, foreign study in the postcolonial period became especially important for graduate-level training. Developments in air transport favored this trend, making international migration convenient and quick for those who could afford to fly. Those who returned from education abroad constituted a small but influential elite in Sudanese society and politics.

Throughout the twentieth century, Egypt remained a powerful magnet for students (academic migrants) even after 1955, when Cairo University established a Khartoum campus (al-Hardallu 1977). (Years later, this "impoverished cousin" [Reid 1990, 197–98] of the Cairene institution was nationalized or "Sudanized" by the Sudan government, becoming al-Nilayn University of Khartoum.) Regarding the Sudanese in Egypt, however, statistical reckonings—for the number of students, workers, and residents—have been ambiguous. In part this is because in the late twentieth century, and in spite of official nationality distinctions, the line between an "Egyptian" and a "Sudanese" remained blurry for many who trace mixed Sudanese-Egyptian origins. Thus complicated by patterns of intermarriage and back-and-forth migration, self-ascribed "national" identity often differed from the labels on passports (Fábos 1994 and 1999). Estimates for the number of "Sudanese" in Egypt reflect this confusion in labeling by ranging widely in 1998 from two to five million (U.S. Committee for Refugees 1998, 67–68).

In the early postcolonial period, the Communist-bloc countries of the Soviet Union and Eastern Europe became major purveyors of higher education to the Northern Sudanese. The Soviet Union during the Cold War was anxious to woo developing countries through offers of economic, technical, and educational assistance (Müller 1964, 101–30). The Sudan was a natural focus for such funding, because it had had a thriving Communist party since the formation of its first student cell in 1946 (Warburg 1978, 93–140). Consequently, after 1957, when Sudanese Communists joined the International Communist Movement, study programs flourished, as Communist-bloc countries delegated leftist Sudanese organizations to allocate scholarships on their behalf. Including trade, student, women's, and farmers' unions, together with the Sudanese Communist Party and its youth wing, these local groups awarded scholarships not only to registered Communists, but to "friendly, sympathetic, and democratic students" in general (Ali 1999).[7] Although the golden age of Sudanese Communism ended in 1970 when the party lost favor under Numayri, these educational migrations continued until the unraveling of the Soviet Union and its allied Communist states in the early 1990s.

In 1973, an official tally stated that 4,286 Sudanese students were attending universities abroad. Egypt accounted for 1,591, or 37 percent, of this total, confirming its historical role as a conduit for peoples and ideas in the Nile Valley. Yugoslavia, the USSR, and Czechoslovakia followed; Britain, the former colonial power, held fifth place (providing for only 4 percent of these students); Bulgaria, Romania, Poland, and East Germany came next. Together, Communist countries (including China) accounted for 1,559, or 36 percent, of Sudanese students abroad. Excluding Egypt, other Arabic-speaking or Muslim-majority countries (including Turkey, Iran, and Pakistan) accounted for only 318 (or 7 percent) of the students (Beshir 1977, 39). These patterns changed in the next twenty years, so that the United States and Canada (which had hosted eighteen and two students respectively in 1973) became important sites for study abroad, as did the Scandinavian countries on a smaller scale (Beshir 1977, 39; Abusharaf 1997).[8]

7. As an international secretary of the Sudanese Youth Union, Rasheed Ali was responsible for selecting students for scholarships. He claims that most of those chosen were not Communist Party members. Rasheed Ali later migrated to Budapest, to represent the Sudan in the World Federation of Democratic Youth. He was still living in Hungary in 1999, along with approximately one hundred other Sudanese migrants. Email correspondence with Rasheed Ali, dated 30 June 1999.

8. Because of their track record of development funding in the Sudan, Scandinavian higher institutions—and notably the University of Bergen in Norway and the University of Uppsala in Sweden—have trained many Sudanese scholars, particularly in the fields of history, anthropology, and development studies.

Academic migration had a major impact on the world-view of Sudanese intellectuals, as al-Tayyib Salih's *Season of Migration to the North*—a classic Arabic novel about two men who return from study in England—reveals (Salih 1969 and 1991).

Beginning in the early 1970s, more Northern Sudanese began to go abroad for employment, looking especially to Arabic-speaking oil-rich countries including Libya, Saudi Arabia, and the Gulf states. Facing a shortage of jobs at home and attracted by higher salaries and living standards elsewhere, university graduates began to migrate, with certain professional sectors moving en masse. By 1978 those working abroad included, for example, an estimated 20 percent to 50 percent of university lecturers, 25 percent of statisticians, and 70 percent of medical school graduates (International Migration Project 1978, 59–61). By 1985, an estimated two-thirds of the country's professional and skilled workers were out of the country (Sidahmed 1996, 195). This trend caused observers to worry about the consequences of "brain drain" for Sudanese national development, and later to lament the impact of this labor "haemorrhage" on the country's economic and political health (International Migration Project 1978, 53; Sidahmed 1996, 195–96).

In fact, attractive salaries in the oil states lured Sudanese workers from every level of the labor force—as construction workers, taxi drivers, domestic servants, and more. In 1968–69, for example, over a third of the Sudanese granted foreign work permits were cooks and domestics, while over a quarter were skilled manual laborers heading for Libya alone (International Migration Project 1978, 47, 50). Migrant workers came not only from big cities, but from rural and small town areas as far west as Darfur (Grawert 1991). Like Nubian and *jallaba* emigrés in the nineteenth century, most of these voluntary migrant workers were males. According to Libya's 1973 census, for example, of 1,448 Sudanese "workers" in the country, only 4 were women; of 336 Sudanese "professionals," only 25 were women (Mahmoud 1983, 229). Similarly, from 1971 to 1979, over 88 percent of emigrés to Saudi Arabia (including workers and their dependents, and pilgrims) were male (Mahmoud 1983, 247). Northern Sudanese female migrants to the oil states were mostly the wives of male workers.[9]

In the postcolonial period the Sudanese government became increasingly concerned about international labor migration and the loss of potential revenues. Hence the government imposed tighter controls (manifest in the transit

---

9. This pattern of low-scale female migration also prevailed in New World migrations of the 1980s and 1990s (Abusharaf 1997).

points of airports), requiring exit visas from 1970, international work permits from 1974, and expatriate income remittances (channeled via the Bank of Sudan) by 1981. In practice, however, rates of evasion were high (Mahmoud 1983, 227–35). Moreover, by transferring their money through unofficial channels, expatriate workers contributed to a hidden or underground economy that remained beyond the control of the Sudanese state (Sidahmed 1996, 195). To make matters worse, the country's faltering economy also prompted the migration of money—a process commonly known as "capital flight"—by which earners sent their money to foreign banks for safekeeping. This process had debilitating effects on the Sudanese economy in the long run (Sidahmed 1996, 195–97). At the same time, it extended the world-view of Sudanese depositors, whose foreign bank accounts gave them personal stakes in the global economy.

The year 1970 was the watershed for the oil-economy migration. On the eve of the boom in 1968–69, 934 Sudanese went abroad as legal guest workers, that is, with work permits granted by the Sudanese Department of Labor. Numbers began to rise in the following year, until by 1975–76 the government granted 12,475 international work permits. These figures do not account for many illegal workers, such as those who went to Arabia on pilgrimage visas but who extended their stay indefinitely. Estimated in toto, it was reckoned that by 1976 somewhere between 52,000 and 62,000 Sudanese were living in the oil-rich states of the Middle East, with Libya and Saudi Arabia as the largest employers (International Migration Project 1978, 47–59; Birks and Sinclair 1978, 77–79).

In light of the restrictive citizenship policies of the oil-rich states, Sudanese workers were de jure temporary migrants in the view of host governments. Hence most regarded their work stays as opportunities to save money for use in the Sudan, to fund marriage, maintain families, build a house for retirement, extend a family business, or contribute to a hometown development project (for example, building a school or clinic) (Abdullahi Ali Ibrahim 1994, 19; Sørbø 1985, 119–35; Mahmoud 1983, 296–97). Remittances from relatives abroad in the oil states and elsewhere were crucial to many Sudan households, accounting in gross terms for an estimated US$3 billion in 1984–85 alone (Sidahmed 1996, 196). This trend even applied to Sudan-based refugee communities, among whom migration to the oil states was common. Viewed on the household level, remittances accounted for over 30 percent of income among Ethiopian refugees living in Port Sudan in the 1980s (Bulcha 1988, 168). Such funds also fed the consumerist appetite for expensive luxury goods. In 1977, for example, eighty households in the Basalwa community of New Halfa had television sets, at a time when the town still had no broadcast reception (Sørbø 1985, 128).

For official temporary workers, durations of time abroad varied. Some men from a community in New Halfa, for example, used air travel to adopt a virtual "commuter lifestyle" between the Sudan and Arabia, going to work for a few months at a time between journeys (Sørbø 1985, 131). Others spent entire careers abroad. The long-term trends are unclear, and prompt the following questions. Will Sudanese workers in the oil states, like West African workers in the Sudan, settle, assimilate, and become "naturalized" (even, perhaps, as noncitizens), remain "permanent pilgrims" for the sake of their livelihoods, or return home for good?

1983–2000

The 1980s and 1990s witnessed acute political, economic, and environmental instability in the Sudan. This period opened in 1983 with an outbreak of severe drought and famine, and with the renewal of civil war in the South. By the mid-1980s the conflict had spread to the Nuba Mountains as well. While war- and famine-related refugee movements were not new to the Sudan (al-Bashir 1991), the crises of the 1980s and 1990s prompted migrations of unprecedented size and scope. While most refugees moved within Sudanese borders, some sought haven in neighboring countries. In 1989, a new round of international migration started when a military coup, backed by a party with Islamist agendas, prompted educated men and women from across the political spectrum to seek exile abroad. At the same time, deteriorating economic conditions made international migration increasingly attractive to students, workers, and their families.

The first civil war between North and South (1955–72) ended with the signing of an agreement in which the government addressed Southerners' long-standing economic and political grievances. Its terms provided for Southern regional autonomy in a federal structure, recognition of English as a principal second language besides Arabic, and generous funding for Southern economic development. Many Southerners became increasingly dissatisfied with the neglect of these provisions and with government plans for the exploitation of Southern water and oil resources. These frustrations fueled the start of the second civil war in 1983 (Woodward 1990; Lesch 1998).

The U.S. Committee for Refugees estimates that from 1983 to 1998 two million Sudanese died from war-related causes (accounting for 20 percent of the Southern population), and more than 80 percent of the Southern Sudanese population had been displaced at different times. These refugees included an estimated 350,000 or more who had fled to neighboring countries and 1.5 million

who were internally displaced in the South (in towns and refugee camps). Significantly, they also included 1.8 million who had migrated to Greater Khartoum—
a process of migration to the North that had not featured in the first civil war
(U.S. Committee for Refugees 1998, 95–96; Hamid 1996, 75). Although most of
the million or so Southerners displaced in the first war returned to their home regions after the 1972 accords, it is open to debate whether mass repatriation will
follow the second civil war—when it ends (Hamid 1996, 66). One view holds that
the likelihood of "repatriation" for refugees living in Greater Khartoum grows
dimmer with time, as refugees assimilate to urban life and as their children, who
come to speak Arabic as a first language, grow up without firsthand experience of
their "homelands" (Miller and Abu-Manga 1992). Another view holds that the
conditions in camps and shanty towns are so bleak, and prospects for employment so dim, that refugees will return once conditions improve (Fouad N.
Ibrahim 1991).

War refugees arrived in Khartoum along with waves of environmental
refugees—migrants escaping drought and food shortages that hit crisis propor-
tions in the western and eastern Sudan between 1983 and 1985. Localized
droughts and famines had occurred in the Sudan on at least a dozen occasions in
the century between 1885 and 1995. However, the 1983–85 drought and famine
were extreme in their demographic impact, prompting an estimated 1.8 million
Northerners to migrate internally, with most heading to Greater Khartoum and
the major Northern towns. Drought, famine, and associated epidemics continued to plague parts of the country in the years that followed (de Waal 1989;
Hamid 1996, 38–39, 75).

The Sudan was not only a producer and exporter of refugees in the postcolonial period. It also received many refugees from abroad, following political
and environmental crises in neighboring countries. Beginning in 1967, for example, thousands of Eritreans sought sanctuary in the Sudan; hundreds of thousands more followed in later years as Eritrea waged its war for independence
against the Ethiopian state. The Sudan government made some provisions for
foreign refugees, establishing a refugee commission in 1967 and passing an asy-
lum act in 1974. In the early 1980s, as it became clear that refugee repatriation
would be slow in coming, the government even sponsored agricultural settlement schemes on a limited scale (Bulcha 1988, 27–30). Like neighboring states,
the Sudanese government assumed that these migrants would be transient. But
for many, repatriation seems unlikely—even for those who cherish hopes of returning (Bulcha 1988, 231). By 1998, for example, there remained in the Sudan an
estimated 320,000 Eritreans, some of whom had been Sudan residents for thirty

years (U.S. Committee for Refugees 1998, 97). Though about 90 percent of these expressed hopes of returning to Eritrea, the loss of their homes and livelihoods, coupled with the devastation of that region, acted as deterrents (U.S. Committee for Refugees 1998, 69). Like the West Africans who are "permanent pilgrims" (Yamba 1995), these Eritreans may become permanent refugees.

The refugee movements of the 1980s and 1990s contributed to a larger process of rural-to-urban migration that had been occurring since the establishment of the Anglo-Egyptian regime in 1898. In the postcolonial era, various economic policies and social trends had accelerated this process, with the result that cities developed at the expense of rural areas. Cities had hospitals, schools, running water, electricity, easily accessible staple goods (for example, cooking oil, sugar, tea), television, and newspapers. Rural areas did not. The "easy life factor" was therefore a major inducement for urban migration, causing the population of Greater Khartoum to grow from an estimated 784,000 in 1973 to 1,343,000 in 1983, and stimulating comparable rates of growth in other large towns (Hamid 1996, 27, 33).

Arabic and Islam added an ideological charge to the politics of the 1980s and 1990s. In 1983 (a watershed year in many respects) Ja'far Numayri, dictator since 1969, declared the imposition of Islamic Shari'a law throughout the country. By this assertion of Islam in the state, Numayri may have hoped to divert attention from the country's economic crisis and from prevailing government corruption (Lesch 1998, 54–55; Sidahmed 1996, 134–35). Because educated Southerners, a majority of whom were Christian, saw this move as another cultural assault from the North, the policy only confirmed their resolution in war.

As the war progressed, Christianity spread in the South among refugees and helped to transcend ethnic differences within the camps (Nikkel 1991). The presence of Christian aid organizations supported this process. On an ideological level, the adoption of Christianity also served as a mode of resistance against the North's Arabic Islamic culture (Marchal 1991; Wheeler 1998). These trends notwithstanding, the civil war appeared to promote Islamization too. Islamic missionary aid organizations also helped refugees and fostered Islam among them. In a well-known essay on religious conversion in Africa, Robin Horton theorized that as microcosmic communities break down and as individuals establish wider geographical and social contacts, their members tend toward broader and stronger notions of the Supreme Being (Horton 1975). Horton used this thesis to explain the dramatic spread of Christianity and Islam in Africa during the colonial period. It may also explain the spread of both creeds among Southern Sudanese war refugees—a highly mobile population in the throes of community breakdown.

Numayri fell from power in 1985, but his Shari'a laws remained. At a time when the idea of secularism had become anathema to many educated Muslim Northerners, Islamic law in theory, if not practice, held wide social appeal. Many Northerners perceived Islam as an authentic indigenous and yet supranational identity that was capable of resisting the spread of Western global culture (El-Affendi 1991; Simone 1994; Sidahmed 1996).

Islam and Islamization became even more important politically in 1989, when the National Islamic Front (NIF), a group affiliated with the Muslim Brotherhood, rose to prominence following the military coup of General 'Umar al-Bashir. Like the Mahdist regime in the late nineteenth century, the NIF regime used pan-Islamic rhetoric to champion causes of *jihad* and anti-imperialism, in this case to wage war against resisters in the South and Nuba Mountains and to condemn the political, economic, and cultural influence of the West. However, the strongly partisan agenda of the NIF-Bashir regime also appeared threatening to many educated Muslim Northerners, and particularly to those, such as Communists, who had a history of political activism (al-Nur 1995). In the aftermath of the 1989 coup, thousands of Muslim Northerners sought exile in Egypt or farther afield.

In 1991, to emphasize its political autonomy and distance from the Western powers, the NIF-Bashir regime decided to support Iraq in the Gulf War. This move led to a chill in Sudanese relations with Saudi Arabia and the Gulf countries, and prompted Kuwait to expel its Sudanese work-migrants at war's end. As Sudanese lost jobs in other oil states, some sought refuge in Iran, Turkey, Syria, and Jordan, while many more looked to Europe, the United States, and Canada (Abusharaf 1997, 520–21).

In the 1990s, the Internet helped Sudanese in the diaspora to build communities across distances. At the same time, hampered by the weakness of the Sudan's internal communications, particularly outside Khartoum, migrants managed to keep in touch with home communities and to send remittances to them. For example, in a new variation on an old theme, one Nubian immigrant in Texas tapped into the World Wide Web to raise money among American donors for potable water facilities in his home village near Dongola (Abdelgadir 2000).[10]

While Sudanese abroad maintained contacts with the Sudan and with Sudanese, they also forged powerful connections in their host countries. Some took

---

10. At first, Awad A. Abdelgadir developed a website devoted to the fund-raising scheme alone, <http://members.aol.com/awadnubia/index.htm>, accessed 31 July 1999. A year later, he started a small e-business with a new commercial website, selling Sudanese hibiscus-mint tea while continuing to advertise the Nubian fund-raising scheme.

new citizenships—ironically not in Arabia and the Gulf States, where citizenship policies remained exclusive, but in the predominantly non-Muslim countries of Europe and North America. Moreover, children of these migrants gained hybrid, hyphenated identities, as Sudanese-Americans, British-Sudanese, and so on. In London, for example, some expatriates founded a special "Sudanese Supplementary School" in 1991 to help Sudanese children, first to retain their ethnic and religious identity (for example, by teaching them to read Arabic newspapers and say their prayers), and second to integrate more smoothly into British society (Mohamed 2000).

In the Sudan, refugee movements constituted the major internal migration of the late twentieth century and contributed to an exodus from the countryside to cities. Army migrations were also important, as soldiers or militia members fighting on both sides of the civil war traveled long distances in the course of battle. But otherwise, short-distance internal migration contracted substantially, as the result of prevailing instability, so that the Sudan lacked political and social coherence within the borders set a century before. By the 1990s, chronic civil war and economic mismanagement had been taking their toll. Domestic communications were breaking down, even as international communications grew stronger. Khartoum had television, radio, newspapers, and fax machines, but outlying regions did not (Boyd 1993, 63). Whereas in the colonial period one could send mail to the remotest corners of the Sudan, this was no longer possible. Instead, speed and dependability favored the mail service between Khartoum and New York or London, regardless of the state of foreign relations. In this country wracked by war, global culture was growing at the expense of national culture.

CONCLUSIONS: MIGRATION AND IDENTITY

The migrations of the past two centuries fostered the expansion of Islamic and Arabic culture in the Sudan. Slavery, urbanization, army recruitment patterns, and educational policies favored this trend. But these developments did not produce cultural homogeneity. Social distinctions remained even within large corporate categories (for example, of "Muslims" or "Arabs"), for at least three reasons. First, people tended to migrate in ethnic clusters, enabling them to stake out small communal identities. Second, many migrants accentuated cultural difference to preserve their separate identities. Often they did so by affirming moral superiority over others around them: hence, for example, the tendency of Blue Nile West Africans to stress the Muslim impiety or laxness of Sudanese, and of Kordofanian *jallaba* to stress the same vis-à-vis local nomads (Yamba 1995, 80;

Beck 1998). Third, many groups undertook multiple migrations, so that identities were always in flux—a feature that impeded assimilation and homogenization.

The case of the Basalwa in the twentieth century illustrates the trend of multiple migration. The Basalwa were poor Egyptian Nubians who migrated to Wadi Halfa in the 1920s to escape from Nile flooding. Inundations on the Sudanese side of the border, caused by the Aswan High Dam, forced them to migrate again in the late 1950s and early 1960s. Some went back to Egypt; others took Sudanese citizenship. In a Sudanese government-planned migration, the latter migrated along with other Sudanese Nubians to a purpose-built town at New Halfa, near the Atbara River (Dafalla 1975). In the 1970s and 1980s many Basalwa men migrated to the oil states as construction workers, earning funds that helped to make their once impoverished families into a prosperous business community. In New Halfa, the Basalwa used their income to establish their own social clubs, mosques, and schools. However, Basalwa migrants, returned from Arabia, found a way to accentuate their own social distinction vis-à-vis non-migrant co-ethnicists by establishing a special club to which members wore Saudi clothes (Sørbø 1985, 119–35). Thus the Basalwa, by the mid-1980s, were able to hold multiple identities, as Egyptians, Sudanese citizens, Nubians, New Halfans, and, in some cases, Saudi returnees.

This study began with the premise that community identities change, along with broader economic, political, and social trends, along routes of contact called migration. In exploring this thesis with reference to the Northern Sudan in the period from 1800 to 2000, the following general conclusions emerge. Global, national, and local identities do not erase each other; they coexist. By extension, large-scale social changes do not homogenize cultures, but rather lead to new, ever-changing, and overlapping cultural formations.

7

Globalization and the Internet

The Malaysian Experience

TOBY E. HUFF

Malaysia's "multimedia super corridor" (MSC) is that country's unique way of joining the "information society" and assisting the transition to the "knowledge economy." Since the Internet is a global construction, it is obviously at the heart of the "second" great transformation that is now going on under the heading of "globalization." Moreover, globalization and modernity today are clearly linked. Efforts to modernize forms of education, commerce, and government are all linked to the new modes of globalized communication and their mastery. At the same time, globalization implies adopting international standards, especially international standards of openness with regard to communication, commerce, and government as well as engineering and science.

From a business and commercial point of view, it is important to recognize that globalization is powered by three inexorable trends: globalization of communication, globalization of labor and commodity markets, and the networking of computers (within firms, between firms, nationally, and internationally). Transactions that in the past would have taken several days to execute—the time to write up an order physically, post it in the mail, and send it to an offsite location—can now be completed within seconds or minutes. All of this is taken for granted now in the United States and the Western world, but it is not yet a reality in most Muslim or other developing countries.

This report benefited from a visit to Malaysia in September 1999, made possible by the Center for Advanced Studies at the National University of Singapore, for which I express thanks. It was further updated by field observations in Malaysia between July and November 2001, made possible by a sabbatical leave granted to me by the University of Massachusetts, Dartmouth, for which I also express gratitude. This is a modified version of Huff 2001.

138

However, the leaders of Malaysia recognized some of the early signs of this great transformation in the early 1990s, and they proceeded quickly to create an Internet infrastructure that would adequately connect Malaysia to the Internet and lay the foundations for the transition to a knowledge-based economy. They hoped that their MSC would become a new engine of economic growth. The project was launched in 1996 and by 1999 it was up and running, clearly far ahead of all other Muslim-majority countries. The many current references to "failed modernity" in the Muslim world do not apply to Malaysia.[1]

THE MSC STORY

The MSC story begins with the "Vision 2020" statement and its commitment to making Malaysia a fully developed country by the year 2020. The Vision 2020 statement (Mahathir 1998, chap. 1) was created in 1991 by consultants at the Institute for Strategic and International Studies and later fully embraced by Prime Minister Mohammad Mahathir. But it was realized soon thereafter that bringing Malaysian average income up to that of a "fully developed" state by 2020—which was estimated to be about $US10,500 (in 1994 dollars) (McKinsey and Associates, as reported in John 2001, 16)—could not be achieved by focusing mainly on significant increases in manufacturing (projected to grow by approximately 7 percent per year and topping out at 38 percent of Gross Domestic Product in the mid-1990s (see fig. 7.1). To make the grade and to bring Malaysian wages up to the level of a fully developed country would require another strategy and another "engine" of economic growth. Consultants and advisers to the prime minister pointed out that the incipient Information and Computer Technology (ICT) revolution, then becoming apparent, was giving birth to a "new economy," the "information age" of the global economy. In a word, the advisers argued that the ICT revolution had within it the seeds that would give rise to the "knowledge economy" and that this would be the new engine of economic growth. If Malaysia could position itself to be part of this new global, knowledge-based economy, then it would be able to harness the new technology and propel itself into the status of a fully developed country by 2020.

It is interesting to note that a team of Australian experts had proposed a similar project in the late 1980s. It was called "multifunctional polis" but was turned down by the government because it was thought that creating a platform "to fast-

1. For a compelling analysis of the struggles that Middle Eastern and North African countries have been having in adjusting to globalization, see Henry and Springborg 2001.

FIGURE 7.1 MALAYSIA ECONOMIC GROWTH PROJECTION

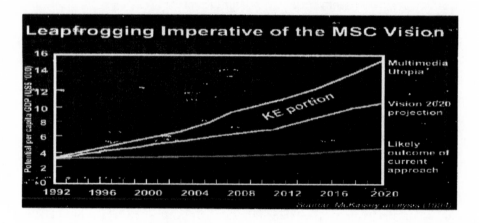

track next generation industries" was a task for private enterprise (*The Edge/Netv@lue2.0* 2001, 2). Consequently, one of the original team members, Dr. Terry Cutler, later became a member of the International Advisory Panel of the MSC and continues to serve on it.

In any event, the Malaysian plan centered on creating a new "platform" of information technology, a local, Malaysian-based version of the Internet-Web platform. It was finally conceived as a "multimedia super corridor," an ICT Utopia that would be a test-bed for all sorts of new multimedia/ICT applications. This new infrastructure and its products would create new jobs, produce new kinds of value-added products and services, and transform government, communication, and commerce in Malaysia. In the process it would (potentially) attract big multinational ICT corporations, ICT leaders such as Intel, Microsoft, Oracle, Compaq, HWP, and so forth. If the venture were successful, it would allow Malaysia to achieve its goal of being fully developed *and* would position Malaysia as a major ICT hub in Southeast Asia, even in the world.

In the end, the concept of a multimedia super corridor was adopted and its construction begun in 1996. By the summer of 1999 the fiber-optic core had been laid and was up and running at 2.5 gigbits/sec (expandable to 10 gigbits/sec) in the fifty-kilometer corridor stretching from the Petronas Twin Towers in Kuala Lumpur south to the newly opened Kuala Lumpur International Airport. In addition, MIMOS (the Malaysian Institute of Microelectronic Systems) had leased a high-speed telecommunication line from Penang in the north (the location of Malaysia's microchip facilities) south through the MSC/Kuala Lumpur corridor all the way to the southernmost city of Jahor Bahru, just a stone's throw across the straits from Singapore. Not only that, several private telecommunication companies had installed other high-speed lines connecting the north and south of the Malaysian peninsula with the MSC. Furthermore, MIMOS maintains four international lines running from the MSC to Japan, Canada, and the West coast of the United States (to San Francisco and Los Angeles). In the summer of 1999, the Japan-Malaysia connection was providing a heavily trafficked connection to users in China. Locally, Internet cafes were everywhere, and their charge for Internet service ranged between 60 cents and one US dollar an hour (RM [Malaysian Ringgits] 2, in September 1999 outside Kuala Lumpur). By the end of 1999, nearly 63,000 kilometers of fiber-optic cable had been laid (Malaysia 2001, 375).

During this first phase of the MSC, there were grand hopes for it that were stated in various brochures and Web pages. The MSC was to be:

• A vehicle for attracting world-class technology-led companies to Malaysia, and developing local industries;

• A multimedia Utopia offering a productive, intelligent environment within which a multimedia value chain of goods and services would be produced and delivered across the globe;

• An island of excellence with multimedia-specific capabilities, technologies, infrastructure, legislation, policies, and systems for competitive advantage;

• A test-bed for invention, research, and other ground-breaking multimedia developments spearheaded by seven multimedia applications;

• A global community living on the leading edge of the Information Society;

• A world of Smart Homes, Smart Cities, Smart Schools, Smart Cards, and Smart Partnerships. (http://www.mdc.my/index.html)

Despite the hype, the original conception of the MSC and its initial execution deserve high marks. If we make a comparison between the Malaysian MSC project and those of other parts of the Muslim world, then Malaysia looks very good indeed, as it is the most Internet-developed Muslim country (see tables 7.1 and 7.2). Table 7.1 indicates that the Middle East and North Africa region lags considerably behind Sub-Saharan Africa as well as East Asia and the Pacific region. The Middle East and North African region falls into the Middle Income range of countries but its Internet development is far below that of Middle Income countries. In Table 7.2 we see that among the Muslim countries listed, Malaysia is the most Internet-developed using the Internet host measure.

MALAYSIA'S MULTIMEDIA SUPER CORRIDOR

The MSC began as a physical corridor fifteen kilometers wide and fifty kilometers long stretching from Kuala Lumpur south to the Kuala Lumpur International

TABLE 7.1

INTERNET HOSTS BY REGION PER 10,000 PEOPLE,
JANUARY, 2000

Region	Internet Hosts per 10,000 Pop.
Middle East and North Africa	0.55
Sub-Saharan Africa	2.73
South Asia	0.22
East Asia & Pacific	2.69
Low Income	0.37
Middle Income	9.96
High Income	777.22
Low and Middle Income	5.40
World	120.02

Source: World Bank 2000/2001, Table 19, 310–11.

Airport. It also included two new cities: Putrajaya and Cyberjaya. The former is now the new government headquarters, opened for viewing on 21 June 1999 and fully occupied in the summer of 2001. Cyberjaya, the new "e-commerce center," was officially declared open on 8 July 1999 and has now attracted over 550 local and international ICT businesses. Between these new cities and Kuala Lumpur, a high-speed, high-capacity fiber-optic Internet backbone was laid with the official intention of providing all the technology and points of access that any individual, educational institution, or business enterprise would need to have full access to the Web. It is evident that Malaysia, as a developing country, does not have the resources to install all the technological infrastructure that would be required to enable the whole country to be wired for the Internet.[2] Consequently, the development of this corridor represents a limited social experiment that promises to enable Malaysia to become part of the information-age economy, a society in

2. The Malaysian government originally rejected the idea of simply opening up the development of the Internet to private enterprise. Their feeling was that private enterprise would develop the infrastructure in a very uneven fashion, and that it would be far less committed to the values of Malaysian society and a principled attempt to provide equality of access. However, the telecommunications industry in Malaysia is now fully privatized.

TABLE 7.2

INTERNET HOSTS BY COUNTRY PER 10,000 PEOPLE,
JANUARY 2000

Country	Internet Hosts per 10,000 Pop.
Algeria	0.01
Egypt	0.73
Iran	0.09
Jordan	1.27
Kuwait	20.5
Lebanon	10.93
Morocco	0.33
Saudi Arabia	1.28
Syria	0.0
Tunisia	0.1
Turkey	13.92
Yemen	0.02
Malaysia	25.43

Source: World Bank 2001, 310, table 19.

which the free flow of information of all kinds provides the basic resource for economic development and productivity. The Malaysian leadership knows that joining the ranks of the global "information society" will lead to a completely open-ended and unknown terrain, and therefore the establishment of this corridor of unfettered access to the Web is a social and economic experiment. The political authorities and Prime Minister Mahathir Mohamad are fully supportive of this leap into cyberspace and the information age.

Behind this leap of faith is the fear that with the emergence of the information-age economy and a postindustrial world, Malaysians will be perpetually stuck in an underdeveloped condition; wealthy countries will continually shed unattractive "sunset" industries, assigning them to poor countries such as Malaysia. Thus, in order to attain the status of a fully developed country by the year 2020, the government has adopted the hi-tech strategy that they believe will enable them to arrive at the forefront of social, economic, and technological development in the early twenty-first century.

To accomplish the aims of the MSC project in twenty years, there were to be three phases of activity. During the first phase the Multimedia Development Corporation (MDC) would successfully create the MSC and attract a core group of world-class companies. Next it would establish new "intelligent cities" (Cyberjaya and Putrajaya) and launch seven "Flagship Applications" that would give content to the MSC and draw people to it for Web-based services. In the third and final phase Malaysia would be transformed into a knowledge-based society (http://www.mdc.my/index.html). Moreover, the Malaysian leadership and those in charge of developing the MSC (that is, MDC), have attempted to address the whole range of technical, economic, manpower, and legal questions that have to be resolved in order for the MSC to become a functioning and viable economic reality.

For example, the MDC has issued a series of directives and legal initiatives that would guarantee no censorship on the Internet within the MSC. Likewise, traditional foreign ownership regulations have been lifted for business firms located on the MSC. Recognizing the shortage of "knowledge workers" in Malaysia, the MDC has set up a knowledge workers exchange (KWX) and allowed virtually unrestricted entry of such workers employed by MSC-status companies. Knowledge workers are defined as those who "create, collect, manipulate and disseminate information and knowledge using electronic technologies and computer tools" (MDC press release, 12 November 1998). These workers are further categorized as Core Service, Support Service, and Supplementary Service workers. This exchange facility has established a central database (and website) so that business enterprises can quickly find the workers they need, recognizing that Malaysia itself cannot provide the vastly expanded pool of workers for this new information-age society based on the use of information technology (IT). It is estimated that by the year 2003, an additional 32,000 such knowledge workers will be needed, which is projected to be 20 percent of the labor force (MDC press release, 12 November 1998). To further cope with that impending labor shortage, a Multimedia University has been established (on two campuses, one in Cyberjaya and the other in Malacca) with a student body of five thousand. This privately-operated institution, which plans to increase enrollment to eight thousand, now recruits only from the top 5 percent of pre-university students and puts them through a rigorous program in math and science training when they first arrive on campus, prior to their actual training in the "new skill set" required by the emerging knowledge-based economy.

VISIONS OF THE INFORMATION SOCIETY

In addition to these strategic considerations, a series of papers addressing the political, social, and economic implications of the MSC have been written and delivered before a variety of audiences in Malaysia and Southeast Asia, including Japan. These papers, written by a major participant in the MSC development project, Dr. Tengku Azzman Sheriffadeen, provide a sociological emphasis and reflect the degree to which the Malaysians have thought out the larger political, economic, and global implications of their project. The following discussion, however, touches on only part of the extensive literature generated by the leadership of the MSC, especially by those associated with MIMOS and the National Information Technology Council (NITC)

On one level, the innovative MSC project deliberately attempts to build upon the profound shift in social, political, and economic relations that we refer to as globalization. On the other hand, the rise of the information age and the information-based economy will undoubtedly lead to significant internal transformations of all societies that embrace the Internet. Accordingly it is striking and promising that a major figure in the transformation of Malaysia has developed such an optimistic and progressive outlook on the impact of this new global phenomenon. This view has been articulated by Dr. Sheriffadeen, a Malaysian CEO and thinker, trained in engineering, who has served on various advisory boards governing the MSC. As the CEO of MIMOS, Sheriffadeen has played a major role in shaping the original conception, design, and ideology of the MSC.

Among the first strategic initiatives undertaken by MIMOS (and hence by Sheriffadeen and his associates) in the early 1990s was the creation of the NITC. That body quickly moved to create a National Information Technology Agenda (NITA).[3] Thereafter MIMOS served as the secretariat for NITC, and together they worked to create the project that came to be known as the MSC.

In the early 1990s, Sheriffadeen wrote a series of papers that explore the social, political, and economic dimensions of the new information technology and that make recommendations about the particular direction that the MSC should take. That direction can be called "human intelligence enhancement." It should be noted that all of the ideas set out by Sheriffadeen were formulated in the early 1990s and before the end of 1997, illustrating how prescient the Malaysian leadership was in coming to terms with ICT and the global transformation.

3. This agenda is fully published on various web pages; see <http://www.nitc.org.my/resources/papers.html>.

In a paper titled "Moving Toward a More Intelligent Use of Human Intelligence" (Sheriffadeen 1995), Sheriffadeen focuses both on the technical possibilities of IT and on the ability of the new IT to enhance human capacity, human values, and economic well-being—which appear to be his main interest. Speaking of the technical wonders of the new digital forms of communication, he mentions the so-called "Negroponte switch" that allows digital information "that is on the ground to go into the air [via satellites] and that which is now in the air will go into the ground. We may therefore envision," he continues, "fully mobile untethered multimedia communication to be soon widely available in the true spirit of anyone, anywhere, anytime, and anything" (1995, 3). Sheriffadeen sees this purely technical advance as having a number of radical social, economic, and political implications. For example, "Widespread ownership of information processing tools and information content will democratize societies in new ways. Societies in general will see greater sharing of rights and responsibilities due to the wider and more rapid diffusion of information. Corporations can no longer operate as hierarchical organizations where decisions are only made at the top. Even governments will not be able to claim exclusivity over major national issues in this democratizing process under the onslaught of IT" (Sheriffadeen 1995, 3).

At the same time, Sheriffadeen realizes that technology per se will not solve all our problems, but that we as social actors must take the initiative—a sort of "social pull" responding to a "technological push"—to create the information society that we wish to live in. He is explicit that this technological revolution is a "paradigm shift [that] is fundamentally a social and cultural phenomenon" (1995, 4).

From a strictly economic point of view, the old paradigm focused on land, labor, and capital has undergone a radical shift. Now the underlying source of value is neither land nor labor, but information. It is this contemporary shift that underlies the emerging "new growth theory" in economics, especially in the work of the American economist Paul Romer (1990). Likewise, the recently published World Bank study (1997) advances this argument. As Sheriffadeen puts it, "Economic and social value will increasingly accrue from human assets. Intelligence and creativity of the people will determine the economic and political status of whole nations. Henceforth the generation and application of new knowledge and technology will set the competitiveness level of their industries" (1995, 4). Underlying this view is the deeper insight that ideas are commodities and that because ideas are basically infinite in supply, the so-called law of diminishing returns is overturned.

Sheriffadeen also holds the view that there will be multiple versions of the information society: "just as there are many cultures, languages, and civilizations there will be many different kinds of Information Society" (1995, 3). What each society needs is an "infostructure," a technical cum human infrastructure that will maximize the human potential to access information and to create value-added commodities and services. In addition, Dr. Sheriffadeen points out that with the new global marketplace based on the flow of information, individuals, corporations, and governments can get the information they need from any service provider, located anywhere in the world. Earlier Sheriffadeen linked this development to the Uruguay round of GATT agreements and the issue of tradability. With the new information-based products, there is a "blurring of the line between core and peripheral" countries, and "IT based services can now be generated anywhere or other and then consumed at any other location" (Sheriffadeen 1994, 3). This statement seems to suggest that all potential local providers are put on notice that they must compete on a level set by international, global standards, not by those of any one country.

CHALLENGES AHEAD

This sketch of Internet development in Malaysia serves to highlight the huge challenges that now confront all societies. In the Malaysian case, we see a Muslim majority state that relatively quickly saw the implications of the Internet for economic development and rapidly prepared the way for its implementation.[4] Malaysian leaders have chosen the emerging set of hi-tech/information technologies as a supplementary engine of economic growth for the purpose of achieving the status of a fully developed country. By the early 1990s, as pointed out earlier, the political and business elite of Malaysia realized that even fully developing the manufacturing sector would not be sufficient to make Malaysia a fully developed country by 2020 as Prime Minister Mahathir planned. Consequently Malaysia opted to make Internet-based industries a major component of its national innovation system (Freeman 1995; Lundvall 1988; Nelson 1993). Because a focus on developing national systems of innovation is a very recent phenomenon (only identified in the economics literature of the late 1980s), Malaysia's efforts in this direction constituted a bold undertaking and forced its

4. The 1991 census gave a breakdown of the population as follows: 57 percent Malay and indigenous descent (who are presumed to be Muslims), 27 percent Chinese, about 8 percent Indian, and the balance composed of non-Malays and non-Malaysians. As reported in Europa Publications 1996, 2069.

leaders to plunge into the technicalities of defining just what a knowledge-based economy entails and how to get there (among others see NITC/MIMOS 1999 and 2000).

But there are also obvious worries regarding the potential political uses of the Web, anxieties that are shared no doubt by all political leaders. Although the study of the political uses of the Internet is only just beginning, early indications suggest that the Internet is used by many individuals to express political and anti-government sentiments.

However, in their inquiry based on the analysis of messages posted on the various Usenet news groups by country, Kevin Hill and John Hughes found that only 33 percent of all messages posted could be labeled as "political" (1998, 81). Of those messages that were political in nature, about 24 percent were anti-government messages, while 19 percent of all such messages were pro-government. As a percentage of all messages posted in the Usenet groups, anti-government messages accounted for only 8.5 percent. Conversely, of all posted messages, pro-government political messages accounted for only 6.4 percent (Hill and Hughes 1998, 84). While the Internet is a medium of anti-regime expression, anti-political messages are not a major portion of all messages posted, as judged by these results. This finding leads to the question of how much public expression of political opinions, especially negative ones, can governments in transition to democracy withstand without collapsing. At the same time Kevin Hill and John E. Hughes found that there is a significant correlation between the level of anti-government postings by country and democratization: as the level of democracy increases, the rate of anti-government postings drops (1998, 87–88).

In this connection, Malaysia's recent experience of political turmoil surrounding the deposition of former deputy prime minister Anwar Ibrahim is an interesting test case. For despite the early threats of the Malaysian government to monitor Internet cafes, it remained faithful to its promise not to censor any aspect of Internet communication. The MSC remained fully operational and free of censorship. There is little doubt that this was connected to the promises made by Prime Minister Mahathir and the careful monitoring of developments in Malaysia by the international board of directors who serve as advisers to the MSC. These directors are drawn from the ranks of the CEOs of high-profile global corporations, including Compaq, Microsoft, Sun MicroSystems, Cisco Systems, among many others, and internationally recognized technology experts. Hence, Malaysia's leaders realized that Malaysia was now tightly bound into the new "network society" and global economic system; even during the political crisis surrounding Anwar, the government encouraged all potential users of the Internet to use it. Indeed, the political struggles surrounding the Anwar affair spawned the first fully online Malaysian newspaper, *Malaysiakini* (http://www.malaysiakini.com), that still thrives. It publishes a broader range of opinions than does the regular print press, though it seems to attract mainly a highly literate and educated segment of the population.

Practically speaking, there are serious technical and manpower issues. On a technical level, the Internet cannot operate without an efficient telecommunications system and, increasingly, without wide bandwidth or fiber-optic cable networking. Installing such a system is expensive and can only be achieved by drawing upon the resources of private industry. Privatizing, thus allowing private industry to take over the telecommunications system, is, as noted earlier, a major hurdle for developing countries everywhere.

The manpower demands of the new information-based economy and the Internet world are daunting. As noted, the Malaysians began to address this challenge by creating the KWX and launching a new kind of university, the Multimedia University, devoted to teaching the new skill set. At the same time, the Malaysians have allowed, and sometimes sponsored, research on the present state of manpower resources in Malaysia. A World Bank report, for example, highlighted the fact that the demand for highly skilled workers exceeds the supply (World Bank 1997). In short, the manpower recruitment problem is essentially global today. It is well known that American corporations, representing the largest economy in the world, recruit IT workers globally, especially from India (Saxenian 1999). Malaysia has to compete with Singapore's high demand for IT/knowledge workers and their program of recruiting high school students in India before they can be snatched by global corporations.[5]

SUMMARY

The arrival of the new global network and global economy based on IT has ushered in a radically new social and cultural era. The new information-based economy is clearly becoming established globally. For countries that wish to join this new economy, the price of admission is connecting to the Internet and establish-

5. I thank my colleagues at the National University of Singapore, Zaheer Baber and Ho Kong Chong, for these insights learned from conversations with them in August 1999 while I was a Fellow at the Center for Advanced Studies.

ing transparency of economic activities. Many countries are averse to such transparency of economic information.

Setting aside all the political and practical difficulties that face any country attempting to transform itself into an information-based economy, the case of Malaysia reveals the fundamental challenges that must be confronted by countries around the world. These challenges stem from the fact that the world economy is being transformed in a radical way, and that all of the old assumptions about the conduct of business as well as the conduct of government are being transformed. Once the (Internet) infrastructure is in place, start-up costs for entering this new world economy seem to be especially low, but in the long run, only those societies that freely enter that electronic world using the latest IT will be able to achieve the highest levels of development that the new IT makes possible. Those who do not enter this new information-based marketplace may be confined to exporting raw materials and manufacturing low-level, labor-intensive commodities of modest value added.

All of these challenges suggest that the relationship between science, technology, and economic growth (as well as between legal structures and economic growth) will have to be rethought in Muslim societies as well as in others. Malaysia perhaps has an advantage because it was able to eliminate the most onerous gender-based disparities while transforming the basic structure of traditional Islamic law (Horowitz 1994).

Although economists since the 1950s have emphasized the importance of technological factors as inputs in the process of economic growth (as shown by Robert Solow's work of the 1950s), the latest version of the theory has redefined "technology" to mean "instructions that we follow for combining raw materials" (Romer 1990, 72; Nelson and Romer 1996, 14 ff.). This version suggests that (1) ideas are economic commodities, and (2) economic growth remains virtually unlimited, so long as nations promote the social conditions that are conducive to creativity and innovation. These conditions are intimately tied to what I call the "public sphere," a completely open (and open-ended) sphere in which all individuals can express their thoughts and pursue their ideas and interests unfettered by political or religious censors (Huff 1997). Moreover, in Tengku Azzman Sheriffadeen's view, this new constellation of IT constitutes a "shift from the traditional centralized power structure to the flatter distributed, web-like networks of communities [and] will require new forms of governance to evolve where the individual is empowered and government intervention is greatly reduced" (Sheriffadeen 1997, 10).

Ideally, Sheriffadeen imagines a "self-regulating society, with virtually unlimited access to information, where the wise rule and the people actively participate in determining their destiny, [and create] a caring society with the notion of human dignity forming the cornerstone of the individual's inalienable right against poverty and starvation" (1997, 10).

Prime Minister Mahathir has given considerable support and funding to the new International Islamic University located on the outskirts of Kuala Lumpur. Its new campus in Gombak is projected to increase enrollment from about twelve thousand to twenty thousand students in the near future. Though the International Islamic University has adopted an agenda of "Islamizing" its curriculum, it in fact conforms to the American model with English as the primary language of instruction. It is this university, according to some reports, that promises to project Malaysian students onto an "international level of achievement" (Hassan 2001). At the same time, the Malaysian government has founded several new universities and technological institutes. Indeed, the MDC accredits more than twenty institutions of higher learning (public and private) with "MSC status," implying that they are either heavy users or significant trainers of ICT personnel (http://www.mdc.com.my).

On the economic level, this new network of communication seems to be indispensable for achieving the highest and most efficient levels of economic as well as political development. In any event, there are good reasons for thinking that scientific and technological innovation are intimately tied together and that both are tied to economic development. As Paul Romer puts it, in the next several decades, "the features that will increasingly differentiate one geographic area (or city or country) from another [economically] will be the quality of public institutions. The most successful will be the ones with the most competent and effective mechanisms for supporting collective interests, especially the production of new ideas" (Romer 1993, 89).

It is just this task of creating the cultural and institutional conditions conducive to creativity and innovation that poses the greatest challenge. It raises in the most fundamental way the old issues of censorship, but now the medium of exchange is increasingly electronic. While people often imagine that this is a venue of free-flowing and anonymous communication, there are indeed monitoring issues that transcend those of political censorship. The need for secure communication means both that private transactions have to be guaranteed privacy and that the possibility of tracking potential criminals (and purveyors of highly destructive viruses) must also be possible. These are issues that far transcend the aims of political leaders who wish to control communication and prevent public expression of anti-government sentiments (Huff 2000; Lessig 1999, among others). A variety of models for the control of Internet communication are now being fashioned. Not surprisingly, they range from the authoritarian to the open-ended. The Malaysians have instituted various "cyberlaws" that seek to guarantee copyright protection as well as the free and uncensored flow of information on the MSC. The most significant evidence that Malaysia intends to keep this promise is the fact that during its first Internet-age political crisis, the deposition of former deputy prime minister Anwar Ibrahim, there was no state-sponsored Internet censorship. However, like many other countries, the Malaysians plan to create a "cyber police force" to monitor criminal acts taking place on the Internet, just as the Germans have created a "cyber sheriff" who is to be in charge of investigating cyber crimes (as cited in Corey 1998, 17). Singapore has installed various proxy servers that function to monitor the "broadcasting" of certain kinds of messages that are deemed socially or politically harmful, while foreign businesses are allowed unrestricted Internet communication (Corey 1998, 10–13; also see Lingle 1998, 157–89; Davies 1999, 77–107). Likewise, it is claimed that email communication in Singapore is not monitored by the government, while the government itself makes unannounced and unauthorized entries into individuals' computers.[6] In Saudi Arabia, officials have installed a variety of software-blocking mechanisms that prevent access to various forbidden sites, which are always changing (Jehl 1999).

All of these issues suggest that the big political issues of freedom of expression and democracy in the Muslim world (as elsewhere) in the twenty-first century will be fought out within the context of the radically new medium of exchange that we call the Internet.[7]

6. "More than 2,000,000 SingNet and Singtel Magix customers' computers, or close to half of all Internet subscribers here, are being scanned without their knowledge to see if their systems are vulnerable to hacker attacks." Spokesmen for the companies then have the audacity to claim, "There is no invasion of privacy at all. Basically what we did was to check if the systems had open windows through which hackers can exploit" (Chong Chee Kin 1999).

7. The really big issues concerning the "architecture" of the Web, including all of the hidden means of tracking and surveillance, especially by commercial agents, have only just become visible and have been set out with striking verve by Lawrence Lessig (1999). Consequently, at the moment the threat of surveillance of individuals on the Web is far greater than the threats to political regimes, authoritarian or otherwise.

8

The Global Mufti

JAKOB SKOVGAARD-PETERSEN

In the fall of 1998, the newspaper *al-Hayat* advertised a new religious program to be aired on al-Jazeera television channel: "The Shari'a and Life are Inseparable," said the headline, and the advertisement continued: "Ahmad Mansur presents the program *Al-shari'a wa-al-haya* [Shari'a and Life] in a style radically different from the traditional format of religious programs. He will host the honorable Shaykh Dr. Yusuf al-Qaradawi and a number of great *'ulama'*. They will give the verdict [*hukm*] and the view [*ra'y*] of the Shari'a on contemporary issues and events in the spheres of life, economy, and politics. In the program *Shari'a and Life* the great *'ulama'* of the tolerant Shari'a will answer questions put to them by viewers."

The new program was broadcast on the satellite channel al-Jazeera, and it was announced in the international newspaper *al-Hayat*. Both *al-Hayat* and al-Jazeera are major players in the new global Arab media. Although dating back to the 1940s, *al-Hayat* was relaunched in the late 1980s from its new headquarters in London and rose in the early 1990s to become the newspaper of choice for Arab intellectuals all over the world. Its standard of reporting is consistently high, and its opinion pages are truly international in terms of scope and contributors.

Even more momentous is the rise of al-Jazeera. Taking advantage of the 1996 breakup of the alliance between the Saudi-owned Orbit channel and the BBC, the Qatar-based al-Jazeera was able to sign up a team of skillful and courageous journalists from the BBC project, among them the Syrian Faysal al-Qasim, whose program *Opposite Direction* has scandalized the political establishment of every Arab country with the exception of Lebanon. Among the program's recent scoops are live speeches by Saddam Hussein, revelations of King Hussein's secret relations with Israel—leading Jordan to close al-Jazeera's office in Amman—and an interview with terrorist leader Usama bin Ladin. In December 1998 the

Arab States Broadcasting Union gave al-Jazeera six months to conform to the Arab media code of honor. So far, however, Qatar's young emir Hamad ibn Khalifa al-Thani has valiantly defended the channel, which runs on a five-year government grant.

Opposite Directions features live debates between two opponents who under the current systems of censorship in the Arab world are unlikely to exchange views in any other medium, and questions and comments are phoned in from Arabs all over the world. Berber nationalists and Libyan officials, representatives of Morocco and the Polisario, of Kuwait and Iraq, and Islamists and secularists are seated opposite one another, and compete through words and gestures for the sympathy of the audience. Al-Jazeera also features other programs, such as *More than One Opinion,* based on similar potentially explosive talk show formats. The channel certainly lives up to its slogan of "One View, Another View."

Needless to say, this is an important expression of a new kind of globalization. Telecommunications is a central component, if not the very essence, of the current drive for globalization. And satellite television, which makes ample use of phone-in programs and succeeds in defying states and governments, is a truly revolutionary phenomenon in the Arab world. In terms of audience, issues, and style, al-Jazeera is evidence of, and certainly furthers, a cosmopolitan Arab identity in which Arabs in Europe and the United States are no longer at the margins but are participants in one huge Arab public sphere.

John Anderson and Dale Eickelman characterized al-Jazeera as "TV on an internet model" because it is marked by audience fragmentation, diversity, and active seeking over passive receiving (1999, 59–61). With its emphasis on consumer choice and the breakdown of state-sponsored "great narratives," this description seems to be in line with some characterizations of postmodernism, a theme to which I shall return.

This article will investigate the impact of the al-Jazeera phenomenon on contemporary Arab understandings of Islam. How does "One View, Another View" translate into the language of religion and Islam? Is *Shari'a and Life* a radical break with tradition, as it claims—and, if so, in what ways? In the following, I will contrast the program and its center of gravity, Yusuf al-Qaradawi, with the greatest star of Arab Islamic state-sponsored television, Shaykh al-Sha'rawi.

YUSUF AL-QARADAWI—THE NEW MEDIA SHAYKH

The choice of Yusuf al-Qaradawi for al-Jazeera's religious program seems obvious on several accounts. Yusuf al-Qaradawi is an Egyptian *'alim,* based in Qatar, where he is dean of the Shari'a faculty. He is a scholar of international reputation, the author of some ninety books, and one of the prominent figures in the current Islamic awakening.

Yusuf al-Qaradawi studied theology at al-Azhar and was involved in student strikes and demonstrations—and he claims to have taken part in the fighting against the British in the Azhar student battalion in the Suez Canal area—in the turbulent years prior to the revolution. In 1953 he founded a youth organization at al-Azhar with the goals of modernizing the university, admitting female students, and introducing English into the curriculum. Its main vision, however, was to instill an activist identity in the Azhar student body. This was the main theme that al-Qaradawi, encouraged by his mentor Muhammad al-Ghazzali, propounded in its program, entitled "Your Mission, Sons of Azhar" (al-Qaradawi 1984, preface).

Because of his links to the Muslim Brotherhood, al-Qaradawi was sent to a prison camp in 1954. Since then, he has spent most of his time outside Egypt, but he is a frequent visitor and commentator in the Islamist press. His standing as an 'alim and mujahid and his independence from the state-run Egyptian religious establishment have made him one of the most respected 'ulama' in the Arab world. His books have sold in the hundreds of thousands. The fact that he has been on the editorial board of such widely different publications as the Oxford Journal of Islamic Studies and al-Da'wa, Egypt's radical Islamist magazine of the 1970s, closed down by Sadat, gives evidence of his standing today.

Many of al-Qaradawi's books are centered around the phenomenon of the Islamic awakening, hailed by him as the most important and positive event of our age. His full endorsement of the present awakening's slogan, "Islam is the Solution," has recently led Armando Salvatore to characterize him as a "solutionist" (1997, 84–89). It is, however, a central tenet of al-Qaradawi's that the 'ulama' must be in charge of the awakening. This idea runs contrary to the understanding of many young activists, who see the 'ulama' as backward government stooges, but it is not far from the Egyptian government's idea of tackling the problem of militant Islamism. Consequently, in 1989, al-Qaradawi was one of a small group of 'ulama' who tried to mediate between the government and the Islamists.

According to al-Qaradawi, the Islamic awakening, bereft of 'ulama' leadership, would lead to extremism; there are already elements in the awakening, he argues, who envision themselves as prophets, unwilling to listen to or compromise with others and unable to distinguish between what is haram and what is simply best avoided (al-Qaradawi 1984, 94). It is only the 'ulama' who can provide mature leadership, because of their knowledge of scripture and the Islamic disciplines.

But this leadership requires that the *'ulama'* abandon their secure state-sponsored positions and learn about contemporary issues from other Muslim specialists. The *'ulama'*, then, are not a priesthood but simply people who have had the privilege of studying Islam and who have a duty to share their understanding with laymen, and with each other. Islam, says al-Qaradawi, is only realized in critical and public discussion. Freedom of thought and speech is thus a prerequisite of true Islam.

It is no coincidence that this sounds like the *islah* movement of the early twentieth century. Al-Qaradawi is a product of al-Maraghi's reform plans for al-Azhar, and he often quotes Salafis such as Muhammad 'Abduh, Muhammad Khidr Husayn, Mustafa al-Maraghi, and 'Abd al-Majid al-Salim. He has also taken up their internationalism and sees al-Azhar as a potential beacon for Muslims all over the world. Finally, like them he is a believer in the new media and recognizes this potential for Islam, even though there may be drawbacks. As he explained in Qatari television's first broadcast of its religious program *Huda al-Islam:* media are not evil in themselves, they can only be put to evil use. They can, however, also be used to spread useful, moral, and religious teachings. This instrumentalist view of the media—that we know also from the Christian Right in America—has allowed him to transform himself into a media mufti. It does not, however, endorse an uncritical use of the media. On the contrary, al-Qaradawi insists that the individual Muslim must take responsibility and choose for himself, or, as he puts it, "each man must be his own *mufti*" (al-Qaradawi 1984, preface).

SHARI'A AND LIFE

Let us turn now from the TV station and al-Qaradawi to his program itself. *Shari'a and Life* is an eighty-minute weekly call-in talk show with two men sitting at a table, Yusuf al-Qaradawi with his spectacles, Azhari turban, and *galabiyya*, and the host, Hamid al-Ansari, in regular Gulf attire. While this is not exactly innovative, the questions raised in the program often are, as illustrated, for example, by the session on "contemporary *fiqh*" on 28 February 1999.

The issue was abortion. A woman calling from the United States was four months and two weeks pregnant. Several doctors had told her that the fetus had severe brain damage and would be heavily mentally retarded or perhaps die. Everybody advised her to have an abortion, but she wanted al-Qaradawi's endorsement.

Al-Qaradawi began by noting that the woman's plight is a good example of contemporary *fiqh* because it presupposes new medical techniques. But he could not endorse an abortion because the fetus was old enough to be a human being, complete with spirit. Thus, he adhered to what amounts to a consensus today among the *'ulama'*, that abortion is endorsed by Islam in the first four months if the fetus is seriously defective (Rispler-Chaim 1993, 15).

There is a small addition to the story, though. Feeling that he could not leave it at that, al-Qaradawi consolingly told of a similar incident when in a *fatwa* he had refused to allow an abortion, but later received a photo of a healthy boy. He therefore advised the woman to leave the matter to God and to trust in Him.

Phrases such as "leave it to God" (*khalliha ila Allah*) and "trust in God" *(tawakkul)*, however, are rare in al-Qaradawi's writing; he habitually scorns Sufis and conservative *'ulama'* alike for their fatalism and apathy. In his books, al-Qaradawi also maintains that analysis and scientific investigation should not be conducted over the mass media, but in specialist publications (al-Qaradawi 1990, 31). The proper role of television and radio then is to allow discussion and to educate. Al-Qaradawi's consoling remarks are revealing of an emotional quality of television with which he is perhaps not quite at ease, but which others, like al-Sha'rawi, have skillfully exploited.

Yet, this is still television with a human dimension, a program worth watching for many Muslims. The format is fixed: in the first half hour, al-Ansari and al-Qaradawi discuss the subject in a broad sense, while the phone number of the program is displayed on the screen. In the second part of the program, al-Qaradawi is consulted over faxes and phones—roughly two-thirds from Europe and the rest from the various Arab countries. The predominance of Europe does not, however, reflect lack of access to the program in the Arab world; rather, it has to do with a lack of alternatives—both of muftis and of Islamic programs—in Europe, and with greater affluence and experience in long distance calls there. And some of the issues, such as democracy, human rights, and the Islamic legitimacy of Arab governments, are perhaps best commented upon by Muslims living in Europe.

Many of the people who phone in do not seem to be particularly interested in asking questions, but simply seek to air a view. Often they succeed, at least in part, before al-Ansari asks them to state their question. Sometimes the questioner is interrupted, or al-Ansari and al-Qaradawi refuse to answer or comment. Occasionally, callers are severely rebuked, as was a man in Paris who had sworn by the Qur'an to stop gambling but had fallen back into his old habits and now contritely asked what to do (al-Qaradawi 1999, 7 March). On the not infrequent occasion when people complain about being forced to resort to bribery, they are told to direct their complaints to the appropriate authorities. The overall impression is certainly that of a relatively free forum for opinions, enhanced by al-Ansari's open role as a moderator who seeks to make people stick to the issue and ask questions. Some of these questions—such as the one on abortion—were slightly embarrassing to al-Qaradawi and seem to indicate that the program is not prefabricated.

But compared with the other talk shows on al-Jazeera, al-Qaradawi's does not really adhere to the slogan "One View, Another View." Yusuf al-Qaradawi's opinions are certainly the correct ones, he is the expert, and he is not there to entertain but to educate. There is the occasional minor challenge, for example, when a man from Mecca stated that it is the Muslim scholars (al-'ulama' wa-al-mujtahidun) who created the internal strife (fitna) in the umma, or when al-Ansari teasingly asked al-Qaradawi why he has not produced one single first-class 'alim in all his years in Qatar. But these are just small exceptions. All in all, Yusuf al-Qaradawi represents the Shari'a, and everybody else represents Life.

Let me end this characterization of the program with an account of a session that clearly would not have been possible on an Egyptian or, for that matter, any other traditional state-run channel. It was called "The Violence of the Islamic Groups, and the Violence of the Regimes," and it specifically addressed the problem of violence as counter-violence of the Arab regimes. Yusuf al-Qaradawi dismissed explanations of violence that stressed poverty and misery as "overly materialistic," and explanations based on conspiracy theories as "evading responsibility." To him, the core of the problem was lack of moral leadership, that is, the absence of morally committed and moderate 'ulama'. As it was now, there were, on the one hand, the 'ulama' of the government, and on the other, ignorant youngsters (shabab), each considering himself to be shaykh al-islam, a recurrent theme in al-Qaradawi's writings on the Islamic awakening. But this phenomenon was in itself related to the lack of dialogue, democracy, and debate in the whole of the Arab world, where dissent is not tolerated and elections are rigged. Pressure always generates counter-pressure. Added to this is the "Shari'a masquerade," where Islam is officially declared the religion of the country and the Shari'a the main source of legislation. Moreover, it was very often the security forces who caused the violence to escalate, for instance in Algeria and in the Egyptian south, where the tradition of blood feud will ensure that the cycle of violence could go on forever (al-Qaradawi 1999, 21 Feb.).

This statement provoked a number of phone calls—most of them sympathizing with the radical groups—but al-Qaradawi referred to Ibn Taymiyya's famous fatwa about the Mongols' mixing of laws and pointed out that even Ibn Taymiyya mainly appealed to the Mamluks to change things: changing laws is solely the responsibility of the state.

At the end al-Qaradawi turned to the issue of government-sponsored media campaigns against Islamist groups. It was clear, he said, that the official media could not reach the violent groups. The problem was that their programs and serials were unconvincing. At this point he became so upset that he spoke in Egyptian vernacular about a film he had seen, in which a young Islamist terrorist was paid forty Egyptian pounds a day to spread his terror. All this was nonsense. What a wrong use of the media! True Islamic media should be edifying.

THE GLOBAL *UMMA*

As already mentioned, the Jazeera phenomenon is an important component in the process of globalization, as is the very format of *Shari'a and Life.* Globalization is also sometimes explicitly mentioned in the program, at times derided as little more than a euphemism for Westernization, common in the Arab media (al-Qaradawi 1999, 28 Feb.).

What is more important, however, is that globalization is constantly reflected in the idea of Islam as it is espoused in the program. In *Shari'a and Life,* God is rarely mentioned, apart from a small introductory invocation. Yusuf al-Qaradawi prefers to speak of Islam, or rather, of the Shari'a and of the *umma,* the world Muslim community, and its recent history. The unity of all Muslims is of central concern to al-Qaradawi. Naturally, this was the theme after the *'Id al-Adha*—the feast observed by all Muslims in the world, as well as by the hundred of thousands of pilgrims during the yearly pilgrimage. Unlike the more militant Islamists, al-Qaradawi seems convinced that Muslims by and large are religious and committed to following the Shari'a, even if they do not know it well enough and are in need of guidance. To al-Qaradawi, the word *umum* (pl. of *umma*) should not be used, for there is only one *umma.* The Shari'a demands that Muslims unite, and at a time when the Europeans and the Americans set up interstate bodies, it is only natural that the same should be done in the Islamic world, which, because of Islam, is already culturally united (al-Qaradawi 1999, 28 Mar.). For al-Qaradawi, Islam is very much identical with the contemporary *umma* of more than one billion people, who are juxtaposed with other civilizations of the globe.

This is also the view of the program as a whole, which became evident in a broadcast in which al-Qaradawi's substitute was 'Abd al-Rahim 'Ali, president of the African World University, and Hamid al-Ansari's substitute was Ahmad Mansur, host of another al-Jazeera talk show. The subject was Africa. A major issue was that Africa's Arab heritage was unknown to the Arabs, because European colonialism had successfully cut Africa off from the Arab world. This isolation still endures, and the Arabs should strive to break the spell and to become acquainted with African Islam. This point, in turn, led to a long discussion of the reliability of statistics, and of Christian missions. A number of people called in and complained about Christian missionary activity, especially in schools, but they were dismissively told that the missionaries were simply doing their job, and that it was up to the Muslims to do a better job.

Both missions, we were told, were mainly targeting "tribal religion." At this point Ahmad Mansur wanted to know what tribal religion was. He was told that this was the worship of idols, stars, and talismans, and he exclaimed, "Oh, you mean all those things we see among the fans at the African Soccer Cup?" (al-Qaradawi 1999, 28 Dec.). What is striking here is not only Ahmad Mansur's representing the intellectual horizon of the ordinary Arab soccer-loving male, apparently expecting his viewers to have the same reference. More to the point, it is also the—from an Islamic perspective—completely neutral, even curious, discussion of African religion as tribal religion, without any condemnation or even use of classical Islamic terms for idolatry. Africa—displayed on maps in the program—was seen as the arena of a battle for the souls of simple-minded people, caught between two world giants, Islam and Christianity, who were both simply doing their job. People belong to one or the other religion, and only one of them is right. They might be best understood as opponents in a game of influence. This seems to confirm Peter Beyer's observation that in the current phase of globalization a new interdependence in the identities of the religions has evolved (Beyer 1994).

Arab state broadcasters were set up to cater to national audiences and occasionally to spread national propaganda to neighboring states. Al-Jazeera is quite clearly also operating with a national audience, only this is the national community writ large: *al-watan al-'arabi,* consisting of anybody who can speak Arabic in the Arab world and beyond. It may use new images, but it quite clearly sees itself as serving an imagined community that is a national audience with common interests, sentiments, and allegiances.

To Yusuf al-Qaradawi and his program, this imagined community is the *umma.* Ultimately, the *umma* encompasses all Muslims whatever their language, but the program constructs its audience as the Arab *umma.* Arabic is important—we saw how the Arabic culture of African Muslims was stressed. What is new and interesting is that this virtual *umma* does not have a ruler; it has many, and this means that no state can control it. The Western Muslims are suddenly of pivotal importance, and al-Qaradawi wants them to break the links to their countries of origin: he advises them to set up a council (*majlis*) in each country to solve their own problems, and to make their own observation of the new moon instead of each group of immigrants following the observations in their countries of origin (al-Qaradawi 1999, 21 Mar.). At the same time, al-Qaradawi emphasizes that social security fraud in Western countries is as great a sin as in a Muslim country (al-Qaradawi 1999, 21 Mar.). Muslims should be good citizens in these countries, and their only other allegiance should be to the *umma*.[1] The pan-Islamic universalism of the Salafiyya movement is given a new lease on life through the new global medium.

THE MEDIUM AND THE MESSAGE

For Yusuf al-Qaradawi, as mentioned, television is a mere instrument, a medium in the original sense of the word, with little impact on the message itself. But two sessions devoted to the media themselves, the first about the new satellite channels and the other about the Internet, make it clear that matters are not as simple as that.

The program about the satellite channels, aired in June 1999, was fairly critical of the content of the new channels. Al-Qaradawi—who appeared to be watching a great many of them—maintained that these new channels did not serve the interests of the *umma,* either in their news coverage or in their entertainment programs. Even in terms of language, they let the Muslims down by using too much of the vernacular, the *'ammiyya.* Callers appeared to agree with al-Qaradawi and complained that the satellite programs were only practicing a mindless copying *(taqlid)* of the West, insisting on issues that run counter to the Shari'a, such as homosexuality. Almost everybody ended their contribution by demanding more hostesses wearing headscarves *(muhajjabat)* on al-Jazeera—and its directors agreed to this demand by fax at the end of the program.

A Syrian man stated that the satellite channels must be used to topple infidel regimes, but was interrupted by al-Ansari, who said that politics was not being discussed on this program (al-Qaradawi 1999, 13 June). Characteristically, al-Qaradawi ended by calling for an international board of *'ulama'* to supervise the ethics of the new transnational channels. His main point, however, was that all programs must have an Islamic message or appeal: "We must make use of all

---

1. Ironically, the emergence of al-Jazeera, MBC, and similar Arabic-language channels is probably a threat to the Islamic and Arabic programming on local TV stations.

genres, dramas, serials, etc., but all must have a *risala* and an Islamic culture. We must grant an hour for your heart and an hour for your Lord" (al-Qaradawi 1999, 13 June).

In this last formulation, we witness the emergence of a television policy. Apart from specifically missionary programs, it appears that most other types of program, such as dramas and serials, if they contain nothing reprehensible, can also be considered Islamic. Any program that adopts Islamic symbolism, such as the headscarf, and avoids or denounces certain controversial issues, such as homosexuality, seems to qualify as Islamic. Again, this seems akin to the path taken by American televangelism since the 1950s, which appropriated popular formats—such as the talk show—and made them Christian by adding religious symbolism, talk, and paraphernalia. As pointed out by Bobby Alexander, this eclecticism enabled marginal religious groups to adapt to some of the views and lifestyles of mainstream American society, with the potential to win greater acceptance and inclusion (Alexander 1997, 195).

American televangelism is often credited with a pioneering role in fundraising via television, thus specifically developing techniques of appealing to its viewers that were later reused by the advertising industry (Lindermann 1996, chap. 1). Yusuf al-Qaradawi, too, is now the figurehead of a cluster of medias promoting a specific Islamic mission. He had had a popular home page on the Internet for years, but in October 1999 a broader Internet service, <islam-online.net>, was launched, which aimed at becoming the gate of choice for Muslims on the Internet. The idea was to create "a trustworthy global *minbar* [pulpit]" at a time when many Islamic sites on the Internet were in fact operated by "enemies of Islam, such as Jews, Bahais or Qadyaniyya" (al-Qaradawi 1999, 3 Oct.).

Like al-Jazeera, <islam-online.net> enjoys financial support from the emir of Qatar, but it is expected to break even in five years. Achieving this goal, of course, means fund-raising. Amidst *fatwa*s allowing such novelties as sexually mixed chat rooms, al-Qaradawi was asked whether contributions to the project could count as *zakat*. He answered that this was an important new dimension of the Islamic mission *(da'wa)*, and as such may be supported by *zakat, sadaqa*, legacies, or other funds (al-Qaradawi 1999, 3 Oct.).

Inserted several times in the program was an advertisement for the new service. Yusuf al-Qaradawi appeared in the middle of his own program, promoting the Internet site and asking, subtly, for contributions to it. Al-Qaradawi was obviously relying on his dignity and status in the program to render his appeal efficient. This is a novelty. Islamic television—and especially *'ulama'* who appeared on it—had not before resorted to appealing to audiences for funding. But this is yet another instance where the logic of the media is making itself felt in the content of the message.

POSTMODERNISM OR PUBLIC SERVICE

This leads me to the last theme of this chapter, namely postmodernism. Here I will compare the introduction of *Shari'a and Life* to that of Shaykh al-Sha'rawi's program *With Shaykh al-Sha'rawi* on national Egyptian television on 26 August 1993.

The contrasts are clear: the al-Sha'rawi introduction features a ceiling in a mosque, the camera slowly following the arabesques, while the text is written in very elaborate calligraphy, accompanied by classical Arabic oud music. *Shari'a and Life,* by contrast, is introduced by a series of pictures flowing at high speed, allowing us glimpses of dollars, soldiers, veiled women demonstrating, oil, arrests, a bathroom, and (curiously) royal horse guards, all along accompanied by a portentous kind of music reminiscent of the music CNN uses for momentous events (and of a type that would certainly have met with Atatürk's approval). All these images are glimpsed through the Arabic letters of the word "Shari'a," which thereby functions as a prism through which to watch and evaluate these contemporary features.

I think it can be safely said that *Shari'a and Life* is consciously setting itself off against the Sha'rawi program and its various epigones in other Arab countries. These programs represent two very different ideas of what kind of religious message should be transferred via television. But can the difference between them be framed in terms of modernism and postmodernism? Is *Shari'a and Life* a good example of television on an Internet model? I will argue that it is not.

The Sha'rawi program features only his person, placed in a mosque, with an audience around him, relating some event in the life of the prophets. The introduction is revealing: Islam here is seen as the venerable tradition, as *turath.* Sha'rawi will not look at contemporary events, but takes us back into sacred history. When Sha'rawi uses *'ammiyya,* the vernacular, it is not because he is upset, as was the case with al-Qaradawi, but because he uses direct speech, playing the role of the prophet Joseph or some other Qur'anic figure. Or he switches to *'ammiyya* to break with the fictional framework and give a contemporary comment. But as anyone who has watched him will confess, this is just one of his artistic effects: his voice, his gesticulation, his facial expressions are mesmerisingly used to convey the importance and intensity of his message. It is these telegenic gifts that have earned him his colossal audience around the world. When he died in the summer of 1998, thousands of weeping Egyptians followed the funeral procession.

Sha'rawi, then, is easily the most popular Islamic television star ever, having appeared at least once a week on Egyptian television for almost twenty-five years. Like al-Qaradawi, he was an Azhari who went abroad to Saudi Arabia and Algeria and made his career there, but he was never a refugee and always kept up good relations with the Egyptian government. When he returned to Egypt, he went into the administration, and in the late 1970s even served for a time as minister of *awqaf*. His literary output was enormous, consisting of print runs totaling more than 700,000, but his work was not well respected in *'ulama'* circles: his books were clearly an offshoot of his television fame, unlike those of al-Qaradawi. There was a huge public interest in Sha'rawi's private life, and he could confide in the press about his favorite food, his old age, and his lifestyle; there were even critical books brought out that tried to portray him as a hypocrite who had enriched himself on the naïveté of his audience.

The Sha'rawi program, then, may look traditionalist—at least if we remember that traditionalism itself is in many ways a product of modernity—but there is something approaching the televangelic in Sha'rawi the media phenomenon, with its components of stardom, audience identification, and consumerism. Admittedly, none of these is new. But, at least to a European like myself, these qualities of televangelism do seem to be increasingly important features of the kind of television that we are watching in the postmodern age.

In comparison, this emotional and charismatic quality seems to be lacking in *Shari'a and Life*. In fact, there is something curiously familiar about the channel: al-Qaradawi insisting on dialogue and argument, on educating and edifying the public and imbuing it with a rational, universal, and democratic Islam. And perhaps this observation should be extended to the whole of the Jazeera channel: men sitting and discussing serious issues for hours, only interrupted by news—is not this the ultimate channel of the old modernist intellectual?

If postmodernity is characterized by features such as the eclectic mixing of hitherto antagonistic spheres such as high and low culture, the breakup of national consensus and paternalism, consumerism, and individual constructions of identities, then al-Jazeera does not seem to qualify; indeed it seems to be the very opposite. It very much resembles that icon of European modernism, national public television. Only here the nation is *al-watan al-'arabi*, consisting of some twenty states plus substantial Arab minorities in the Western world. In both media and Islamic thinking, modernism had its own brand of globalism, namely universalism. Just as Yusuf al-Qaradawi is a latter-day Salafi who can now make use of yet another medium to further his universalist pan-Islamism, so the ideals of al-Jazeera are reminiscent of a modernist globalism that came to the fore in the Arab world a hundred years ago, but ever since has had to fight to establish a platform free of political control.

9

Where Does Globalization Take Place?

Opportunities and Limitations for Female Activists in
Turkish Islamist Non-Governmental Organizations

CATHARINA RAUDVERE

While visiting a women's meeting place for religious education on the outskirts of Istanbul in 1997, I found myself in a room covered on one side with religious decorations (mainly brought back from *hac* tours or ostentatious gifts from wealthy relatives who had migrated to Germany) and covered on the other with bookshelves containing Qur'ans, selections of *hadis* editions, *tefsir* collections by famous Sufi *şeyh*s, Said Qutb and other Islamist classics (in Turkish), along with university textbooks by Foucault, Habermas, and Sontag. A prayer meeting had just finished in another room and the participants were now relaxing, drinking tea, and chatting. The hot topic of the week was the upcoming trial of Istanbul's mayor, Tayyıp Erdoğan, and the daily demonstrations in his favor. At the same time a teenage girl was using the television remote control to switch between the Islamist channel 7 and Kral (the Turkish answer to MTV), where Madonna's latest video was being shown. The girl sang along for a while, then pushed the buttons again and the screen gave us a glimpse of a Chechen *şeriat* execution on the news from the national television company.

The blend of political topics, intense prayer, pop music, and social networking, together with the ease with which the women moved between the activities while effectively planning new Qur'an lessons and food distribution to the poor, and passing on information about new demonstrations, seemed to bother no one except me, the essay-writing outsider. The flow of information, ideas, sounds, and pictures was obviously a manageable part of the women's everyday life.

It is interesting to contemplate the changes in women's lives compared with twenty years before. Prayer meetings in secluded places for women only had certainly not been uncommon then, but other aspects of the present gathering were novel: women who cross the megacity in order to attend particular religious meetings, the political debate, and, perhaps most important, religious women taking charge of activism with instant impact on their local life. Because there are many more women's circles of this kind, their influence is no longer limited to the immediate vicinity. Can theories of globalization and late modernity explain the living conditions and activities of these women? In relation to globalization, keywords such as access, volume, and speed are frequently used. In the milieu described above, the world is certainly entering the women's meeting place via new media and personal narratives, and there are conspicuous reactions and responses to the global flow.

ONLY CONNECT

When discussing the conditions of globalization in relation to Muslim women in the late twentieth century, we can, with Alan Scott (1997), ask whether globalization should be characterized as a social process or political rhetoric. Is it an analytical concept or an ambiguous metaphor in praise or condemnation of a worldwide free-market economy?

This chapter takes a close look at the framework of globalization, especially in relation to small local groups, in order to approach—not answer—the question of where globalization actually takes place. It takes for granted that there are processes of change termed "globalization" that de facto take place and influence both macro and micro levels of community life in every corner of the world. But what are the products of globalization and what is productive of globalization (Roseneil 1997, 5)? Questions of this kind bring up issues of a rather paradoxical character.

The terms "opportunities" and "limitations" in the title of this paper are used not just in an attempt to focus on gender, but also to reflect the impact of social status and access to education in relation to globalization. My second intention in what follows is to oppose the conventional image of women as victims of processes such as urbanization and globalization, not accepting the view that their religion, poverty, lack of education, or gender necessarily predetermine them to lead subordinate lives. Rather than being heard as a pitiful undertone, religious women activists are here seen as contributing to the changes connected with globalization. They may not always employ the expected modes of communication, instead choosing new forums that are not so easily detected. Once I was asked at a seminar whether I thought these women's groups were "really important." One's answer obviously depends on one's perspective. The public emergence of religious women in an increasingly complex society has a certain cumulative effect. Little by little, groups that not long ago were marginal have now been incorporated into the mainstream; new media are not as easily controlled as the old, neither by state authorities nor male family members. Approaching the issues put forward in this volume, the aim will largely be "to locate postmodern culture in a context of disorganized capitalism, of consumer society and cultural mass production" (Turner 1990, 5) in a Turkish context.

The empirical material for this essay comes from fieldwork in Istanbul, where I studied a small Muslim women's group over a period of five years in the mid-1990s.[1] The women organize their activities in the form of a religious foundation *(vakıf)*, offering regular prayer meetings, basic religious education, and charity work to other women in their neighborhood. The women's use of the term *vakıf* in everyday language refers both to the formal organization and to their meeting place. The importance of the organization as such should not be underestimated. The foundation gives the women independence and the opportunity to accumulate capital for investment in new large-scale projects, both cultural and financial. The women are well known locally, but are in an ambiguous position—not because of the form of their programs, but rather because of their extent. They are respected as pious, yet they have transgressed the borders of what convention thought it possible for women to accomplish. In a few years in the 1990s, activities grew from private house meetings to major events publicly advertised. Women's ability to stretch given social and religious boundaries has made it obvious how very direct the impact of the megacity is on individual women's lives. Through negotiations within the given Muslim system, freedoms and opportunities previously unthinkable were obtained.

In the present example, an inner circle of twelve women, two with university degrees, reaches approximately 150 women per week through their programs. They thus form an elite in relation to their local community, and most of the leading women have a family history with a solid base in the Muslim middle class.[2] It

1. The results of the fieldwork (1993–97) have been published in Raudvere 2002.

2. The Muslim middle class in Turkey should be regarded not only as a novelty, caused by rapid urbanization and the development of the educational system, but also as a group muted during the heydays of Kemalism and only recently visible in mainstream society. In certain districts of the major cities, well-educated members of religious families have conveyed Muslim scholarship and learning for generations. The contemporary Islamist-oriented middle class is certainly not constituted solely of social climbers, as some secularist debaters claim, but also of transmitters of tradition firmly rooted in urban environments. Göle 1997a and 1997b.

is the values and norms of this social stratum that dominate the promulgations of the group. The *vakıf* is one of many women's groups in the district, the city, and the Muslim world, and it is naturally difficult to assess their impact in any way. The various associations are far from united in approach or attitude; each one leaves the mark of women's presence in its local culture. Increasingly, groups are making use of traditional media as well as the Internet. The combination of formal and informal ways of communicating and sharing information makes it almost impossible to determine whether, and how, the groups interconnect. Furthermore, many groups are temporary.

The weekly performance of the repetitive and intense *zikir* prayer constitutes the core of activities, and the teachings and theology of the leading women are clearly based on Sufi *(tasavvuf)* thought. The focus of the fieldwork was on the collective forms of ritual life, and its significance for the women's profile as a group. The women of the *vakıf* identify themselves as the keepers of Sufi traditions, but without any formal connection to, or initiation into, any established order *(tarikat)*. When discussing the orders that are active in the immediate vicinity, the members always stress independence: the women have no living theological authority and no formal internal hierarchies. They refer to a deceased teacher, *hoca,* and have filed notes from his sermons in their records. The *vakıf* has published an edited volume of these and the exegesis that follows the communal readings of the *hoca*'s words forms the basis of the ideological statements of the women. The group is an example of the many independent religious nongovernmental organizations (NGOs) that have come to light in Turkey since the early 1980s and that are often viewed as a product of a new turn in the Turkish modernization process.

The women expressly do not define themselves primarily as "modern women" or as part of any "modern movement," but rather as keepers of traditional values. "Modern" in their vocabulary is used primarily as a pejorative term—when not used in praise of new technical equipment. Their proclaimed goal is to restore what has almost been destroyed by the modern world, and especially by Kemalism. The "return" they advocate is not only to religion, but correspondingly to what is conceived as a "true national heritage." In times of cultural fragmentation the women of the *vakıf* perceive themselves as guards of *tevhid,* unity, and the key concept used when defending this position is *gelenek,* tradition. With a glance at the world bustling around them, such a tradition is regarded as indisputably Muslim, Turkish, and homogeneous. "Modernity" in this context is used as a rhetorical figure, as the name of an opposed alien ideology that only religion can conquer.

When Bryan S. Turner (1990, 11) writes, "It is possible to be postmodern (without nostalgia for *Gemeinschaft*) without being anti-modern (without rejecting the achievements of bourgeois civil society; that is, the achievements of social relations based on *Gesellschaft*)," it could be added that the religious activism of contemporary Turkey is, from an analytical perspective, entirely incorporated into late modern society, although it is discursively anti-modern and holds nostalgia as one of its rhetorical key concepts. In another context, when discussing the pluralism and relativism of postmodernity in relation to the universalism of many contemporary religious movements, Turner states: "Fundamentalism is therefore the cultural defense of modernity against postmodernity" (1994, 78). In order to emphasize the ability of self-expression among the Muslim NGOs, the term "late modernity" is perhaps a more pertinent term when trying to grasp the conditions faced by religious activists in contemporary Turkey.

The women's mission prompts a return to the sources, the Qur'an and the *hadis*, in order to accomplish the desired restoration, at both personal and societal levels. In this aspect they must be considered part of the current Islamist movement understood in the broadest sense. Islamism is a movement of the counterculture, stressing Muslim values as the basis for a future good society. Various groups in Turkey are united by a firm but diffuse desire to "return to the sources" and by a vision of being able to live like the pioneers of Islam. An image of the *selef,* the first three generations of believers representing "authentic" theology and practice, emerges from the normative literature. These people were indisputably Arabic, but this seems to be more of a problem for me than for my informants, who gladly integrate the *selef* in their nationalistic discourse as a pure and righteous beginning. The women do not hail the current Zeitgeist, which they define as depraved and repulsive. Instead they point to institutions and practices that have from their point of view stood firm and unaffected by the influence of Kemalism and modernization. They build their world-view on a double historical Utopia, on the Medinan model derived from readings of the holy scriptures (Raudvere 1998) and on images of Ottoman life. The Ottoman *millet* system (a complicated categorization of people according to religion, in "nations") has been brought forward as an ideal of a stable and well-structured mode of community life. Historically it was "typical of all pre-modern systems of social stratification by social order" (Gülalp 1999, 39). It clearly defined a person in terms of relations and duties toward family and community and therefore serves well as a rhetorical counter-image in contrast to contemporary negotiable identities. Neo-Ottomanism is a strong trend among Turkish Islamist intellectuals, as recently discussed by Hakan Yavus, and it has also spread in more general religious circles and strengthened the nationalistic bias of Turkish Islamism. Yavus argues that "the processes of democratization and capitalist development carried the dominant, traditional Ottoman-Islamic worldview and culture of Turkish Anatolia from the periphery to the center of the political forum" (1998, 20).

The women organize their activities according to their conception of Ottoman ideals. The grand complexes of religious and social institutions, *külliye*, that surrounded the major mosques in pre-republican times function as their historical mirror. Using the *külliye* as prototype, the women preach, teach, nurse, and feed, always paying close attention to the spiritual and material needs of their local community, a crowded district of central Istanbul that displays most of the characteristics of late modern society. The attitude is a pronounced "antimodernism" on a local discursive level, but a late modern phenomenon in the analytical model used in the study.

ENCOUNTERING THE GLOBAL—AND SHARING IT

In comparison with the situation in Turkey some ten or fifteen years ago, the activities of female religious activists are not only larger in scale but also considerably more visible and public. They are also undoubtedly part of global events. This has a paradoxical effect in more than one way. On one hand, in contemporary Turkey there are more possible choices of religious life than ever; an apparent individualization with the emphasis on personal preferences exists at least in the major cities. In poor areas too, often viewed with a biased gaze as culturally homogeneous, there are options for variety in religious life. Different Muslim associations compete with various theological and ideological programs for attention and support. On the other hand, not everything that comes after high modernity is pluralism: what the highly visible religious groups teach today is often quite authoritarian, more or less radical, Islamist universalism. The women in the present study are empowered, from the perspective of their local community, but they seldom claim formal power at an institutional level.

To put the paradox in other words, there are parallel processes occurring among the religious groups in contemporary Turkey. There is an endeavor to achieve homogeneity, at least at a discursive level, although opinions differ considerably about what the content of "the Muslim alternative" should be. Yet there are also frequent calls for the right to religious diversity. The most striking example perhaps is the increasing Alevi consciousness. Despite the obvious fact that they constitute a highly heterogeneous group, distinctive Alevi debaters and groups present themselves as a united alternative to mainstream Sunni orthodoxy and as a religious and political opposition to the establishment, whether embodied as representatives of the secular state or as Sunni clergymen (Vorhoff 1994). The Alevis pronounce a counter-narrative against the grand narratives of both Turkish nationalism and Islamism. There are also rifts within Sunnism. The traditional *tarikats*, not the least the Nakşbendis, have always belonged to influential political circles. Still today various Sufi groups have taken political stands against the Islamist Refah/Fazilet Partisi, most notably the Nurcus and groups associated with Fethulla Gülen. Along with these comparatively large and public groups there are numerous associations of more or less formal character that make the Muslim map of Turkey quite motley. As an additional critique of the often claimed privatization thesis,[3] it must be remembered that women's religious activism in Turkey is more public than ever. This is true not only in the formal sense, through organizations and meetings, but also through the very presence of women's expression of religious values through dress code and behavior at all levels of society. Variations in the female *tesettür,* decent garment, in which minor details—buttons, pleats, reveres, and cut, not to mention color of the coat and whether or not the headscarf is patterned—reveal much about the wearer and the group(s) she is associated with. Even the most resolute Kemalist must admit that "religious people" cannot be dismissed as a single category, and all of them are certainly not country people, *köylüler,* a frequently used insult. In the ongoing ideological battle over which direction the Muslim movement will take, the women of the *vakıf* studied are, from the perspective of their local community, empowered. They have opportunities to organize activities and have access to hold meetings in some mosques and *mescits.* Nevertheless, by convention women's religious activities are as such defined as private. Few Islamist women have reached the status of a public persona, and even fewer have remained in that role for any length of time.

In May 1999, Turkish politics flared up when the Fazilet Partisi representative, Merve Kavakcı, was about to take her seat in parliament. Wearing a headscarf, and knowing full well that she was thereby violating established dress rules for an official representative, she was forced to leave the assembly hall. The Kavakcı affair involved many actors. All parties were aware of the fact that any hostile attack on her would cause international media interest. University-educated and English-speaking, Merve Kavakcı could answer foreign journalists herself; she could speak for herself as an independent Muslim woman. Never-

3. For further discussions of secularization and privatization see Robertson 1992, 85 ff.; Beyer 1994, 70 ff.; Turner 1994, 80 ff.; Davison 1998, 134 ff.

theless, Kavakcı is not primarily an example of women's influence or position in the Islamist party. Although many women worked hard in the campaigns before the December 1995 elections, no woman was deemed eligible to stand for election, and the chairman at the time, Necmettin Erbakan, adopted a scornful and patronizing manner, and belittled the very idea of female representation. Kavakcı was chosen as a token woman not only to escalate the headscarf conflict, but also to call international attention to the Turkish Islamists' political struggle. Undoubtedly the headscarf has been the major icon in the polarization of secularists and Islamists. More than that, it has split the secularists. Younger people seem ready to accept the variety of religious dress and seem to be more aware that *başörtü*, covering, can signify a multitude of religious and ideological positions. International influence on this variety has hitherto not been very well studied. In the social sciences, alongside discussions about globalization is a marked interest in local versions of a hyperculture, in this case, Islam. To be able to approach the space where globalization takes place and where cultural products are generated and staged, it is important to identify which spaces have traditionally been open to female participants and which have been opened up and how. The globalization of everyday activities for the *vakıf* women is located in very different spheres of life (Beyer 1994, 70), depending on age, education, and social background.

In the following, three fields of localized globalization will be discussed as well as examples of dramatic sociopolitical changes that have taken place in Turkey since the early 1980s, particularly as they relate to religious women's groups.

MOBILITY AND VISIBILITY

The first examples will show that there is a highly apparent new mobility for religious women, and hence also a new visibility. Not long ago, the home of a woman's own family—or of her close relatives and friends—was the given arena for her collective religious activities. The local mosque was hardly a woman's place. For most women, a visit to a saint's shrine, *zaviye,* on a minor pilgrimage together with a women's group or with the extended family was the only time they would enter a space exclusively set aside for religious use.

The changes in women's religious arenas have a coarse economic background. Due to rapid urbanization, women in all strata of society work outside their homes to a much larger extent than before. They are thus of necessity exposed to lifestyles and attitudes not represented in their own families. They meet groups whose members are professional, but who nevertheless follow the rules of *edep* and use the code of *tesettür*. Among the urban pious women there is no necessary correlation between employment and not leading a religious life. Quite the opposite, the more activist Muslim groups are well oriented in the urban landscape. Women move around extensively to go to work and to participate in religious activities, and are accustomed to commuting across cities by means of public transport. Women who work also have money of their own, albeit limited, to spend on religious activities. This new visibility contests the routine dichotomy of public-private, men-women that is prevalent in many secularization/modernization theories. Modernization (in terms of widespread education, urbanization, professional careers, and so forth) has made women's religious life more public, and the late modern reaction against large-scale programmatic secularization campaigns has created new space for Muslim activities (Göle 1997a).

Traveling is of course an obvious example of mobility, and going abroad is a major achievement for most women in Turkey. A trip abroad is an ambiguous undertaking because it is commonly supposed to contaminate a woman with foreign influence. Women's travelling for religious reasons must therefore be carefully prepared in order not to cause suspicion; it must be both legitimate and protect the travelers' decency. The women of the *vakıf* organize their own *hac* tours to Mecca at least once a year for themselves and women in the vicinity.[4] The number of *hac* permits granted in Turkey is limited and the allocation is by quotas. When a package tour is bought, the bureaucratic matters are supervised by the travel agent. At least twenty women at a time travel on a charter basis with a token man as their leader, staying away for two or three weeks. Depending on the scheme of other activities in the group, both the obligatory *hac* (which may be undertaken only during the month of pilgrimage, Zilhicce) and the minor *umre* (which can be performed at any time of the year) are organized. Thanks to these tours, women who would not have had a chance to go on such a journey are given the opportunity to fulfil the demand, *şart,* of pilgrimage.

The central state authority for the *hac* tours is the Directorate for Religious Affairs (DIB), which operates through local organizations. The number of pilgrims is restricted and each would-be pilgrim must acquire individual approval, *izin*. It is apparently the case that an application processed via the *vakıf* increases the chances of being among the selected, even for women without the company of a close male relative. The *hac* is much easier to accomplish than it was just a few

---

4. For further discussions of women's *hac* tours, see Delaney 1990; Tapper and Tapper 1991; Kamalkhani 1998, 102 ff.

decades ago. It used to be a sign of considerable economic well-being and social status, and few women went. Nowadays there are convenient flights and well-planned sojourns. Charter travel is both fast and affordable. Even married women with family responsibilities can make a full *hac* and be back within a fortnight. Although it is nowadays within reach of many more people, the performance of the *hac* still lends a certain prestige within religious circles.

The *vakıf* takes the initiative and thus awakens and encourages the idea (and dream) that the *hac* is feasible among less affluent women. Members of the group also help with the practical arrangements of the pilgrimage, such as advice on how to get economic support, and share knowledge and experience about the *hac* as a religious event. The *hac* as an opportunity for global encounters should not be overestimated, however. There is no absolute correlation between traveling and actually meeting. From what can be understood from the discussions held after the pilgrims have returned, the women keep more or less to themselves while in Saudi Arabia, and direct, substantial contacts with Muslims from other countries are rare. In her study of the *hac*, Carol Delaney has brought up the issue of language barriers.[5] It would not be sensible to argue that the *hac* tours by necessity constitute an arena for actual meetings and interaction with the international Muslim world. The significance of the *hac* is of another character. Mostly the returning women's sense of "Muslim otherness" is based on visual perception, and they bring back memories of the *hac* that linger for a long time. When scenes from Indonesia or Africa are shown on television, the *hacı*s often start referring to observations made in Mecca and Medina, and the *hac* develops into a collective international experience.

The *hac* tours are certainly not only of significance for those who travel. The individual traveler shares the many aspects of the experience with family, friends, and the groups with which she is associated. The homecoming parties are an important part of the pilgrimage. The structure of the *hac* is almost paradigmatic with its three marked phases, and with the reintegration being as important as the separation. The liminal phase is the *hac* experience itself and the individual is prepared to return to society with a new status: *hacı*. The pilgrims are to be received back into the community whose members have prayed for the travelers during

5. In this essay Carol Delaney compares the migrant workers' annual journey back to Turkey with the *hac* tour, using empirical material gathered during her fieldwork in Anatolia in 1980–82. The context is obviously very remote from the world of the *vakıf* women, and Delaney's emphasis on the marginalization of women is of course not relevant in the present case. Nevertheless, interesting comparisons can be made.

their absence. The women at home follow the daily special *hac* broadcasts on television during the month of pilgrimage. When hundreds of thousands are shown circulating the Kâbe in packed crowds, someone invariably shouts with warmth, "Oh, there they are!" Even though it is absolutely impossible to catch any individual faces, the television viewers at the *vakıf* feel connected to these events, thanks to their participating friends. The introduction of high-tech telecommunication has also facilitated direct reports from Medina of both personal and religious importance, creating an emotional bond of simultaneous experience, temporarily invalidating the differences between "here" and "there."

The memories of the *hac* are reproduced in direct verbal discourse but can also be manifested in tangible objects, such as souvenirs purchased in Medina. The flow of consumer goods is always accentuated in postmodern theory, and it is certainly a vital part of the symbolic universe of the community studied here. It is all too easy to dismiss the souvenirs as knickknacks because they are often mass-produced in China or Malaysia: the Kâbe or the Prophet's mosque in a multitude of materials and forms. But the *hac* presents are of immense importance when establishing and maintaining social relations after a completed pilgrimage. Acts of giving and receiving are highly formalized at the homecoming parties held immediately after the pilgrims are picked up at the airport or within the next few days. The act of gift-giving is a ritualized way of showing respect to the recipient and transferring the blessing, *bereket,* from one location to another in concrete form. The *zemzem* water brought back in recycled five-liter cans is a clear example of the commemorative and highly tangible aspects of all the rituals connected with the *hac.* This blessed water is distributed as long as it lasts at the closure of prayer meetings and prolongs the feeling of being in the pilgrimage month. It is also a widely held opinion that the *zemzem* water has a healing quality. The water is served in tea glasses from a tray, and the women rise from the prayer circle to face Mecca. When everyone has a tea glass in hand, a collective formulaic prayer is said and the water is drunk, swallowed in one gulp.

Seemingly banal objects (framed pictures, key-rings, pencils, purses, and so forth) loaded with social and religious meaning are distributed in large quantities. Personal gifts function as a sign of affection and confirm an emotional and social bond between two individuals. The recipient's status is also affected. The gift signals that the owner is, if not a *hacı* herself, a comparatively close friend of one. Souvenirs are also kept to be sold further on at the sales and fairs *(kermes)* that are organized twice a year to bring in money for the programs and charity work of the *vakıf.* On these occasions objects purchased in Medina and Mecca are piled up at the center of the tables of goods for sale among homemade and handmade articles and merchandise donated by manufacturers known to the women, often family businesses with one or more women active in the *vakıf*. The Mecca souvenirs thus spread a certain dignity over the whole event.

The women also bring back memorial narratives that are spread orally in the vicinity and support the status of the group. Both the departure and the return are the subjects of conversation: who is going, who gave what to whom, and so forth. Miracles that took place in Saudi Arabia are related, for example, stories about people who were lost in the immense crowds and then found again. Prayers spoken at Mecca are answered, recitations from the Qur'an are interpreted as answers to current problems. Stories from the *hac* told and retold at the different kinds of *vakıf* meetings are slowly integrated in the social memory of the group, connecting this little *cemaat* with the universal center of all Muslims. *Hac* narratives are frequently brought up as comments on news from the Muslim world on television or in the press as testimony that there really are Chinese Muslims or Black Muslims in the United States. Late modernity is often related to a multipolar world and set within a discussion of postmodernity. In the present discussion, Mecca can be added to the centers competing for global significance. Within the Islamist discourse the place challenges the West on ideological and cultural terms, and in a Middle Eastern political context this cultural nexus diminishes the importance of the nation-state. Both aspects are apparent in contemporary Turkey where "the new religious consciousness" with all its contradictions is united in a vague anti-Westernism along with an even more vague rhetorical, far from always practiced, aspiration for the global *ümmet*. In popular imagination, Carol Delaney writes, Mecca is "a place displaced beyond the horizon, creating a desire to bridge the distance; it is also a presence that is absent, engendering a pervasive mood of longing" (Delaney 1990, 516). However, it must be remembered that the *hac* was a mass event (and the nexus of a highly eloquent international mass culture) by definition long before the introduction of concepts like modernity or postmodernity. What has changed is the increased number of people (and for our purpose here, the increased number of women) who have the opportunity to go and the efficiency with which their going is handled. To this may also be added the impact of modern media that can transmit simultaneous eyewitness reports.

For the majority of the women associated with the *vakıf*, it is the only journey abroad they have made; and in some cases it is the only kind of travel outside Turkey that is conceivable because of family conventions. Even for educated women (with both economic and social opportunities) a trip abroad, even to a Muslim country, is out of the question. The only legitimate reason for travel is pilgrimage and to visit close relatives. Organizing a *hac* is a meritorious act, *sevap,* for the *vakıf* and extends the possibilities for women to go to Mecca. The *hac* tours also serve as an important icon in fund-raising campaigns and have given the women a high-profile local identity as being full of enterprise. The tours give them an ambiguous local authority. Men are ambivalent about whether women should travel in this way, and more importantly, whether women should take the lead in this manner—breaking the norm that a woman should not perform the *hac* without the company of a close male relative. There have been rather vehement debates by the more educated women, who defend their way of organizing pilgrimage in response to fathers and brothers who bring up theological arguments in order to make the women understand that it is righteous to submit to tradition. In order to emphasize local diversity, it must be added that a number of women also oppose this particular form of activity, but often more from a social or moralistic than from a theological point of view. More than once, the negotiation skills of the *vakıf* women have calmed the storm.

Although my fieldwork was set within only one district of the city, even in this limited area religious groups compete at both the ideological and the economic level. Offering *hac* tours and other opportunities for more limited pilgrimage adds fuel to a neighborhood debate from which the women gain power and prestige even as some turn away from them. Negotiation has lately been a favored term in social sciences as well as in cultural studies. From a local perspective, space for negotiation has been one of the most considerable social changes: women are the cause for theological debate and as individuals they give powerful answers to that debate. This situation, when women formulate religious arguments on their own behalf, cannot be explained simply by the level of general education. The fact that many more women have graduated from the religious colleges and İmam Hatip schools, and that some of them have gone on to academic theological studies at the *ilahiyat* faculties at the major universities, has an impact too. There are still very few Turkish women who take up a public role as theologians in publishing and other forms of media, but in a semi-public space with retained gender divisions, such as the *vakıf,* younger women do not hesitate to share their learning and have confidence in their scholarly ambitions. "A woman's voice should not be heard" is often claimed by women, with reference to the *hadis* literature, as an argument against "loud," *gürültülü,* participation. But within gender-separated spheres, theological arguments are seldom raised against a female's interpretation of tradition.

Another aspect of the new mobility that brings the world to the *vakıf* is the extensive labor migration from Turkey and the subsequent return of migrants.

These people in general have a highly ambiguous status in their mother country, especially young women (Robins and Morley 1996). On one hand, many people come back with considerable wealth. They often invest their money in local enterprise and thereafter live a good life. On the other hand, the returning migrants are often looked upon with suspicion in cultural terms. The longer they have been away, the more likely it is that they will be considered foreigners, *yabancı*. The reunion can be more painful than expected, and on a personal level even a tragedy. In the present case study, returned and invested money has played a crucial role in the *vakıf*'s potential to develop new projects.

In relation to religious activism, the returnees bring back capital in all of Bourdieu's four senses. Clear-cut economic capital is perhaps the most immediately visible and includes money and prestige goods as well as management know-how. Economic support from returned families is of fundamental importance to the *vakıf* group, which would never be able to keep up with its ambitious programs if it relied only on traditional fund-raising such as *kermes* or subscriptions. Cultural capital returns in the sense that young women who have been to school in Europe often also have some basic knowledge of English, and their general standard of education is higher. These qualifications put them in a better position if they want to take up a professional career or consume global media such as international television channels or the Internet. In this sense they serve both as introducers and as cultural and linguistic translators. As for social capital, there are connections to Turkish Muslim groups abroad, often in Germany and Holland, albeit less frequent when it comes to women's groups. These groups can have various aims and directions: some are more religious in orientation and others are of more nationalistic character. Altogether, however, they strengthen the young Muslims' networks. Publicly active young women may be rejected as individuals (especially among their relatives staying in Turkey), but in the long run groups with international contacts gain increasing status, even in their local context. Symbolic capital is manifested in dress codes and attributes as much as it is in the self-confidence with which the programs are carried out.

The contacts described above are most often family-based. The people involved (and here those who actually migrate are included as well as those who stay at home receiving telephone calls and summer visitors, and watching international news with new eyes as it relates to family and friends abroad) acquire in the long term a more complex understanding of other ways of life. Turkish labor migration is an excellent example of transnational flows of people, money, consumer goods, knowledge, and information. The German diaspora is thereby mirrored in local Turkish surroundings. Female returnees, as well as male, pass on knowledge so as to conquer secular space while retaining their pride and dignity. The very presence of Muslim attitudes that are in line with late modern living conditions could be considered *dava,* mission, in the immediate vicinity. Encounters with, and access to, modernity are not of necessity a farewell to religion, even though they may give rise to conflicts within the local religious establishment.

MUSLIM DIVERSITY

A second aspect of globalization is that as a result of social as well as spatial mobility, women are constantly confronted with other ways of life. The question of the consequences of the urban conglomerate (Hannerz 1980) highlights the cultural conflicts between rural migrants and the daughters of the megacity within a small group such as the one under study. Both secularism and Islamism constantly challenge what newcomers to the city hold to be traditional and sound. Many women are surprised to discover that they have to defend themselves against other Muslims: they may realize, for example, that their brightly patterned rural headscarf is less bothering to the secular lady for whom they are cleaning than to the women with whom they want to pray. In almost all Turkish Muslim women's groups, differences in education are notable when social and spatial mobility is considered. Yet the impact of informal education should not be underestimated, as the women understand their assignment to inform and advise about the true path, *doğru yol,* not only in the Sufi sense but also as part of Muslim lifestyle. In this sense the informal education undertaken by the religious NGOs is a very direct form of socialization. It is not only of individual importance: the behavior and attitudes of a collective are constantly judged by the people around them. In a society where core issues of the political debate are the length of coats, personal manners, and attitudes toward the needy, collective action must be founded in theological arguments to manage the potential critique from the neighborhood. In a society of "disorganized capitalism," to use Turner's phrase, charity work is badly needed, not only in an economic sense as a means of easing poverty and pain, but also as a means of reaching people, of making them understand the conditions of modern religion. "Religiously-based social movements therefore constitute distinct possibilities for bridging the gap between privatized religious function and publicly influential religious performance" (Beyer 1994, 107). Serving the poor is the prime legitimate reason for religious women to become involved in social life beyond the control of family members. It is very apparent that these encounters are inducements for self-reflection, even though the new experiences are seldom articulated in conversations at the *vakıf.*

A third example of globalization is of course the new media market in

Turkey. The religious television channels have undergone rapid development and harsh competition with each other. The style of the programs has progressed from very solemn Qur'an recitations to the whole variety of television genres: jingles, trailers, television personalities, talk shows, and soap operas. The explosion of television channels, magazines, and other popular media has brought a greater knowledge of the world, not only in a general sense but, more importantly for our purposes here, in greater knowledge of how other Muslims live. Despised or embraced, Muslims of other countries have come alive in a way that was not the case before the mid-1980s. Changes in modes of communication play a vital part in this process. Religious messages are expressed in new media that not only affect the sender, but also make new demands of the receiver. One example is the mass-produced easy reading material aimed at young females. These publications are often in the form of short novels focused on a single individual and with a moralistic twist at the end where a Muslim lifestyle and values are presented as the solution to the main character's problems. This consumer culture, with its strong ideological bias, indicates "a consumption of signs and images in which the emphasis upon the capacity to endlessly reshape the cultural or symbolic aspect of the commodity makes it more appropriate to speak of commodity-signs" (Featherstone 1995, 75).

The women of the *vakıf* are both big consumers of the new communication technology and producers of information. The activities of the *vakıf* are highly dependent on faxes, mobile telephones, computers, and quick printing facilities for flyers, posters, and booklets. The women advertise their weekly activities within limited strata and areas, but with the utmost efficiency. The new forums for expression are not solely a reflection of global impact, but also provide an impetus to find new ways to make imprints on the local public sphere. The women participate in creating (more or less consciously) debate by means of their presence or non-presence, all the while maintaining the rules of *tesettür,* decent dress code. They have also published extracts of the didactic conversations *(sohbetler)* of a locally famous *hoca.* The notes and cassette recordings on which the book is based were made in the 1980s by the now senior women. This publication has, as much as the *hac* tours, gained the women a certain renown. The theology expressed in it connects them with a well-established Sufi legacy, and this connection legitimates their *zikir* practices, which could otherwise be questioned. Although it is the women who have selected and edited the texts in line with their present ambitions, the voice is formally male. The collection is read from at all kinds of meetings arranged by the *vakıf.* Copies have been sold in hundreds to new attendants, and the book must be considered the most successful of all products from the group.

It is only among the political elite of Islamist intellectuals that any explicit formulations are found of what it takes to be a global individual in a more technical sense. The women under study act out of loyalty to their group and to their friends and avoid relating to the world at large. Many active Muslims in Turkey define themselves as a sort of diaspora in relation to mainstream secular society. A rhetorical twist is often made when they present themselves both as the representatives of a genuine Muslim Turkish heritage and, owing to Kemalistic politics over the last seventy years, perforce as marginal players. The conception of a global Muslim community, *ümmet,* serves them as both ideal and comfort.

Whenever Islamist activism is analyzed, there is the risk that people's devotion will be reduced to the question of politics; individuals accordingly tend to underemphasize the strength of their religious attachment. Studies of groups with an Islamist orientation seldom call attention to personal belief as a driving force, whereas studies of Sufism tend to avoid the political aspects of dervish activism and instead cover theological concepts such as spiritual development, guidance, and so forth. The *vakıf* of the present study is certainly at the crossroads between Islamism and Sufism, where religion goes along with politics; Sufism is political and Islamism is spiritual.

Alberto Melucci's arguments in favor of integrating the question of individual needs into analyses of social movements in complex societies are thus very appealing. In his book *Nomads of the Present: Social Movements and Individual Needs in Contemporary Society* (1989), Melucci points out that social phenomena such as the developing NGOs have dimensions, emotional and symbolic relations, that cannot be interpreted as political because they function according to a radically different logic. He energetically underscores the fact that the conditions of these affective relations must be regarded as fundamental whenever social movements of a religious character are analyzed. Using Melucci's framework, three principal aspects stand out when considering the religious women's activist movement as part of a trend as well as demonstrating the impact of the *vakıf* as an organization.

Melucci combines micro and macro analyses and does not conceive of global processes and major political changes as solely national concerns, but insists on one local meaning and interpretation. Accordingly, clear-cut rhetorical conflicts are not petrified; rather the complexity of variation is emphasized. The liberal market economy opened Turkey not only to a more globalized economy, but also to substantial cultural and economic changes. The relativization that follows in the wake of globalization in many ways contests the more rigid nation-state identity. Melucci speaks of "the democratization of everyday life" when he approaches attempts to regulate the complexity of contemporary rapid change. The social movements of late modernity offer models within which individuals may socialize and rules for transforming liberty and relativism into stable identities. These processes infrequently emphasize the authoritarian character of smaller groups. Over the years I have witnessed how networks of women's groups have acquired the capacity for very fast mobilization. The demonstrations in favor of religious schools or in defense of Istanbul's Islamist mayor Tayyıp Erdoğan serve as good examples of this capacity. Young Islamists have not only been able to bring together fifty thousand demonstrators in forty-eight hours, but also to organize them into gender-divided ranks in processions, carrying well-designed streamers and placards. Second, Melucci stresses both synchronic and diachronic elements in his analytical framework, which brings up the importance of history in the study of people's interpretations of the present. As discussed above, the historical mirror is of the utmost importance when confirming legitimacy in a local context. Third, variability is a key term for Melucci, which has been developed further in Peter Beyer's discussion of the relativization of religion. In order not to be misunderstood as inconsistent or paradoxical, the moves of individual agents are aligned with choice and change of "commodity-signs," to borrow Featherstone's term. Within a single day the religious identity of the modern individual can face a number of situations whose essential features are changed.

Despite his contributions to the study of social movements Melucci, and other theorists of globalization, are highly gender-blind in their search for the meaning of religion in late modern society (Scott 1997). When planning and arguing for their programs, the women are forced into a battle on two fronts: one against the Muslim, male-dominated community and its traditionalistic conventions, and the other against mainstream secular society. They have to deal with local religious authorities, formal representatives of the DIB, and more informal *imam*s and *hoca*s, as well as with representatives of state and the municipality.

In conclusion, some of Fredric Jameson's efforts to distinguish what constitutes the postmodern (or, preferably, late modern) condition (Jameson 1983, 1991, 1998a) will be brought up.[6] The focus is primarily on Jameson's interest in urban living conditions in megacities and his discussions of the controversial shift from high modernity to whatever may come after.

Jameson speaks of local reactions to the established forms of high modernism. From this perspective the *vakıf* is part of a major trend in Turkish society over the last twenty years (if not longer) toward alternative understandings of modern living. Or, to use a favorite postmodern expression, the Kemalistic mas-

6. Quotations are taken from Jameson 1998a.

ter narrative is being challenged by Muslim alternatives. As discussed above, the Islamist counter-narrative of the past and the present aims at the foundation of a Muslim society as described in the *hadis*. This historical Utopia, the Medinan model, combines synchronic and diachronic aspects that aggressively contradict the progressive evolutionism of the Kemalistic ideology and other forms of high modernism. The local character and the diversity of this trend have also limited its political influence. As an umbrella organization, the Refah/Fazilet Partisi has had surprisingly little ideological influence on parliamentary politics. Rather, the party has supported a biased protectionism of a generally conservative character.

Jameson and others speak of the blurred or contested boundaries of high and low culture. This feature has a certain gendered aspect and can be exemplified by the new modes and genres of both spoken and written text. In the local context of the present fieldwork, authoritative speech and authoritative interpretation have traditionally had their specific and highly respected time, place, agents, and symbols. "Discursive authority is not so much an entity as it is (1) an effect; (2) the capacity for producing that effect; and (3) the commonly shared opinion that a given actor has the capacity for producing that effect" (Lincoln 1994, 10 f.). Public prayer ceremonies, Friday sermons, formal didactic speeches, *sohbet,* and other statements of normative character (*fetva*s, moral advice, and so forth) are carried out by male bearers of tradition. Within the *tarikat*s, discursive authority is institutionalized and embodied in the *şeyh,* who is regarded as a living link in a historical chain, *silsile,* of divine guidance. In these conservative milieus, tradition is to a great extent understood as faithful reproduction, and novel interpretation, *ictihâd,* is considered a major sin. The lay women's appearance on the semi-public scene (along with other Muslim/Islamist NGOs) has certainly blurred those distinctions. Not only have they transgressed the gender borders as public speakers, they have also brought into public modes of speech that not long ago were limited to the private sphere.

Furthermore, Jameson uses the postmodern as a periodizing concept. Although criticized, this aspect is interesting, because Jameson emphasizes that the "break" is also a continuation. Applied to Turkey, the introduction of a liberal economy in the early 1980s by Prime Minister Turgut Özal could serve as an example of such a radical shift (Özal 1991). It definitively globalized the economy of Turkey and affected social and cultural life; it was the express end to large-scale state-dominated projects, and late modernity has unambiguously made cultural processes take another turn. In its wake, numerous NGOs were established in all fields of interest, manufacturing local, transnational, and other identities. Choice and diversity are hailed by many Turkish intellectuals as the road to a more thoroughgoing democratization. From the perspective of a less prosperous district, the importance of education is more than ever the key to accessing the benefits of a changing society. If globalization is supposed to be more than just another term for internationalism, colonialism, or hegemonic aspirations, it must comprehend chronological aspects. There is a temporal aspect of globalization that indicates a new phase of modernity as a force in social and cultural processes as well as an ideology.

Jameson's adoption of the term "pastiche" (without any mocking or satirical connotations) should also be noted when considering the coded systems of the Turkish Muslim NGOs, and when discussing the use of history or the fad for nostalgia and retro in secular as well as religious circles. Both neo-Ottomanism and the *selef* ideals are representations of the ideals or cultural stereotypes of the past. Although it is the secularist interpretation of nationalism that has been the dominant ideology for the better part of this century, a new mode of nationalism has emerged with an apparent orientation toward the Muslim world, as regards both cultural identity and foreign policy (Yavus 1998).

Finally, a condition arising under the pretext of postmodernity that is more difficult to apply to the ideology of the women of the *vakıf* is "the death of the subject." It might to some extent go well with the Sufi theology of taming the self and conceptions of "die before you die," while a normative, more Islamist discourse demands a stable, responsible, humble self. It leaves us with the discussion of the relation between a globalized world with ever more options and the trend towards particularization and emphasis on local life worlds, "the interplay of the particular and the universal" in the process of globalization (Beyer 1994, 14).

LATE MODERNITY AS A LIVING CONDITION AMONG RELIGIOUS WOMEN ACTIVISTS IN CONTEMPORARY ISTANBUL

Islam has traditionally always been understood as a universal religion. The salvation preached is a concern for all of humankind, and consequently the concept of *tevhid* has always been a cornerstone in all forms of theological discourse. Here globalization has been discussed as an effect rather than a cause. Above all it has focused on women as agents in response to the global impact on their religious lives in a male-dominated context.

As indicated in the scenario outlined at the beginning of this essay, the conditions for women's religious activism have changed rapidly over the last fifteen to twenty years. A proper female space for prayer meetings and social events of a similar kind is hard to accept within a strict private/public dichotomy. While still following the rules of spatial gender division, *tesettür,* and *edipli* behavior, women have nevertheless amazed (if not shocked) their local environment with their intense activism and their ability to conquer new arenas. The activism is to a large extent dependent on individual women's skills and powers of endurance. The potential for women's groups to act in a more visible mode has been realized thanks to women with both secular and religious education enabling them to deal with authorities (establishing a *vakıf*) and to formulate valid theological arguments (defending the *hac* tours).

However, the ability to cope with the flow of information, propaganda, and leisure from competing, not to say combating, media conglomerates is not a question of education alone. There is a substantial difference between the generations. The younger women use the new media technology with competence, and also show that their apprehension of the world is in turn thereby deeply affected. The technical competence of the younger generation is the means by which an older generation of women partakes in the global flow.

Finally, it must be stressed that no contemporary Turkish issue or event can be discussed without considering the impact of nationalism, which, as the election in April 1999 testified, is perhaps the most forceful ideology today. When considering the conditions for religious activities, it must not be forgotten that nationalism is a strong bond between laicists and Islamists. The gaze of the founding father is still omnipresent; the portrait of Kemal Atatürk, watching over his republic, hangs in every public room. But identity politics today differ radically from those of the heyday of Kemalistic modernism. Everyday life has become a battleground for structure, discourse, and a vibrant counter-discourse. Most Turkish NGOs (religious or other) define themselves as representatives of values that in one way or another oppose the hegemonic claims made by the state for decades. Liberal economic policy, globalization, and the various NGOs have effectively contradicted such claims. The focus here is on a grassroots organization, and no clear-cut center of conflicts can be identified. Even within the Islamist movement goals and means differ dramatically. Melucci's use of the concept of "complex society" is therefore advocated when staging individual actors in a context; micro and macro levels of society are not easily distinguished when one tries to grasp groups in constant motion. The group studied here is constantly testing its collective identity in relation to other women's groups, the local religious establishment, and the secular society of the majority—and therefore sometimes acts in a way that may seem contradictory. Adding to the complexity, it must also be taken into account that individuals simultaneously belong to several (sometimes conflicting) social systems; any local woman as an individual is certainly more than a representative of the category "female religious activist."

Whether the present development of multivocal Muslim NGOs deepens democracy or is a step toward a more authoritarian society is still a topic of inflamed debate in contemporary Turkey.

10

From Postmodernism to "Glocalism"

Toward a Theoretical Understanding of Contemporary
Arab Muslim Constructions of Religious Others

P A T R I C E   C .   B R O D E U R

Whether real or imagined, Islam(s) and Muslim identities are constantly being defined and redefined by Muslims, generations after generations, in order to provide an integrated self-understanding in the midst of an increasingly complex world. These various competing definitions are always the result of world-views made up of or influenced by a variety of other concepts and identities, whether religious or ideological. They are never generated solely on the basis of "pure" internal Islamic developments; they are rather the fruit of a binary self/Other interdependent process that is best understood as existing somewhere in between local and global, past and future, here and there. Neither modernity nor postmodernity, however defined, explains this human desire for a meaningful integrated self-understanding that is both rooted in the history and future of one's primary community of identity and open to the integration of time and space. For this reason, I suggest using the term "glocalism," a concept that offers some utility in addressing complex, multicultural and multi-loci phenomena such as Arab Muslim constructions of religious Others. In brief, I define "glocalism" as a constant reflexive process by which a human being's philosophy/ideology/belief/perception and corresponding praxes understand and integrate reality.

This paper examines the usefulness of this definition of "glocalism" for understanding contemporary Arab Muslim constructions of religious Others. It is divided into three parts. First I draw a parallel between the dialectic of self/Other and that of modernity/postmodernity. Second, I survey different definitions of "glocalism" and propose my own in order to enable a synthesis of the above two dialectics. Third, I apply this concept to a unique twentieth-century Arabic literature on "religious Others" to illustrate how the concept of "glocalism" enhances our understanding of contemporary Arab Muslim constructions of religious Others. I conclude with a few questions regarding the changing nature of Islamic studies and the need to move beyond a modern/postmodern theoretical dichotomy in order to avoid the present ideological and theoretical pitfalls rooted in dichotomous conceptual patterns.

THE DIALECTIC OF SELF/OTHER
REPRESENTATION AND ITS PARALLEL TO THE
DIALECTIC OF MODERNITY/POSTMODERNITY

In the 1994 publication of her doctoral dissertation on the history of the dialectic between self and Other in Western philosophy, published under the title *De l'autre: Essai de typologie* (1994), Françoise Mies suggests the interplay between three levels of self/Other interaction. On the first level, the self coexists within the Other in a state of undifferentiation. It is, for example, the fetus inside the mother's womb, the teenager within a rock concert crowd, a pilgrim circumambulating the Ka'ba on the Hajj. On the second level, the self meets the other (small *o*) face to face, bringing out the uniqueness of the self that leads to differentiation. It is Adam "seeing" Eve after the fall in the cosmological biblical story, Majnun greeting Layla in the famous medieval Islamic literary story, Iranian President Mohammed Khatemi meeting Pope John Paul II on 11 March 1999. On the third level, the self interacts with the Other (capital *O*) in all of its general and ambiguous forms. It is a black person walking into an all-white congregation or vice versa, a *muhajjaba* (Muslim woman wearing a headscarf) entering an American fitness center, a non-Arabic-speaking Muslim man listening to a Friday noon *khutba* in a local Cairo mosque. While those three distinctions are valuable, Mies's explanation of their interplay does not account for the powerful ways in which dialectics function in both cognitive and perceptual human processes. For this reason, I prefer using the middle-path approach of the French philosopher Paul Ricoeur.

In his 1990 introduction to *Soi-même comme un autre* (*Oneself as Another*, 1992), Paul Ricoeur develops a hermeneutics of the self that avoids the two dialectically opposed Western philosophical traditions that would have the "I" either, on the one hand, as the founding principle of reality (Descartes's "cogito ergo sum" that inaugurated a philosophy of the subject) or, on the other hand, as the ultimate seat of its illusion (Nietzsche). Ricoeur's hermeneutics of the self rests on the constant dialectical interplay between *idem*-identity (unchanging) and *ipse*-identity (changing), thereby formulating a principle by which identity integrates both sameness and difference, identity and alterity. Whether the dialectic is strictly tripolar (Mies's approach) or bipolar (Ricoeur's approach) does not change the reality that any identity construction, Muslim identity being one of numerous possible examples, relies on the constant dialectical interplay between self and Other. My purpose is to examine, with the help of Ricoeur's theory, where and how this interplay happens.

The dialectic between self and Other takes place within what I call "differential space through time." "Differential space through time," or "gap-time," is the invisible time-space that allows the fluid and constantly changing constructions of any identity. "Gap-time" is at the center of where and how meaning is produced, from the semantics of the sentence (Derrida), to the hermeneutics of the text (Ricoeur), to the understanding of genres (Beebee 1994), to the workings of power (Dyrberg 1997). The use of "gap-time" also avoids a problem that can easily arise when using the expression "differential space through time": the word "differential" may resonate with similar foundational concepts such as "differentiation" (Fornäs 1995, 31), "disjuncture" (Appadurai 1990, 304), "rupture" (David Harvey 1989, 79), "fragmentation" (Featherstone 1995, 13, 76), or *"différance"* (Irene Harvey 1986). I do not, however, mean to emphasize difference over sameness. After all, Ricoeur's choice of *idem*-identity and *ipse*-identity within his hermeneutics of the self does not privilege the self over the Other, sameness over difference. By carefully balancing these two oppositional forces of sameness and difference, Ricoeur rejects both the more recent emphasis on difference as formulated through the philosophies of Lévinas and Derrida, for example, and the lingering philosophies of the subject associated with modernist and essentializing frameworks of inquiry. In a similar fashion, the concept "gap-time" reflects the integration of the vectors of both time and space so as to highlight the location where, and the process by which, identity construction happens.

The parallel between the dialectic of self/Other and that of modernity/ postmodernity is clear. From Fornäs (1995, 35) we learn of the continuity between modernity and high-modernity or late consumer capitalism. The emphasis is on the continuity or sameness, that is, on *idem*-identity. From Featherstone (1995, 84) we learn of the discontinuity between modernity and postmodernity. In this case, the stress is on rupture or on the Other per se, that is, complete alterity. From Jameson (1998a, 18) we learn of a middle ground between modernity as *idem*-identity and postmodernity as the Other, thus the resulting *ipse*-identity. Using Ricoeur's hermeneutics of the self therefore throws light on the process by which nomenclature, in particular when used for periodization, is inextricably linked to a process of differentiation through conceptual dichotomies that constantly interplay with each other, changing the nature of each polar concept. Therefore, the dichotomy modernity/postmodernity may not be the most useful point of entry to describe present changes worldwide in general and in the Islamic world in particular. To overcome this dichotomy, I propose the term "glocalism."

DEFINING "GLOCALISM"

The concept "glocalism" is an integration of the words "globalism" and "localism." Because the many issues surrounding the dialectic modernity/postmodernity and self/Other have to do with a *rapport de force* between two seemingly oppositional concepts/factors/elements/tendencies and so forth, I suggest the use of the term "glocalism" in order to resolve those dialectical tensions for four reasons. First, this approach is not new; it reflects a Hegelian process of thesis/antithesis/synthesis. "Glocalism" becomes the conceptual synthesis for the thesis "modernity" and the antithesis "postmodernity." Second, the combination of the two original words into one neologism is a reflection of hybridity in its form and integration in its content. Third, the simplicity of its dual origin makes it easily accessible to a large public, a rare occurrence in the realm of theoretical thinking. Fourth, the concept "glocalism" also makes sense of "the way that Foucault . . . stresses how modernity has opened our eyes to the discontinuous aspects of history; its interruptions, fractures and holes" (Fornäs 1995, 21, n. 3), without having to define himself (or be defined by others) as either a modernist or a postmodernist. These four reasons should be sufficient to increase the use-value of this new word that explains more precisely the complex interaction between local and global forces shaping the process of identity construction.

There are, however, at least two limitations to the concept of "glocalism." First, keeping in mind Michel de Certeau's suspicion of our Western philosophical dependency upon the Hegelian model—the Parmedian principle of the identity of thought (epistemology) and being (ontology) (Godzich 1986, viii-ix)—it may well be that any effort at theorizing "glocalism" is only doomed to lack a degree of heterology necessary to sustain its viability in contemporary Western philosophical discourse. Second, the word "glocalism" implicitly emphasizes spatial integration of opposites, whatever their referential boundaries may be, over the vector of time. In order to remedy this second deficiency, I combine "glocalism" with the concept of "gap-time" mentioned in the previous section. The combination of these two neologisms de-emphasizes dialectical images of opposites and linear spectra in favor of circular and spiral metaphors: "learning processes for human societies . . . [are] more like an accelerating spiral than a straight line" (Fornäs 1995, 27). The human learning processes go back and forth between local and global perspectives, in the same way as our vision constantly moves back and forth between the near and far. They respond to various forces that shape the speed, shape, and content of any spiral. The present globalization of religion (Beyer 1994) may well be a sign of this age-old mystical desire for integrating "gap-time" and "glocal" space. This contemporary religious/spiritual quest reflects a desire to transcend all dichotomies such as time and space, self and Other, sameness and difference, verbal representation and physical reality, or modernity and postmodernity. The present "Rumi phenomenon" in North America is one of many such examples (Lewis 2000).

This search for transcendence and integration is clearly demonstrated in the various ways in which the term "glocalism" has been defined over more than a decade. Since it was first coined in the mid-1980s, the term "glocalism" has spread rapidly from its initial Japanese business context to a wide variety of geographical areas as well as fields of knowledge, including sociology, education journalism, political science, economics, environment, art and architecture, and development, as well as religion. Its use is more visible on the Internet than in print media, itself an important indication of the effects of the new cybertechnology on the development of neologisms that seek to integrate various conceptual perceptions of reality. The definitions vary greatly, although they tend to emphasize the power of the local over the global.

In the second section of his Web article "An Entrepreneurial City in Action: Hong Kong's Emerging Strategies in and for (Inter-)Urban Competition," Bob Jessop, professor of sociology and political theory at Lancaster University, UK, gives a short and critical history of the use of the term "glocalization." He places its emergence in the mid-1980s when Japanese businessmen developed the term *dochaku* to explain an approach to global export of goods that uses marketing techniques tailored to local cultural sensitivities (Featherstone 1995, 9). In other words, the concept initially referred to the strategy of global localization in which inter-firm as opposed to intra-firm division of labor is fostered, a strategy of globalization favored by American businesses. Jessop argues that "glocalization is a strategy pursued by global firms that seek to exploit local differences to enhance their global operations." He suggests that such firms tend to reverse, or at least confuse, the motto "think globally, act locally" (http://tina.lancs.ac.uk/sociology/soc045rj.html).

In the field of education, two articles are noteworthy. In "Towards a Glocal

Language Curriculum," Diana Hicks differentiates between globalization and glocalization. Globalization, on the one hand, is the process whereby multinationals and international government organizations rapidly spread products, technologies, and ideas around the world. Glocalization, on the other hand, is a process that starts in the local community and then spreads outside. The English language learning curriculum, Hicks argues, should be the starting point in glocalization. Although English is a global language, students will "learn more about their own local language and their own use of language through learning another one." Likewise, the context in which the English language is taught will teach students about their local world. "Whatever the topic the starting point is the world of the student" (http://www.disal.com.br/nroutes/nr4/pgnr4_05.htm). In "Crafting a 'Glocal' Education: Focusing on Food, Women, and Globalization," Deborah Barndt argues that "glocal education" aims to help women understand the way their local practices as food providers for their families connect with the growing global forces of food production and distribution. "At the root of the current ecological and cultural crisis is a mechanistic paradigm promulgated by modern science and exemplified by the Cartesian separation of the human mind from the human body." Barndt's "glocal education" tries to transcend such dualities as mind/body. Her article also exemplifies the transdisciplinarity necessary to cover such a topic from the perspectives of both education and environmental studies (http://www.yorku.ca/faculty/academic/dbarndt/glocalarticle.html).

Overlapping between education and journalism, the PSB Broadcasting site in Pusan, South Korea, lists its goals: "to be a leader in the glocalization age; to promote public welfare; to renovate education and further the local culture; to help develop Pusan." It aims to "execute a primary role in developing local society" and to "lead local society into internationalization." Like the VilaWeb site described below, this site is devoted to using global communication techniques in order to promote local culture (http://www.psb.co.kr/eng/about/aboutPSB/aboutPSB.html). Similar to PSB's site, the city of Nakajo, Japan, has opened an office in Tokyo with the purpose of introducing more businesses to the industrial park in Nakajo and offering Nakajo's local products and industries to the wider public. I believe that this is an example of the original glocalization concept mentioned in Jessop's article mentioned above (http://www.town.nakajo.niigata.jp/Eng/glocal.html).

In "Glocal Journalism: Using the Tools of Globality for the Information of Proximity," the unnamed author goes one step further than PSB or the city of Nakajo. He uses "glocalism" to illustrate a new method of reporting the news. The electronic newspaper VilaWeb is "defined by the objective of permanently informing the human community that was closest to us, at the same time using the tools of the internet to create a participative model, different from the classic media." VilaWeb is a Catalonian site dedicated to bringing together websites managed in Catalonia and those that make reference to that area. It aims to report local news accurately by providing viewers with links to all available reports on a particular event (http://partal.com/welcome/glocal/English.html).

In contrast to education or journalism, an unnamed South Korean political scientist (in a speech delivered at Taejon University in Taejon, South Korea) theorized "glocalism" by defining it as a new paradigm in which "global federations, nation states, and local governments coexist in the international community, cooperating and competing with each other and dynamically playing their respective roles." This author's supporting example of glocalization dates back to 1988 when the mayor of Kuji City protested against Mikhail Gorbachev's Soviet military intervention in Lithuania. Because the two cities were closely related through the production of amber, the mayor helped out Klaveida, Kuji City's sister city, by sending medicine worth fifteen million yen to Lithuania. He thus responded to an international issue with local concerns and consequences in mind. This article may illustrate the original meaning of the term as developed within political science by emphasizing the importance of local government in maintaining national and global security (http://www.eco.shimane-u.ac.jp/~tomino/gdlg.txt).

Mixing politics and economics, Veli-Matti Hynninen's short article "Effeto Finlandia—First Steps Towards Glocalism," calls for Finland to take a more global stance by participating in the European community while still retaining Finnish cultural heritage and values. "Finland, the northern fringe of Europe, is no longer the fringe, but the heart . . . The best way to further local issues is to think globally. Glocalism means local action in a global framework. The new Europe is glocal. The new Finland is glocal. Today local must also be global" (http://www.kolumbus.fi/pater/finlandi.htm). A more straightforward example of the application of glocalism to economics is the way the Russian software company Akella has localized a video game by simply making a high-quality translation of the "POD" game into the Russian language. This example follows the early Japanese model of global localization whereby a large multinational makes decisions that affect local markets (http://www.akella.ru/English/glocal.html).

The opposite approach is reflected in the following example emerging from a concern for the environment. An editorial in a German student magazine argues that the town of Siegen must take its own actions in environmental issues because

Bonn is not doing enough about global warming. If Siegen were to set its own energy agenda, it would be acting locally through global knowledge and thereby affecting the global situation (http://glocal.avmz.uni-siegen.de/loccult/locculted.html). Paraphrasing another website, glocal action by local governments such as the town of Siegen would prevent global warming (http://www.earthday-j.org/English/about_edj.html). Both of these environmental examples reflect a similar tension between universal ethics and individual human responsibility, which leads one site to refer to environmental issues as glocal problems (http://www.bicc.de/sef/events/1998/symposium/kuschel.html). In these three cases, the use of the word "glocal" strictly refers to local initiatives that are both based on global knowledge and linked to global impact.

The same emphasis is shared in the following three examples taken from the world of art and architecture. Benjamin Genocchio reviews the art of Laurens Tan, a multimedia artist who fuses old and new technology in a process Tan calls "historic futurism." Gennochio finds in Tan's work "a desire to explore the social and ideological implications of technological change, in particular global unification and a corresponding loss of individual and cultural identities. One could describe this process as "glocalism"—the local experience of global phenomena." (http://www.artasiapacific.com/articles/glocalism/index.html). In "Glocal Scents of Thailand," an art exhibit in Sweden of ten young Thai artists, the curator, Shukit Panmongkol, writes: "the starting point of 'Glocal scents of Thailand' is the existence of an artistic consciousness which, however implicitly, creates images that are compelling in the present and relevant in an international and contemporary discourse but equally strongly grounded in local, cultural, and historical aspects of Thailand." Whether glocalization is a good or bad phenomenon remains ambiguous, as the article points out both the cohesion and the tension between new and old, modern and traditional (http://www.edsvikart.com/utstallningar/glocalshukit.html). A similar stress on integrating old and new runs through Professor Celestino Soddu's architectural plan to build throughout Italy a network of twenty thousand "telematic piazzas." These structures would unite "virtual communities" by offering Internet access, email, video-conferences, e-commerce, and so forth. While the greater Italian community would be brought together through the network, so would the smaller towns because the townsfolk would meet at the piazza. In this way, these piazzas would globalize and localize the communities all at once, creating social cohesion and new sources of tensions on both global and local levels. The local authorities would decide on the basis of local needs which technological standards and types of multimedia and telematic services are to be provided at the piazza. This project aims to promote economic and social cohesion, promotion and development of cultural heritage, and balanced competition all over Italy. Soddu notes the evolution from "local village" to "global village" to our present "glocal village" (http://www.piazzetelematiche.it/doc_e_genart.html and http://www.artscene.de/mv/eo/1999).

Another example in which values are one of the outcomes of a glocal application of knowledge comes from the field of development. In "Glocal: An Integrated Community Development Program," a Baha'i husband-and-wife team started a program to develop a local Indian community, aiming to teach technological communication skills in order to help the community share local values with the world. This unidirectional movement from the local to the global fails to explain how the access to global technology is going to impact the local values in the medium to long range (http://www.racz-net.com/glocal).

In the area of religion, a new group called "Glocal: The Global/Local Electronic Communications Networks of Faith Communities and Non-Governmental Organizations" defines the term by writing: "The effects of globalization are quite diverse in different local situations and cultures. They are both global in origin and local in impact, hence the word 'glocal'. . . . Religious communities are by their very nature mediating forces on the global scene. Few other kinds of organizations have such deep local roots and global reach" (http://glocal.peacenet.or.kr/about/about.htm). Indeed, religious communities are uniquely placed for monitoring all forces, whatever the directions of their movement might be (http://www.passiochristi.org/intering.html). For example, in "Zen Buddhism in Brazil: Japanese or Brazilian?" published in the *Journal of Global Buddhism,* "The global expansion of Zen Buddhism carried Shin Bukkyoo [Nationalistic Buddhism] ideas with it. However, they were appropriated by Brazilians and hybridized locally. Similarly, Brazilian Zen took part of this process of Zen Buddhism's 'glocalization' " (http://jgb.la.psu.edu/1/derocha001.html).

From my survey of these and other usages in the Internet of the words "glocal" and "glocalism," four characteristics emerge. First, at the center of perception is the individual: all individuals are at their own center of perception. In that sense, there is no longer any center/periphery dichotomy. Second, the use of either "local" or "global" to describe the locality of any individual at any point in time is inadequate. A person may be traveling worldwide and give the impression of globality or never move beyond the neighborhood and give the impression of locality. Yet, a multinational business executive who is affecting global forces more directly through constant traveling may be reproducing mostly local cultural practices from his or her local "home." The reverse is equally true: many villagers may be physically "static" all their lives, yet through their exposure to the rest of the world, through radio and television in particular, not to mention local marketing campaigns, they participate in shaping global trends through material and conceptual consumption patterns visible in their local markets as well as through their ideological aspirations expressed through conversations affecting local politics and self-understanding. The in-between cases are countless, such as seasonal migrants who give the impression of globality because they move over sometimes large distances while remaining minimally affected by their new but impermanent local environments. Despite much effort at integrating into their local environments, many students on "year abroad programs" exhibit similar tendencies.

This collapse in referential space (that is, from an analytical perspective, there is no longer any isolated "local" space nor any isolated "global" trend) is linked to a third characteristic: collapse in referential time. Past and future collapse into one ever-changing present both in the case of multimedia art, which fuses old and new technology in a process Tan calls "historic futurism," and in Panmongkol's artistic consciousness, which "creates images that are compelling in the present and relevant in an international and contemporary discourse but equally strongly grounded in local, cultural, and historical aspects of Thailand" (see note 7). Both of these examples reflect a fourth characteristic: the collapse of material/form and meaning/content on both the material and the conceptual level. In short, these four characteristics lead me to conclude that the dichotomy local/global is too crude to help as a tool of analysis. Moreover, Celestino Soddu's note on the evolution from "local village" to "global village" to our present "glocal village" can only help to the extent that we continue developing useful definitions of what "glocal" might mean.

Toward this end, I propose to define "glocalism" as a constant reflexive process by which a human being's philosophy/ideology/belief/perception and corresponding praxes understand and integrate reality perceptually, materially, and symbolically in ways that, though not always conscious, try to overcome constantly the gaps between various dichotomies, conceptual and pragmatic, as presented in linguistic representations of reality, that live with interdependent community circles. In the next section, I will apply this definition to contemporary Arab Muslim constructions of religious Others. Then, I will conclude by "flipping the mirror around," so as to examine glocally some of our own methodological concerns as scholars of Islam(s) working from various disciplinary perspectives.

APPLYING "GLOCALISM" TO CONTEMPORARY ARAB
MUSLIM CONSTRUCTIONS OF RELIGIOUS OTHERS

In the course of the twentieth century, especially in its latter half, a rapid increase
in the number of writings on various religions of the world emerged in the Middle East (Brodeur 2000, 116). The importance of these twentieth-century Arab
Muslim constructions of religious Others is at least threefold: first, this new, or
for some renewed, literature represents a link to a thousand-year-old history of
Arabic literary efforts at making sense of religious diversity through understanding religious Others from an Islamic perspective. Second, the name given to this
medieval literature is debated: Guy Monnot has called it "l'histoire musulmane
des religions" (1986, 21) while Steven Wasserstrom referred to it as an "islamicate
history of religions" (1988, 405–11). I suggested elsewhere a third alternative
with the aim of linking both medieval and modern literatures: "a generic system
of religious Others" (2000, 22). These three suggestions intend to displace the
still prevalent expression "Islamic heresiography" that has been used by Orientalists for over one and one-half centuries. Through such debate, I hope to illustrate below how the process of naming this literature can serve as a comparative
mirror through which Western historians of religion and Islamicists in particular
can better look at the history of their own discipline. Third, this literary production reflects one angle of the continuous and turbulent twentieth-century
process of Muslim identity formation. Whether Arab or not, Muslims have confronted many challenges: colonialism and postcolonialism, Cold War and post-
Cold War *pax americana,* as well as premodern, modern, and postmodern
competing world-views. Each one of these factors has played a different role in
defining what Islam ought to be and what being a Muslim means.

Apart from explaining why this literature is important, these three reasons
also reflect my effort at simultaneously integrating questions pertaining to both
modern and postmodern frameworks, indicative of a glocal analysis. For example, a modern reading of twentieth-century Arab Muslim constructions of religious Others asks of this literature a number of straightforward questions: what
do Arab Muslims write on religions other than Islam? Are those descriptions ac-
curate or not? How closely do these authors follow the methodological norms
for precise scientific analysis? As for a postmodern reading of the same literature,
it leads to a different set of questions: how do Arab Muslims write about religions
other than Islam? What assumptions about each author's own self-identity can be
made from their descriptions of religious Others? How far can my understanding of each one's intention go, given the limitations of my own hermeneutical

horizon as the researcher? Who controls the means of production of such writings and benefits from their sale? What kinds of power dynamics are reflected in
the ways in which I, as a Western Christian Islamicist, relate to my Arab Muslim
literary object of analysis? Finally, a glocal reading of this literature raises yet another set of questions that includes and builds on the previous ones: who am I
when I embark on writing the present article? What identity categories do I implicitly and explicitly use in the process of generating my own understanding of
how Arab Muslims write on religious Others? How do I select and write about
twentieth-century Arab Muslim writings on religious Others in relationship to
the authors behind this literature, given that most of them are alive? In other
words, how do I bridge the difference between me as researcher and "them" as
both object and subject of analysis? How do my own philosophy/ideology/be-
lief/perception and corresponding praxes as a writer within a North American
academic context shape the reality I wish to describe? Are my desires to integrate
my perceptions with those of the authors under study motivated by ideology (my
need to have them recognize how their own perceptions of religious Others need
to be rooted in a methodology that sustains the political ideology I subscribe to),
material gain (my need to publish in order to get tenure and secure my own financial well-being), or symbolic meaning (my need to promote a Christian gospel
of love that requires me to "love as I would like to be loved," translated as "describe the Other as I would like my Christian self to be described by Arab Muslims")? What ethics sustains this whole endeavor when, upon reflection, it seems
so narcissistic? What are the benefits of my analysis for the authors I study? And
how do I acknowledge, within my own limited consciousness, the efforts I am
making to overcome the gaps between various dichotomies, conceptual and
pragmatic, as presented in linguistic representations of reality?

One way to analyze twentieth-century Arab Muslim constructions of religious Others glocally and to try answering some of these questions is by examining the use of nomenclature. First, a close examination of medieval Arab Muslim
writings on religious Others reveals that there was no agreed-upon category of
genre for this kind of literature. The most frequently used category was that of
polemical refutation *(radd 'ala)*, which was used in just over a third of the surviving eighty-one cases of book titles produced between 729 and 912 C.E. (Brodeur
2000, 51). In subsequent centuries, this usage continued but decreased in favor of
various other names, such as "divisions and sects" *(al-milal wa-al-nihal)*, popular-
ized by al-Shahrastani's (1076–1153 C.E.) famous *Kitab al-milal wa-al-nihal*. Besides never acquiring a set nomenclature for itself, this literature was
heterogeneous in ideology: from polemics to apologetics to more critical ap-

proaches foreshadowing the nineteenth-century Western European historical-critical methodology. It is not until the later part of the nineteenth century that Western European Orientalists, borrowing from Christian terminology, applied the term "heresiography" to describe all of this diverse Islamic literature on religious Others. Only then the naming process imposed by the Orientalist outsiders for their own analytical purposes de facto created a set category of analysis not previously generated by Muslims themselves. The need for applying such a category was thus a projection from a mostly Western European modern Christian hermeneutical horizon onto a medieval Islamic one, revealing more about the Orientalist world-view than about medieval Islamic understandings of the non-Muslims purported to be described.

By the middle of the twentieth century, a slow but steady revival of Arab Muslim writings on religious Others began to emerge, a phenomenon that has grown exponentially, especially in the last twenty years (Brodeur 2000, 116). The modern Orientalist assumption that there is a clear dichotomy between the medieval and modern constructions of religious Others because of the break between the two periods of production reflects an Enlightenment paradigm that dichotomizes between medieval and modern world-views. There was indeed a break in the production of such literature on religious Others during the eighteenth and nineteenth centuries. However, the twentieth-century revival production is not as different from its first developments a thousand years ago as it may appear on the surface. There is a greater degree of integration that seeks to overcome the gap between medieval and modern world-views in both conceptual and material terms. In order to analyze this point in particular, it is useful to turn to Arjun Appadurai's first two of five new concepts built on an analogy with landscapes: technoscapes, ideoscapes, mediascapes, ethnoscapes, and finanscapes (Appadurai 1990, 296–300).

According to Appadurai, "technoscapes" refer to global configurations of technology. This "technology, both high and low, both mechanical and informational, moves at high speeds across various kinds of previously impervious boundaries" (1990, 297). In our case, Western book technologies and scientific writing styles have become normative and ubiquitous for all twentieth-century Arab Muslim writers on religious Others (Brodeur 2000, 112–14). In terms of high technology, the modern means of production that was made available through the Arabic printing press revolution has completely replaced the premodern means of production. Simultaneously, in terms of low technology, twentieth-century Arab Muslim authors seeking to be taken seriously have come to use scientific writing styles. The whole system of source referencing with quotes, footnotes, and bibliography became the normative format in Arab Muslim writings on religious Others during the course of the twentieth century, mimetically reproducing what had become the powerful Western academic writing norm. Therefore, the technoscape of the production on religious Others, both high and low, has drastically changed between the formative medieval and modern periods.

As for "ideoscapes," they are "concatenations of images, but they are often directly political and frequently have to do with the ideologies of states and the counter-ideologies of movements explicitly oriented to capturing state power or a piece of it. These ideoscapes are composed of elements of the Enlightenment world-view" (Appadurai 1990, 299). Examples of ideoscapes pervade a majority of Arab Muslim writings on religious Others, especially concerning Judaism. Representations of Jews as seekers of world power, heavily influenced by the popular revival of the Protocols of the Elders of Zion (Bronner 2000, 136), is one clear example of a concatenation of images that sustains a counter-ideology to undermine the state of Israel. In all cases of modern Arab Muslim writings on religious Others, these ideoscapes contain elements of the Enlightenment. Whether developed or not in classical Arabic, contemporary concepts always appear in modern standard Arabic under the influence of Western thought translated into Arabic (Ayalon 1987). For example, the expressions "comparative religions" *(muqaranat al-adyan)* and "history of religions" *(ta'rikh al-adyan)* only appear in modern Arabic. Thus, a similar trajectory of transformation in the essentializing of the meaning of the word "religion" that took place in Western Europe during the period of the Enlightenment (Smith 1962, 38) happened in the Arab world under the influence of colonialism between the latter half of the nineteenth and the first half of the twentieth century (Brodeur 2000, 252–81).

What Appadurai does not include in his above definition is that ideoscapes, in addition to including elements of the Enlightenment, never completely lose premodern characteristics. For instance, the modern spectrum of representations of religious Others overlaps closely with the premodern spectrum, from polemics to apologetics to historical-critical textual approaches. In fact, the concept of a concatenation of images holds as much for a concatenation of genres: in the present literature, many genres coexist even though they come from different historical time zones. The wholesale reproduction of medieval Arabic books on religious Others, not necessarily as the result of careful philological and historical re-editing but for popular modern consumption, points toward this collapse of past and present as distinct categories. In addition, the availability of those works through global distribution channels owned and managed by Muslims and non-Muslims alike, although often for radically different purposes, reflects countless examples of how gap-time functions.

In short, the difference between Arab Islamic technoscapes and ideoscapes of religious Others is remarkable. While the mimetic appropriation in the realm of technoscape has enjoyed a high degree of success, in the area of ideoscape there was a move from the mimesis of the colonial period to the mimicry of the postcolonial and "glocal" times. If pastiche is "the imitation of a peculiar or unique style, the wearing of a stylistic mask" (Jameson 1998a, 5), I would argue that the majority of the modern twentieth-century Arab Muslims who have written books on religious Others in the last thirty years are practicing such pastiche. Even though the variety of genres used to represent religious Others has increased, the category of polemics still remains the predominant genre. The heritage of decades of Orientalism on this phenomenon of representation of religious Others consolidated this tendency toward the judgmental and essentializing approaches to self/Other representation in Muslim history. Even though such polemical writings may constitute the predominant voice in the modern and contemporary Arab Muslim constructions of religious Others, the historical-critical voice, tiny in the medieval period, is now growing. With this voice comes a more self-reflective interrelationship that creates the characteristics necessary to move from the dialectics of modernity/postmodernity to the integrated reflexive process of "glocalism."

This process requires a broader focus of analysis, which can only be mentioned here in passing. Twentieth-century Arab Muslim literature on religious Others overlaps with three broader literary areas: modern Arab constructions of the Other in general, modern Islamic constructions of the Other in a variety of languages, and modern reproduction of medieval Arabic writings on religious Others. The relationship between these three overlapping areas implies not only a "gap-time" but also a "glocal space." The "gap-time" is reflected in the implicit differentiation between various ethnic, linguistic, nationalist, and/or religious identities at play in these three overlapping areas. The "glocal space" emerges from the fact that some of the Arab Muslim authors that produced this literature did not necessarily live in the Arab world at the time of their writing, nor had their lives been confined to it before writing (Brodeur 2000, 134–38). The differential space between physical geographical movement and intellectual geographical movement (through books, media, and so forth) implies a "glocal space."

Therefore, by developing the concept of glocalism as a reflexive discursive process, I hope to have enriched our understanding of twentieth-century Arab Muslims' philosophy/ideology/belief/perception and corresponding praxes regarding book production on "religious others." Arab Muslim authors have developed various ways to integrate perceptually, materially, and symbolically the varieties of religious Others around them.

The changing nature of Islam as an object of study, materially and ideologically (Nanji 1997), and of Muslims as primary interpreters of what Islam means, requires that both Westernized Muslim and especially non-Muslim scholars creatively integrate many of their descriptive categories in order both to be more sensitive to internal Islamic classificatory schema and to move away from Orientalist categories, as in the case of "heresiography." Yet my suggestion to replace "heresiography" with the expression "religious Others" as well as my definition of "glocalism" may be criticized as equally Western, given that they emerge from a Western philosophic tradition rooted in the theorized dialectic between self and Other. It could not be otherwise according to the Gadamerian notion that the "interlacing of horizons cannot be methodologically eliminated" (Ormiston and Schrift 1990, 221). Indeed, there is no escape from my own hermeneutical circle bound between the movement of a composite Western tradition and that of an equally composite Islamic tradition as reflected, for example, in contemporary Arab Muslim constructions of religious Others. The increase in scholarly inquiry on the relations between the Islamic world and other cultures and religions (Waardenburg 1999) stems as much from the subjectivities of the predominantly non-Muslim Western European and North American researchers of this topic as from the subjectivities of a growing number of contemporary Muslims around the world who write about and research non-Muslims and their relations to Muslims and Islam. All writers, whether authors of contemporary Arabic Muslim writings on religious Others or academic inquirers on such a topic now share a common glocal reality whose internal boundaries of perception, though, often vary sharply. It is the constant search for more suitable linguistic representations of reality to overcome such differential space and gap-time that leads to creative yet highly debated new forms seeking a greater degree of conceptual integration.

THE IMPLICATIONS OF "GLOCALISM"
FOR SCHOLARS OF ISLAM

We are finally able to "flip the mirror around" so as to examine the integration of local with global forces in our own methodological concerns as scholars interested in Islam(s). Indeed, it is no longer possible to say that what brought together many of the authors of this book's articles for the Harvard workshop on "Muslims and Islam(s) in the Age of Postmodernity and Globalization" was a

common professional or disciplinary identity as Islamicists. The Orientalist localism of a European-based academic discipline concerned with a clearly demarcated *dar al-islam* Other as the object of study is a bygone era. Yet the localisms of
institutions rooted in material and symbolic power, such as the premise of this
book's initial conference at Harvard University, continue their influence on shaping reality. The participation of Muslims and non-Muslims in the construction of
academic representations of Islam(s) reflects a healthy intersubjectivity that is
another revealing factor of the multiplicity of ways in which Muslims today deal
with religious diversity. The very nature of our inquiry into the relationship between Islam(s) and postmodernity at once requires multiple tools, yielding an interdisciplinary and inter-communicative audience, as proven by the composition
of this book. As for the non-Muslim scholars of Islam among us, whether our
own scholarly efforts are just a pastiche of Islam as understood by many practicing Muslims today, whether they are fellow scholars or not, we can never escape
the interdependence between our own subjectivities as non-Muslim researchers
and that of our Muslim "subjects" of inquiry. The reverse is equally true, tying us
all into a complex web of symbiotic interrelationships.

What is less obvious for most Westerners, especially the non-Muslims like
myself, and this may be for fear of acknowledging our own past lingering into the
present, is the growing hybridization in what was once a local European production of well-crafted historical-philological tools used to serve the needs of a burgeoning scientific discipline called Oriental Studies. Such tools have not only
been reused as secondhand methods handed down to the younger (and often
economically poorer) Muslim brothers (rarely sisters). These tools have also, in
this process, been reinvented to suit the immediate needs of radically different
audiences. To the extent that this process applies to the usage of Orientalist paraphernalia by Muslims themselves around the world, thereby producing a distorted mirror phenomenon of Occidentalism (Tavakoli-Targhi 2001), as scholars
of Islam we have no choice but to acknowledge how localized versions of secondhand Orientalisms are now breeding their own transmutations. These localisms also have their own ways of propagating themselves, especially through
human and electronic transmigrations, therefore making it more appropriate to
call them "glocalisms."

The degree of exposure to one another across cultures, underlined by the
concomitant increase in competition to control the earth's resources, has led
many people to question and write about their own identity and their unavoidable
mutual relations with various Others. We are faced with one another as mirrors in
which to recognize our own selves, to imagine our respective identities in their

similarities and differences, whether religious or disciplinary. Indeed, "the mutual relations of the disciplines is never one of autonomy or of heteronomy, but some sort of complicated set of textual relations that needs to be unraveled in each instance" (Godzich 1986, x). This book is one such instance where gap-time and glocalism fuse into what Mark Taylor calls a "moment of complexity" reflecting our "emerging network culture" (Taylor 2001).

11

The Scandal of Literalism in Hamas, the Israeli-Palestinian Conflict, and Beyond

ANNE MARIE OLIVER

CONTEMPORARY LITERALISMS

The migration and dispersal of populations, the electronic extension of the human sensorium, the progressive abstraction of matter, an encroaching mono-lingualism, cultural and economic homogenization, communications traversing the earth at unknown rates: these hallmarks of dematerialization and globalization do more than smudge territorial and bodily boundaries, they threaten the very conditions of identity, the signatures of individuals and entire collectives, provoking as they do crises in traditional notions of word and world. The material world sheds its substance, becomes etherized, while everyday language, deprived of opportunities for instantiating itself, becomes an object of doubt and cynicism. At the same time, we witness a counter-phenomenon. For many peoples around the globe, what was once a cluster of mutually supportive common-alities—common territory, common origin, and so forth—has been severely reduced. Language constitutes one of the last remaining embodiments of collective identity—ethnic, cultural, religious—and is thus forced to carry the major burden of identity-conferment, even as it becomes increasingly subject to crises of verification.

The current preoccupation with various tensions—universalism and partic-ularism, relativism and absolutism, globalization and authenticity, unity and dis-persal—can be seen as a symptom in and of itself of this incarnational crisis. The

I thank Zsuzsa Baross, Kanan Makiya, and Mira Zergani for reading and commenting on this essay.

paradox at work is that precisely at the moment when "diversity" and "pluralization" are celebrated, diversity and pluralization announce their absence from the
scene, their very impossibility, in much the same way that globalization can be
said to herald a radical constriction of the world. The old singular forms disinte-
grate, and across their sacred corpses swarm a host of particles whose power lies
almost solely in number—crowds, colonies, throngs, hordes—as in the Last
Days, when, it is written, masses, both demonic and angelic, will overwhelm the
earth—Gog and Magog, the Army of God, the ingathered faithful, the masses of
the quick and the dead arrayed before the eye of God in Jerusalem at "the Hour"
(al-sa'a), bees, rain, clouds, stones.

The disintegration of traditional unities and the rise of "the masses" as political force are not unrelated movements, for we can say that it is precisely the latter that by sheer number produces the appearance, if not the concrete reality, of
the former. Within the power center itself of the new globalizing order, we see a
similar dyad—the dematerialization of traditional unities and the emergence of
masses that simulate unity but find expression in less overtly political terms, that
is, in terms of biologies and technologies—swarming viruses, biologic and electronic; superorganisms from corporate entities to dreams of human hives, capital in the form of informational hordes traversing the earth at the speed of light;
potentially infinite clones—all of which express a fundamental transformation
in the notion of material unity. At the moment when identity-as-unity falls apart,
indeed, when the material world itself seems on the verge of disappearance, the
swarm appears. In the old forms, the swarm was believed to manifest an invisible
spirit; in many of its new incarnations, the swarm itself has become invisible.[1]

Is it any wonder that we look with ever-increasing wonder at revolutions,
mass movements, religion? And is it any wonder that the old textual forms of
"fundamentalism" have become the subject of renewed interest, the hoped-for
solution to linguistic crisis, the basis for political action? Indeed, can we not entertain the paradox that one of the most remarkable characteristics of the time is
precisely "fundamentalism," a particular type of determinism that dreams of a
fundamental isomorphism between codes and their referents, and believes that it
can mine down to a primeval layer of reality and discover essences? Preoccupied
with origins, correspondences, series, and sequences of exact precision, we thus
find ourselves once again in the realm of pure form, semiotic magic.

One might even speak of warring fundamentalisms, for we should distin-

---

1. It was Elias Canetti's opinion (1962, 42–47) that religions possibly begin with such invisible
crowds.

guish textual literalism, or textual fundamentalism, from the far newer literalist techniques of power and control, which might be called biotechnic. In this essay, I will be interested primarily in textual forms of literalism—the transformation of seemingly stable symbols and allegories into prophetic signs—as a basis of resistance to new codes, new totalizing principles, new religions that do not announce themselves as such. The return to textual literalism, or fundamentalism, should not be seen as simple nostalgia or as a simple expression of resistance to the constriction of the world that globalization announces. Involving the resurrection of particularist scripts, literalist systems constitute "deglobalizing reactions," to use Featherstone's (1995) phrase, but they themselves often aspire to a universalism on a par with that of the ideological systems they oppose. My example is Islamism, and, in particular, the Islamic Resistance Movement (Hamas), its literalization of sacred scripts of sacrifice, martyrdom, and apocalypticism within the Israeli-Palestinian conflict, that most literary and (alternately) literalist of conflicts.

ISLAMISM AS LITERALIST PROJECT

"Is Islamism driven by religious fervor, social protest, or nationalist xenophobia? Is the rise of Islamism a threat to stability, tolerance, and order? Or is it the first step toward reform, participation, and democratization? Does repression of Islamists radicalize them or tame them? Are Islamists in power guided by their ideals or their interests? Does Islamism have the momentum to remake the future, or is it a rearguard action that is already failing?" (Kramer 1997, 7).

Here are the questions that initiate a typical book on the subject of Islamism. Let me say from the beginning that these questions, which regularly crop up in essays on the subject, are important questions, but perhaps, in the end, the wrong questions, or rather, the most uninteresting questions that might be asked of Islamism, for Islamism has inaugurated not only a political and religious revolution in the Middle East and elsewhere, but also a linguistic and aesthetic one. I am not speaking simply of a renaissance of dead copy, although such a revival can be seen within Islamism, but rather of the return of a new old aesthetic of power and identity inseparable from language. I could choose another word to describe the phenomenon in question—politics, order, system, ideology, religion, 'aqida—but have chosen this one because it privileges *affect* over *fact*. For this reason alone, we cannot speak so soon of "the failure of political Islam," or, for that matter, of any other form of twentieth-century fundamentalism, religious or other; quite possibly, we will never be able to do so. For with Islamism, we are not dealing with error, error that once detected and made manifest would bring

down an entire system, but rather with a particular resurgence, a vertical revivalism virtually immune to error and human judgment in general. We would speak
instead of the return of a movement that bears witness to the force of literalism
as a means of subverting the established order, of radically interrupting mundane life, of introducing once again the eternal universal, of instantiating language if not God Himself, before consuming itself—an eventuality that will be
interpreted not as evidence of "failure" but rather of power, efficacy, realization,
and divine judgment.

This essay, then, can be seen as a response of sorts to a particular trend in
studies on Islamism—and Hamas, my particular interest here—which is the oc-
clusion of language. It is a response to all those who believe that by eliminating
language or by treating it simply as ornament, transitional object, or
instrument[2]—strategy or tactic—they are getting at the facts. For whether taking
the form of apologetics or catastrophism, these works proceed from the illusion
that one can separate word and act, raw materials and their transformation,
through language, desire, poetry. After these have been pushed out of the picture, there is nothing significant that can be said about the phenomenon in question, just as the Holy Land can hardly be said to exist outside the bizarre collective
fantasies that have amassed and constellated around it over the centuries.

Questions such as whether Islamism is a political or religious phenomenon
are even less illuminating. They make no sense outside language; indeed, one can
question whether they make any sense at all, particularly when they are directly
correlated with pragmatics and fanaticism, respectively, for the operative assumption is that if groups like Hamas are primarily political phenomena, then
they are capable of being co-opted and domesticated; if, on the contrary, they are
religious phenomena, then perforce they are essentially resistant to any co-optive
move. The division of the political and the religious along these lines is an artificial one, and by that I do not refer so much to the concept of *din wa-dawla,* but to
the more general fact that religion cannot be adequately separated from politics,
law, or any other system of judgment outside the realm of language.

What I want to do here is simply to pose a series of questions with regard to

2. A "content analysis" of Islamist rhetoric, for instance, is sometimes called for, but such an
exercise cannot possibly yield anything other than a term's frequency of usage. The sheer fact that
the term *"jihad"* appears frequently in the Islamist lexicon, for instance, does not show us when it
must be considered, first and foremost, as signifying certain authoritative conditions of speech,
nor, conversely, when its literalist force is dominant. During times of conflict and war, needless to
say, the literalist immediacy of the term prevails, and to argue then that its meaning is purely formal
or that, as is more often, the term refers solely to "the greater *jihad,*" an interiorized or spiritual
struggle, is pure silliness.

the move from symbols to signs, or from the literary, or metaphorical, to the literal, as it relates to the problem of judgment—a move that is not limited to Hamas, but rather is symptomatic of the Israeli-Palestinian conflict as a whole—if not perhaps of a more widespread condition whose operative fantasy is radical desymbolization. Like the suicide bomber, who constitutes his shadow, the contemporary subject seeks both to confirm himself through language, history, and judgment, but also to be rid of them completely;[3] in short, we might speak of the anxiety of civilization—a civilization (debt and inheritance) whose cradle and grave, I want to suggest, have been rediscovered in ostensibly political form in the twentieth century in and through that great morality play, Manichaean drama, and scene of judgment called the Israeli-Palestinian conflict.

VERTICAL LITERALISM; OR, THE ISRAELI-PALESTINIAN CONFLICT

Countless people the world over see the Israeli-Palestinian conflict not only as an "ancient" antagonism but, more problematically, as the dramatic fulfillment of sacred texts and prophecies, a modern-day reenactment of the battle between the Sons of Light and the Sons of Darkness; that is, we are dealing with a primary form of literalism, and we could raise the question as to what function is served by transforming a twentieth-century conflict into a primeval rivalry.[4] The parties to the conflict themselves embrace this type of prefiguration as key to their identity and distinction, while at the same time seeking escape from the resultant anxiety and judgment through various "riddance responses" and preemptive strikes, which the suicide bomber can be said to epitomize. That these responses express themselves through the selfsame authorized literary and cultural forms that catalyzed the process of overdetermination in the first place—tragedy, Manichaenism, sacrifice, martyrdom, and apocalypticism—shows the double-edged or ambivalent nature of such forms, their capacity for engendering radical reversals of means and ends.

    This profound overdetermination suggests an intense anxiety; let us call it again "the anxiety of civilization," a civilization whose determinative weight

    3. I mean "the contemporary subject" in its originary sense as one subject to forces beyond his or her control—language, fate, world.

    4. As with the phenomenon of déjà vu, which this prefiguring resembles, we must ask what is being repressed, and what enables the *affect* of a return? What type of collective fantasy, in other words, is at work?

threatens to make us all into hunchbacks, as in the hunched man carrying Jerusalem on his back in Sliman Mansour's famous painting entitled *Carry On.* Why does the little man not just throw the thing off his back and walk away? The thought must surely pass through his mind now and again. The little man, who is neither properly Arab nor Jew, Palestinian nor Israeli, can we not say, is the carrier of something, and what is that something but "the world" or "civilization"—the sheer "perseveration of cultural forms," as Bakan (1971, 29 f.) would have it, that is, all those defense strategies of collective life embedded in language that persist through time even when—or perhaps especially when—they have become obstacles in the way of envisioning alternative futures and alternative modes of transformation. The little man, in short, carries the law, as in Divine Law, and as such, he is both the object of inestimable esteem and abject resentment if not despisal.

If the Israeli-Palestinian conflict is a preeminent judicial topos of the late twentieth century, it is also the place where "the ultimate insolubility of all legal problems," to quote Walter Benjamin,[5] is displayed in exaggerated form. Its subjects are emblematic of this ambivalence toward language and judgment: they are treated as superjudicial—that is, as carriers of the Law, avatars of monumentalism—and, alternately, as prelegal, the latter occurring under two conditions. The first occurs whenever passion, that oldest and greatest of mitigating circumstances, rules discourse about them as well as their own discourse about themselves, leveling everything in its path. The second, which is paradoxical and far more interesting, occurs whenever they become not only carriers of Divine Law, but attempt to fulfill that law in the here-and-now, to realize it completely.

We might go so far as to say that the Israeli-Palestinian conflict has become, at least for those under its influence, one of the last vestiges of the Real (indeed, perhaps of God Himself); that is, it is instinctually turned to whenever Language, Truth, and Judgment have become critically indeterminate. More than this, it speaks of and to an intense nostalgia for vertical monumentalism, or "vertical

---

5. "How would it be, therefore, if all the violence imposed by fate, using justified means, were of itself in irreconcilable conflict with just ends, and if at the same time a different kind of violence came into view that certainly could be either the justified or the unjustified means to those ends, but was not related to them as means at all but in some different way? This would throw light on the curious and at first discouraging discovery of the ultimate insolubility of all legal problems (which in its hopelessness is perhaps comparable only to the possibility of conclusive pronouncements on 'right' and 'wrong' in evolving languages). For it is never reason that decides on the justification of means and the justness of ends, but fate-imposed violence on the former and God on the latter" (Benjamin 1968, 293–94).

madness," as Jean Baudrillard might put it, for what distinguishes this conflict is precisely its vertical elements;[6] that is, the horizontality of history is punctuated by ascensions, descensions, sublime deaths, resurrections, and God-directed originary events, as in the divine time lines beloved by the faithful that begin with "The Creation of Adam" and then move on through a series of firsts, ending finally with that most vertical of all vertical events, or rather, series of events—Armageddon, the End of the World, the Last Judgment.

In a completely vertical universe, there are no accidents, errors, forgettings, chance. Indeed, the very notion of accidentality is suspect. Everything is consequential, and no one and nothing escapes the laws of judgment; no one is innocent. At the same time, we can say that everyone is, in fact, inculpable given that individuals within such a system are always in the end subject to the laws of an authority that is itself subjectless, or rather is not a human subject. We must ask what happens to language and judgment in the face of monumental verticality, and how transformation is possible at all within such an overdetermined system. What kinds of devices, that is, are called upon to facilitate movement within such a system? One of those devices, as I have suggested, is literalism.

A Mississippi cattleman reads Numbers 19, and spends the next ten years of his life trying to produce a Red Heifer,[7] a project reportedly aided by U.S. govern-

6. More than any other Palestinian political group, the Islamists emphasize the vertical dimension in tacit recognition of the fact that the Palestinians, like the Jews in exile, possess two strong criteria for identifying themselves as a people and a nation—the possession of a common god and a sacred writing whose subject is that god. The two criteria can be said to be, in actuality, one. Islamists believe that Palestinians will accomplish nothing by borrowing the terms of systems other than Islam; indeed, all other systems constitute perfidious examples of *bid'a* (innovation), under whose rubric are included, for instance, the lexicons of nationalism and international legality— "self determination," "autonomy," "independence," and so forth—as utilized by the Palestine Liberation Organization, as well as the international lexicon of Marxism and Leninism preferred by the left-wing factions (the Popular Front for the Liberation of Palestine, the Democratic Front for the Liberation of Palestine, and the Palestinian Communist Party). Hamas, its adherents claim, has everything that these factions have, but to quote from the movement's *mithaq,* or covenant, "It has more. It has a higher essence that is more significant, for divine causes give it spirit and life. And there is a relation to the source of spirit and the giver of life, which raises the banner of God in the skies of the homeland and so connects the heaven and the earth by a strong bond."

7. In 1990, Clyde Lott of Canton, Mississippi, began corresponding with Rabbi Chaim Richman of the Temple Institute about the exact specifications of the Red Heifer—a red, unblemished heifer upon which a yoke had never been placed and which in ancient times was ritually slaughtered and burned, its ashes mixed with spring water and made into a paste to purify high priests before they entered the Temple. The animal is necessary for purifying the Temple site, and is referred to in Numbers 19:2–7 of the Torah.

Lott successfully bred a pure red heifer, thus exciting those Jews who believe that the discov-

mental agencies and Israeli yeshivot, and a project that will, notably, hasten the dream of reestablishing the Jewish Temple, which, in turn, will entail the destruction of the Islamic holy sites now established on the Mount, if not the actuation of the Armageddon script. This is literalism. A seven-year-old Palestinian boy hears the Qur'anic scripture "And do not think that those who are killed on the path of God are dead; Nay, they are alive and with their Lord, well provided for,"[8] and places himself in a line of fire. This is literalism. An Israeli settler sprays bullets into Palestinian passersby in the Hebron suq, quoting a biblical verse as his imprimatur, "Abraham bought the Cave of the Patriarchs for four hundred shekels of silver . . . No one will return it."[9] This is literalism. A Gaza youth takes as his own the words "And it was not you who slew them, but Allah slew them,"[10] and then goes out and blows himself up, taking as many of the enemy with him as possible. This is literalism.

---

ery of a red heifer will open the way for the rebuilding of the Temple and the coming of the Jewish Messiah—a view shared by those Christians who view the Third Temple as a sign of the return of Jesus. Lott and Richman soon laid the groundwork for what is now called the Canaan Land Restoration of Israel, Inc., with Clyde Lott as president. The organization is said to ship planeloads of red cattle to Israel, 140 heifers per load.

On 15 April 1997, according to London's *Sunday Telegraph,* a team of rabbis confirmed the birth of a red heifer in Israel. Rabbinical opinion up until that time was that no flawless red heifer had been born in Israel since the destruction of Herod's Temple in 70 A.D. by the Roman Emperor Titus. The birth of Melody, as the cow was dubbed, was considered a miracle, particularly given that her mother was a black-and-white cow, her father a dun-colored bull. A spot of white was later discovered on her, and she was declared an unfit sacrifice.

8. The quotation, the most ubiquitous of tributes paid to Palestinian martyrs, nationalist or Islamist, is derived from the Qur'an (3:169). It reproduces a speech delivered in the early days of Islam by Muhammad to his followers who had just suffered a serious military defeat after a number of victories. The speech not only assures the survivors that the fallen are in heaven, but goes on to rebuke the *kuffar* or "unbelievers" who had taunted the followers of Islam with the claim that had they heeded their words and stayed at home, "they would not have died nor would they have been killed."

9. On 1 January 1997, Israeli settler and off-duty soldier Noam Friedman, dressed in his Israel Defense Forces uniform, opened fire on Palestinians in Hebron's Gross Square, near the Jewish enclave of Avraham Avinu, injuring six. Friedman said that the act was meant to prevent an Israeli withdrawal from the West Bank city and to avenge the death of Baruch Goldstein, the American-born settler who in 1994 gunned down dozens of Palestinians praying at al-Ibrahimi Mosque, located in the Second Temple Period building that Jews call the "Cave of the Machpela"—the traditional burial site of Abraham, Isaac, Rebecca, Leah, and Jacob.

10. The verse, Qur'an 8:17, is used by Hamas trainer Muhammad 'Aziz Rushdi to embolden and inspire his charges—members of the cell Force 3—to carry out a suicide operation, and appears on the videotape *The Giants of al-Qassam,* which also features the youths' last testaments.

Suicide bombings are a spectacular example of what we mean when we say that literalism always points to a subversive force at work. Although they are internally justified by scriptural and legal arguments, and the youth who carry them out invariably present themselves as instances of embodied imperative, the very fulfillment of sacred scripts, suicide bombings are, in actuality, explosive dissolutions of self and other, word and world, and can be said to signal a deep crisis in language, religion, and the notions of truth and justice. For we must ask what it might mean for a subject to identify himself completely with a sacred script and then blow himself up, taking not only the enemy with him but the script he is said to embody as well, all in the selfsame moment. In the final analysis, suicide bombings might be said to constitute a subversive phenomenon even perhaps within the ideological system that authorizes them, not because they assume unprecedented form, but because they overliteralize preexisting scripts, thereby bringing them to crisis. Indeed, can we not pose the question as to whether the function of a suicide bombing is to disable or throw off Language, History, and Judgment, indeed, let us say, put an end to them, precisely through their sheer and utter realization? For the final product is not the Dream of a Perfect Language, but rather explosion, ecstatic dissolution, speechlessness, oblivion. When a suicide bomber says that he desires nothing more than Paradise itself, perhaps we should take him at his word, for Paradise is precisely the realm of speechlessness, the place where the tongue becomes a superfluous organ.[11] As there is no time, there is no language; as there is no language, there is no judgment.

If suicide bombings are radical "riddance mechanisms," preemptive strikes that attempt to throw off the burdens of Language, History, and Judgment, they also, however, produce their own system of judgment. The suicide bomber, that is, seeks to become a prelegal subject, a subject incapable of being judged by humans, at the same time as he acquires the status of judge, for death is commonly perceived as something like a vertical or divine judgment, and the suicide bomber, as an agent of death, partakes of that power. Possessed by ancestral spirits and guided by supernatural forces, he is presented as an epic hero, the embodiment of the *umma* in its search for glory, immortality, redemption, rebirth, divinity. His tale is told in a mixture of history and pseudohistory, fact and legend. The endless catalogues of people and things peculiar to his narrative lend it the semblance of a crowd across whose shoulders he rides effortlessly. Indeed,

11. Whether the shiny, metallic version of heaven particular to American Protestantism or the sensuous Islamic paradise, all notions of paradise share the fact that their denizens are upon entry rendered speechless, and happily so.

he might be said to contain a host of crowds within himself—religious, national, angelic, ecstatic—which are condensed in and transfigured through him, and which live through his sacrificial death and vertiginously vertical ascension.

THE FROG AND THE SCORPION: A FABLE

If our subject is literalism, we must speak not only of those subjects who turn to literalism for various purposes, but also of those subjects—or more properly, subject-objects—for whom literalism can be said to be their very mode of existence in the world, those for whom symbols can hardly be said to exist. One would have to speak of the literalism of children, the literalism of animals, the literalism attributed to women, lunatics, and God, and of the ways in which these figures are captured and inhabited whenever transformation in and of itself is an objective, whenever the subject is attempting to move toward a prelegal status. Thus, with regard to the suicide bomber, we can trace a series of conditions—Woman, Animal, Child—through which he passes on his way to reaching the status of Metallic Man and Human Bomb. That this series moves from the animate to the inanimate is remarkable precisely because it represents not only the would-be hero's petrification but also everything he must leave behind on his quest.

I want now to turn to that hackneyed little fable of enemies and tale of murder-suicide called "The Frog and the Scorpion" precisely because its form is fabular rather than prophetic—that is, we are dealing primarily with a horizontal universe—and thus we see judgment as it is made from the bottom up, as it were. The fable, as you may remember, goes something like this:

> Once upon a time, there was a scorpion sitting on the bank of a river. He wanted to cross to the other side, but he could not swim. He saw a frog . . . and an opportunity.
>
> The frog, upon seeing the scorpion, shied away.
>
> "Do not be afraid, dear friend," the scorpion said. "I would like you to take me on your back to the other side of the water."
>
> "What?!" said the frog. "How would I know that you would not sting me?"
>
> "If I were to sting you," said the scorpion, "we would both drown."
>
> The frog could not argue with this logic, and so let the scorpion on his back. Halfway across the water, he felt a stinging pain in his back.
>
> With all the strength he had left, he turned his head and looked at the scorpion, asking, "Why did you do that? Now we both shall die."
>
> The scorpion answered with a sly grin, "It's in my nature."

There are many variants of the fable's ending, but I will mention here only two, both from the Middle East: "We're both Arabs, aren't we?" the ending of the purportedly original Arab version of the fable that takes place on the River Nile, and "This is the Middle East, isn't it?" a popular punch line heard on the streets of Jerusalem and Tel Aviv. Both elicit laughter, and both rely on a particular type of subversive movement, an almost genetic literalism or essentialism that identifies the individual with the crowd rather than with God, for the frog and the scorpion, as the determiners themselves signify, are not a singular frog and scorpion but rather represent types, crowds condensed into representative figures. It is precisely this crowd element that is interrogated and subverted in the rendition of the fable that appears in *The Crying Game,* whose subject is the IRA kidnapping of a British soldier. I saw a version of the film in west Jerusalem, and have wanted to write about "The Frog and the Scorpion" ever since witnessing the wild applause and even tears that followed the fable's telling. A Palestinian audience might well have responded in the same way, for what the British soldier does to the fable is to de-essentialize and individualize its message, thereby forcing his executioner to ask of himself, Is murder in my nature? Can I kill this man before me? or perhaps even, Can I overcome the crowd within myself?

"The Frog and the Scorpion" is a story about the complicating force of language, for what is at work is not only an essential distrust of the enemy, who is virtually genetically encoded as such, but equally, an essential distrust of language. The frog dies, after all, because of words, the very medium through which he might have escaped with his life. It is as if he cannot think straight because he is sitting on the bank of the river, that primeval slaughtering ground of animals, rather than in the river or on dry land. The frog has been transformed by language to the extent that it has become capable of completely overriding instinctual demand, even demands as hardwired as fear and self-preservation, but just as he cannot swim in water and hop about on land at the same time, he cannot completely bridge the two realms. The problem is not that he is forced to operate either within the logic of language or the logic of instinct, with one of the two simply overriding the other, but rather that the relay systems between the two are lagged and unpredictable.

The scorpion, in contrast to the frog, seems fundamentally immune to transformational grammars of any sort; this is Gilles Deleuze's point in his analysis of Welles's cinematic rendition of the fable (Deleuze 1989, 126–55). When he utilizes the language of infantile beseechment, the language of small things—the "Help me!" implicit in his request to the frog—he does not become a child, not even for a moment, but remains himself throughout, for, according to the fable, the scorpion can never be anything other than what he is. The "genetic language" of the scorpion, accordingly, seems merely to piggyback and further instinctual drive, and the drive in question is as primal as self-preservation. Whether one calls it "the Organ of Destructiveness," "the death drive," or "mimetic repetition," or prefers to talk instead of self-extinction, ego-annihilation, or simply maladaptation, the fact remains that the scorpion seems willing to kill and die for no reason whatsoever.

Such an analysis, however, perhaps misses the central point I would want to make about "The Frog and the Scorpion," which has to do with the predicament of the human amphibian, that is, with the relations obtaining between language, deceit, and consciousness. What both the frog and the scorpion display is a certain language-generated schizophrenia—homicidal, suicidal, at odds with survival. If the frog is kindly schizoid, the scorpion seems simply cruel, and this cruelty cannot be separated from his attitude toward language.

Although it is presumably the frog who represents the human in the fable—only a human could croak forth a pitiful ontological "Why?" while dying—the fable is, nevertheless, not on the side of the poor frog, but rather on the side of the scorpion, who has learned how to transform himself and his world precisely through language; to exploit, indeed, perhaps relish the new types of bifurcations, deceits, incongruities, and fabulations that language makes possible, even though this new skill will bring about his very death. And it is, notably, the scorpion, the creature ostensibly incapable of asking "Why?" who is given the last word. His reply to the "Why?" of the frog—"It's in my nature"[12]—is simple and irrefutable, and effectively reduces the frog to speechlessness. This essentialism, or primary literalism, constitutes the greatest challenge to the purported moralism of the fable, for if the scorpion is only doing what scorpions do, how then can he be held accountable for what he does? What is the "lesson,"[13] then, of "The Frog and the Scorpion" but "Watch out for language!!!" The scorpion is capable of being judged only because he speaks, and it is only language that tinges his actions with a particular odium.

12. A variant ending: "I can't help myself. I'm a scorpion. That's who I am, that's what I do."

13. Fables always possess such "lessons," and if we look at the "nature show," a modern American transmutation of the animal fable, we see numerous changes in the type of lessons that Nature is supposed to teach us, whether maternalism, capitalism, power, frugality, or "good instinct." The protagonists themselves being speechless, it has traditionally been the function of the voice-over to inform the viewer that what she is witnessing is a universe orchestrated by a higher force. The ever-increasing graphicism of the nature show, however, suggests a different philosophy in which language is seen as extraneous to raw power and impersonalism constitutes the most fundamental of truths.

THE SALVATION OF POETRY

It is tempting to see "The Frog and the Scorpion" as a fable about the origins of language, that is, a fable about metaphor, or perhaps about "natural" language itself, that is, the turn from the presemiotic to the semiotic. And we must ask who is the real literalist in the fable, for if the frog on one level seems the very embodiment of metaphor, or the carrier function, he is nevertheless a literalist in that he expects some kind of correlation between what the scorpion says he will or will not do, and what will or will not be done. The scorpion, on the other hand, is the very incarnation of a type of literalism that is incapable of transporting its subject elsewhere, but rather simply and irreversibly unfolds according to the laws of a predetermined pattern, and can never be anything other than what it is destined to be. The scorpion utilizes a type of *argument,* a consequential logic based upon result or compulsion of the type "If . . . then," and guaranteed, as it were, by the threat of death. The fact that this logic is couched in the subjunctive case and thus entails an "as if" quality, a tension between memory and imagination capable of opening up a road to other fates, is what ostensibly escapes the scorpion altogether.

The problem lies perhaps less within the "nature" of the frog or that of the scorpion than within the space between them. The world of the fable can be said to be moral, or pure, only in the sense that it is strictly kosher. The various life forms that inhabit it remain separate and insular; they can never truly mate. The scorpion, stinger raised and ready, riding atop the back of the frog, submerged but for its eyes frantically scoping the horizon, is sexual parody, and we are far away here from myth, which, in contrast to the fable, relishes promiscuous interminglings of disparate matters. The logic of myth is unabashedly recombinant. Monstrous pluralisms threaten categories of every sort. If, in the end, we are returned to the proper, the singular creatures that populate the form—Centaurs, griffons, manticores—nevertheless express a potentially infinite multiplicity.

In contrast, nothing, "The Frog and the Scorpion" suggests, can ever change the essential incompatibility of the frog and the scorpion: they inhabit different universes tangential but impermeable. Mutually beneficial transformations are virtually inconceivable, as are accidents. There simply are no such things as accidents. This is, of course, the tragic vision, and this is why the fable is a tragic, or tragicomic, form. One should raise the question as to what function is served by such a vision, which notably permeates all discourse about the Israeli-Palestinian conflict. In some respect, might tragedy itself represent an attempt at escaping judgment, for in tragedy, as in "The Frog and the Scorpion," there are no true surprises, only Fate, and this certitude, this "prewritten" quality, has a paradoxically soporific effect on players and spectators alike. Tragedy, notes Jean C. Anouilh in *Antigone* (1957), is "restful" precisely for the reason that "hope, that foul, deceitful thing, has no part in it." We might say that tragedy, in its insistence on the compulsions of fate, is a particularly literalist form, or perhaps, that the tragic figure is a literalist but only partially conscious of that fact. He will be judged solely on the basis of his attempted escape from literalism, from fate—the poetry of that attempt, let us say.

If we imagine different linguistic interactions between the frog and the scorpion, we are left with very different affects, and, accordingly, very different moral and juridical implications. Would the meaning of the fable change if the scorpion said nothing to the frog before stinging him to death? If the phrase "with a sly grin" were omitted, as in some versions? If the frog did not croak "Why?" before dying? What would happen to the story if the scorpion spoke in poetry rather than prose? What if he offered mitigating circumstances for his deed, which would provide a "before" and an "after," effectively changing what is a fable of enemies into a fable of revenge and accentuating its judicial implications? Or what if he uttered some cryptic remark like "The waters sing lullabies," or said simply, "I hate you"? What if he said "Just because!" or murmured sweet endearments in the ear of the frog as he stung him to death? In each case, everything about the fable would be changed; indeed, in many instances, the story of the frog and the scorpion could no longer be said to constitute a fable at all.

As is, however, the fable lacks a strong vertical element, and judgment of the frog and scorpion is made on the perception of excess. "Evil," as opposed to the merely "bad," one could say, always signifies its presence in excess, a peculiarly surplus value. The fine line between "killing" and "murder" ("warfare" and "terror," "clean war" and "dirty war," and so forth) is drawn on the basis of excess, or decadence. A verdict, for instance, might be made according to the excessive number of stab wounds found on the body of a victim or by the superfluous fact that the accused laughed. What is important to note here is the fact that acts are capable of being judged only when they exhibit the structure of a story, and we must question the connection between excess and meaning; that is, we must ask under what conditions might hyperbole be necessary for meaning, interpretation, and judgment to take place. One might even question the connection between "poetics" and judgment. Indeed, does one not see in the very idea of premeditation a recognition of a linkage between the two? The true criminality of the crime lies less in the act itself than in its fantastic preludes and imaginative orchestrations, which indicate that the agent has lent his sickness a narrative and meaning. This "literary" or "poetic" capacity in and of itself announces the fact that the agent possesses a "moral faculty"—a means of jumping beyond the present, of envisioning and judging the possible trajectories and ramifications of act. The more "poetic" the crime, the harsher the judgment.

The essential, paradoxically, is glimpsed in and through excess. The sly grin of the scorpion signals such an excess and, like his fluorescence, constitutes something of a biological puzzle, an unknown function. In each of the possible variants of "The Frog and the Scorpion," our contempt for the scorpion can be said to increase in direct proportion to the sadistic surplus that he exhibits through word and deed. Similarly, our opinion of the frog would change radically were his relation to language different. If the frog had said to the scorpion in the middle of the water, for instance, "Kill me, rend me, drown me in my blood!"[14] such a masochistic provocation might even be understood by the reader as justifying his death. And if the sadism of the scorpion and the masochism of the frog seemed perfectly congruent, we would feel almost nothing for either of them.

But perhaps we attribute to the frog and the scorpion more self-knowledge than they actually possess. We assume that because they speak, they know what they are doing. The most haunting quality of the animal fable, its truth and power, lies perhaps in the fact that humans, like animals, go through life not knowing exactly what is happening to them, nor exactly what they are doing, until it is too late. It is only at the moment of his death that the frog sees, recognizes, what has happened to him. This fundamental tardiness, this belatedness, this logic of the posthumous, is at the heart of tragedy as well as all apocalyptic scenarios. The full meaning of what we do is always too late in coming. Here is the pathos inherent in all tragedy and all judgment. If upon stinging the frog in the middle of the river, the scorpion had said, "Forgive me, dear friend, for I do not know what it is I am doing," as if to say, "I am a literalist against my will," he, too, would belong in the realm of tragedy (again, perhaps in the end an attempted evasion of judgment, but with the salvation of poetry), and we could only recognize ourselves in him and turn our heads in shame.

POSTSCRIPT

A friend suggests upon reading this piece that the altruism of the frog is false, and that it is the frog rather the scorpion that might best be compared to the sui-

14. The line of a song appearing on a June 1992 videotape of *The Battalions of 'Izz ad-Din al-Qassam, The Islamic Resistance Movement* (Hamas).

cide bomber. In her reading, the frog knows exactly what will happen if he lets the scorpion upon his back; he also knows that the only way that he can possibly kill his enemy is to kill himself at the same time. I find this reversal intriguing but would insist on the preeminence of language in interpreting the fable. In the end, I find it difficult to dispense with the notion that the frog risks more than does the scorpion and that the risk he imposes on himself is superfluous, and for this reason alone, he excites pity, admiration, and contempt, all at once; that is, in the end, I would insist on seeing "The Frog and the Scorpion" primarily through the lens of that curious conflation of Bloom and Freud that I have called "the anxiety of civilization"—the intense ambivalence catalyzed by verticalism, even a verticalism as "idiotic"[15] as that of a frog.

15. "Behind the frog, the epitome of the truthful animal, there is the scorpion, the animal sick with itself. The first is an idiot and the second is a bastard" (Deleuze 1989, 141).

WORKS CITED

INDEX

Works Cited

Abaza, Mona. 2002. *Debates on Islam and Knowledge in Malaysia and Egypt: Shifting Worlds.* Richmond, UK: Curzon Press.

'Abd al-Rahim, Muhammad. 1936. *Nafathat al-yara' fi al-adab wa-al-ta'rikh wa-al-ijtima'.* Khartoum: Sharikat al-tab' wa-al-nashr.

Abdelgadir, Awad A. 2000. "The Village of Kolomiseed (Az-Zawrat) Fundraising Projects." *Gateway to Nubia,* 18 Sept., <http://nilevalleyherbs.com/projects.htm>.

Abduh, Muhammad. 1966. *The Theology of Unity.* Translated by Ishaq Masa'ad and Kenneth Cragg. London: Allen and Unwin.

Abrahamian, Ervand. 1993. *Khomeinism: Essays on the Islamic Republic.* Berkeley: Univ. of California Press.

Abu Salim, Muhammad Ibrahim. 1991. *Ta'rikh al-khartum.* 3d ed. Beirut: Dar al-jil.

Abul-Fadl, Muna. 1991. "Beyond Cultural Parodies and Parodizing Cultures: Shaping Discourse." *American Journal of Islamic Social Sciences* 8, no. 1: 15–43.

Abusharaf, Rogaia M. 1997. "Sudanese Migration to the New World: Socio-economic Characteristics." *International Migration* 35, no. 4: 513–36.

Aciman, André. 1994. *Out of Egypt: A Memoir.* New York: Farrar, Straus and Giroux.

Adams, William Y. 1977. *Nubia: Corridor to Africa.* Princeton, N.J.: Princeton Univ. Press.

Adler, Glenn. 1996. "Global Restructuring and Labor." In *Globalization: Critical Reflections,* edited by James H. Mittelman. Boulder, Colo.: Lynne Rienner.

Adorno, Theodor. 1978. *Minima Moralia.* Translated by E.F.N. Jephcott. London: Verso.

El-Affendi, Abdelwahab. 1991. *Turabi's Revolution: Islam and Power in Sudan.* London: Grey Seal.

Ahmed, Akbar S. 1992. *Postmodernism and Islam: Predicament and Promise.* New York: Routledge.

Ainslie, George. 1986. "Beyond Microeconomics." In *The Multiple Self,* edited by Jon Elster. Cambridge, UK: Cambridge Univ. Press.

Alatas, Syed Farid. 1993. "On the Indigenization of Academic Discourse." *Alternatives* 18: 307–38.

———. 1995. "The Sacralization of the Social Sciences: A Critique of an Emerging Theme in Academic Discourse." *Archives de Sciences Sociales des Religions* 91 (July-Sept.): 89–110.

Alatas, Syed Hussein. 1972. "The Captive Mind in Development Studies." *International Social Science Journal* 24, no. 1: 9–25.

Alexander, Bobby. 1997. "Televangelism." In *Rethinking Media, Religion, and Culture*, edited by Stewart M. Hoover and Knut Lundby. London: Sage Publications.

Ali, Rasheed. 1999. Email correspondence, Budapest, 30 June 1999.

al-Alwani, Jabir Taha. 1991. "Taqlid and Ijtihad." *American Journal of Islamic Social Sciences* 8, no. 1: 129–42.

———. 1993. "The Crisis of Thought and Ijtihad." *American Journal of Islamic Social Sciences* 10, no. 2: 234–37.

———. 1996. "Authority: Divine or Qur'anic?" *American Journal of Islamic Social Sciences* 13, no. 4: 536–50.

Amin, Samir. 1976. *Unequal Development: An Essay on the Social Formations of Peripheral Capitalism*. Hassocks, UK: Harvester Press.

Amis, Martin. 1991. *Time's Arrow*. New York: Harmony.

Anderson, Benedict. 1991. *Imagined Communities: Reflections on the Origin and Spread of Nationalism*. Rev. ed. London: Verso.

Anderson, Jon, and Dale Eickelman. 1999. "Media Convergence and Its Consequences." *Middle East Insight* 12 (Apr.): 59–61.

Anouilh, Jean C. 1957. *Antigone*. Paris: Table Ronde.

Appadurai, Arjun, ed. 1986. *The Social Life of Things: Commodities in Cultural Perspective*. Cambridge, UK: Cambridge Univ. Press.

———. 1990. "Disjuncture and Difference in the Global Cultural Economy." In *Global Culture: Nationalism, Globalization, and Modernity*, edited by Mike Featherstone, 295–311. London: Sage Publications. Also published in *Theory and Society* 7, no. 2/3: 295–310.

Appiah, Anthony. 1992. *In My Father's House*. New York: Oxford Univ. Press.

Arendt, Hannah. 1958. *The Human Condition*. Chicago: Univ. of Chicago Press.

Ashcroft, Bill, Gareth Griffiths, and Helen Tiffin. 1998. *Key Concepts in Postcolonial Studies*. London: Routledge.

Atal, Yogesh. 1981. "The Call for Indigenization." *International Social Science Journal* 33, no. 1: 189–97.

Austin, Dennis. 1980. "The Transfer of Power: Why and How." In *Decolonisation and After: The British and French Experience*, edited by W. H. Morris-Jones and Georges Fischer, 3–34. London: Frank Cass.

Ayalon, Ami. 1987. *Language and Change in the Arab Middle East: The Evolution of Modern Political Discourse*. Oxford, UK: Oxford Univ. Press.

Aydin, Cemil. 1995. "The Conception of 'Civilization' and 'Science' in the Journals of Mecmua-i Funun (1862–1867) and Mecmua-i Ulum (1880–1882)." Master's thesis, Institute of Social Sciences, Istanbul University.

Ayubi, Nazih. 1991. *Political Islam: Religion and Politics in the Arab World*. London: Routledge.

al-Azm, Sadik. 1993–94. "Islamic Fundamentalism Reconsidered." *South Asia Bulletin* 13, nos. 1 and 2: 92–121; 14, no. 1: 73–98.

al-Azmeh, Aziz. 1981. *Ibn Khaldun in Modern Scholarship.* London: Third World Center for Research and Publishing.

———. 1993. *Islams and Modernities.* New York: Verso.

Bakan, David. 1971. *Disease, Pain, and Sacrifice: Toward a Psychology of Suffering.* Boston: Beacon Press.

Balamoan, G. Ayoub. 1981. *Peoples and Economics in the Sudan, 1884–1956.* Rev. ed. Cambridge, Mass.: Harvard Univ. Center for Population Studies.

Bales, Kevin. 1999. *Disposable People.* Berkeley: Univ. of California Press.

Baran, Paul. 1957. *The Political Economy of Growth.* New York: Monthly Review Press.

Barber, Benjamin. 1996. *Jihad vs. McWorld.* New York: Ballantine Books.

Bartov, Omer. 1996. *Murder in Our Midst.* New York: Oxford Univ. Press.

al-Bashir, Abdel Rahman A. 1991. "People on the Move: Immigrants, Refugees and Displaced Masses, and Their Impact on Society." In *Sudan: Environment and People,* Second International Studies Conference papers, 8–11 Apr. 1991, held at Univ. of Durham. *International Sudan Studies Conference,* vol. 2, 35–55. Durham: Sudan Studies Society of the United Kingdom.

Bauman, Zygmunt. 1989. *Modernity and the Holocaust.* Ithaca, N.Y.: Cornell Univ. Press.

———. 1990. "Modernity and Ambivalence." In *Global Culture—Nationalism, Globalization and Modernity. A Theory, Culture and Society* special issue, edited by Mike Featherstone, 143–69. London: Sage Publications.

———. 1995. "Violence, Postmodern." In *Life in Fragments.* Oxford: Blackwell.

———. 1998. *Globalization.* New York: Columbia Univ. Press.

Bayat, Asef. 1997. *Street Politics.* New York: Columbia Univ. Press.

Baykara, Tuncer. 2000. "Bir kelime-ıstılah ve zihniyet olarak 'medeniyet' in Türkiye'ye girişi." In *Osmanlılarda medeniyet kavramı ve ondokuzuncu yuzyıla dair arastırmalar,* by Tuncer Baykara. Bornova, Izmir: Akademi Kitabevi.

Beck, Kurt. 1998. "The Struggle over a Proper Lifestyle in Northern Kordofan." In *Kordofan Invaded: Peripheral Incorporation and Social Transformation in Islamic Africa,* edited by Endre Stiansen and Michael Kevane, 254–79. Leiden: Brill.

Beck, Ulrich. 1994. "The Reinvention of Politics." In *Reflexive Modernization,* edited by Ulrich Beck, Anthony Giddens, and Scott Lash. Stanford, Calif.: Stanford Univ. Press.

Beebee, Thomas. 1994. *The Ideology of Genre: A Comparative Study of Generic Instability.* University Park: Pennsylvania State Univ. Press.

Beetham, David. 1999. *Democracy and Human Rights.* Cambridge, UK: Polity Press.

Beinin, Joel, and Joe Stork, eds. 1997. *Political Islam.* Berkeley: Univ. of California Press.

Bellah, Robert N. 1970. "Religious Evolution." In *Beyond Belief: Essays on Religion in a Post-Traditional World,* 168–89. New York: Harper and Row.

Benhabib, Seyla. 1999. "Sexual Difference and Collective Identities." *Signs* 24, no. 2: 335–62.

Benjamin, Walter. 1968. "The Work of Art ..." In *Illuminations,* edited by Hannah Arendt, translated by Harry Zorn. New York: Harcourt Brace Jovanovich.

Berger, Peter L. 1967. *The Sacred Canopy: Elements of a Sociological Theory of Religion.* Garden City, N.Y.: Doubleday.

———. 1996. "Secularism in Retreat." *National Interest* 46: 3.

Berger, Suzanne, and Ronald Dore, eds. 1996. *National Diversity and Global Capitalism.* Ithaca, N.Y.: Cornell Univ. Press.

Beshir, M. O. 1977. *Educational Policy and the Employment Problem in the Sudan.* Khartoum: Khartoum Univ. Press.

Best, Steven, and Douglas Kellner. 1991. *Postmodern Theory.* New York: Guilford Press.

Beswick, Stephanie. 1994. "Non-Acceptance of Islam in the Southern Sudan: The Case of the Dinka from the Pre-Colonial Period to Independence." *Northeast African Studies* 1, nos. 2–3: 19–47.

———. 1998. "The Ngok: The Emergence and Destruction of a Nilotic Protostate." In *Kordofan Invaded: Peripheral Incorporation and Social Transformation in Islamic Africa,* edited by Endre Stiansen and Michael Kevane, 145–64. Leiden: Brill.

Beyer, Peter. 1994. *Religion and Globalization.* London: Sage Publications.

Beynon, John, and David Dunkerley. 2000. *Globalization: The Reader.* New York: Routledge.

Bhabha, Homi K. 1986. "The Other Question: Difference, Discrimination and the Discourse of Colonialism." In *Literature, Politics and Theory,* edited by Francis Barker, Peter Hulme, Margaret Iversen, and Diana Loxley. London: Methuen.

———. 1994. *The Location of Culture.* New York: Routledge.

Bhagwati, Jagdish, and Richard A. Brecher. 1980. "National Welfare in an Open Economy in the Presence of Foreign-Owned Factors of Production." *Journal of International Economics* 10, no. 1: 103–16.

Bielefeldt, Heiner. 2000. " 'Western' Versus 'Islamic' Human Rights Conceptions?" *Political Theory* 28, no. 1: 90–121.

Bilgrami, Akeel. 1995. "What is a Muslim?" In *Identities,* edited by Kwame Anthony Appiah and Henry Louis Gates Jr. Chicago: Univ. of Chicago Press.

Binder, Leonard. 1988. *Islamic Liberalism.* Chicago: Univ. of Chicago Press.

Birks, J. S. 1978. *Across the Savannas to Mecca: The Overland Pilgrimage Route from West Africa.* London: C. Hurst and Company.

Birks, J. S., and C. A. Sinclair. 1978. *Human Capital on the Nile: Development and Emigration in the Arab Republic of Egypt and the Democratic Republic of the Sudan.* Geneva: International Labour Organization.

Bitterli, Urs. 1985. "Der 'Edle Wilde.' " In *Wir und die Wilden,* edited by Thomas Theye, 270–87. Hamburg: Rowohlt.

———. 1989. *Cultures in Conflict: Encounters between European and non-European Cultures, 1492–1800.* Translated by Ritchie Robertson. Cambridge, UK: Polity Press.

———. 1991. *Die "Wilden" und die "Zivilisierten": Grundzüge einer Geistes—und Kulturgeschichte der europäisch-überseeischen Begegnung.* Munich: Beck.

Bjørkelo, Anders. 1989. *Prelude to the Mahdiyya: Peasants and Traders in the Shendi Region, 1821–1885.* Cambridge, UK: Cambridge Univ. Press.

Black, Antony. 2001. *The History of Islamic Political Thought: From the Prophet to the Present.* New York: Routledge.

Bloom, Harold. 1992. *The American Religion.* New York: Simon and Schuster.

Blumenberg, Hans. 1985. *The Legitimacy of the Modern Age.* Translated by Robert M. Wallace. Cambridge, Mass.: MIT Press.

Boorstin, Daniel J. 1993. "Apostles of Novelty." *New Perspectives Quarterly* 10, no. 3 (summer): 60.

Borges, Jorge Luis. 1998. "Funes, His Memory." *Collected Fictions.* Translated by Andrew Hurley. New York: Viking.

Boroujerdi, Mehrzad. 1996. *Iranian Intellectuals and the West: The Tormented Triumph of Nativism.* Syracuse, N.Y.: Syracuse Univ. Press.

———. 1997. "Iranian Islam and the Faustian Bargain of Western Modernity." *Journal of Peace Research* 34, no. 1 (Feb.): 1–5.

Bose, Sugata. 1997. "Unsettled Frontiers of Asian History." In *Unsettled Frontiers and Transnational Linkages: New Tasks for the Historian of Asia,* edited by Leo Douw. Amsterdam, The Netherlands: VU Univ. Press.

Bourdieu, Pierre. 1977. *Outline of a Theory of Practice.* Cambridge, UK: Cambridge Univ. Press.

———. 1990. *The Logic of Practice.* Translated by Richard Nice. Stanford, Calif.: Stanford Univ. Press.

———. 2000. "The Historicity of Reason." *Pascalian Meditations.* Translated by Richard Nice. Stanford, Calif.: Stanford Univ. Press.

Boyd, Douglas A. 1993. *Broadcasting in the Arab World: A Survey of the Electronic Media in the Middle East.* 2d ed. Ames: Iowa State Univ. Press.

Boyer, Robert, and Daniel Drache, eds. 1996. *States Against Markets.* New York: Routledge.

Braudel, Fernand. 1993. *A History of Civilizations.* Translated by Richard Mayne. New York: Penguin.

Brennan, Timothy. 1997. *At Home in the World.* Cambridge, Mass.: Harvard Univ. Press.

Brenner, Louis. 2001. *Controlling Knowledge: Religion, Power and Schooling in a West African Muslim Society.* Bloomington: Indiana Univ. Press.

Brenner, Robert. 1998. "The Economics of Global Turbulence." *New Left Review* 229: 1–265.

Brodeur, Patrice. 2000. "From an Islamic Heresiography to an Islamic History of Religions: Modern Arab Muslim Literature on Religious Others with Special Reference to Three Egyptian Authors." Ph.D. diss., Univ. of Michigan. Available from UMI Dissertation Services, Ann Arbor, Michigan.

Bronner, Stephen Eric. 2000. *A Rumor about the Jews: Reflections on Antisemitism and the Protocols of the Learned Elders of Zion.* New York: St. Martin's Press.

Brook, Timothy, and André Schmid, eds. 2000. *Nation Work: Asian Elites and National Identities.* Ann Arbor: Univ. of Michigan Press.

Brown, Daniel. 1996. *Rethinking Tradition in Modern Islamic Thought.* Cambridge, UK: Cambridge Univ. Press.

Bulcha, Mekuria. 1988. *Flight and Integration: Causes of Mass Exodus from Ethiopia and Problems of Integration in the Sudan.* Uppsala, Sweden: Scandinavian Institute of African Studies.

Bulliet, Richard. 1994. *Islam: The View from the Edge.* New York: Columbia Univ. Press.

Bürger, Peter. 1992. *The Decline of Modernism.* University Park: Pennsylvania State Univ. Press.

Burke, Edmund III, and Ira Lapidus. 1988. *Islam, Politics, and Social Movements.* Berkeley: Univ. of California Press.

Calasso, Roberto. 1994. *The Ruin of Kasch.* Cambridge, Mass.: Belknap Press of Harvard Univ. Press.

Calhoun, Craig. 1995. "Nationalism and Civil Society." In *Social Theory and the Politics of Identity,* edited by Craig Calhoun. Cambridge, Mass.: Blackwell.

Callaghy, Thomas. 1993. "Vision and Politics in the Transformation of Global Politics." In *Global Transformation and the Third World,* edited by Robert O. Slater, Barry M. Schutz, Steven R. Dorr. Boulder, Colo.: L. Rienner Publishers.

Canetti, Elias. 1962. *Crowds and Power.* Translated by Carol Stewart. New York: Farrar, Straus and Giroux.

————. 1979. *The Tongue Set Free.* Translated by Joachim Neugroschel. New York: Seabury Press.

Carter, Steven L. 1998. *Dissent of the Governed.* Cambridge, Mass.: Harvard Univ. Press.

Casanova, José. 1994. *Public Religions in the Modern World.* Chicago: Univ. of Chicago Press.

Cerny, Philip G., and Mark Evans. 1999. *New Labour, Globalization, and the Competition State.* Cambridge, Mass.: Minda de Gunzburg Center for European Studies, Harvard Univ.

Cesari, Jocelyne, ed. 1996. *Réseaux transnationaux entre L'Europe et le Maghreb.* 2 vols. Brussels: European Commission.

————. 1997. *Etre Musulman en France aujourd'hui.* Paris: Hachette.

————. 1998. *Musulmans et républicains: Les jeunes, l'Islam et la France.* Brussels, Editions Complexe.

————. 2000a. "Islam in European Cities." In *Minorities in European Cities: The Dynamics of Social Integration and Social Exclusion at the Neighbourhood Level,* edited by Sophie Body-Gendrot and Martin Martiniello, 88–99. New York: St. Martin's Press.

————. 2000b. "Islam and Globalization: The Necessity of a New Approach." Paper presented at the International Political Science Association Congress, Quebec City, Canada, 1–5 Aug.

————. In press. "Muslim Minorities in Europe: The Silent Revolution." In *Islamization or Reislamization?* edited by François Burgat and John Esposito. Gainesville, Fla.: Univ. Press of Florida.

————. Forthcoming. *Islam in the West.* New York: Palgrave.

Chakrabarty, Dipesh. 2000. *Provincializing Europe: Postcolonial Thought and Historical Difference.* Princeton, N.J.: Princeton Univ. Press.

Chomsky, Noam. 1999. *The New Military Humanism*. Monroe, Maine: Common Courage Press.

Chong Chee Kin. 1999. "Singet Scanning Computers." *Straits Times,* 30 Apr.

Choueiri, Youssef. 1990. *Islamic Fundamentalism*. Boston: Twayne Publishers.

Cohen, Jean. 1997. "Interpreting the Notion of Civil Society." In *Toward a Global Civil Society,* edited by Michael Walzer. Providence, R.I.: Berghahn Books.

Colas, Domique. 1997. *Civil Society and Fanaticism*. Translated by Amy Jacobs. Stanford, Calif.: Stanford Univ. Press.

Collins, Robert O. 1983. *Shadows in the Grass: Britain in the Southern Sudan, 1918–1956*. New Haven, Conn.: Yale Univ. Press.

———. 1988. "Africa Begins at Malakal." Paper presented at the conference on "Religion and Politics in the Sudan," Centre de recherches africaines, Paris, 22–24 June.

Comaroff, John L., and Jean Comaroff. 1992. "The Colonization of Consciousness." In *Ethnography and the Historical Imagination*. Boulder, Colo.: Westview Press.

Conklin, Alice L. 1997. *A Mission to Civilize: The Republican Idea of Empire in France and West Africa, 1895–1920*. Stanford, Calif.: Stanford Univ. Press.

Corey, Kenneth. 1998. "Electronic Space: Creating and Controlling Cyber Communities in Southeastern Asia and the United States." <http://www.ssc.msu.edu/~Dean>.

Cro, Stelio. 1990. *The Noble Savage: Allegory of Freedom*. Waterloo, Ont.: Laurier.

Cvetkovich, Ann, and Douglas Kellner, eds. 1997. *Articulating the Global and the Local: Globalization and Cultural Studies*. Boulder, Colo.: Westview Press.

Dabashi, Hamid. 1993. *Theology of Discontent*. New York: New York Univ. Press.

Dafalla, Hassan. 1975. *The Nubian Exodus*. London: Christopher Hurst.

Dallmayr, Fred. 1996. *Beyond Orientalism: Essays on Cross-Cultural Encounter*. Albany: State Univ. of New York Press.

Daly, M. W. 1986. *Empire on the Nile: The Anglo-Egyptian Sudan, 1898–1934*. Cambridge, UK: Cambridge Univ. Press.

———. 1991. *Imperial Sudan: The Anglo-Egyptian Condominium, 1934–1956*. Cambridge, UK: Cambridge Univ. Press.

Daniel, E. Valentine. 1996. *Charred Lullabies*. Princeton, N.J.: Princeton Univ. Press.

Danto, Arthur C. 1999. "History and Representation." *The Body/Body Problem*. Berkeley: Univ. of California Press.

Davies, Derek. 1999. "The Press." In *The Singapore Puzzle,* edited by Michael Haas, 77–107. Westport, Conn.: Praeger Press.

Davis, Mike. 1999. "Magical Urbanism." *New Left Review* 234: 3–43.

———. 2001. *Late Victorian Holocausts*. New York: Verso.

Davison, Andrew. 1998. *Secularism and Revivalism in Turkey*. New Haven, Conn.: Yale Univ. Press.

Decker, David F. 1998. "Females and the State in Mahdist Kordofan." In *Kordofan Invaded: Peripheral Incorporation and Social Transformation in Islamic Africa,* edited by Endre Stiansen and Michael Kevane, 86–100. Leiden: Brill.

Delaney, Carol. 1990. "The 'Hajj': Sacred and Secular." *American Ethnologist* 17, no. 3: 513–30.

Deleuze, Gilles. 1989. *Cinema 2: The Time-Image.* Translated by Hugh Tomlinson and Robert Galeta. Minneapolis: Univ. of Minnesota Press.

Deringil, Selim. 1991. "Legitimacy Structures in the Ottoman Empire: Abdülhamid II, 1876–1909." *International Journal of Middle East Studies* 23: 345–59.

———. 1999. *The Well-Protected Domains: Ideology and the Legitimation of Power in the Ottoman Empire, 1876–1909.* London: I. B. Tauris.

Derrida, Jacques. 1995. *The Gift of Death.* Translated by David Wills. Chicago: Univ. of Chicago Press.

Dirlik, Arif. 2000. "Is There History after Eurocentrism? Globalism, Postcolonialism, and the Disavowal of History." In *History after the Three Worlds,* edited by Arif Dirlik, Vinay Bahl, and Peter Gran, 25–47. Lanham, Md.: Rowman and Littlefield.

Dolan, Michael. 1993. "Global Economic Transformation and Less Developed Countries." In *Global Transformation and the Third World,* edited by Robert O. Slater, Barry M. Schutz, and Steven R. Dorr. Boulder, Colo.: L. Rienner Publishers.

Dorfman, Ariel. 1998. *Heading South, Looking North.* New York: Penguin.

Duerr, Hans Peter. 1987. *Dreamtime. Concerning the Boundary Between Wilderness and Civilization.* Oxford, UK: Blackwell.

Dunn, Ross E. 1989. *The Adventures of Ibn Battuta: A Muslim Traveler of the Fourteenth Century.* Berkeley: Univ. of California Press.

Durkheim, Emile. 1995. *Elementary Forms of Religious Life.* New York: Free Press.

Dyrberg, Torben Bech. 1997. *The Circular Structure of Power.* London: Verso.

Economist. 2000. "NGOs: Sins of the Career Missionaries," 29 Jan.

The Edge/Netv@lue2.0. 2001. 24 Sept.

Eichengreen, Barry. 1996. *Globalizing Capital.* Princeton, N.J.: Princeton Univ. Press.

Eickelman, Dale F. 1999. "The Coming Transformation of the Muslim World." Foreign Policy Research Institute Wire, <http://www.fpri.org/fpriwire/0709.199908.eickelman.muslimtransform.html>.

Eickelman, Dale F., and James Piscatori, eds. 1996. *Muslim Politics.* Princeton, N.J.: Princeton Univ. Press.

Eisenstadt, Shmuel N., and Wolfgang Schluchter. 1998. "Introduction: Paths to Early Modernities—A Comparative View." *Daedalus* 127, no. 3: 1–18.

Elias, Norbert. 1978–82. *The Civilizing Process.* Translated by Edmund Jephcott. Oxford: Blackwell.

Elster, Jon. 1999. *Alchemies of the Mind.* New York: Cambridge Univ. Press.

Enayat, Hamid. 1982. *Modern Islamic Political Thought.* Austin: Univ. of Texas Press.

Entelis, John. 1986. *Algeria: The Revolution Institutionalized.* Boulder, Colo.: Westview Press.

Esping-Andersen, Gøsta, ed. 1996. *Welfare States in Transition.* Thousand Oaks, Calif.: Sage Publications.

Esposito, John, ed. 1990. *The Iranian Revolution.* Miami: Florida International Univ. Press.

Euben, Roxanne. 1999. *Enemy in the Mirror.* Princeton, N.J.: Princeton Univ. Press.

Europa Publications. 1996. *Europa World Yearbook 1996.* London: Europa Publications.

Evans-Pritchard, E. E. 1949. *The Sanusi of Cyrenaica.* Oxford, UK: Clarendon Press.

Ewald, Janet J. 1990. *Soldiers, Traders, and Slaves: State Formation and Economic Transformation in the Greater Nile Valley, 1700–1885.* Madison: Univ. of Wisconsin Press.

Fábos, Anita. 1994. "Discourse of Dominance: Refugees and Subnational Identity in Sudan." Paper presented at the Third International Meeting of the Sudan Studies Associations, Boston, 21–24 Apr.

———. 1999. "Ambiguous Ethnicity: Propriety *(adab)* as a Situational Boundary Marker for Northern Sudanese in Cairo." Ph.D. diss, Boston Univ.

Fanon, Frantz. 1963. *The Wretched of the Earth.* New York: Grove Press.

Farmer, Paul. 1999. *Infections and Inequalities.* Berkeley: Univ. of California Press.

Al-Faruqi, Ismail Raji, and AbdulHamid AbuSulayman. 1989. *Islamization of Knowledge: General Principles and Work Plan.* Herndon, Va.: International Institute of Islamic Thought.

Featherstone, Mike, ed. 1990. *Global Culture: Nationalism, Globalization, and Modernity.* London: Sage Publications.

———. 1995. *Undoing Culture: Globalization, Postmodernity, and Identity.* London: Sage Publications.

Featherstone, Mike, Scott Lash, and Roland Robertson, eds. 1995. *Global Modernities.* Thousand Oaks, Calif.: Sage Publications.

Finley, M. I. 1960. *Aspects of Antiquity.* New York: Viking Press.

Fischer, Michael. 1980. *Iran: From Religious Dispute to Revolution.* Cambridge, Mass.: Harvard Univ. Press.

Fish, Stanley. 1999. *Trouble with Principle.* Cambridge, Mass.: Harvard Univ. Press.

Flax, Jane. 1990. *Thinking Fragments.* Berkeley: Univ. of California Press.

Fleischer, Cornell. 1984. "Royal Authority, Dynastic Cyclism, and 'Ibn Khaldunianism' in Sixteenth-Century Ottoman Letters." In *Ibn Khaldun and Islamic Ideology,* edited by Bruce B. Lawrence. Leiden: Brill.

Fornäs, Johan. 1995. *Cultural Theory and Late Modernity.* London: Sage Publications.

Forsythe, David. 1991. *The Internationalization of Human Rights.* Lexington, Mass.: Lexington Books.

Foucault, Michel. 1972. *The Archeology of Knowledge and the Discourse on Language.* Translated by A. M. Sheridan Smith. New York: Pantheon Books.

———. 1980. *History of Sexuality.* Translated by Robert Hurley. Vol. 1. New York: Vintage Books.

———. 1988. "Iran." In *Politics, Philosophy, Culture,* translated by Alan Sheridan and others; edited by Lawrence D. Kritzman. New York: Routledge.

Frank, A. G. 1969. *Capitalism and Underdevelopment in Latin America.* New York: Monthly Review Press.

Freeman, Chris. 1995. "The 'National System of Innovation' in Historical Perspective." *Cambridge Journal of Economics* 19, no. 1: 5–24.

Friedrich, Otto. 1982. *The Kingdom of Auschwitz*. New York: HarperPerennial.

Frisby, David. 1986. *Fragments of Modernity*. Cambridge, Mass.: MIT Press.

Fukuyama, Francis. 1989. "The End of History." *National Interest* 16: 3–18.

Gallagher, Catherine, and Stephen Greenblatt. 2000. *Practicing New Historicism*. Chicago: Univ. of Chicago Press.

Geertz, Clifford. 1971. *Islam Observed*. Chicago: Univ. of Chicago Press.

———. 1996. *After the Fact: Two Countries, Four Decades, One Anthropologist*. Cambridge: Harvard Univ. Press.

Gellner, Ernest. 1979. *Spectacles and Predicaments*. Cambridge: Cambridge Univ. Press.

Genovese, Eugene. 1979. *From Rebellion to Revolution*. Baton Rouge: Louisiana State Univ. Press.

Gergen, Kenneth, Aydan Gulerce, Andrew Lock, Girishwar Misra. N.d. "Psychological Science in Cultural Context." <http://www.massey.ac.nz/~ALock/culture/culture.htm>.

Geuss, Raymond. 1981. *The Idea of a Critical Theory*. New York: Cambridge Univ. Press.

———. 1998. "Art and Criticism in Adorno's Aesthetics." *European Journal of Philosophy* 6, no. 3: 297–319.

Ghandi, Leela. 1998. *Postcolonial Theory: Critical Introduction*. New York: Columbia Univ. Press.

Giddens, Anthony. 1991. *Modernity and Self-Identity: Self and Society in the Late Modern Age*. Stanford, Calif.: Stanford Univ. Press.

Giesen, Bernhard. 1998. "Cosmopolitans, Patriots, Jacobins and Romantics." *Daedalus* 127, no. 3: 221–50.

Gilligan, James. 1996. *Violence*. New York: Vintage Books.

Godzich, Wlad. 1986, "The Further Possibility of Knowledge." Foreword to *Heterologies: Discourse on the Other*, by Michel de Certeau, translated by Brian Massumi. Minneapolis: Univ. of Minnesota Press.

Goldberg, Ellis. 1992. "Smashing Idols and the State." In *Comparing Muslim Societies*, edited by Juan R. I. Cole. Ann Arbor: Univ. of Michigan Press.

Goldhagen, Daniel. 1996. *Hitler's Willing Executioners*. New York: Knopf.

Göle, Nilüfer. 1996. *The Forbidden Modern*. Ann Arbor: Univ. of Michigan Press.

———. 1997a. "The Gendered Nature of the Public Sphere." *Public Culture* 10, no. 1: 61–81.

———. 1997b. "The Quest for the Islamic Self within the Context of Modernity." In *Rethinking Modernity and National Identity in Turkey*, edited by Sibel Bozdogan and Resat Kasaba. Seattle: Univ. of Washington Press.

Goonatilake, Susantha. 1995. "The Self Wandering Between Cultural Localization and Globalization." In *The Decolonization of Imagination*, edited by Jan Nederveen Pieterse and Bhikhu Parekh. Atlantic Highlands, N.J.: Zed Books.

Gourevitch, Philip. 1998. *We Wish to Inform You That Tomorrow We Will Be Killed with Our Families: Stories from Rwanda*. New York: Farrar, Straus and Giroux.

Gowan, Peter. 1999. "Neo-Liberalism and Civil Society." *The Global Gamble.* New York: Verso.

Grafton, Anthony. 1995. *New Worlds, Ancient Texts.* Cambridge, Mass.: Belknap Press of Harvard Univ. Press.

——. 1997. *The Footnote.* Rev. ed. Cambridge, Mass.: Harvard Univ. Press.

Grawert, Elke. 1991. "Impacts of Male Rural Outmigration and Women's Work on Food Security: Case Study of Kutum, Northern Darfur, Sudan." Paper presented at International Sudan Studies Conference, Sudan Studies Society of the United Kingdom, Univ. of Durham, 8–11 Apr. *Sudan: Environment and People: Second International Studies Conference papers,* vol. 2, 64–69.

Greenblatt, Stephen. 1991. *Marvelous Possessions.* Chicago: Univ. of Chicago Press.

Greider, William. 1997. *One World, Ready or Not.* New York: Simon and Schuster.

——. 1998. *Fortress America.* New York: Public Affairs.

Gretty, Myrdal. 2000. "The Construction of Muslim Identities in Contemporary Europe." In *Islamic Words, Individuals, Societies and Discourse in Contemporary European Islam,* edited by Felice Dassetto, 35–47. Paris: Maisonneuve et Larose.

Griffin, Jasper. 2000. "Bizarre New World." *New York Review of Books,* 15 June.

Griffiths, Ieuan L. 1994. *The Atlas of African Affairs.* 2d ed. London: Routledge.

Guizot. M. François. 1829–32. *Histoire de la civilisation en France depuis la chute de l'empire romaine.* Paris: Pichon et Didier.

Gülalp, Haldun. 1999. "The Poverty of Democracy in Turkey: The Refah Party Episode." *New Perspectives on Turkey* 21 (fall): 35–60.

Habermas, Jürgen. 1991. *The Philosophical Discourse of Modernity.* Cambridge, Mass.: MIT Press.

——. 1994. *Postmetaphysical Thinking.* Cambridge, Mass.: MIT Press.

——. 1997. "Kant's Idea of Perpetual Peace with the Benefit of 200 Years' Hindsight." In *Perpetual Peace: Essays on Kant's Cosmopolitan Ideal,* edited by James Bohman and Matthias Lutz-Bachmann. Cambridge, Mass.: MIT Press.

——. 1999. "Bestiality and Humanity." *Constellations* 6, no. 3: 263–72.

Hacking, Ian. 1999. *The Social Construction of What?* Cambridge, Mass.: Harvard Univ. Press.

Hafez, Sabry. 2000. "The Novel, Politics, and Islam." *New Left Review,* 2d ser., 5 (Sept./Oct.): 117–41.

al-Hajj, M. A. 1967. "The Thirteenth Century in Muslim Eschatology: Mahdist Expectations in the Sokoto Caliphate." *Research Bulletin, Centre of Arabic Documentation* (Ibadan) 3, no. 2: 100–115.

Hale, Sondra Dungan. 1979. "The Changing Ethnic Identity of Nubians in an Urban Milieu: Khartoum, Sudan." Ph.D. diss., Univ. of California at Los Angeles.

Halliday, Fred. 1994. "The Politics of Islamic Fundamentalism: Iran, Tunisia and the Challenge to the Secular State." In *Islam, Globalization and Postmodernity,* edited by Akbar S. Ahmed and Hastings Donnan, 91–113. London: Routledge.

Hamad, Khidir. 1980. *Mudhakkirat Khidir Hamad: al-haraka al-wataniyya al-sudaniyya, al-is-tiqlal wa-ma-ba'dahu*. N.p.: Matba'a sawt al-khalij.

Hamid, Gamal Mahmoud. 1996. *Population Displacement in the Sudan: Patterns, Responses, Coping Strategies*. New York: Center for Migration Studies.

Hannerz, Ulf. 1980. *Exploring the City: Inquiries Toward an Urban Anthropology*. New York: Columbia Univ. Press.

———. 1996. *Transnational Connections*. New York: Routledge.

Hanssen, Beatrice. 2000. *Critique of Violence*. New York: Routledge.

al-Hardallu, Ibrahim. 1977. *Al-ribat al-thaqafi bayna misr wa-al-sudan*. Khartoum: Khartoum Univ. Press.

Hardt, Michael, and Antonio Negri. 2000. *Empire*. Cambridge, Mass.: Harvard Univ. Press.

Hargey, Taj. 1981. "The Suppression of Slavery in the Sudan, 1898–1939." D.Phil. thesis, Univ. of Oxford.

Hartmann, Martin. 1914. *Reisebriefe aus Syrien*. Berlin: N.p.

Harvey, David. 1989. *The Condition of Postmodernity: An Enquiry into the Origins of Cultural Change*. Cambridge, Mass.: Blackwell Publishers.

———. 1996. *Justice, Nature and the Geography of Difference*. Cambridge, Mass.: Blackwell Publishers.

Harvey, Irene. 1986. *Derrida and the Economy of Différance*. Bloomington: Indiana Univ. Press.

Hasan, Yusuf Fadl. 1967. *The Arabs and the Sudan: From the Seventh to the Early Sixteenth Century*. Edinburgh: Edinburgh Univ. Press.

Hassan, M. Kamal. 2001. *Intellectual Discourse at the End of the Millennium: Concerns of a Muslim-Malay CEO*. Kuala Lumpur: International Islamic Univ. Press.

Hastings, Adrian. 1997. *The Construction of Nationhood: Ethnicity, Religion and Nationalism*. Cambridge, UK: Cambridge Univ. Press.

Held, David. 1995. *Democracy and the Global Order*. Stanford, Calif.: Stanford Univ. Press.

Held, David, et al. 1999. *Global Transformations*. Stanford, Calif.: Stanford Univ. Press.

Heller, Agnes. 1999. *A Theory of Modernity*. Malden, Mass.: Blackwell Publishers.

Henderson, K.D.D., and T.R.H. Owen, eds. 1963. *Sudan Verse*. London: Chancery Books.

Henry, Clement M., and Robert Springborg. 2001. *Globalization and the Politics of Development in the Middle East*. New York: Cambridge Univ. Press.

Herzfeld, Michael. 1993. *The Social Production of Indifference*. Chicago: Univ. of Chicago Press.

Hill, Kevin, and John E. Hughes. 1998. *Cyberpolitics: Citizen Activism in the Age of the Internet*. Lanham, Md.: Rowman and Littlefield.

Hill, Richard, and Peter Hogg. 1995. *A Black Corps d'Elite: An Egyptian Sudanese Conscript Battalion with the French Army in Mexico, 1863–1867, and Its Survivors in Subsequent African History*. East Lansing: Michigan State Univ. Press.

Hill, Richard. 1959. *Egypt in the Sudan, 1820–1881.* London: Oxford Univ. Press.

Hirschman, Albert O. 1991. *Rhetoric of Reaction.* Cambridge, Mass.: Belknap Press of Harvard Univ. Press.

Hitchens, Christopher. 1993. *For the Sake of Argument: Essays and Minority Reports.* London: Verso.

Hjärpe, Jan. 1999. "Revolution in Religion: From Medievalism to Modernity and Globalization." In *Globalizations and Modernities: Experiences and Perspectives of Europe and Latin America,* edited by Göran Therborn. Report 99:5. Stockholm: Swedish Council for Planning and Coordination of Research.

Hochschild, Adam. 1998. *King Leopold's Ghost.* Boston: Houghton Mifflin.

Hoffman, Eva. 1989. *Lost in Translation.* New York: Penguin.

Hoffmann, Stanley. 1977. "An American Social Science: International Relations." *Daedalus* 106, no. 3 (summer): 41–60.

Holt, P. M. 1970. *The Mahdist State in the Sudan, 1881–1898: A Study of Its Origins, Development and Overthrow.* Oxford, UK: Clarendon Press.

Hont, Istvan. 1995. "The Permanent Crisis of a Divided Mankind." In *Contemporary Crisis of the Nation State,* edited by John Dunn. Cambridge, Mass.: Blackwell Publishers.

Hoodbhoy, Pervez. 1991. *Islam and Science. Religious Orthodoxy and the Battle for Rationality.* London: Zed Books.

Horowitz, Donald. 1994. "The Qur'an and the Common Law: Islamic Law Reform and the Theory of Legal Change." *American Journal of Comparative Law* 42: 233–93 and 545–80.

Horton, Robin. 1975. "On the Rationality of Conversion (Part I)." *Africa* 45: 219–35; and "On the Rationality of Conversion (Part II)." *Africa* 45: 73–99.

Hourani, Albert. 1983. *Arabic Thought in the Liberal Age, 1798–1939.* Cambridge, UK: Cambridge Univ. Press.

———. 1992. "Lebanese and Syrians in Egypt." In *The Lebanese in the World: A Century of Emigration,* edited by Albert Hourani and Nadim Shehadi, 497–507. London: Centre for Lebanese Studies in association with I. B. Tauris Publishers.

Huff, Toby E. 1997. "Science and the Public Sphere: Comparative Institutional Development in Islam and the West." *Social Epistemology* 11, no. 1: 25–37.

———. 2000. "The Internet and the Public Sphere: Technologies of Control or Liberation and Development." *Hybridity. Journal of Culture, Texts and Identities* 1, no. 1: 2–16.

———. 2001. "Globalization and the Internet: Comparing the Middle Eastern and Malaysian Experiences." *Middle East Journal* 55, no. 3: 439–58.

Humphrey, Michael. 1998. *Islam, Multiculturalism and Transnationalism: From the Lebanese Diaspora.* Oxford, UK: Centre for Lebanese Studies in association with I. B. Tauris Publishers.

Humphreys, R. Stephen. 1999. *Between Memory and Desire.* Berkeley: Univ. of California Press.

Huntington, Samuel. 1996. *Clash of Civilizations.* New York: Simon and Schuster.

Husain, Mir Zohair. 1995. *Global Islamic Politics*. New York: HarperCollins College Publishers.

Huyssen, Andreas. 1986. *After the Great Divide*. Bloomington: Indiana Univ. Press.

Ibrahim, Abdullahi Ali. 1994. *Assaulting with Words: Popular Discourse and the Bridle of Shariah*. Evanston, Ill.: Northwestern Univ. Press.

Ibrahim, Fouad N. 1991. "Hunger among the Southern Sudanese Migrants in the Shanty Towns of Greater Khartoum." Paper presented at International Sudan Studies Conference, Sudan Studies Society of the United Kingdom, Univ. of Durham, 8–11 Apr. *Sudan: Environment and People: Second International Studies Conference papers,* vol. 2, 76–89. Durham: Sudan Studies Society of the United Kingdom.

Ibrahim, Hasnayn, ed. 1992. *Zahira al-'unf al-siyasi fi al-nuzum al-'arabiyya*. Beirut: Markaz dirasat al-wahda al-'arabiyya.

Ignatieff, Michael. 1998. *The Warrior's Honor*. New York: Metropolitan Books.

Inglehart, Ronald. 1997. *Modernization and Postmodernization*. Princeton, N.J.: Princeton Univ. Press.

International Migration Project. 1978. *International Migration Project: Country Case Study,* by R. I. Lawless. Durham, UK: International Migration Project, Univ. of Durham.

Irwin, Robert. 1996. "The Emergence of the Islamic World System, 1000–1500." In *The Cambridge Illustrated History of the Islamic World,* edited by Francis Robinson, 32–61. Cambridge, UK: Cambridge Univ. Press.

Jameson, Fredric. 1983. *The Political Unconscious: Narrative as a Socially Symbolic Act*. London: Methuen.

———. 1991. *Postmodernism, or, The Cultural Logic of Late Capitalism*. Durham, N.C.: Duke Univ. Press.

———. 1998a. *The Cultural Turn: Selected Writings on the Postmodern, 1983–1998*. London: Verso.

———. 1998b. "Notes on Globalization as a Philosophical Issue." In *The Cultures of Globalization,* edited by Fredric Jameson and Masao Miyoshi. Durham, N.C.: Duke Univ. Press.

Jameson, Fredric, and Masao Miyoshi, eds. 1998. *The Cultures of Globalization*. Durham, N.C.: Duke Univ. Press.

Jehl, Doug. 1999. "The Internet's 'Open Sesame' Is Answered Warily." *New York Times,* 18 Mar.

John, K. J. 2001. "The Malaysian GEM Story: Leapfrogging to a K-Society." 7 May, <http://www.nitc.org.my/resources/papers.html>.

Johnson, Douglas. 1989. "The Structure of a Legacy: Military Slavery in Northeast Africa." *Ethnohistory* 36, no. 1: 72–88.

Jones, Peter. 1994. "Bearing the Consequences of Belief." *Journal of Political Philosophy* 2: 24–43.

Kakar, Sudhir. 1996. *The Colors of Violence*. Chicago: Univ. of Chicago Press.

Kamalkhani, Zahra. 1998. *Women's Islam: Religious Practice among Women in Today's Iran*. London: Kegan Paul International.

Kandiyoti, Deniz, ed. 1991. *Women, Islam and the State.* Philadelphia, Pa.: Temple Univ. Press.

Kant, Immanuel. 1970. "Perpetual Peace." In *Political Writings,* edited by Hans Reiss; translated by H. B. Nisbet. New York: Cambridge Univ. Press.

al-Karsani, Awad al-Sid. 1998. "Religion, Ethnicity and Class: The Role of the Tijaniyya Order in al-Nahud Town." In *Kordofan Invaded: Peripheral Incorporation and Social Transformation in Islamic Africa,* edited by Endre Stiansen and Michael Kevane, 180–96. Leiden: Brill.

Kaplan, E. Ann, ed. 1988. *Postmodernism and Its Discontents.* New York: Verso.

Kapteijns, Lidwien. 1985. *Mahdist Faith and Sudanic Tradition: The History of the Masalit Sultanate, 1870–1930.* London: KPI.

Karrar, Ali Salih. 1992. *The Sufi Brotherhoods in the Sudan.* London: C. Hurst.

al-Kawakibi, 'Abd al-Rahman. 1991. *Umm al-qura: wa huwa daht mufawadat wa-muqarrarat mu'tamar al-nahda al-islamiyya al-munaqid fi makka al-mukarrama sana 1316.* Beirut: Halab.

Keane, John. 1996. *Reflections on Violence.* New York: Verso.

Keddie, Nikki R. 1972. *Sayyid Jamal ad-Din "al-Afghani": A Political Biography.* Berkeley: Univ. of California Press.

———. 1998. "The New Religious Politics." *Comparative Society and History* 40, no. 4: 696–723.

Kepel, Gilles. 1991. *La Revanche de Dieu.* Paris: Editions du Seuil.

Kermode, Frank. 1971. *Modern Essays.* London: Collins.

Khairallah, Khairallah T. 1912. *La Syrie.* Paris: Leroux.

———. 1919. *Le Problème du Levant.* Paris: N.p.

Kim, Jim Yong, et al., eds. 1999. *Dying for Growth.* Monroe, Maine: Common Courage Press.

Kleden, Ignas. 1986. "Social Science Indigenisation: National Response to Development Model and Theory Building." *Prisma* 41:27–38.

Kleinman, Arthur. 1999. "Experience and Its Moral Codes." Vol. 20 of *The Tanner Lectures on Human Values,* edited by Grethe B. Peterson. Salt Lake City: Univ. of Utah Press.

Kleinman, Arthur, and Joan Kleinman. 1997. "The Appeal of Experience." In *Social Suffering,* edited by Arthur Kleinman, Veena Das, and Margaret Lock. Berkeley: Univ. of California Press.

Knoke, David, and James H. Kuklinski. 2000. *Network Analysis.* London: Sage Publications.

Kohn, Hans. 1936. *Western Civilization in the Near East.* Translated by E. W. Dickes. London: Routledge.

———. 1962. *The Age of Nationalism: The First Era of Global History.* Westport, Conn.: Greenwood Press.

Koselleck, Reinhart. 1985. "The Historical Political Semantics of Asymmetric Counterconcepts." In *Futures Past,* translated by Keith Tribe. Cambridge, Mass.: MIT Press.

Kramer, Martin, ed. 1997. *The Islamism Debate*. Tel Aviv: Moshe Dayan Center for Middle Eastern and African Studies, Tel Aviv Univ.

Kramer, Robert S. 1991. "Holy City on the Nile: Omdurman, 1885–1898." Ph.D. diss., Northwestern Univ.

Krasner, Stephen D. 1999. *Sovereignty: Organized Hypocrisy*. Princeton, N.J.: Princeton Univ. Press.

Krauss, Rosalind. 1993. *The Optical Unconscious*. Cambridge, Mass.: MIT Press.

Kreiser, Klaus. 1983. "Weisser Elefant oder Milchkuh? Ein neuer Beitrag über die Türken im Jemen." *Jemen Report* 14, no. 1: 12–14.

Krieger, Joel. 1999. *British Politics in the Global Age*. Cambridge, UK: Polity Press.

Lane, Edward William. 1863. *An Arabic-English Lexicon*. London: Williams and Norgate.

Laqueur, Walter. 2001. "Fundamentalism." *Partisan Review* 68, no. 3 (summer): 499–503.

Latour, Bruno. 1993. *We Have Never Been Modern*. Translated by Catherine Porter. Cambridge, Mass.: Harvard Univ. Press.

Lauren, Paul Gordon. 1998. *The Evolution of International Human Rights: Visions Seen*. Philadelphia: Univ. of Pennsylvania Press.

Lawrence, Bruce B. 1984. "Ibn Khaldun and Islamic Reform." In *Ibn Khaldun and Islamic Ideology*, edited by Bruce B. Lawrence. Leiden: Brill.

———. 1989. *Defenders of God*. San Francisco: Harper and Row.

Lears, T. J. Jackson. 1981. *No Place of Grace*. New York: Pantheon Books.

Lee, Robert D. 1997. *Overcoming Tradition and Modernity: The Search for Islamic Authenticity*. Boulder, Colo.: Westview Press.

Lesch, Ann Mosely. 1998. *The Sudan: Contested National Identities*. Bloomington: Indiana Univ. Press.

Lessig, Lawrence. 1999. *Code and Other Laws of Cyberspace*. New York: Basic Books.

Levi, Isaac. 1986. *Hard Choices*. Cambridge, UK: Cambridge Univ. Press.

Lévi-Strauss, Claude. 1979. *Myth and Meaning*. New York: Schocken Books.

Lewis, Bernard. 1998. *The Multiple Identities of the Middle East*. New York: Schocken Books.

Lewis, Franklin D. 2000. *Rumi: Past and Present, East and West*. Boston: Oneworld.

Ley, Hermann. 1982. "Société bedouine et société citadine dans l'oeuvre d'Ibn Khaldoun." *Actes du Colloque International sur Ibn Khaldoun: Alger 21–26 Juin 1978*, 115–31. Algiers: Société nationale d'édition et de diffusion.

Lifton, Robert. 1986. *The Nazi Doctors*. New York: Basic Books.

Lincoln, Bruce. 1994. *Authority: Construction and Corrosion*. Chicago: Univ. of Chicago Press.

Lindermann, Alf. 1996. *The Reception of Religious Television*. Stockholm: Almqvist and Wiksell International.

Lingle, Christopher. 1998. *The Rise and Decline of the Asian Century*. Hong Kong: Asia 2000 Limited.

Löwith, Karl. 1949. *Meaning in History*. Chicago: Univ. of Chicago Press.

Lundvall, B. A. 1988. *National Innovation Systems.* London: Pinter.

Luttwak, Edward. 1999. *Turbo Capitalism.* New York: HarperCollins Publishers.

Lyotard, Jean-François. 1984. *The Postmodern Condition.* Minneapolis: Univ. of Minnesota Press.

MacEwan, Arthur. 1999. *Neo-Liberalism or Democracy?* New York: Zed Books.

MacLeod, Arlene. 1991. *Accommodating Protest.* New York: Columbia Univ. Press.

Mahathir, Mohamad. 1998.*Mahathir Mohamad on the Multimedia Super Corridor.* Subang Jaya, Malaysia: Pelanduk Publications.

Mahmoud, Fatima Babiker. 1984. *The Sudanese Bourgeoisie: Vanguard of Development?* London: Zed Books.

Mahmoud, Mahgoub El-Tigani. 1983. "The Impact of Partial Modernization on the Emigration of Sudanese Professionals and Skilled Workers." Ph.D. diss., Brown Univ.

Makdisi, Ussama. 2000. *The Culture of Sectarianism: Community, History, and Violence in Nineteenth-Century Ottoman Lebanon.* Berkeley: Univ. of California Press.

Malaysia. 2001. *Eighth Malaysia Plan, 2001–2005.* Kuala Lumpur: Government of Malaysia, <http://www.epu.jpm.my/rm8/front_rm8.html>.

Malek, Mark M. 1991. "The Arabization of the Names of People in the Southern Sudan." Paper presented at International Sudan Studies Conference, Sudan Studies Society of the United Kingdom, Univ. of Durham, 8–11 Apr. *Sudan: Environment and People: Second International Studies Conference papers,* vol. 2, 29–34. Durham: Sudan Studies Society of the United Kingdom.

Malik, Muhammad Mahjub. 1987. *Al-Muqawama al-dakhiliyya li-harakat al-mahdiyya (1881–1898).* Beirut: Dar al-jil.

Mamdani, Mahmoud. 1996. *Citizen and Subject.* Princeton, N.J.: Princeton Univ. Press.

Mandaville, Peter. 2000. "Information Technology and the Changing Boundaries of European Islam." In *Paroles d'Islam: Individus, sociétés et discours dans l'Islam européen contemporain,* edited by Félice Dassetto, 281–97. Paris: Maisonneuve et Larose.

Manger, Leif, ed. 1999. *Muslim Diversity: Local Islam in Global Contexts.* Richmond, UK: Curzon.

Marchal, Roland. 1991. "Remarques sur le développement de l'Eglise catholique et la 'vernacularisation' du christianisme au Soudan." In *Sudan: History, Identity, Ideology/Histoire, identités, idéologies,* edited by Hervé Bleuchot, Christian Delmet, and Derek Hopwood, 181–94. Reading, UK: Ithaca Press.

Marcus, George, and Michael Fischer. 1986. *Anthropology as Cultural Critique.* Chicago: Univ. of Chicago Press.

Mardin, Şerif. 2000. *The Genesis of Young Ottoman Thought.* Syracuse, N.Y.: Syracuse Univ. Press.

Margalit, Avishai. 2000. "The Odds Against Barak." *New York Review of Books,* 21 Sept.

Margolis, Joseph. 1999. *What, After All, Is a Work of Art?* University Park: Pennsylvania State Univ. Press.

Martin, B. G. 1976. *Muslim Brotherhoods in Nineteenth-Century Africa.* Cambridge, UK: Cambridge Univ. Press.

Martinez, Luis. 1998. *La guerre civile en Algérie.* Paris: Karthala.

Marty, Martin, and R. Scott Appleby. 1992. *The Glory and the Power.* Boston: Beacon Press.

Marx, Karl. 1978. *Marx-Engels Reader.* Edited by Robert C. Tucker. New York: W. W. Norton.

McCole, John. 1993. *Walter Benjamin and the Antinomies of Tradition.* Ithaca, N.Y.: Cornell Univ. Press.

McHugh, Neil. 1994. *Holymen of the Blue Nile: The Making of an Arab-Islamic Community in the Nilotic Sudan, 1500–1850.* Evanston, Ill.: Northwestern Univ. Press.

Melucci, Alberto. 1989. *Nomads of the Present: Social Movements and Individual Needs in Contemporary Society.* Edited by John Keane and Paul Mier. Philadelphia, Pa.: Temple Univ. Press.

Memmi, Albert. 1965. *The Colonizer and the Colonized.* Translated by Howard Greenfeld. New York: Orion.

Messaoudi, Khalida. 1995. *Une Algérienne debout.* Paris: Flammarion.

Mies, Françoise. 1994. *De l'autre: Essai de typologie.* Namur: Presses Universitaires de Namur.

Mignolo, Walter D. 2000. *Local Histories/Global Designs: Coloniality, Subaltern Knowledges, and Border Thinking.* Princeton, N.J.: Princeton Univ. Press.

Mill, John Stuart. 1973. *Essays on Politics and Culture.* Edited by Gertrude Himmelfarb. Gloucester, Mass.: Peter Smith.

———. 1989. *On Liberty.* Edited by Stephan Collini. New York: Cambridge Univ. Press.

Miller, C. 1991. "Le changement linguistique à Juba et à Khartoum." In *Sudan: History, Identity, Ideology/Histoire, identités, idéologies,* edited by Hervé Bleuchot, Christian Delmet, and Derek Hopwood, 153–80. Reading, UK: Ithaca Press.

Miller, Catherine, and Al-Amin Abu-Manga. 1992. *Language Choice and National Integration: Rural Migrants in Khartoum.* Khartoum: Khartoum Univ. Press.

Miller, James. 1999. "Of Choice." *Social Research* 66, no. 4: 1121–35.

Mitchell, Timothy. 1991. *Colonising Egypt.* Cambridge, UK: Cambridge Univ. Press.

Mohamed, Tibyan. 2000. "Sudanese Supplementary School." *Sudan Dispatch: Journal of Sudanese Development* 3, no. 9: 10–14.

Monnot, Guy. 1986. *Islam et religions.* Paris: Maisonneuve and Larose.

Moody, Kim. 1999. *Workers in a Lean World: Unions in the International Economy.* London: Verso.

Moore, Barrington Jr. 1978. *Injustice.* White Plains, N.Y.: M. E. Sharpe.

Moras, Joachim. 1930. *Ursprung und Entwicklung des Begriffs der Zivilisation in Frankreich, 1756–1830.* Hamburg: Seminar für romanische Sprachen und Kultur.

Moretti, Franco. 1987. *The Way of the World.* London: Verso.

———. 2001. "Planet Hollywood." *New Left Review,* 2d ser., 9: 90–101.

Mosse, George. 1978. *Toward the Final Solution.* New York: Howard Fertig.

Moten, Abdul Rashid. 1996. *Political Science: An Islamic Perspective*. New York: St. Martin's Press.

Mottahedeh, Roy. 1985. *The Mantle of the Prophet: Religion and Politics in Iran*. New York: Pantheon Books.

Motyl, Alexander J. 1999. *Revolutions, Nations, Empires*. New York: Columbia Univ. Press.

MSANEWS. 2000. 28 Aug., <http://msanews.mynet.net>.

Mueller, John. 1989. *Retreat from Doomsday*. New York: Basic Books.

Muhammad, Fida. 1998. "Ibn Khaldun's Theory of Social Change: A Comparison with Hegel, Marx and Durkheim." *American Journal of Islamic Social Sciences* 15, no. 2: 25–45.

Müller, Kurt. 1964. "Soviet and Chinese Programmes of Economic and Technical Assistance to African Countries." In *The Soviet Bloc, China and Africa,* edited by Sven Hamrell and Carl Gösta Widstrand, 101–30. Uppsala, Sweden: Scandinavian Institute of African Studies.

Murqus, Yuwaqim Rizq. 1984. *Tatawwur nizam al-idara fi al-sudan fi ahd al-hukm al-thuna'i al-awwal, 1899–1924*. Cairo: Hay'at al-misriyya al-ʿamma li-al-kutub.

Mutahhari, Ayatullah Murtaza. 1986. *Social and Historical Change: An Islamic Perspective*. Translated by R. Campbell. Berkeley, Calif.: Mizan Press.

Nagel, Thomas. 1986. *The View from Nowhere*. New York: Oxford Univ. Press.

Najila, Hasan. 1964. *Malamih min al-mujtama ʿal-sudani*. 3d ed. Beirut: Dar maktabat al-hay'a.

Nandy, Ashis. 1991. "Secularists on the Run." *Mantham,* June.

Nanji, Azim, ed. 1997. *Mapping Islamic Studies: Genealogy, Continuity and Change*. Berlin: Mouton de Gruyter.

al-Naqar, Umar. 1985. "The Historical Background to the Sudan Road." In *Sudan in Africa,* edited by Yusuf Fadl Hasan, 98–108. 2d ed. Khartoum: Khartoum Univ. Press.

Nasr, Ahmad ʿAbd al-Rahman. 1979. *Al-idara al-baritaniyya wa-al-tabshir al-islami wa-al-masihi fi al-sudan: dirasa awaliyya*. Khartoum: Wizarat al-tarbiyya wa-al-tawjih, al-shuʿun al-diniyya wa-al-awqaf.

National Records Office (Khartoum). NRO Personnel 3A/6/13 (file for Hamza al-Malik Tambal, 1923–32) and NRO Personnel 1A/2/4 (file for Da'ud Iskandar, 1928–55).

Nelson, Richard, ed. 1993. *National Innovation Systems: A Comparative Analysis*. New York: Oxford Univ. Press.

Nelson, Richard R., and Paul Romer. 1996. "Science, Economic Growth, and Public Policy." *Challenge* 40, no. 2: 9–21.

Niblock, Tim. 1987. *Class and Power in Sudan: The Dynamics of Sudanese Politics, 1898–1985*. Houndmills, Basingstoke, Hampshire, UK: Macmillan Press.

Nietzsche, Friedrich. 1998. *On the Genealogy of Morality: A Polemic*. Translated by Maudemarie Clark and Alan Swensen. Indianapolis, Ind.: Hackett.

Nikkel, Marc R. 1991. "Aspects of Contemporary Religious Change among the Dinka."

In *Papers of the Second International Sudan Studies Conference,* vol. 1, 90–100. Durham, UK: Univ. of Durham.

NITC/MIMOS. 1999. "The K-Economy and Its Implications." 17 Dec. Technology Park, Malaysia: Mimos Berhard.

———. 2000. *Access, Empowerment and Governance in the Information Age.* Building Knowledge Societies Series, vol. 1. Technology Park, Malaysia: Mimos Berhard.

al-Nur, Faruq Muhammad Ibrahim. 1995. Conversation in the Sudanese Studies Center, Cairo, 6 Nov.

O'Fahey, R. S. 1990. *Enigmatic Saint: Ahmad ibn Idris and the Idrisi Tradition.* Evanston, Ill.: Northwestern Univ. Press.

O'Fahey, R. S., and J. L. Spaulding. 1974. *Kingdoms of the Sudan.* London: Methuen.

Offe, Claus. 1984. *Contradictions of the Welfare State.* Edited by John Keane. Cambridge, Mass.: MIT Press.

———. 1987. "Challenging the Boundaries of Institutional Politics." In *Changing Boundaries of the Political,* edited by Charles Maier. New York: Cambridge Univ. Press.

———. 1996. *Modernity and the State.* Cambridge, Mass.: MIT Press.

Ormiston, Gayle L., and Alan D. Schrift, eds. 1990. *Transforming the Hermeneutic Context.* Albany: State Univ. of New York Press.

Outlaw, Lucius. 1996. *On Race and Philosophy.* New York: Routledge.

Özal, Turgut. 1991. *Turkey in Europe and Europe in Turkey.* Nicosia, Cyprus: Rustem and Brother.

Palmer, Richard. 1969. *Hermeneutics.* Evanston, Ill.: Northwestern Univ. Press.

Perkins, Kenneth J. 1993. *Port Sudan: The Evolution of a Colonial City.* Boulder, Colo.: Westview Press.

Pick, Daniel. 1989. *Faces Of Degeneration.* New York: Cambridge Univ. Press.

Pieterse, Jan Nederveen, and Bhikhu Parekh. 1995. "Shifting Imaginaries." In *The Decolonization of Imagination,* edited by Jan Nederveen Pieterse and Bhikhu Parekh. Atlantic Highlands, N.J.: Zed Books.

Piscatori, James. 1986. *Islam in a World of Nation-States.* New York: Cambridge Univ. Press.

Piven, Frances, and Richard Cloward. 1979. *Poor People's Movements.* New York: Vintage Books.

Pogge, Thomas. 1989. *Realizing Rawls.* Ithaca, N.Y.: Cornell Univ. Press.

———. 1992. "Cosmopolitanism and Sovereignty." *Ethics* 103: 48–75.

———. 2002. *World Poverty and Human Rights: Cosmopolitan Responsibilities and Reforms.* Cambridge, UK: Polity.

Polanyi, Karl. 2001. *The Great Transformation.* Boston: Beacon Press.

Portes, Alejandro, and Ruben Rumbaut. 1996. *Immigrant America.* Berkeley: Univ. of California Press.

Poster, Mark. 1997. *Cultural History and Postmodernity: Disciplinary Readings and Challenges.* New York: Columbia Univ. Press.

Potter, Jonathan. 1996. *Representing Reality: Discourse, Rhetoric and Social Construction.* London: Sage Publications.

Press, Eyal. 2000. "Human Rights—the Next Step." *Nation* 271, no. 21: 13–18.

Putnam, Hilary. 1995. "The Permanence of William James." In *Pragmatism*. Cambridge, Mass.: Blackwell.

al-Qaddal, Muhammad Sa'id. 1992. *Al-Imam al-Mahdi: Muhammad Ahmad ibn 'Abd Allah (1844–1885)*. Beirut: Dar al-Jil.

al-Qaradawi, Yusuf. 1984. *Risalat al-Azhar*. Cairo: Maktabat Wahbah.

———. 1990. *Fatawa Mu'asira*. Kuwait: Dar al-Qalam.

———. 1999. *Al-Shari'a wa-al-haya*. TV program, Al-Jazeera, Qatar.

Quine, W. V. 1981. "Five Milestones of Empiricism." In *Theories and Things*. Cambridge, Mass.: Harvard Univ. Press.

———. 1987. *Quiddities*. Cambridge, Mass.: Belknap Press of Harvard Univ. Press.

Ramadan, Tariq. 1999. *To Be a European Muslim: A Study of Islamic Sources in the European Context*. Leicester, UK: Islamic Foundation.

al-Rahman, Muhammad Fawzi Mustafa. 1972. *Al-thaqafa al-'arabiyya wa-athruhu fi tamasuk al-wihda al-qawmiyya fi al-sudan al-mu'asir*. Khartoum: Al-dar al-sudaniyya.

Raschke, Carl. 1989. "Jacques Lacan and the Magic of Desire." In *Lacan and Theological Discourse*, edited by Edith Wyschogrod, David Crownfield, and Carl A. Raschke. Albany: State Univ. of New York Press.

Raudvere, Catharina. 1998. "Urban Visions and Religious Communities: Access and Visibility." In *Alevi Identity: Cultural, Religious and Social Perspectives*, edited by Tord Olsson, Elisabeth Özdalga, and Catharina Raudvere. Istanbul: Swedish Research Institute in Istanbul.

———. 2002. *The Book and the Roses: Sufi Women, Visibility, and Zikir in Contemporary Istanbul*. Istanbul: Swedish Research Institute in Istanbul.

Reid, Donald Malcolm. 1990. *Cairo University and the Making of Modern Egypt*. Cambridge, UK: Cambridge Univ. Press.

Reynolds, David. 2000. *One World Divisible*. New York: W. W. Norton.

Ricoeur, Paul. 1990. *Soi-même comme un autre*. Paris: Le Seuil.

———. 1992. *Oneself as Another*. Translated by K. Blamey. Chicago: Univ. of Chicago Press.

Rida, Rashid. 1927. *Khulasat al-sira al-muhammadiyya wa-haqiqa al-da'wa al-islamiyya*. 2d ed. Cairo: Matba'a al-manar.

Rispler-Chaim, Vardit. 1993. *Islamic Medical Ethics in the Twentieth Century*. New York: E. J. Brill.

Risse-Kappen, Thomas, ed. 1995. *Bringing Transnational Relations Back In*. New York: Cambridge Univ. Press.

———, et al., eds., 1999. *The Power of Human Rights*. New York: Cambridge Univ. Press.

Robertson, Roland. 1989. "Globalization, Politics, and Religion." In *The Changing Face of Religion*, edited by James A. Beckford and Thomas Luckmann. London: Sage Publications.

———. 1992. *Globalization: Social Theory and Global Culture*. London: Sage Publications.

Robins, Kevin, and David Morley. 1996. "Almancı, Yabancı." *Cultural Studies* 10, no. 2: 248–54.

Robinson, Ronald. 1972. "Non-European Foundations of European Imperialism." In *Studies in the Theory of Imperialism,* edited by Roger Owen and Bob Sutcliffe. London: Longman.

Romer, Paul. 1990. "Endogenous Technological Change." *Journal of Political Economy* 98, no. 5, part 2: S71-S102.

———. 1993 . "Two Strategies for Economic Development: Using Ideas and Producing Ideas." In *Proceedings of the World Bank Annual Conference on Development Economics 1992.* Washington, D.C.: World Bank.

Roseberry, William. 1996. "The Rise of Yuppie Coffees and the Reimagination of Class in the United States." *American Anthropologist* 98, no. 4: 762–75.

Rosenberg, Justin. 2000. *The Follies of Globalisation Theory.* New York: Verso.

Roseneil, Sasha. 1997. "Contesting Global Forces." In *The Limits of Globalization,* edited by Alan Scott. London: Routledge.

Roth, Philip. 1997. *American Pastoral.* New York: Vintage.

Rothschild, Emma. 1999. "Globalization and the Return of History." *Foreign Policy* 115 (summer): 106–16.

Rousseau, Jean-Jacques. 1987. *The Basic Political Writings.* Translated and edited by Donald A. Cress. Indianapolis, Ind.: Hackett.

Roy, Olivier. 1994. *The Failure of Political Islam.* Translated by Carol Volk. Cambridge, Mass.: Harvard Univ. Press.

Ruay, Deng D. Akol. 1994. *The Politics of Two Sudans: The South and the North, 1821–1969.* Uppsala, Sweden: Nordiska Afrikainstitutet.

Rudé, J. 1964. "La Germania d'Enea Silvio Piccolomini et la 'réception' de Tacite en Allemagne." *Etudes germaniques* 19, no. 3: 274–81.

Rudolph, Susanne Hoeber. 2000. "Dissing the State? Religion and Transnational Civil Society." Paper presented at the International Political Science Association Congress, Quebec City, Canada, 1–5 Aug.

Rudolph, Susanne Hoeber, and J. Piscatori, eds. 1997. *Transnational Religion and Fading States.* Boulder, Colo.: Westview Press.

Rudy, Sayres S. 2000. "A Political Economy of Globalization." Unpublished paper available from author.

Ruggie, John. 1998. *Constructing the World Polity.* New York: Routledge.

Saavedra, Martha. 1998. "Ethnicity, Resources, and the Central State: Politics in the Nuba Mountains, 1950 to the 1990s." In *Kordofan Invaded: Peripheral Incorporation and Social Transformation in Islamic Africa,* edited by Endre Stiansen and Michael Kevane, 223–53. Leiden: Brill.

Sadowski, Yahya. 1987. "Egypt's Islamist Movement." *Middle East Insight* 4, no. 4: 37–44.

———. 1996. "Just a Religion." *Brookings Review* (summer): 34–35.

———. 1998. *The Myth of Global Chaos.* Washington, D.C.: Brookings Institution Press.

Safi, Louay M. 1994. *The Challenge of Modernity: The Quest for Authenticity in the Arab World.* Lanham, Md.: Univ. Press of America.

———. 1996. *The Foundation of Knowledge. A Comparative Study in Islamic and Western Methods of Inquiry.* Petaling Jaya, Malaysia: International Islamic Univ. Malaysia Press/International Institute of Islamic Thought.

Said, Edward. 1978. *Orientalism.* New York: Pantheon.

———. 1993. *Culture and Imperialism.* New York: Knopf.

Salamé, Ghassan, ed. 1994. *Democracy Without Democrats?* New York: I. B. Tauris Publishers.

Salih, al-Tayyib. 1969. *Mawsim al-hijra ila al-shamal.* Cairo: Dar al-hilal.

———. 1991. *Season of Migration to the North.* Translated by Denys Johnson-Davies. Portsmouth, N.H.: Heinemann.

Salih, Kamal el-Din Osman. 1982. "The British Administration in the Nuba Mountains Region of the Sudan, 1900–1956." Ph.D. thesis, School of Oriental and African Studies, Univ. of London.

Salvatore, Armando. 1997. *Islam and the Political Discourse of Modernity.* Reading, UK: Ithaca Press.

Sanderson, Lilian Passmore, and Neville Sanderson. 1981. *Education, Religion and Politics in Southern Sudan, 1899–1964.* London: Ithaca Press.

Sassen, Saskia. 1991. *The Global City: New York, London, Tokyo.* Princeton, N.J.: Princeton Univ. Press.

Saxenian, Ann Lee. 1999. "Silicon Valley's New Immigrant Entrepreneurs." June, <http://www.ppic.org/publications/PPIC120/index.html>.

Schaebler (Schäbler), Birgit. 1996a. "Universale Zivilisationsmission in der europäischen Phase außereuropäischer Expansion: Anregungen aus der Globalisierungsdebatte." *Loccumer Protokolle* 26, 187–97.

———. 1996b. *Aufstände im Drusenbergland. Ethnizität und Integration einer ländlichen Gesellschaft Syriens vom Osmanischen Reich bis zur Unabhängigkeit.* Gotha, Germany: Perthes.

———. 2004. "From 'Urban Notables' to 'Noble Arabs': Shifting Discourses in the Emergence of Nationalism in the Arab East (1910–1916)." In *From the Syrian Land to the States of Syria and Lebanon,* edited by Thomas Philipp and Christoph Schumann. Beirut/Wurtberg: OIB/Ergon.

Schama, Simon. 1996. *Landscape and Memory.* New York: Vintage.

Scheuerman, William. 1999. "Economic Globalization and the Rule of Law." *Constellations* 6, no. 1: 3–25.

Schiller, Friedrich von. 1972. "The Nature and Value of Universal History." *History and Theory* 11, no. 3: 321–34.

Schneewind, J. B. 1998. *The Invention of Autonomy.* New York: Cambridge Univ. Press.

Schoelch, Alexander. 1991. "Der arabische Osten im neunzehnten Jahrhundert, 1800–1914." In *Geschichte der arabischen Welt,* edited by Ulrich Haarmann, 365–431. Munich: C. H. Beck.

Schofield, Norman. 1999. "The Heart of the Atlantic Constitution." *Politics and Society* 27, no. 2: 173–215.

Schorske, Karl. 1998. *Thinking with History.* Princeton, N.J.: Princeton Univ. Press.

Schulze, Reinhard. 1990. *Islamischer Internationalismus im 20. Jahrhundert.* Leiden: Brill.

———. 2000. *A Modern History of the Islamic World.* New York: New York Univ. Press.

Scott, Alan. 1997. "Introduction: Globalization Social Process or Political Rhetoric?" In *The Limits of Globalization,* edited by Alan Scott. London: Routledge.

Scott, James. 1998. *Seeing Like a State.* New Haven, Conn.: Yale Univ. Press.

Sen, Amartya. 1999. *Development as Freedom.* New York: Alfred Knopf.

———. 2000. "East and West." *New York Review of Books,* 10 July.

Sharabi, Hisham. 1970. *Arab Intellectuals and the West: The Formative Years, 1875–1914.* Baltimore: Johns Hopkins Univ. Press.

Sharkey, Heather J. 1994. "Ahmad Zayni Dahlan's *al-Futuhat al-Islamiyya:* A Contemporary View of the Sudanese Mahdi." *Sudanic Africa: A Journal of Historical Sources* 5: 95–110.

———. 1998. "Colonialism and the Culture of Nationalism in the Northern Sudan, 1898–1956." 2 vols. Ph.D. diss., Princeton Univ.

Sharkey-Balasubramanian, Heather J. 2000. "The Egyptian Colonial Presence in the Anglo-Egyptian Sudan, 1898–1932." In *White Nile, Black Blood: War, Leadership, and Ethnicity from Khartoum to Kampala,* edited by Jay Spaulding and Stephanie Beswick, 279–314. Lawrenceville, N.J.: Red Sea Press.

Shayegan, Daryush. 1997. *Cultural Schizophrenia: Islamic Societies Confronting the West.* Syracuse, N.Y.: Syracuse Univ. Press.

Sheffer, Gabi. 1996. "Whither the Study of Ethnic Diasporas? Some Theoretical, Definitional, Analytical and Comparative Considerations." In *The Networks of Diasporas,* edited by Georges Prévélakis, 37–46. Paris: L'Harmattan.

Sheriffadeen, Tengku Azzman. 1994. "The Malaysian Development Experience." Paper presented at National Institute of Public Administration, Kuala Lumpur.

———. 1995. "Moving Toward a More Intelligent Use of Human Intelligence." Paper presented at "INFOTECH 95 Malaysia," Kuala Lumpur, 1–5 Nov.

———. 1997. "Beyond Information Literary: A Malaysian Experiment." Paper presented at APEC "Conference on Information Literacy '97," Tokyo, 4 Nov.

Shklar, Judith. 1990. *Faces of Injustice.* New Haven, Conn.: Yale Univ. Press.

Shoch, James. 2000. "Contesting Globalization." *Politics and Society* 28, no. 1: 119–50.

Shuqayr, Na'um. 1972. *Jughrafiyat wa-ta'rikh al-sudan.* 2d ed. Beirut: Dar al-thaqafa.

Sidahmed, Abdel Salam. 1996. *Politics and Islam in Contemporary Sudan.* London: St. Martin's Press.

Sikainga, Ahmed Alawad. 1996. *Slaves into Workers: Emancipation and Labor in Colonial Sudan.* Austin: Univ. of Texas Press.

Silverstein, Ken. 1999. "High-Caliber Carnival." *Mother Jones,* July-Aug. San Francisco: Foundation for National Progress.

Simmel, Georg. 1955. *Conflict.* Translated by Kurt H. Worlff; and *The Web of Group Affiliations.* Translated by Reinhard Bendix. New York: Free Press.

Simone, T. Abdou Maliqalim. 1994. *In Whose Image?: Political Islam and Urban Practices in Sudan.* Chicago: Univ. of Chicago Press.

Simpson, Lorenzo. 1995. *Technology, Time, and the Conversations of Modernity.* New York: Routledge.

Sirma, Ihsan Süreyya. 1980. *Osmanlı Devleti'nin Yıkılışında Yemen İsyanları.* Istanbul: Düsünce Yayınları.

SISS. 1997–98. *Catalog.* Leesburg, Va.: Graduate School of Islamic and Social Science.

Sivan, Emmanuel. 1985. *Radical Islam.* New Haven, Conn.: Yale Univ. Press.

Sklair, Leslie. 1995. *Sociology of the Global System.* Baltimore: Johns Hopkins Univ. Press.

Smith, Steven. 1989. *Hegel's Critique of Liberalism.* Chicago: Univ. of Chicago Press.

Smith, Wilfred Cantwell. 1962. *The Meaning and End of Religion: A New Approach to the Religious Traditions of Mankind.* New York: Macmillan Company.

Sontag, Susan. 1981. *Under the Sign of Saturn.* New York: Vintage.

Sørbø, Gunnar M. 1985. *Tenants and Nomads in Eastern Sudan: A Study of Economic Adaptations in the New Halfa Scheme.* Uppsala, Sweden: Scandinavian Institute of African Studies.

Sorush, Abdolkarim. 1995. "Mana va Mabnay-e Sekularism [The Meaning and Basis of Secularism]." *Kiyan* 26 (Aug.-Sept.): 4–13.

Soto, Hernando de. 1989. *The Other Path.* Translated by June Abbott. New York: Harper and Row.

Spaulding, Jay. 1982. "Slavery, Land Tenure, and Social Class in the Northern Turkish Sudan." *International Journal of African Historical Studies* 15, no. 1: 1–20.

———. 1998. "Early Kordofan." In *Kordofan Invaded: Peripheral Incorporation and Social Transformation in Islamic Africa,* edited by Endre Stiansen and Michael Kevane, 46–49. Leiden: Brill.

Spaulding, Jay, and Lidwien Kapteijns. 1991. "The Orientalist Paradigm in the Historiography of the Late Precolonial Sudan." In *Golden Ages, Dark Ages: Imagining the Past in Anthropology and History,* edited by Jay O'Brien and William Roseberry, 139–51. Berkeley: Univ. of California Press.

Spengler, Oswald. 1939. *The Decline of the West.* New York: Knopf.

Spivak, Gayatri Chakravorty. 1999. *A Critique of Postcolonial Reason: Toward a History of the Vanishing Present.* Cambridge, Mass.: Harvard Univ. Press.

Stenberg, Leif. 1996. *The Islamization of Science: Four Muslim Positions Developing an Islamic Modernity.* Stockholm: Almqvist and Wiksell International.

———. 2000. "Science in the Service of God: Islamizing Knowledge." *ISIM Newsletter* (Leiden) 6: 11.

Stevens, Jacqueline. 1999. *Reproducing the State.* Princeton, N.J.: Princeton Univ. Press.

Stiansen, Endre. 1993. "Overture to Imperialism: European Trade and Economic Change in the Sudan in the Nineteenth Century." Ph.D. diss., Univ. of Bergen.

Stoddard, T. Lothrop. 1917. "Pan-Turanism." *The American Political Science Review* 11, no. 1: 12–23.

Strange, Susan. 1971. "The Politics of International Currencies." *World Politics* 23, no. 2: 215–31.

———. 1996. *The Retreat of the State.* New York: Cambridge Univ. Press.

Subrahmanyam, Sanjay. 2000. *Daedalus.* "Multiple Modernities" special issue 129, no. 1.

Sudan Government, 1905, 1907, 1909, 1911. *Reports on the Finance, Administration and Condition of the Sudan.* Khartoum: Sudan Government.

Sulayman, Muhammad. 1985. *Dawr al-azhar fi al-sudan.* Cairo: Al-hay'a al-misriyya al-'amma li-al-kutub.

al-Tahtawi, Rifa'at. 1265/1848. *Takhlis al-ibriz ila talkhis bariz.* Cairo: Bulaq.

Tapper, Nancy, and Richard Tapper. 1991. "Religion, Education and Continuity in a Provincial Town." In *Islam in Modern Turkey: Religion, Politics, and Literature in a Secular State,* edited by Richard Tapper. London: I. B. Tauris.

Tavakoli-Targhi, Mohamad. 2001. *Refashioning Iran: Orientalism, Occidentalism, and Historiography.* Basingstoke, UK: Palgrave.

Taylor, Charles. 1989. *Sources of the Self.* Cambridge, Mass.: Harvard Univ. Press.

———. 1995. *Philosophical Arguments.* Cambridge, Mass.: Harvard Univ. Press.

Taylor, Mark C. 2001. *The Moment of Complexity: Emerging Network Culture.* Chicago: Univ. of Chicago Press.

Thelen, Kathleen, and Ikuo Kume. 1999. "The Effects of Globalization on Labor Revisited." *Politics and Society* 27, no. 4: 476–504.

Thompson, John B. 1990. *Ideology and Modern Culture.* Stanford, Calif.: Stanford Univ. Press.

Thuermer-Rohr, Christina, et al., eds. 1989. *Mittäterschaft und Entdeckungslust.* Berlin: Orlanda Frauenverlag.

Tibi, Bassam. 1987. *Arab Nationalism: Between Islam and the Nation-State.* New York: St. Martin's Press.

———. 1998. *The Challenge of Fundamentalism: Political Islam and the New World Disorder (Comparative Studies in Religion and Society).* Berkeley: Univ. of California Press.

Tignor, Robert L. 1987. "The Sudanese Private Sector: An Historical Overview." *Journal of Modern African Studies* 25, no. 2: 179–212.

Tilly, Charles. 1978. *From Mobilization to Revolution.* Reading, Mass.: Addison-Wesley.

Tocqueville, Alexis de. 1969. *Democracy in America.* Edited by J. P. Mayer, translated by George Lawrence. New York: Harper.

———. 1983. *The Old Regime and the French Revolution.* Translated by Stuart Gilbert. Garden City, N.Y.: Doubleday.

Todorov, Tzvetan. 1996. *Facing the Extreme.* Translated by Arthur Denner and Abigail Pollak. New York: Metropolitan Books.

Tomlinson, John. 1999. *Globalization and Culture.* Chicago: Univ. of Chicago Press.

Touraine, Alain. 1995. *Critique of Modernity.* Cambridge, Mass.: Blackwell.

Trilling, Lionel. 1979. *Beyond Culture.* New York: Harcourt Brace Jovanovich.

Tripp, Charles. 1999. "Can Islam Cope with Modernity?" *Times Literary Supplement,* 23 Apr.

Troutt-Powell, Eve Marie. 1995. "Colonized Colonizers: Egyptian Nationalists and the Issue of the Sudan, 1875–1919." Ph.D. diss., Harvard Univ.

Turnbull, Peter. 2000. "Contesting Globalization on the Waterfront." *Politics and Society* 28, no. 3: 367–91.

Turner, Bryan S. 1990. "Introduction: Defining Postmodernity." In *Theories of Modernity and Postmodernity*, edited by Bryan S. Turner, 1–13. London: Sage Publications.

———. 1994. *Orientalism, Postmodernism, and Globalism.* New York: Routledge.

UNDP. 1999. "Human Development Report 1999: Globalization with a Human Face," <http://hdr.undp.org/reports/gobal/1999/en>. New York: United Nations Publications.

Ursinus, Michael. 1993. "Nicht die Türken siegten über Byzanz, sondern Byzanz über die Türken." *Periplus* 3: 47–60. Munster.

———. 1994. *Quellen zur Geschichte des Osmanischen Reiches und ihre Interpretation.* Istanbul: Isis Verlag.

U.S. Committee for Refugees. 1998. *World Refugee Survey 1998.* New York: U.S. Committee for Refugees.

Vattimo, Gianni. 1997. *Beyond Interpretation.* Stanford, Calif.: Stanford Univ. Press.

Vertovec, Steven, and Ceri Peach, eds. 1997. *Islam in Europe: The Politics of Religion and Community.* New York: St Martin's Press.

Voll, John Obert. 1982. *Islam: Continuity and Change in the Modern World.* Boulder, Colo.: Westview Press.

Vorhoff, Karin. 1994. *Zwischen Glaube, Nation und neuer Gemeinschaft: alevitische Identität in der Turkei der Gegenwart.* Berlin: Schwarz.

de Waal, Alex. 1989. *Famine that Kills: Darfur, Sudan, 1984–1985.* Oxford, UK: Clarendon Press.

Waardenburg, Jacques. 1999. *Muslim Perceptions of Other Religions: A Historical Survey.* New York: Oxford Univ. Press.

Waldner, David. 1999. *State Building and Late Development.* Ithaca, N.Y.: Cornell Univ. Press.

Wallerstein, Immanuel. 1974. *The Modern World System I: Capitalist Agriculture and the Origins of the European World Economy in the Sixteenth Century.* New York: Academic Press.

Walz, Terence. 1979. *Trade Between Egypt and Bilad as-Sudan, 1700–1800.* Cairo: Institut français d'archéologie orientale du Caire.

Warburg, Gabriel. 1971. *The Sudan under Wingate: Administration in the Anglo-Egyptian Sudan, 1899–1916.* London: Frank Cass.

———. 1978. *Islam, Nationalism and Communism in a Traditional Society: The Case of Sudan.* London: Frank Cass.

Wasserstrom, Steven. 1988. "Islamicate History of Religions?" *History of Religions* 27, no. 4: 405–11.

Weber, Eugen. 1976. *Peasants into Frenchmen. The Modernization of Rural France 1870–1914.* Stanford, Calif.: Stanford Univ. Press.

Weber, Max. 1976. *From Max Weber: Essays in Sociology.* Translated and edited by H. H. Gerth and C. Wright Mills. New York: Oxford Univ. Press.

Weiss, Linda. 1999. "Managed Openness: Beyond Neoliberal Globalism." *New Left Review* 238: 126–40.

Westney, D. Eleanor. 1987. *Imitation and Innovation: The Transfer of Western Organizational Patterns to Meiji Japan.* Cambridge, Mass.: Harvard Univ. Press.

Wheeler, Andrew. 1998. "Gateway to the Heart of Africa: Sudan's Missionary Story." In *Gateway to the Heart of Africa: Missionary Pioneers in Sudan,* edited by Francesco Pierli, Maria Teresa Ratti, and Andrew C. Wheeler, 10–25. Nairobi, Kenya: Paulines Publications Africa.

White, Hayden. 1978. *Tropics of Discourse. Essays in Cultural Criticism.* Baltimore: Johns Hopkins Univ. Press.

White, Stephen K. 1991. *Political Theory and Postmodernism.* New York: Cambridge Univ. Press.

Wild, Stefan. 1990. "Triumph and Resignation: Arab Intellectuals and the Nineteenth-Century European Image of the Arabs." Unpublished paper, cited with permission of the author.

Williams, Raymond. 1973. *The Country and the City.* London: Chatto and Windus.

Winch, Peter. 1958. *The Idea of a Social Science and Its Relation to Philosophy.* 2d ed. London: Routledge.

Wittrock, Björn. 2000. "Modernity: One, None, or Many? European Origins and Modernity as a Global Condition." In *Daedalus,* "Multiple Modernities" special issue 129, no. 1: 30–60.

Wolf, Eric. 1982. *Europe and the People Without History.* Berkeley: Univ. of California Press.

Wolin, Richard. 2000. "Untruth and Method." *New Republic,* 15 May.

Wollheim, Richard. 1984. *The Thread of Life.* New Haven, Conn.: Yale Univ. Press.

Wood, Allen. 1990. *Hegel's Ethical Thought.* New York: Cambridge Univ. Press.

Woodward, Peter. 1990. *Sudan, 1898–1989: The Unstable State.* Boulder, Colo.: Lynne Rienner Publishers.

World Bank. 1997. *Malaysia: Enterprise Training, Technology and Productivity.* Washington, D.C.: World Bank.

———. 2001. *World Development Report 2000/2001.* New York: Oxford Univ. Press.

Yamba, C. Bawa. 1995. *Permanent Pilgrims: The Role of Pilgrimage in the Lives of West African Muslims in Sudan.* Edinburgh: Edinburgh Univ. Press.

Yavus, Hakan. 1998. "Turkish Identity and Foreign Policy in Flux: The Rise of Neo-Ottomanism." *Critique* 12 (spring): 19–41.

Zelizer, Vivian. 1997. *The Social Meaning of Money: PIN Money, Paychecks, Poor Relief, and Other Currencies.* Princeton, N.J.: Princeton Univ. Press.

Zizek, Slavoj. 1999. *Ticklish Subject.* New York: Verso.

———. 2000. *The Fragile Absolute, or, Why Is the Christian Legacy Worth Fighting For?* New York: Verso.

Zubaida, Sami. 1993. *Islam: The People and the State.* New York: I. B. Tauris.

Index

Italic page number denotes a table or chart.